••• **Second edition**

CAMBRIDGE

Objective

Louise Hashemi
Barbara Thomas

PET

Student's Book
with answers

CAMBRIDGE LEARNER CORPUS
REAL ENGLISH GUARANTEE

CAMBRIDGE
UNIVERSITY PRESS

CAMBRIDGE
UNIVERSITY PRESS

University Printing House, Cambridge CB2 8BS, United Kingdom

Cambridge University Press is part of the University of Cambridge.

It furthers the University's mission by disseminating knowledge in the pursuit of education, learning and research at the highest international levels of excellence.

www.cambridge.org
Information on this title: www.cambridge.org/9780521732666

© Cambridge University Press 2010

First published 2003
Second edition published 2010
13th printing 2015

Printed in Dubai by Oriental Press

A catalogue record for this publication is available from the British Library

ISBN 978-0-521-73268-0 Student's Book without answers with CD-ROM
ISBN 978-0-521-73266-6 Student's Book with answers with CD-ROM
ISBN 978-0-521-73269-7 Teacher's Book
ISBN 978-0-521-73274-1 Audio CDs (3)
ISBN 978-0-521-73270-3 Workbook without answers
ISBN 978-0-521-73271-0 Workbook with answers
ISBN 978-0-521-73272-7 Self-study pack
ISBN 978-0-521-16827-4 For Schools Pack without answers
ISBN 978-0-521-15724-7 Classware

Cover concept by Dale Tomlinson and design by David Lawton
Produced by Kamae Design, Oxford

Acknowledgements

The authors and publishers would like to thank the teachers and students who trialled and commented on the material:
Argentina: Liliana Luna, Claudia Cecilia Muniz, Marite Stringa, Sylvia Trigub; Australia: Jacque Byrne; Brazil: Angela Cristina Antelo Dupont; Cyprus: Peter Lucantoni; France: Virginie Petit, Robert Wright; Italy: James Douglas, Sarah Ellis, Monica Flood; Malta: Matthew Bonnici; Mexico: Jan Isaksen, Universidad Latino-Americana; Spain: Elizabeth Bridges, Samantha Lewis, Nick Shaw; Switzerland: Nancy Hersche, Julia Muller, Jean Rudiger-Harper, Fiona Schmid; United Arab Emirates: Christine Coombe, Philip Lodge, Anne Scullion; UK: Jenny Cooper, Lynda Edwards, Joe Gillespie, Jane Hann, Roger Scott, Tony Triggs; USA: Gregory Manin. They would also like to thank Maria Adduono, Alejandro Cervantes, Patricia Cervantes de Brofft, Rachel Connabeer, Fiona Dunbar, Alison Hayman, Emma Heydermann, David Jay, Rosalie Kerr, Alex Latimer, Stuart McDonald, Peter McLaren, Kristina Renée Noto, Rebecca Place, Patricia Quintana, Roger Scott, James Terrett, Valerie Walder, Gaye Wilkinson, Marilyn Wilson, Claire Wood, for their comments on the second edition.

Picture research by Hilary Fletcher, Val Mulcahy and Kevin Brown.

The publishers are grateful to Annette Capel and Wendy Sharp for permission to reproduce their original course book concept in Objective PET and in all other Objective examination course books.

The authors would like to thank Alyson Maskell, Laila Friese and Niki Donnelly at Cambridge University Press for their unfailing support and efficiency. They would also like to thank the following people for all kinds of assistance: Rowland, Rhiannon and Rebecca Thomas, Abbas Hashemi, Oliver Knight, Laurie McGeoghegan and David Aluwahlia, Jacqueline Clark, Patrizia Congedo, Joanne Hunter, Nick Kovaios, Justyna Matwiejczyk, Olga Sands, Paul Shields, Chie Obata Sibley.

The authors and publishers acknowledge the following sources of copyright material and are grateful for the permissions granted. While every effort has been made, it has not always been possible to identify the sources of all the material used, or to trace all copyright holders. If any omissions are brought to our notice, we will be happy to include the appropriate acknowledgements on reprinting.
The following are reproduced by permission of:
Cambridge University Press for the front cover and for the extract on p 79 from The Double Bass Mystery by Jeremy Harmer. Copyright © 1999, 2007; Jean Greenwood for the adapted activity on p 145 'Who am I?' from Activity Box published by Cambridge University Press, 1997; Global Friendship for the text on p 151 The Friendship Page from http://www.friendship.com.au.; Topic Records Ltd for the printed lyrics on p 174 and original recording Somewhere the Sun is Shining. Words and music by John Tams, performed by John Tams. Copyright © Topic Records Ltd. All rights of the producer and of the owner of the works reproduced reserved. Unauthorised copying, hiring, lending, public performance and broadcasting of this record is prohibited; D C Thomson & Co Ltd for the text on p 193 and the audio recording from 'Mind Reader' from Shout Magazine. Copyright © D C Thomson & Co Ltd.

The publishers are grateful to the following for permission to include photographs and other illustrative material:
A1Pix p53 (Chris Walsh); Action Plus pp50(a), 192(bl &tl) /Matthew Clarke; Advertising Archives pp168, 171(r); Alamy pp11(c) /Stefan Hunziker, 28(a) / Chuck Franklin, 34(taxi) /©FCL Photography, 55(d) /Olga Sapegina, 86(d) /David L. Moore – Studio, 90(1) /David Young-Wolff, 90(5) /Anna Yu, 97 / dbphots, 100(bc) /Nick Chaldakov, 124(Daniel) / Rob Wilkinson, 141 / Sofia Goff, 148(br) /John Henshall, 162(c) / terry harris just greece photo library, 180(4) / Fincher Files, 205a /chicagoview, 205(b) / Oliver Knight, 174(tl) / Sally and Richard Greenhill; "Aquilia desk lamp" is from Alliance Optotek Corp p86(f); Alvey & Towers pp34 (helicopter, lorry, ship, tram), 35(b & c, coach); Art Directors & TRIP pp22(c), 38(2), 124 (Angela), 162(e); BSH Home Appliances Ltd p171(l); Bossaball Sports sl p11(b); Bubbles Photolibrary p30(l) /Nikki Gibbs; Camera Press p154(f); Alan Chambers p76; Corbis pp13(b) /Scott Bales/Icon SMI/Icon SMI, 38(5) /Roy Botterell, 93(b right) /Hulton-Deutsch Collection, 110(tr) /Kelly-Mooney Photography, 133 / Rob Lewine, 137(r) /Larry Williams, 142(d) /Frank Lukasseck, 180(2) / Obama For America/Handout/Reuters, 183(c) /Francoise Gervais, 66(7) / Macduff Everton; Mary Evans Picture Library pp43, 143(b, t), 154(h); Eye Ubiquitous /Hutchinson pp50(c),174(tr); Fortean Picture Library p142(a, b, c); Getty Images pp16(a) /Barros & Barros, 16(b) /Gregg Segal, 16(f) / Julie Troy, 22(a) /Emily Shur, 22(e) /Holly Harris, 27(A) /Kathrin Ziegler, 28(b) /Alvis Upitis, 28(c) /M. Llorden, 38(4) /Pando Hall, 41(bl) /Peter Cade, 41(br) /Chabruken, 41(t) 42(e) /Arthur Tilley, 42(a) /Terry Doyle, 42(c) /Euan Myles, 42(d) /Alistair Berg, 48(tr) /Ken Chemus, 50(d, g) /Martin Barraud,

50(e) /Mike Powell, 58(bl), 74(r) /Erik Dreyer, 75 /AFP, 86(a) /Bridgeman Art Library, 86(c) 204(a) /White Packert, 90(2) / Dimitri Vervitsiotis, 93(a left), 93(a right) /Hulton Archive, 93(b left) /Joseph McKeown, 98 / AFP, 100(tl) /Brian Erler, 110(bl) /Ed Freeman, 124(Anna) /Daniel Bosler, 124(Clare) /Johner Royalty Free, 124(Emily) /Matthias Clamer, 124(Joelle) / Gustavo Di Mario, 124(Michael) / Chaz Kiba, 125(bl) /Popperfoto, 148(tc) / DreamPictures, 178(3) /David Young-Wolff, 180(a) /Steve Jennings; Ronald Grant Archive pp28(f) /EON Productions, 116(a) /Working Title, 116(b, d) /Universal Pictures, 116(c) /LucasFilm, 116(e, g) /20th Century Fox; Designer: Christen Halter, Formart Industrial Design, Germany, www.formartdesign.com p154(g); Robert Harding Picture Library pp55(a), 162(a) /Walter Rawlings, 174(bl); Steve Henesy/photographersdirect.com p202; Imagestate pp50(f), 174(br); Istockphoto.com p34(scooter); Masterfile p60(b) /Matthew Plexman, Book Cover from Dracula by Stoker B (2009) by permission of Oxford University Press p78(c); PA Photos pp28(d) / Yui Mok, 74(c, l) 183(l) 193(l) /John Birdsall Photo Library, 178(4 & 5 Posed by models) /John Birdsall Photo Library, 180(e); Courtesy of the Penguin Group (USA) Inc book cover of When It Happens by Susane Colasanti p78(b); Photodisc p42(b); Photofusion Picture Library pp22(f) /Pam Isherwood, 55(c) / Maggie Murray, 124(Sarah) / Ulrike Preuss, 162(d) /Lisa Woollett, 192(br) /Melanie Friend, 192(c) /Brenda Prince; Photolibrary.com pp15(b) /Jon Feingersh, 16(d) /Photodisc, 16(e) 22(d) 27(b) /Image Source, 22(b) 55(b) 126 /Digital Vision, 26(b) /Will Woods, 26(t) /Big Cheese, 30(r) 204(b) /Bananastock, 36(l) /Stockbroker, 38(1) /J Lange/ Modelreleaseco.uk, 38(3) /Caroline Woodham, 42(f) 107(t) /Creatas, 58(a) / Nigel Blythe, 58(bl) /Corbis, 60(t) Odilon Dimier, 61 /Mixa Co Ltd, 72(tr) / Mike Berceanu, 90(3) /Diane Macdonald, 90(4) /I Love Images, 100(bl) / Reinhard Dirscherl, 110(br) /moodboard, 124 (Bob) / Noel Hendrickson, 124(Leo) /Tay Jnr, 124(Maria) /Don Mason, 124(Nick) /Westend61, 148(bc) / Eric Cahan, 148(bl) /Rolf Bruderer, 148(tl) /Granger Wootz, 177 /Frank and Helena, 190 / Luca Invernizzi Tettoni; Now Wait for Last Year by Philip K Dick, published by Gollancz, an imprint of the Orion Publishing Group, London p78(e); Photoshot p180(c) / Slaven Vlasic/Everett; Courtesy of Plexus Publishing book cover of River Phoenix: A Short Life by Brian J Robb p78(a); Punchstock p15(t) /Digital Vision; Reuters p11(a); Rex Features pp13(t) /Sipa Press, 19(l) /© Sony Pictures/Everett, 19(r) /Everett Collection, 28(e) /Donald Cooper, 50(b), 54 /D Geraghty/Newspix/ 58(b), 58(d) 148(tl) /Image Source, 87(c), 93(c), 100(br), 116(f) /© Warner Bros/Everett, 116(h) /© Focus/Everett, 129 /David Fisher, 154(e) /Roger Viollett, 180(1) /White & Reed, 180(3) /East News, 180(b) /Action Press, 180(d) /Ron Sachs; ©Sainsbury Archive, Museum of London p166; Science & Society Museum p154(d); Science Photo Library p110(tl) /Graeme Ewen; Shutterstock.com pp16 /Piotr Marcinski, 40(c) /Monkey Business, 40(l), 193(tr) /Michael Jung, 40(r) /Dotshock, 124(Caroline) James.R.Martin, 124(Lily) /Monkey Business, 124(Tony) (Cassie) /Roman Gorielov, 124(Hugh), 178(2), 192(tr) /auremar, 195 /Edyta Pawlowska; South West News Service p87(b); Superstock pp22(g) / age Fotostock, 200 /Francis Frith; Topfoto p11(d); VIEW Pictures p162(b) / Denis Gilbert; Courtesy of the publisher Virago, an imprint of Little, Brown Book Group, the book cover of Cat's Eye by Margaret Atwood illustrated by David Cutter p78(f); www.wenn.com p180(5).

The following photographs were taken on commission: Gareth Boden p82, 169; Olivia Brown p125(tl);Trevor Clifford for p86(e, h), 93(d)111, 112, 113 (br); Abbas Hashemi for p186; Louise Hashemi for pp66, 86, 88, 137; Barbara Thomas p125(br); Anna Vaughan p 125(tr).

We have been unable to trace the copyright holders for the following items and would be grateful for any information to enable us to do so: Page 87 (a, b) Page 154 (a, b and e).

We are grateful to the following companies for permission to use copyright logos:
'Coca-Cola' and 'Coke' are registered trade marks of The Coca-Cola Company p 168 (top); McDonalds Restaurants Limited p 168 (top); Mercedes-Benz UK p 168 (top); Virgin Atlantic p 168 (top)

Illustrations by:
Adz 24, 44, 65, 78, 163; Kathryn Baker 119; Debbie Boon 187; Kathy Baxendale 32(m), 70(tl), 134(ml, bl); Tim Davies 164; Kamae Design 13, 88, 154(tr), 157(t); Karen Donnelly 20, 32(bl), 38, 70(tr, m), 89, 134(bl); Mark Duffin 14, 48, 60, 66, 103, 120; Nick Duffy 31, 36, 42, 54, 69, 157(b); Stephen Elford 23, 25,153; Tony Forbes 12, 80, 130, 131, 171; Gecko Ltd 49(tl), 72, 138(t); Dylan Gibson 10, 32(t), 49(tr), 107, 117, 134(t, middle r), 183(b), 201; Peter Greenwood 37; Ben Hasler 106; Julian Mosedale 62, 81; Lisa Smith 18, 40, 51, 57, 104, 132, 138, 139, 165, 189; David Tazzyman 92, 176; Sam Thompson 173;

Corpus research by Julie Moore.

Map of Objective PET Student's Book

TOPIC	GRAMMAR	FUNCTIONS AND VOCABULARY	PRONUNCIATION	REVISION
Unit 1 **A question of sport** 10–13 Sports and hobbies	Present simple / to be + frequency adverbs	Definitions and explanations; a kind of + -ing/noun; sports; hobbies; expressing attitude	/aɪ/ as in like /iː/ as in steep /ɪ/ as in big	Present simple; the alphabet; like + -ing
Exam folder 1 14–15 Reading Part 1 Speaking Part 1				
Unit 2 **I'm a friendly person** 16–19 People	like/enjoy + -ing; want / would like + to; to be + a(n) + occupation	Describing people: appearance, personality, interests; inviting and responding to invitations	/ɒ/ as in pop /ʌ/ as in fun /juː/ as in university	have got
Exam folder 2 20–21 Listening Part 3 Writing Parts 1, 2 and 3				
Unit 3 **What's your job?** 22–25 Work	Present simple vs. present continuous (for present actions); state verbs; short answers	Saying what people are doing; jobs	/æ/ as in cat /ɑː/ as in cart /ʌ/ as in cut	Present simple (Unit 1)
Exam folder 3 26–27 Speaking Part 3 Reading Part 5				
Unit 4 **Let's go out** 28–31 Entertainment	Prepositions of time; present continuous for future plans	Entertainment; making appointments; dates	Saying days and months	would you like + to? (Unit 2); present continuous for present actions (Unit 3)
Exam folder 4 32–33 Listening Part 1 Writing Part 2				
Unit 5 **Wheels and wings** 34–37 Transport	need; countable and uncountable nouns; expressions of quantity	Transport; airport language; compound nouns	Unstressed a, of, to and some	Frequency adverbs and present simple (Unit 1); compound nouns from Units 1–4
Exam folder 5 38–39 Reading Part 2				
Unit 6 **What did you do at school today?** 40–43 Education and history	Past simple; short answers; adjectives ending in -ing and -ed	School life; school subjects; describing feelings and opinions; dates (years and decades)	Final sound of regular verbs in past tense: /t/, /d/ and /ɪd/	Expressing opinions
Exam folder 6 44–45 Listening Part 2 Writing Part 3				
Units 1–6 Revision 46–47				
Unit 7 **Around town** 48–51 Towns and buildings	Prepositions of place and movement; comparative adjectives; commands	Places/buildings in towns; directions; polite questions; saying you don't understand	/aʊ/ as in out /ɔː/ as in or	Adjectives from earlier units; spelling rules
Exam folder 7 52–53 Reading Part 3				
Unit 8 **Let's celebrate** 54–57 Special days	Present perfect simple; just, already, yet	Describing experiences and recent activities; celebrations, festivals and parties; giving good wishes	Dates	Dates (Unit 4); talking about pictures (Unit 3); present tenses

TOPIC	GRAMMAR	FUNCTIONS AND VOCABULARY	PRONUNCIATION	REVISION
Exam folder 8 **58–59** Speaking Parts 3 and 4 Writing Part 2				
Unit 9 **How do you feel?** **60–63** Health and fitness	Short answers in the present perfect	Parts of the body; illnesses; giving advice; expressions with *at*	/eɪ/ as in *say* /e/ as in *tell*	Present tenses; past simple; present perfect; short answers
Exam folder 9 **64–65** Reading Part 4 Speaking Part 2				
Unit 10 **I look forward to hearing from you** **66–69** Letters and emails	Present perfect and past simple; *ago, for, since, in; been* and *gone; have you ever...?*	Letters and emails, etc.	Final sound of plural nouns /s/, /z/ and /ɪz/	Past simple; present perfect; short answers
Exam folder 10 **70–71** Listening Part 1 Writing Part 3				
Unit 11 **Facts and figures** **72–75** Geography, nationality and numbers	Superlative adjectives; present simple passive	Countries, nationalities, languages; large numbers and measurements; what to say when you're not sure	/tʃ/ as in *cheese* /ʃ/ as in *shoe*	Comparative adjectives (Unit 7); descriptive adjectives (Units 2 and 6)
Exam folder 11 **76–77** Reading Part 5				
Unit 12 **A good read** **78–81** Books	Past continuous; past continuous vs. past simple; *while/when* + past continuous	Telling a story; saying what happened and what was happening; kinds of books; book reviews	/uː/ as in *two* /ʊ/ as in *took*	Saying what you like and why; giving opinions
Exam folder 12 **82–83** Speaking Part 1 Writing Part 3				
Units 7–12 Revision **84–85**				
Unit 13 **A place of my own** **86–89** Furniture and homes	Modals (probability and possibility): *it could/might/ must/can't be*; prepositions of place	Describing styles and saying what you prefer; price; rooms and furniture	/ʒ/ as in *television* /dʒ/ as in *joke*	Present and past tenses; prepositions (Unit 7) advice (Unit 9)
Exam folder 13 **90–91** Reading Part 2				
Unit 14 **What's in fashion?** **92–95** Clothes	*used to; too* and *enough* with adjectives; adjective order	Guessing unknown words; clothes; colours	Pronunciation of *gh* and *ph*	Describing things; years and decades (Unit 6); superlative adjectives (Unit 11); adjectives
Exam folder 14 **96–97** Listening Part 4 Writing Parts 2 and 3				
Unit 15 **Risk!** **98–101** Adventures	Modals (permission and obligation): *can, can't; have to, don't have to; had to* and *didn't have to*; adverbs	Rules; phrasal verbs with *get*; activities and experiences; adjectives and adverbs	Pronunciation of *ou*	Adjectives from earlier units; past simple (Unit 6)
Exam folder 15 **102–103** Reading Part 1				
Unit 16 **Free time** **104–107** Making plans	*going to* future; present tense after *when, after* and *until* in future time	Study and leisure; the time; invitations; making arrangements	Saying times	Invitations (Unit 2); present continuous for future plans (Unit 4)

TOPIC	GRAMMAR	FUNCTIONS AND VOCABULARY	PRONUNCIATION	REVISION
Exam folder 16 108–109 Listening Part 2 **Writing Part 1**				
Unit 17 **Next week's episode** 110–113 Predictions	*will* future; *will* vs. *going to*; *everyone, no one, someone, anyone*	Saying what will happen; TV and radio	/ɑː/ as in *car* /ɔː/ as in *sore* /ɜː/ as in *third*	*need* (Unit 5); telling a story; present continuous for present actions (Unit 3)
Exam folder 17 114–115 Reading Part 4				
Unit 18 **Shooting a film** 116–119 Films	Past perfect; past perfect vs. past simple	Talking about the order of past events; films; telling a story	/ə/ at the end of words	Past simple (Unit 6); giving opinions (Units 2 and 6)
Exam folder 18 120–121 Listening Part 3 **Writing Part 2**				
Units 13–18 Revision 122–123				
Unit 19 **Happy families** 124–127 Family life	Verbs and expressions followed by *to* and *-ing*; *make* and *let*	Families; agreeing and disagreeing; giving opinions	/ð/ as in *their* /θ/ as in *thirsty*	Advice (Unit 9)
Exam folder 19 128–129 Reading Part 5				
Unit 20 **So you think you've got talent?** 130–133 Music	Comparison of adverbs; *so* and *such*; connectives	Music, musical instruments; congratulating; saying what you like and prefer; jobs	Homophones	Comparative adjectives (Unit 7); superlative adjectives (Unit 11)
Exam folder 20 134–135 Listening Part 1 **Writing Part 3**				
Unit 21 **Keep in touch!** 136–139 Communicating	*Have something done*; reported commands and requests; possessive pronouns and adjectives	Making phone calls	Telephone numbers	Present simple (Unit 1); commands (Unit 7); plans (Unit 16)
Exam folder 21 140–141 Reading Part 3				
Unit 22 **Strange but true?** 142–145 The unexplained	Reported speech	Saying what you (don't) believe; reporting verbs; science fiction	Silent consonants	modals: *it could/might/must/can't be* (Unit 13); present and past tenses; giving opinions, agreeing and disagreeing
Exam folder 22 146–147 Listening Part 4 **Writing Part 1**				
Unit 23 **Best friends?** 148–151 Friendship	Relative clauses; adjectives + prepositions	Friendship; introducing people	Linking words ending in a consonant	Personality adjectives (Units 2 and 6)
Exam folder 23 152–153 Reading Part 1 Speaking Part 2				
Unit 24 **I've got an idea** 154–157 Inventions	Past simple passive; future passive	Describing objects; talking about things you don't know the name of; guessing vocabulary	Linking words ending in *r* and *re*	modals: *it could/might/must/can't be* (Unit 13); *a kind of* (Unit 1); present simple passive (Unit 11); dates (years) (Units 6 and 14)

TOPIC	GRAMMAR	FUNCTIONS AND VOCABULARY	PRONUNCIATION	REVISION
Exam folder 24 158–159 Listening Part 3 Writing Part 3				
Units 19–24 Revision 160–161				
Unit 25 **Shop till you drop** 162–165 Shopping	Reported questions; *too much, too many, not enough*; verbs with two objects	Shops and shopping; asking for things; trying on clothes	Stress: correcting what people say	Reported speech (Unit 22); clothes (Unit 14)
Exam folder 25 166–167 Reading Part 3				
Unit 26 **Persuading people** 168–171 Advertising and persuasion	First conditional; *unless*; *if* and *when*	Understanding writer or speaker purpose; advertising; reporting verbs	Stress in common short phrases	Making plans (Unit 16); telling a story (Unit 12)
Exam folder 26 172–173 Speaking Parts 1 and 2 Writing Part 3				
Unit 27 **Travellers' tales** 174–177 Travel experiences	Adverbs at the beginning of a sentence; reflexive pronouns: *myself, yourself,* etc; *every, each, all*; using the passive	Saying why people do things; travel; word building	/eə/ as in *chair* /ɪə/ as in *here*	Guessing unknown words; present and past simple passive (Units 11 and 24); giving advice (Units 9 and 19)
Exam folder 27 178–179 Reading Part 2				
Unit 28 **What would you do?** 180–183 Celebrities	Second conditional	Jobs; expressions with prepositions	Auxiliaries	Modals: *it could/might/ must/can't be* (Units 13 and 24); agreeing and disagreeing, opinions (Unit 19); *if* and *when* and first conditional (Unit 26)
Exam folder 28 184–185 Listening Part 2 Writing Part 1				
Unit 29 **What's on the menu?** 186–189 Food and restaurants	*So do I, Neither/Nor do I*; polite question forms	Asking politely; food; restaurants; apologising	Unstressed words	Reported questions (Unit 25)
Exam folder 29 190–191 Reading Part 4 Speaking Parts 3 and 4				
Unit 30 **Blue for a boy, pink for a girl?** 192–195 Boys and girls	*hardly*; *before/after* + *-ing*	Informal language; saying goodbye	Revision of /ʌ/, /æ/, /ɒ/, /ɑː/, /aʊ/, /ɔː/, /e/, /eɪ/, /ɪ/, /iː/, /ʊ/, /uː/, /ɜː/, /aɪ/, /eə/	Tenses and vocabulary from previous units
Exam folder 30 196–197 Listening Part 4 Speaking Parts 3 and 4 Writing Parts 1, 2 and 3				
Units 25–30 Revision 198–199				

Visual materials   200–205

Grammar folder   206–214

Key to phonetic symbols   215

Irregular verb list   216

Answers and recording scripts   217

Content of the Preliminary English Test Examination

The PET examination consists of three papers – Paper 1 Reading and Writing, Paper 2 Listening and Paper 3 Speaking. There are four grades: Pass with Merit (about 85% of the total marks); Pass (about 70% of the total marks); Narrow Fail (about 5% below the pass mark); Fail. For a Pass with Merit and Pass, the results slip shows the papers in which you did particularly well; for a Narrow Fail and Fail, the results slip shows the papers in which you were weak.

Paper 1 Reading and Writing 1 hour 30 minutes

(50% of the total marks: 25% for Reading and 25% for Writing)
There are eight parts in this paper and they are always in the same order. You write your answers on the answer sheet.

Part	Task Type	Number of Questions	Task Format	Objective Exam folder
Reading Part 1	Multiple choice (A, B or C)	5	You answer multiple-choice questions about five short texts (notices, postcards, labels, messages, emails, etc.).	1, 15, 23
Reading Part 2	Matching	5	You match five descriptions of people to eight short texts.	5, 13, 27
Reading Part 3	True/false	10	You answer ten true/false questions about a longer text.	7, 21, 25
Reading Part 4	Multiple choice (A, B, C or D)	5	You answer five multiple-choice questions testing opinion, detail and general meaning in a text.	9, 17, 29
Reading Part 5	Multiple choice (A, B, C or D)	10	You choose the correct words to fill ten spaces in a short text.	3, 11, 19
Writing Part 1	Rewriting sentences	5	You write one to three words in a gapped sentence so it means the same as the sentence given above it.	2, 16, 22, 28, 30
Writing Part 2	A short message	1	You write a short message (35–45 words) which includes three pieces of information.	2, 4, 8, 14, 18, 30
Writing Part 3	Either a letter or a story	1	You write either a letter or a story (about 100 words) in response to a short text or instruction.	2, 6, 10, 12, 14, 20, 24, 26, 30

Paper 2 Listening about 30 minutes (plus 6 minutes to copy answers onto the answer sheet)

(25% of the total marks)
There are four parts in this paper and they are always in the same order. You listen to some recordings. You hear each recording twice. You write your answers on the answer sheet.

Part	Task Type	Number of Questions	Task Format	Objective Exam folder
Listening Part 1	Multiple choice (A, B or C)	7	You answer seven multiple-choice picture questions about seven short recordings.	4, 10, 20
Listening Part 2	Multiple choice (A, B or C)	6	You answer six multiple-choice questions about a recording with one speaker or one main speaker and an interviewer.	6, 16, 28
Listening Part 3	Gap fill	6	You complete six gaps in a text by listening to a recording with one main speaker.	2, 18, 24
Listening Part 4	True/false	6	You answer six true/false questions about a conversation between two speakers.	14, 22, 30

Paper 3   Speaking   10–12 minutes for a pair of students

(25% of the total marks)

There are four parts in the speaking test and they are always in the same order. There are two students taking the examination and two examiners.

Part	Task Type	Number of Questions	Task Format	Objective Exam folder
Speaking Part 1	The examiner asks both students some questions.	2–3 minutes	You are asked to give information about yourself.	1, 12, 26
Speaking Part 2	The students have a discussion together.	2–3 minutes	You are given some pictures about a situation and you discuss it with the other student.	9, 23, 26
Speaking Part 3	Each student talks in turn to the examiner.	3 minutes	You are each given a different colour photograph which you talk about for up to a minute.	3, 8, 29, 30
Speaking Part 4	The students have a discussion together.	3 minutes	You have a discussion with the other student about a topic connected with the photographs in Part 3.	8, 29, 30

New for the second edition of Objective PET

As well as adding new exercises, pictures and a Grammar Folder, the authors have used the Cambridge Learner Corpus for the second edition. A CD-ROM and website give extra support.

⊙ Cambridge Learner Corpus

When you see this icon in the book, it means that this language area has been identified in the Cambridge Learner Corpus (CLC) as an area in which learners often need extra practice. The CLC is a collection of over 30 million words taken from student exam papers from Cambridge ESOL. It shows real mistakes students have made in their exams. The mistakes the authors focus on are typical of learners at this level and that is why this book provides further practice in using these features of the language accurately.

◉ CD-ROM

On the CD-ROM there are 90 exercises, six for each pair of units, giving extra practice in vocabulary, grammar, reading, listening, writing and pronunciation. There is also an interactive word game and a PET Practice Test, as well as additional resources for both teachers and students, such as wordlists and teaching tips for using these and photocopiable recording scripts for some of the Listening tasks.

Website

www.cambridge.org/elt/objectivepet

On this website you will find a number of useful resources for both students and teachers: an additional free photocopiable PET Practice Test with audio, a further interactive word game to test your vocabulary (Vocabulary Trainer), photocopiable wordlists and teaching tips as well as photocopiable recording scripts for classroom use.

1 A question of sport

Grammar present simple + frequency adverbs
Vocabulary sports; hobbies; *a kind of*
Revision *there is/are*

cycling

Introduction

1 Put the letters in order to make the names of sports.
You can write the name of the sport by its picture above.

I S IN ALL T FA GN A S K E R D U
N S L G K L T O O S Y R O H R R G
G K I C Y C A B E S B B L M Y C I H C H I S G N B Y

IN NG TA N OL L D FU E LAS
L G I U E L S S B A L N R I H S T
I A S F R B N T N E T E N V Y L W G N T C I

2 Read the statements about sport. Tick (✓) the statements that are true for you.

I play football.	
I go swimming.	
I do athletics.	
I never do any sport.	
I watch lots of sport on television.	
I never watch sport.	
I sometimes watch sport.	

Compare answers round the class.
Does anyone in the class not like sport?
What does he/she like doing instead?

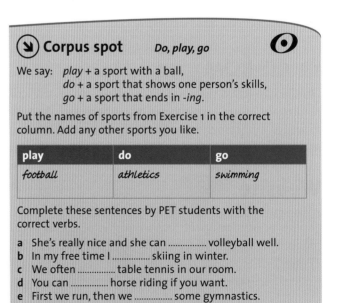

⬎ Corpus spot *Do, play, go*

We say: *play* + a sport with a ball,
do + a sport that shows one person's skills,
go + a sport that ends in *-ing*.

Put the names of sports from Exercise 1 in the correct column. Add any other sports you like.

play	do	go
football	athletics	swimming

Complete these sentences by PET students with the correct verbs.

a She's really nice and she can .... volleyball well.
b In my free time I .... skiing in winter.
c We often .... table tennis in our room.
d You can .... horse riding if you want.
e First we run, then we .... some gymnastics.

3 Work with a partner. Look below at the names of equipment used in sport. Match the equipment to the sports in Exercise 1 and write the name of the sport(s) next to the equipment. Some equipment matches more than one sport. Use your English–English dictionary if necessary.

basket	*basketball*	bat	....
bike	....	board	....
boat	....	helmet	....
net	....	racket	....
sail	....	skis	....
stick	....		

Listening

1 Look at the photographs. They show some unusual sports – bossaball, curling, snowfering and karting. Can you guess which sport is in each photograph?

a ☐　b ☐　c ☐　d ☐

2 **1 02** Listen to four people talking about these sports. Which sport is each person talking about? Write 1, 2, 3 or 4 next to each photo.

3 **1 03** Listen to some more information about these sports. Write the answers to these questions.

Bossaball
a What do they always wear? *They always wear shorts.*
b When do they usually play this?

Curling
c What do they use?
d What do people sometimes say?

Karting
e How fast can you go indoors?
f What is a kart?

Snowfering
g Where do they do this?
h What do they use?

4 Listen again. The speakers say how they feel about these sports.
Which words do they use?

1 ....
2 ....
3 ....
4 ....

Can you suggest any more words like these?

Language focus

a kind of

Answer these questions. Use *It's a kind of* and the words in the box.

a What's a helmet?
   It's a kind of hat.
b What's a racket?
c What's windsurfing?
d What's table tennis?
e What's rugby?
f What's a kart?
g What's snowfering?

| tennis |
| hat |
| team game |
| car |
| windsurfing on the snow |
| bat |
| surfing on water |

Present simple + frequency adverbs

+	I He	*sometimes*		**play** football. **plays** football.
−	We She	**don't** **doesn't**	*usually*	**play** football.
?	**Do** **Doesn't**	you she	*often*	**play** football?

To be + frequency adverbs

+	She We	**is** **are**	*usually*	happy.
−	He They	**isn't** **aren't**	*always*	happy.
?	**Is** **Are**	he you	*never*	happy?

> ### ⬎ Grammar spot   Frequency adverbs
>
> Look at the table above. Circle the correct words to complete this sentence:
>
> Frequency adverbs go *before / after* a main verb but *before / after* an auxiliary verb and *to be*.

1 Look at the table above. Rewrite each sentence below, adding one of the adverbs in the box in the correct place. Do other people agree with your answers?

| never   sometimes   often   usually   always |

a Basketball players are tall.
   Basketball players are often tall.
b Cyclists go very fast.
c Footballers are very rich.
d Surfers get wet.
e Gymnasts wear helmets.
f There are two people in a tennis match.
g Good athletes smoke.

2 Work with a partner. Use the adverbs in the box in Exercise 1. Ask and answer questions like these:

Do you often finish your homework?
Yes, always!
Does your dad sometimes play tennis?
Yes, often.
Are you always tidy?
No, never!

Use these words, or your own ideas:

make breakfast   play computer games
be polite   wear expensive clothes
remember your friend's birthday

> ### ⬎ Corpus spot   Word order ◉
>
> Correct the word order mistakes in these sentences by PET students.
> a She comes often to my house.
> b I meet them sometimes in my free time.
> c At weddings people usually are happy and have fun together.
> d I don't go often to the countryside.
> e He usually doesn't make jokes.
> f We have a basketball team and we play often against other teams.

3 Complete these sentences about yourself and your family and friends. Use the frequency adverbs in the box in Exercise 1. Use *not* in some sentences.

a *I don't often eat* cheese for breakfast.
b *My brother usually plays* football after class.
c .... very tired in the morning.
d .... a sleep in the afternoon.
e .... in the spring.
f .... quiet in English lessons.
g .... sport on television.

4 Now write three true sentences using the frequency adverbs with your own ideas.

⬎ GF page 206

1 Think about the words *like* and *big*. Do they have the same vowel sound as *wheel* and *please*?

2 Say these words aloud and put them into the correct column.

steep quite hill field like knee kind people ice little stick line big street ride rich wheel bike team

/aɪ/	/iː/	/ɪ/
quite	steep	hill

3 **1 04** Listen to the recording and check your answers.

4 Write four ways we can spell the sound /iː/ in English:

....

«Activity» **Free time**

1 Work with a partner. Choose a sport or hobby (it's better if it's unusual!). Write down some information about it. Write sentences like these:

You play in a team. / You can do this alone.

You play in a field. / You usually do this in a swimming pool.

2 Now talk to another pair of students. Don't tell them the name of your sport or hobby. Try to guess their sport or hobby and let them try to guess yours. Ask questions like these:

Do you usually do this in summer?
Do you use a kind of board?
Do you always play with friends?
Do you wear special shoes?
How many people are there in the team?
Is it sometimes dangerous?

You can answer:

Yes, (sometimes / usually / often / always) or *No, (never)* or *We don't know.*

Vocabulary spot

Word trees are a useful way to learn and remember word families. Make a vocabulary tree of words for a sport or activity that you enjoy.

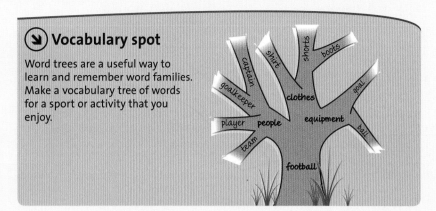

captain shirt shorts boots goalkeeper clothes goal player people equipment ball team football

«Activity» **Make a poster**

Make a poster about a sportsman or sportswoman you admire. Put their picture on it if you can. Write this kind of information on it:

What sport does he/she play?
What does he/she usually wear?
What equipment does he/she use?
What does he/she often/sometimes/never do?
How do you feel about this sport?

Exam folder 1

Reading Part 1

1 Look at these texts. Before you read them, say which is:

- a text message
- a telephone message
- an email
- a notice.
- a Post-it note

This sports camp is great but the changing room is small and dirty. Also, the café is always crowded, so my friends and I eat in the park.
Maria

The swimming pool opens at 6.30am except Sundays when it opens at 7am

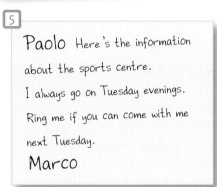

It's too cold for football practice tonight ☹ but come to the gym for fitness training ☺
M.Collins

CONTINUE   MORE

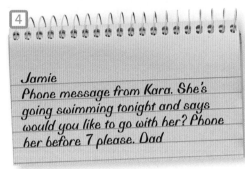

Jamie
Phone message from Kara. She's going swimming tonight and says would you like to go with her? Phone her before 7 please. Dad

Paolo Here's the information about the sports centre.
I always go on Tuesday evenings.
Ring me if you can come with me next Tuesday.
Marco

2 Now read the texts. Were you right?

Exam Advice

Look at the texts and decide what they are, e.g. a Post-it note, an email, etc. It will help you to answer the questions.

3 Read text 1 again. Look at these three sentences about it. Which one says the same as the email?

A Maria meets her friends in the café.
B Maria eats outdoors.
C Maria likes the changing room.

B is correct. Underline the words in text 1 which tell you about where she eats.

Why are A and C wrong? Underline the words in text 1 which tell you about Maria's friends and the changing room.

4 Now choose the correct answers for the other texts.

2 A The swimming pool opens at 6.30 every day.
B The swimming pool opens at 7 on Sundays.
C The swimming pool opens early at weekends.

3 A Football practice is cancelled tonight.
B There isn't time for fitness training tonight.
C The footballers can't meet tonight.

4 A Dad wants Jamie to phone him.
B Kara wants to meet Jamie at 7.
C Kara wants to go swimming with Jamie.

5 A Marco goes to the sports centre every week.
B Paolo and Marco often go to the sports centre together.
C Paolo sometimes goes to the sports centre on Tuesdays.

Speaking Part 1

1   Make some questions to ask Pablo and Cristina. Use these words.

What / your surname?   Where / come from?
Where / live?   What part of / live in?
How / old?   How many languages / speak?
How / travel to school?   What / like doing in your free time?

2   Read these texts and find the answers to your questions.

> My name is Pablo. My surname's Suarez.
> I'm Spanish. I live in a village near a large city
> called Seville. It's in the south of Spain.
> I usually drive to college. I'm 19 years old.
> I speak Spanish and English. I like playing
> football and going to the cinema.

> My name is Cristina Lopez. I'm
> Mexican. I live in the centre of the
> capital, Mexico City. I usually walk
> to school. I'm 16 years old. I speak
> Spanish, English and a little Italian.
> In my free time, I like shopping, reading
> and going out with friends.

3   Work with a partner. One of you is Pablo and the other is Cristina.
    Ask and answer the questions in Exercise 1.

4   Think of the answers you can give about yourself to the questions
    in Exercise 1.

5   Now ask your partner the same questions. Your partner answers
    about himself or herself. Then your partner asks you. Answer about
    yourself.

6   Write a text about yourself, like the texts by Pablo and Cristina. Use
    your answers to the questions to help you.

Exam Advice

The examiner asks you questions about
yourself. Learn how to talk about yourself,
where you live and what you like doing.

2 I'm a friendly person

Grammar	like/enjoy + -ing; want / would like + to
Vocabulary	describing people and personality; inviting and responding to invitations
Revision	have got

Introduction

1 Look at this page from a college website. What does it tell you about these students? What do they look like? Can you describe them?

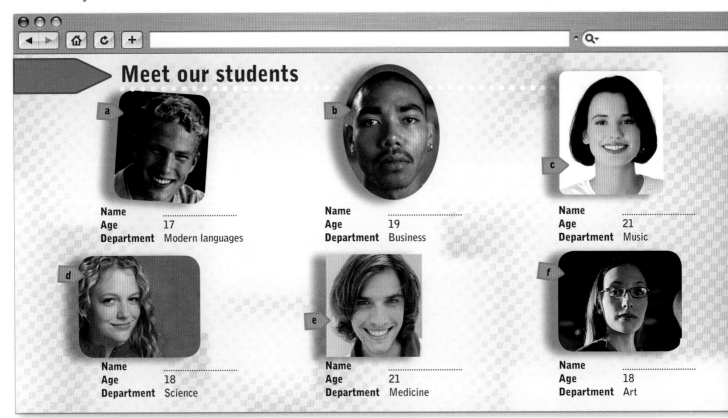

Meet our students

a	Name		
	Age	17	
	Department	Modern languages	

b	Name		
	Age	19	
	Department	Business	

c	Name		
	Age	21	
	Department	Music	

d	Name		
	Age	18	
	Department	Science	

e	Name		
	Age	21	
	Department	Medicine	

f	Name		
	Age	18	
	Department	Art	

2 🔘05 When a new student arrives, another student goes to meet them. They talk on their mobiles before they meet.

Listen to two conversations and write each speaker's name in the space below their photo. The students' names are in the box below. Which two don't you hear?

Anastasia	Julia	Kurt	Mandana	Mike	Stefan

Describing people

I**'ve got** brown eyes.

She **hasn't got** long hair.

Have you got fair hair?

She**'s** short and slim **with** short hair.

3 Work with a partner.
Imagine you are Kurt (a boy) and Anastasia (a girl). Describe yourselves to each other. Use the language in the box above to help you.

4 Write a short description of someone famous on a piece of paper but don't write their name on it.
Write the names on the board.
Put all the descriptions together.
Take them out in turn and read them aloud.
Match each description to one of the names on the board.

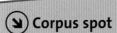 **Corpus spot**

Describing people
Underline the correct word in these sentences by PET students.
a She is *long / tall / high* and slim.
b He's got short, fair *hair / hairs*.

Reading

1   The college website has pages where students can put notices about things like accommodation, travel, etc. Read these notices and write *Travel*, *Contacts* or *Accommodation* above each one to show which page it is from.

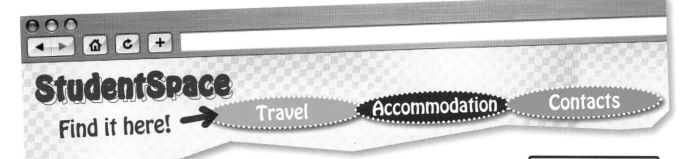

StudentSpace
Find it here! ➔   Travel   Accommodation   Contacts

1 Travel

Hi! I'm a medical student and I work in London on Sundays. I need a lift. I start work at 7.30 and I mustn't be late, but I haven't got transport. I'm happy to share the cost of petrol. I like rock music and computer games. Text or phone 07777531245 anytime. Elena

4 ....

Does anyone have friends in Portugal or Brazil? I'm a modern languages student and I want to have an email penfriend who speaks Portuguese. I like swimming and pop music. I'm not a serious person. I like going clubbing with my friends. Write to Henry.happyfoot@nunet.com

2 ....

Are you self-confident? Do you like meeting new people? I want to go to Australia in the summer and work there, then visit some other countries. I like doing gymnastics and playing basketball and I enjoy dancing. Do you want to come with me? email AdrianAB23@nunet.com

5 ....

My name's Sandra. I'm hard-working and I want lots of adventures in my life. I like jazz and pop music. I'd like to run my own business when I leave college. I drive to London and back every Sunday to see my boyfriend. Would you like a lift? Share cost of petrol. 07536661259

3 ....

I'm a first-year art student and want to share a flat or house in the city centre. I can pay up to £300 a month. I like shopping and going out. I don't enjoy living in the student hostel. If you share my lifestyle and have a space in your place, phone Carola: 07879345621.

6 ....

I've got a small house near the campus and I want to share it with one other person. You must be a non-smoker and tidy. I like playing chess and listening to classical music. I'm a final-year physics student. Come and see the room on Saturday morning. Maggie, 142 Bennett Road (behind the Science Faculty building).

2   Complete this table by ticking the boxes.

Who	Elena	Adrian	Carola	Henry	Sandra	Maggie
a knows what job he/she wants in the future?	✓					
b has a part-time job now?						
c offers to pay for something?						
d wants to go to another part of the world?						
e wants to find somewhere to live?						
f enjoys sport?						
g likes quiet hobbies?						

3   Do you think any of the students will meet?

Language focus

Personality

Work with a partner. Read the quiz together. Mark your partner's answers.

Look at the bottom of page 19 to find the result, then complete this sentence about yourself:

I'm .... person.

> **a + adjective + person**
> I'm a(n) independent/ friendly/serious **person**. = I'm independent/friendly/serious.

What kind of person are you?

1. **What kind of music do you like?**
   A pop
   B jazz
   C classical

2. **Do you like studying?**
   A no
   B some subjects
   C yes

3. **Would you like to travel round the world?**
   A yes – with my friends
   B yes – alone
   C no, I wouldn't

4. **You're free this evening. What do you want to do?**
   A go clubbing
   B go to the cinema
   C stay at home and read

5. **You want to find a new hobby. What would you like to learn?**
   A to ride a horse
   B to paint
   C to make bread

6. **You'd like to celebrate your birthday. What would you like to do?**
   A have a big party on the beach
   B try a new restaurant
   C invite some friends to dinner

7. **Who would you like to meet?**
   A a famous singer
   B a famous politician
   C a famous writer

8. **How many phone calls do you make every day?**
   A at least twenty
   B between two and ten
   C perhaps one or two

like, enjoy, want, would like and have got

↪ Grammar spot

like, enjoy, want, would like + nouns and verbs
Look at the quiz and fill the spaces with *to go* or *going*.

	films.
We like We enjoy	a .... to the cinema.
	b .... out with our friends.
	a holiday.
She wants She'd (would) like	c .... to the cinema.
	d .... horse riding.

1 Complete the conversations with the correct form of *would like, like* or *have got*.

a **Waiter:** Good morning. What <u>would you like</u> to order?

Woman: Salad for me please, and a steak for Tiddles.

b **Boy:** .... Sophie .... a book for her birthday?

Girl: I think a CD is a better present for her because she .... pop music.

c **Boy:** How many brothers and sisters .... you ....?

Girl: Three sisters, but I .... any brothers.

d **Girl:** .... your dad .... jazz music?

Boy: Oh yes, he .... 200 CDs.

e **Boy:** What .... you .... doing on holiday?

Girl: Oh, I .... swimming in the sea.

f **Boy:** .... you .... to come to the zoo with me this weekend?

Girl: No, thank you. I .... seeing animals in cages.

g **Mum:** I .... to meet your boyfriend.

Girl: Oh, he's very busy. He .... going sailing at weekends so he studies hard all week.

h **Girl:** I .... to buy some running shoes. What .... you ....?

Shop assistant: Sorry, we .... any. We only sell football boots.

2 Write a notice for the college website on page 17. Choose Travel, Contacts or Accommodation. Say what kind of person you are and explain what you want.

↘ GF page 206

«Pronunciation»

1 Look at this sentence. Do the words have the same vowel sound in them?

Stop studying, students!

2 Say these words aloud and put them into the correct column.

university fun pop music
become some Tuesday other
club long you above doctor
discuss want cost future

/juː/	/ʌ/	/ɒ/
university	fun	pop

3 ▸ **1 06** Listen and check your answers.

4 ▸ **1 07** Read these sentences and underline the sounds /juː/, /ʌ/ and /ɒ/. Listen to the recording and repeat.

I want to become a doctor.
Some university students have a lot of fun.
I run a music club above a shop.
His other brother's got long hair.

«Activity» Invitations and replies

1 Write down four things you like doing in your free time.

....

....

....

....

2 Now ask other people in the class about their interests. Say: What do you like doing? When you meet someone who shares one of your interests, suggest doing it together. Accept or refuse other people's invitations. Use the language in the box to help you.

Inviting	Accepting and refusing
Would you like to ... with me this weekend?	*Yes, that'd be great/fun/ interesting.* *Oh, sorry, I'm afraid I'm busy / I can't.*

Notice for
Travel ☐
Contacts ☐
Accommodation ☐

Post your notice here:

Don't forget to give your contact details!

«Activity» What kind of person?

Work with a partner. Choose a character in a film, television programme or book that you both know.
You each write a short text describing the personality of this character. Add some information about what he or she likes doing or doesn't like doing. You can use the quiz results to help you. Read each other's descriptions. Do you agree?

Quiz results

Mainly As: You think life is fun. You're never serious. You're confident and you have lots of friends.

Mainly Bs: You are independent. You like new experiences and ideas. You enjoy meeting new people. You wouldn't like to stay in one place all your life.

Mainly Cs: You like a quiet life. Perhaps you're rather shy. You don't want a lot of adventures. You'd like to have an interesting job.

A mix of As, Bs and Cs: You are a happy mix!

Exam folder 2

Listening Part 3

1 Look at these pictures of Dan. What does he do every day?

2 **1 08** Listen to what Dan says. Does he use exactly the same words as below? Underline the words which are different from what you hear.

a I always <u>cycle there</u>.
  go there by bicycle

b I have a huge breakfast at about half past eight.
  ....

c I'm studying geography.
  ....

d I usually study in my room in the afternoon.
  ....

e I enjoy spending time with my friends.
  ....

f I would like to travel round the world.
  ....

3 Listen again and look at the recording script.

4 Write the words Dan uses under the ones you underlined in Exercise 2.

5 Look at these pictures of Katy. What does she do every day?

6 **1 09** Listen to Katy talking about her day and fill in the missing information below. Remember she may use different words from the ones you see here.

> At 6.30 am she goes to the (1) .... on foot.
> At (2) .... she has breakfast.
> Her subject is (3) ....
> In the afternoon she usually goes to the (4) ....
> There is always a match on (5) .... afternoons.
> In the evening, she likes (6) ....
> When she finishes her course, she wants to be a (7) ....

7 Look at the recording script. Listen again and check your answers.

Exam Advice

The words you write in the spaces are always the same as the words you hear. But the words around the spaces are sometimes different from the words you hear.

Writing folder

Writing Parts 1, 2 and 3

Exam Advice

Correct punctuation is important in your writing. Understanding punctuation also helps you when you read.

1 Work with a partner. Look at the conversation below and answer the questions.

'Would you like a drink?'
'Thanks, but I've got one.'
'My name is Tom. I'm Jane's brother.'
'I'm Julietta, but my friends call me Julie.'

a How many capital letters are there? Why are they there? Can you think of other places where English uses capital letters?
b Find the quotation marks. Mark them in colour. Why are they there?
c How many apostrophes are there? Mark them in a different colour. Why are they there?
d How do we end a statement?
e Where do we use a question mark?
f Where do we use a comma?
g Do you know any other punctuation marks?

2 What's the difference between *the student's books* and *the students' books*?

3 These sentences need apostrophes and capital letters. Can you correct them?

a My brother and ~~j~~ I usually watch football matches at my grandparents flat because their televisions very big.
b On thursday im going to the match between italy and scotland with dad and uncle ian.
c Were travelling in my uncles car to edinburgh and after the match, were staying at the norton hotel.
d Then on friday morning my uncle and i are visiting edinburgh castle and my fathers going to the national gallery and a museum.

4 Correct the punctuation mistakes in this note.

dear pia
how are you i must tell you
about a new club in my town. its
in oxford road and i think youd
love it. we can play tennis and go
swimming and theres a small gym
i made a new friend there last
sunday. her names jessica. shes
from canada and shes got blonde
hair and she makes me laugh. shes
a good dancer too. i hope you
can come here soon and meet her
with love,
Andy

⬎ Corpus spot   Irregular plurals

We usually make plurals by adding *s*, but there are some important exceptions. Correct the mistakes of these PET students.

a In my country, all the womans wear new clothes at weddings.
b I like the London streets with their red telephone boxs.
c There are a lot of friendly persons at the club.
d I look after the childs when their parents are working.
e During the break we talk about our lifes and our friends.

3 What's your job?

Grammar	present simple/continuous; state verbs; short answers
Vocabulary	jobs
Revision	present simple

Introduction

1 🔊 1•10 Look at the photographs and listen to seven people talking about their jobs. Match the speakers to the photographs.

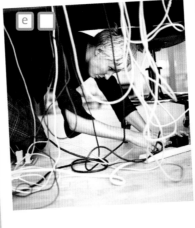

2 What do the people do? Write the names of their jobs.

3 Look at the photographs again. What are the people doing?

Present continuous

I	am (not) wearing	
You/we/they	are (not) wearing	a helmet.
He/she/it	is (not) wearing	
Am I		
Are you/we/they	wearing	a helmet?
Is he/she/it		

4 Would you like to do any of these jobs? Why? / Why not?

Listening

1 Look at this picture. Can you guess what the people's jobs are?

2 Listen to the man talking on the phone. What is his job? Who is he talking to?

3 Listen again. The man is describing the people he can see. Five of them have jobs. Write the names of their jobs.

1 ....
2 ....
3 ....
4 ....
5 ....

Language focus

Present simple and present continuous

1 Look again at the picture of the shopping mall. Decide what the people *are doing* and what they *do*. Put the verbs in the correct form.

a The security officer *is talking* to a police officer.
b The model .... (stand) by a fountain.
c The photographer .... (sell) his photographs to magazines.
d The thief .... (pull) a shopping bag on wheels.
e The thief .... (steal) things from shops.
f The bank guard .... (not look) at the thief.
g The bank guard never .... (do) anything, because he's lazy.
h The photographer .... (take) a photograph of the model.
i The artist .... (sell) her pictures to the children's parents.
j The thief .... (not steal) anything at the moment.
k The journalist .... (write) something in his notebook.

> ### 🢖 Grammar spot
>
> **Present simple and present continuous**
>
> Look at these sentences about picture *e* on page 22 and then choose the correct tense to complete the rules.
> *I design websites.*
> *I'm plugging in my computer.*
>
> We use the *present simple / present continuous* to talk about what we usually do.
> We use the *present simple / present continuous* to talk about what we're doing now.

2 Sonia is an English schoolgirl. She's fifteen. This week she's doing work experience in a hotel. Look at the activities opposite. Make sentences about Sonia using the present simple or the present continuous.

usually	this week only
cycle to school	not go to school
do lessons all day	not do any homework
study at home in the evening	work in a hotel
play volleyball after school	have meals with her colleagues
not wear her best skirt every day	speak French with hotel guests

What does Sonia usually do / not do?
She cycles to school.
....
....
....
....

What is Sonia doing / not doing this week?
She isn't going to school.
....
....
....
....

3 Complete this telephone conversation Sonia had with her granny using the verbs in the box.

do ~~not go~~ get up help like prefer look forward to start stay understand work not work

Sonia: Hi, Granny. How are you?
Granny: Oh, not bad. How's school?
Sonia: (**a**) *I'm not going* .... to school this week.
Granny: Why not? Are you ill?
Sonia: No, I (**b**) .... work experience. I
(**c**) .... in a hotel.
Granny: I hope you (**d**) .... in the kitchen.
You're not good at cooking!
Sonia: No, I'm not in the kitchen. I (**e**) ....
the receptionist and the manager.
Granny: Is that nice?
Sonia: Yes, it is. Well, I (**f**) .... working with
the manager, she's really friendly. But I
(**g**) .... helping the receptionist
because I can talk to the guests. I can practise my French
because some French people (**h**) ....
in the hotel. I (**i**) .... almost everything
they say. Isn't that great?
Granny: Yes, that's very good.
Sonia: Yes. But I am tired. When I go to school, I
(**j**) .... at half past seven, but this week
I (**k**) .... work at seven o'clock.
Granny: Oh, well, you can have a good rest at the weekend.
Sonia: Oh, yes. I (**l**) .... it.

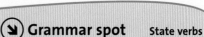 Now listen to the recording and check your answers.

↘ GF page 206

Grammar spot State verbs

Some verbs are not normally used in continuous tenses in English. These are state (or stative) verbs, for example *believe, know, like, think, understand, want.* Keep a list and add to it when you meet new ones.

Correct the mistakes in these sentences.
a ~~I'm not believing~~ you can fly a plane.
I don't believe
b Are those jeans new? I'm liking them very much.
c We're thinking this CD is very expensive.
d Are you wanting some coffee?
e I can't phone you because I'm not knowing your number.
f The teacher is speaking quickly and I'm not understanding what she's saying.
g My friends are watching a pop programme on TV but I'm not liking it, so I'm listening to my MP3 player.

4 Do school students do work experience in your country? Would you like to do it?

Short answers

In English the grammar of the short answer must match the grammar of the question.

1 Match each question to its answer.

   a Do I look OK?
   b Do you live near the school?
   c Does this school open on Sundays?
   d Do they like ice cream?
   e Am I sitting in the right place?
   f Are you studying English?
   g Is the sun shining?
   h Are they working?

   1 Yes, I do. / No, I don't.
   2 Yes, you are. / No, you aren't.
   3 Yes, you do. / No, you don't.
   4 Yes, they are. / No, they aren't.
   5 Yes, it does. / No, it doesn't.
   6 Yes, it is. / No, it isn't.
   7 Yes, they do. / No, they don't.
   8 Yes, I am. / No, I'm not.

2 Work with two other students. Take turns to ask and answer questions. Then listen to the other two students and check their grammar.

   Do you play volleyball? Yes, I do.
   Are we speaking Italian? No, we aren't.

«Pronunciation»

1 **1 13** Listen to the recording and mark these words in the order in which you hear them.

   a cat .... cart .... cut .....*1*......
   b bag .... bug ....
   c carry .... curry ....
   d match .... March .... much ....

2 Listen again and repeat each sentence.

3 **1 14** Now repeat these words after the recording and decide which have the same vowel sound in them as cat /æ/, cart /ɑː/ and cut /ʌ/.

   does   doesn't   can   can't
   must   mustn't   are   aren't

«Activity» Spot the difference

Work with a partner. Don't look at page 23.

Try to find all the differences between this picture and the one on page 23. Say what the people are doing and what they are not doing now.

EXAMPLE: *The photographer isn't taking a photo of the model now, he's taking a photo of the thief.*

When you finish, check your memory by looking at page 23.

«Activity» What's my job?

Work in a group. One person mimes an activity which is part of a job. The others guess what his or her job is.

Ask questions like these about the activity:

Are you making something?
Are you mending something?
Are you opening a door?
Are you answering a telephone?

The answers can only be
Yes, I am or *No, I'm not.*

Ask questions like these about the job:

Do you make things?
Do you talk to other people?
Do you work indoors?
Do you use special equipment?

The answers can only be

Yes, I do.   No, I don't.   or   Sometimes.

Exam folder 3

Speaking Part 3

1 Look at this picture of a young man, Tom. Can you match these questions to their answers?

a Where is he?
b What does he look like?
c What is he wearing?
d What kind of person is he?
e What is he doing?
f How do you feel about doing this kind of thing?
g Why?

1 He's painting something.
2 Because I don't like the smell of paint.
3 He's a friendly person.
4 I wouldn't like to do this.
5 He's wearing white shorts and a red T-shirt.
6 He's outside his house.
7 He's tall and he's got short fair hair.

2 Look at this picture of a young woman. Can you answer these questions?

a Where is she?
b What does she look like?
c What is she wearing?
d What kind of person is she?
e What is she doing?
f How do you feel about doing this kind of thing?
g Why?

Exam Advice

Learn these questions. They do not all fit every exam photograph, but they help you to think of what to say.

3 Now shut your book. Can you remember all the questions?

4   Work with a partner. One of you talks about
    Photograph A and then the other talks about
    Photograph B. Before you start, look at the seven
    questions on page 26. Think about your answers for
    your photograph. Don't say anything now.

    Now cover page 26. Imagine your partner wants to
    know the answers to all seven questions. Tell your
    partner about your photograph. Are you giving your
    partner all the answers?

    When your partner is speaking, listen carefully. Look at
    the questions on page 26. Tick the questions when you
    hear the answers.

Reading Part 5

1   Look again at the photograph in Exercise 1 on page 26.
    Choose the correct word to go in these spaces.

    1 Tom is ......*A*...... .
       A tall   **B** long   **C** high   **D** great
    2 Tom .... wearing a T-shirt.
       A do   **B** does   **C** is   **D** be
    3 Tom's ....a tin of yellow paint.
       A has   **B** got   **C** wants   **D** uses

Exam Advice

If you are not sure which word is correct, try to decide which
words are wrong, and why.

2   Look again at the photograph in Exercise 2 on page 26.
    Choose the correct word to go in these spaces.

    1 Irena .... got a tidy desk.
       A isn't   **B** hasn't   **C** doesn't   **D** aren't
    2 Irena usually .... a sandwich for lunch.
       A eats   **B** eating   **C** have   **D** having
    3 Irena's a ....
       A hairdresser   **B** shop assistant   **C** nurse   **D** secretary

4 Let's go out

Grammar	prepositions of time; present continuous for future plans
Vocabulary	entertainment; making appointments; dates
Revision	present continuous for present actions; *would like*

a

b

Introduction

1 Write the names of the different kinds of entertainment by the photographs.

circus

b..............t

c

m.............. show

d

music fes..............

e

m..............l

f

f..............m

2 🔊 15 Listen to the pieces of music and match them with the photographs.

3 Say what is happening in each photograph. If you don't know a word, use *a kind of ...* .

EXAMPLE: *In picture **c** the magician is putting some money into a hat. He is holding a kind of stick.*

4 Which of these kinds of entertainment would you like to go to? Why? Which would you not like to go to?

Reading

1 You are looking at a website to find out what's on. You can click on different kinds of entertainment and then read about different events. Read about the events A–F quickly. Then decide which entertainment section (Theatre, Cinema, Museums, etc.) each one belongs to.

A _Cinema_   B ....   C ....   D ....   E ....   F ....

wherecanwego.com   A Guide to What's On near you!

What are you looking for?

[Theatre >]   [Cinema >]   [Museums >]   [Clubbing >]

[Music >]   [Children >]   [Dance shows >]

Monday 24 – Sunday 30 August

A

Set in San Francisco, *Meet my Family* stars Jamie Glazer and Francesca Nolte and tells the funny story of a family who run a restaurant. An unexpected visitor alters their lives forever. Things will never be the same again!

This year's best comedy film   Certificate 12
Every evening this week at the Arts Picture House at 7.45 pm. Tickets £6.50.

B

Don't miss the excitement, the comedy and the music of the
CIRCUS OF THE CITY
The Big Top is in Central Park from 26 until 29 August. Afternoon shows start at 2.30 pm and evening shows start at 7 pm. Tickets at a range of prices (£10–£16). Book early.

C

PLUS SIX, a local rock band who are now well known and appear all over the world, are returning to their home town to play in a gig on Saturday evening (29 August at 8 pm) in the Riverside Buildings. Book tickets early as they are very popular. £16.

D

MOJO'S is the best place to enjoy yourself at weekends. If you're feeling energetic, dance the night away on Fridays and Saturdays with DJs Simon and Dave.

For over-16s only. Open 9 pm – 4 am.
Arrive before 11 and pay only £8, after 11 £10.

E

An exciting new group called *Motari* present their fascinating African and Western dances with some flamenco and jazz added. They are performing twice in the Town Hall on Sunday at 4 pm and 8 pm.
All tickets £9. Interval refreshments included.

F

Tickets are still available for a weekend festival of rock music and fun in the gardens of Kingston Manor. Begins at midday on Saturday 29 and finishes at midnight on Sunday 30. Camping available. Tickets £70 weekend, £45 day.

2 Read each text quickly again to answer these questions. Don't worry about any words you don't know.

  a Which events may make you laugh? _A and B_
  b Which events are outdoors?
  c Which event costs £7 or less?
  d Which events are only on one day?
  e What can you go to on Monday evening?
  f What can you go to on Saturday afternoon?

Vocabulary spot

When you read, try to understand the words you don't know before you check them with your teacher or in a dictionary.

What do the words below mean? Look at the words around them in the texts and guess the correct answers.

1 In text A *alters* means   a) changes   b) leaves   c) stops.
2 In text C *gig* means   a) building   b) concert   c) band.
3 In text E *fascinating* means   a) confusing   b) slow   c) interesting.

Corpus spot   *Fun* and *funny*

Match *fun* and *funny* to their meanings.

If something or someone is ...., it/he/she makes you laugh. [fun/funny]
If something is ...., you enjoy doing it. [fun/funny]

Here are some sentences written by PET students. Put *fun* or *funny* in each gap.

a There were lots of .... things to do at the holiday camp like sailing or diving.
b The film I saw was very ....
c We'll have great .... when you come to stay for the weekend.

Language focus
Prepositions of time

1 **1 16** Listen to some conversations with your books closed and decide where the people are going.

1 .... 2 .... 3 ....

2 Now listen again and fill in the missing words.

Conversation 1

Sara: I know. It sounds good. I'd like to go.

Ed: I'm taking my little brother. Would you like to come too?

Sara: That would be great. I love the noise, the music and all the excitement. The last time I went was **(a)** *in 2005* when I was ten.

Ed: Oh, really? Well, I like the clowns best. Are you free **(b)** .... or tomorrow? The afternoon show is best for my brother.

Sara: Sorry, I'm busy then. I'm going to the cinema **(c)** .... – I've got the tickets, so I can't change it – and I'm playing tennis **(d)** ....

Ed: Oh, well … can you go **(e)** ....? It finishes **(f)** .... That's Saturday.

Sara: I'm free **(g)** ....

Ed: Good. I'm free then, too. It only comes once a year, so we mustn't miss it.

Conversation 2

Sam: Hi, Juliet, it's Sam here. Have you got the tickets yet?

Juliet: Yeah, for tonight.

Sam: What time does it start?

Juliet: Just a minute. I'll look. Er, it starts **(h)** ....

Sam: Oh, you know I work in a shop **(i)** ....? In the city centre. Well, there's a sale **(j)** ...., so I'm working late. I have to tidy the shop **(k)** ...., so I'm working till seven thirty this evening. I usually finish **(l)** ...., which is better.

Juliet: Don't worry. There are lots of adverts before the film actually starts.

Sam: OK. See you later then. Outside?

Juliet: See you there. Bye.

Conversation 3

Max: It's so boring here **(m)** ...., Rachel. There's nothing to do.

Rachel: There are lots of good things on **(n)** .... What are you doing **(o)** ....? My mum's going to see a dance show **(p)** .... We can go with her.

Max: Oh, boring. And I don't like going to things like that **(q)** ....

Rachel: Well, there's the rock festival in the park. That looks good. I like listening to music outside **(r)** .... But it's very expensive.

Max: Mm. I've only got £10.

Rachel: Well, would you like to go to the new nightclub? I went there last week **(s)** .... It's only £8 before eleven. We can go **(t)** ....

Max: I'd really like to go to the rock festival, but OK then. Shall we meet at your house?

Rachel: Yeah. About nine?

Max: See you then.

3 Look at Exercise 2 and use your answers to help you complete this table.

on	at	in	no preposition
		2005	today

> ### ⤵ Grammar spot **Prepositions of time**
>
> Choose the correct preposition to complete the rules.
> We use *on / at / in / no preposition* before days of the week and dates.
> We use *on / at / in / no preposition* before times, *the weekend, the end of the day, the moment*.
> We use *on / at / in / no preposition* before months, seasons and years.
> We use *on / at / in / no preposition* before *today, tomorrow (morning), this / next (afternoon, week)*.

4 Put the correct preposition (or nothing) in each space.

  a My friend's taking me sailing ....–........ next Sunday.

  b My team's playing football against yours .... Friday afternoon.

  c I'm visiting my grandmother in Chile .... this summer.

  d Would you like to come to the theatre with me .... Saturday evening?

  e Our friends are arriving .... 7.30.

  f I don't like swimming .... the winter – the water's too cold.

  g I always feel tired .... the afternoon.

  h Jake's taking his driving test .... 23 March.

  i My brother got married .... 2008.

  j This street's very dark .... night.

  k I'm babysitting .... tomorrow evening.

  l I was very bored .... the weekend.

> ↘ **GF page 206**

«Pronunciation»

1 How many syllables are there in these words?

Sunday ...*2*..   Monday ....   Tuesday ....
Wednesday ....   Thursday ....   Friday ....
Saturday ....

2 🔊 **17** Repeat the words after the recording. Were you right?

3 Can you mark the main stress on these words?

January   February   March   April
May   June   July   August
September   October   November   December

4 🔊 **18** Listen to the recording and check your answers.

5 How do we say these dates?

28 April   15 August   3 February

6 🔊 **19** Listen to the recording and check your answers.

7 Choose the correct words to complete this sentence.

We *say* / *write* 15th January or 15 January but we *say* / *write* the fifteenth of January or January the fifteenth.

«Activity» Time expressions

Your teacher will give you a circle with ON, AT or IN in the middle. Work in a group of three. Your teacher will give you a game board. When you land on a square containing a time phrase which matches your preposition, write it in your circle.

Present continuous for future plans

↘ Grammar spot

Present continuous for future plans

Look at these sentences from the conversations on page 30 and then choose the correct tense to complete the rules.
I work in a shop.
I'm playing tennis tomorrow afternoon.

We use the *present simple* / *present continuous* to talk about what we usually do.
We use the *present simple* / *present continuous* to talk about future plans.

The person in the pictures is planning to do things at different times. Write sentences about the things he is planning to do, choosing a time expression from the box for each sentence. You do not need to use all the expressions.

He's travelling to Moscow on Saturday morning.

Saturday morning	next Monday
the weekend	tomorrow afternoon
15th January	the summer
Thursday	6.30

> ↘ **GF page 207**

«Activity» Diary

Work with a partner. One of you is A and one of you is B. Fill in your diary on page 200 or page 202. You can choose some of the events on page 29 or imagine some. Don't show your partner.

Ask your partner *What are you doing on ...?*

Find a time when you are both free so you can go to the cinema together.

Exam folder 4

Listening Part 1

1 Greg and Sophia are talking about something. Look at these three pictures. What do you think they are talking about?

 A ☐    B ☐    C ✓

2 Look at the question.

> **1** What do they decide to do tomorrow?

The box under picture C above is ticked because that is the answer.

🔘20 Listen to Greg and Sophia's conversation and think about why C is the answer. Answer these questions.

a Are they playing tennis tomorrow? Why? / Why not?
b Are they playing hockey tomorrow? Why? / Why not?
c Are they going cycling tomorrow? How do you know?
d Do they both agree? How do you know?

3 Look at these pictures for four other conversations.

Think what the conversations are about. The questions help you too.

2 Which shop are they going to first?

 A ☐   B ☐   C ☐

3 When is Tim meeting his father?

 A ☐   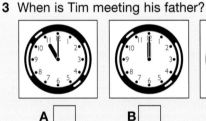 B ☐    C ☐

4 Where are they going on Saturday evening?

 A ☐   B ☐   C ☐

5 When is Paula's birthday party?

 A ☐   B ☐   C ☐

4 🔘21 Now listen to conversations 2, 3, 4 and 5. Decide which picture is correct for each one and put a tick in the box.

Exam Advice

Read the question and look at the pictures before you listen.

Writing folder

Writing Part 2

1 Look at this question. It is an example of the kind of task you will see in Part 2 of the Writing Paper. What does it ask you to do?

> You're spending a day in the capital of your country next Saturday. Write an email to an English friend called Helen. In your email, you should
> - say what you would like to do in the city
> - tell her what time you are arriving
> - suggest where to meet

2 Work with a partner. Read these three answers. Only one answers the question. Which one?

a

Delete   Reply   Reply All   Forward   Print

Dear Helen,
On Saturday I'd like to go shopping because I want to buy a new coat and some shoes. Then I would like to go to the cinema and have an Italian meal. My father is bringing me in the car. You can come in the car with us too. We are leaving home at 9.30.
Love
Maria

b

Delete   Reply   Reply All   Forward   Print

Dear Helen,
I'd like to go to the cinema on Saturday and walk by the river. We can go to a café to have lunch. What do you want to do? I am arriving at 11.30. We can meet outside the station.
Love
Maria

c

Delete   Reply   Reply All   Forward   Print

Dear Helen,
I'd like to go to the museum on Saturday. I'm arriving at 11.30 so we can meet at midday.
Love
Maria

3 In Writing Part 2 you must write 35–45 words.

Add *outside the museum* to answer c. Is this a good answer now?

4 Think about your own answer to the questions.

   a What would you like to do in your capital city?
   b Think about when you will arrive.
   c Think of different places you can meet someone.

5 Write your answer.

Exam Advice

Remember there are always three things you must write about in Writing Part 2.

6 Have you answered the three parts of the question?

   Count the words. Make sure you have 35–45 words.

7 How many lines of your writing is 35–45 words?

5 Wheels and wings

Introduction

1 Look at the photographs of different ways of travelling. Match each one to a clue below and write the words in the crossword. Now finish the crossword. The other clues don't have photographs.

Grammar *need*; countable/uncountable nouns; quantity
Vocabulary transport; compound nouns
Revision present simple + frequency adverbs

Across

1 It takes lots of people to school, to work and around town.

5 It is only found in cities and travels on rails.

7 It carries a few people in the air.

8 It transports goods by road.

9 You need to be fit to travel on it.

11 You often find it outside the railway station.

12 It travels at about 850 kilometres per hour.

13 It goes on long journeys across water, carrying people and goods.

Down

2 It has two wheels, only carries one person and has a very small engine.

3 Many families own one.

4 It takes people across water. It travels quite slowly.

5 It runs on rails and has several carriages.

6 It has no roof and often goes faster than a car.

10 It spends a lot of time on motorways carrying people from one place to another.

2 Work in a group. Compare your crosswords. Can you help the other people in your group?

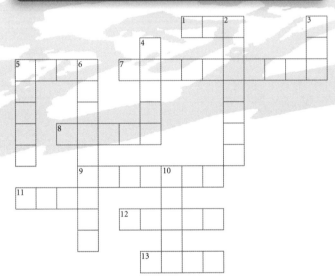

3 How many of the different ways of travelling do you use? Count them.

Write three sentences using *usually*, *sometimes* and *often*.

EXAMPLE: *I often travel by train.*

4 Write each of the words from the crossword under one of these headings: AIR, LAND, WATER.

(⭳) Corpus spot ⊙

Correct these mistakes made by PET students and complete the rule below.

a We always go to the city centre with car.

b We can go there by foot.

We go .... car, train, bicycle, plane, boat but we go .... foot.

(⭳) Vocabulary spot

American English has some different words from British English. What do these words mean in British English? Use your dictionary if you need to.

truck ....   cab ....   freeway ....

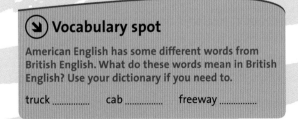
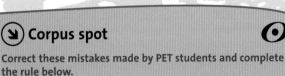

Listening

a ↓ CHECK - IN 🧳

b ↓ CUSTOMS

c ↑ HOTEL RESERVATIONS

d ↑ PASSPORT CONTROL

e 𝒊 INFORMATION ➡

f ← DEPARTURE LOUNGE ✈

g ↓ SHOPS

h ↑ TICKET SALES

1 Where do you find all these signs?

2 🔊 1·22 Listen to six conversations. Each conversation happens at one of the places above. Write the letter to show where the speakers are.

1 .... 2 .... 3 .... 4 .... 5 .... 6 ....

Language focus

Need

1 Listen again and answer these questions.

Conversation 1
a What does the man need?
b What doesn't the man need?

Conversation 2
c What doesn't the woman need?

Conversation 3
d What does the man need to do?

Conversation 4
e What do they need to buy?

Conversation 5
f Does the woman need to pay any tax?

Conversation 6
g When does the man need to come back?
h Does he need to reconfirm his return flight?

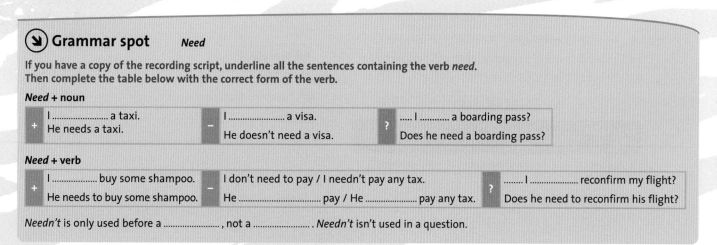

⬇ **Grammar spot** *Need*

If you have a copy of the recording script, underline all the sentences containing the verb *need*. Then complete the table below with the correct form of the verb.

Need + noun

+	−	?
I .... a taxi. He needs a taxi.	I .... a visa. He doesn't need a visa.	..... I .... a boarding pass? Does he need a boarding pass?

Need + verb

+	−	?
I .... buy some shampoo. He needs to buy some shampoo.	I don't need to pay / I needn't pay any tax. He .... pay / He .... pay any tax.	.... I .... reconfirm my flight? Does he need to reconfirm his flight?

Needn't is only used before a ...., not a .... *Needn't* isn't used in a question.

2 Complete these sentences with the correct form of *need*.

a It's very hot here – I _need_ a drink.

b .... (you) a new suitcase to take on holiday?

c .... (we) book a taxi to the airport?

d You .... (not) take the train because I can drive you home.

e Lorry drivers .... stop for a break after a few hours on the road.

f Do .... (I) wear a helmet on a bike?

g My brother .... (not) a car because he catches the bus everywhere.

h You .... (not) come to the station with me – I know where it is.

➘ **GF page 207**

Countable and uncountable nouns

1 Joe is going to stay with a Brazilian family who live by the seaside. Here are some of the things he is planning to take. What are they?

2 Put them into the correct column.

Countable (singular)	Countable (plural)	Uncountable
a camera	some magazines	some shampoo

➘ **Grammar spot**

Countable and uncountable nouns

Complete these rules with the words *countable* and *uncountable*.

.... nouns can be singular or plural.
.... nouns cannot be plural. We use *a* or *an* before .... nouns. We use *some* before .... nouns and plural .... nouns.

With uncountable nouns we often use a countable noun like *bottle*. Match these uncountable nouns to a word below:

shampoo   water   tea   chocolate   bread

a bar   a bottle   a glass   a packet   a loaf

EXAMPLE: *a bottle of shampoo*

3 Joe can't carry his backpack because he has too many things. The weather is hot in January in Brazil. Work in a group. What does Joe need to take? What doesn't he need to take? Make two lists.

Things Joe needs to take	Things Joe doesn't need to take

4 Tell some other students what you decided. Do they agree with you?

5 Work with a partner. Imagine you are going to stay with a friend in Britain for a week in January. What things do you need to take? What things don't you need to take? Write them down. Read your list to another pair of students. Do they agree with you?

I need to take a warm coat. I don't need to take a sun hat or any sunscreen.

➘ **GF page 207**

➘ **Corpus spot**

Countable and uncountable nouns

Correct these mistakes made by PET students.

a I have a lot of works to do at home tonight.

b We can eat fishes and big plates of salad.

c We came to a set of traffic light.

d Listening to English musics is good.

e I have a lot of furnitures in my room.

f My friend Noelia always gives me good advices.

g They travel to other country every year.

Expressions of quantity

↘ Grammar spot — Expressions of quantity

Complete the column headings in the table below.

.... nouns	.... nouns
I've got **a lot of / lots of** bags.	I've got **a lot of / lots of** luggage.
I haven't got **any** bags.	I haven't got **any** luggage.
I haven't got **many** bags.	I haven't got **much** luggage.
I've got **a few** bags.	I've only got **a little** luggage.
I've got **several** bags.	
I've got **a couple of** bags.	

At the airport, Joe meets the woman in the picture. He emails his mum from his laptop. Circle the correct words.

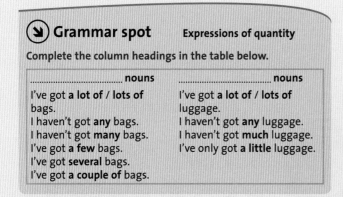

Hi Mum

I'm at the airport now. I'm waiting to check in. There aren't **(a)** (many)/ much passengers waiting for my flight yet – that's probably because I got here so early. I'm so pleased I haven't got **(b)** many / much luggage. There's a woman sitting next to me who's also going to Brazil. I hope her friends meet her at the airport because she has **(c)** lots of / many luggage. She's got **(d)** several / a couple of suitcases, **(e)** a few / a little carrier bags and **(f)** much / a lot of boxes. She's even got **(g)** a few / a couple of backpacks.

I bought a book about Brazil in the airport shop. The one Uncle James gave me didn't have **(h)** many / much information about the area I'm visiting. I've got **(i)** a little / a few English money left, so I'll go and spend it on a coffee now. Talk to you when I get there.

Love,

Joe

 GF page 207

1 Fill in the missing words in these sentences.

   a I need ..*a*.......... visa.
   b I've got .... couple .... suitcases.
   c They need .... take their passports.
   d He's got .... lot .... luggage.
   e Do we need .... book a taxi?
   f You need .... money.

2 **1 23** Listen and repeat the sentences. What do you notice about the words you filled in?

3 Try saying these sentences. Put a circle around the words which are not stressed.

   a I need (a) hotel room.
   b You need to pay tax.
   c I want some shampoo.
   d I'd like to go swimming.
   e He's got a few magazines.
   f I've got a new pair of shoes.

4 **1 24** Listen and repeat the sentences. Were you right?

«Activity» What do I need?

Your teacher will give you a card. Don't show it to the other students. Guess the activity on your friends' cards.

Ask questions like these:

Do I need other people to do this?
Do I need good weather?
Do I need any special equipment?
Do I need to go to a special place?

Answer their questions truthfully. You can answer *Yes, No, Sometimes* or *It doesn't matter*.

«Activity» Compound nouns

Sometimes we put two nouns together to make another, e.g. *address book*. Your teacher will give you some cards with nouns on them. Find the student who has a noun which goes with yours and decide which word comes first.

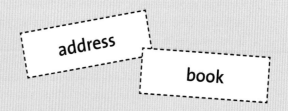

address

book

Exam folder 5

Reading Part 2

1   Look at these five people. They all want to go on holiday.

Now look at the suitcases.

Can you guess which suitcase belongs to each person?
There is one extra suitcase which doesn't belong to anyone.

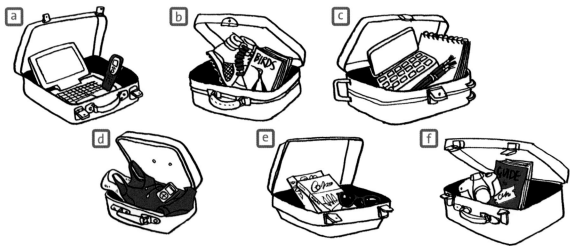

2   Now read some information about the five people and try again to match
them with their suitcases. Underline the words which help you choose.

1   Karen likes pop music and dancing in discos and she would like to find
    a hotel where she can swim every day. She also enjoys using a gym.
2   Tom needs to find a quiet hotel in the country which has a good
    restaurant. He is taking some work on holiday with him and needs to
    hire a room for a business meeting in the hotel.
3   Maggie would like to relax in her hotel, sunbathing, swimming and
    reading. She wants to stay somewhere quiet with a good restaurant.
4   John wants to stay in the mountains. He likes walking and is interested
    in flowers and birds. He wants to stay in a family hotel.
5   Mike wants to spend his holiday sightseeing in the city. He likes taking
    photographs of the places he visits and wants a hotel which can
    organise trips. He would like a hotel with a swimming pool.

3   Read these descriptions of places to go on holiday. Which hotel would you like to go to?

A

The Spring Hotel is a family hotel with a new swimming pool in the centre of the city. It is near all the famous buildings and art galleries. The hotel arranges coach tours to other towns.

B

Hotel Crystal is on the edge of the city with its own gardens and has 200 rooms, a first-class restaurant and three swimming pools. It is ideal for a really relaxing, quiet holiday in the sun.

C

Grand Hotel is a large hotel in the centre of the city. It has evening entertainment including a disco twice a week. There are coach trips to the mountains where visitors can walk and enjoy the flowers and the birds.

D

The Park Hotel has 10 rooms. It is in a quiet spot in the country. It doesn't serve food but there are restaurants in the city, which is about 10 kms away. The hotel arranges coach tours of the city for those people who do not like walking.

E

The Riviera Hotel is a family hotel in the city with its own swimming pool and gym where guests can keep fit. There is a disco in the hotel every night and it also has two restaurants.

F

The Hotel Royal is a large hotel in a village surrounded by mountains and is very quiet and peaceful. It has a gym and a good restaurant. Meeting rooms are available.

G

The Hotel Regent is very old and beautiful. It is in the middle of the city and is close to lots of good restaurants. It has several meeting rooms and is suitable for business conferences.

H

The Palace Regent is a quiet family hotel in the mountains so it is very easy to go for walks without needing to use a car. There are flowers and birds to enjoy all year round and restaurants in the village.

4   Look at page 38 and read the text about Karen again. Look at the words you underlined.

5   Now find a hotel for Karen. Look at the table.

Read the hotel texts again and tick which hotels have a disco. Can Karen swim and use a gym at any of the hotels which have music? Tick the boxes. Which hotel is best for Karen?

Hotels	A	B	C	D	E	F	G	H
disco?								
swimming?								
gym?								

6   Read the text about Tom again and underline any other important information. Check you have underlined the information to look for.

7   Now find a hotel for Tom. Read the hotel texts again and tick which hotels are in the country. Which one has a good restaurant?

Hotels	A	B	C	D	E	F	G	H
in the country?								
good restaurant?								
room for meeting?								

8   Now do the same for Maggie, John and Mike.

Maggie

Hotels	A	B	C	D	E	F	G	H
quiet?								
swimming?								
restaurant?								

John

Hotels	A	B	C	D	E	F	G	H
family hotel?								
walking in the mountains?								
flowers and birds?								

Mike

Hotels	A	B	C	D	E	F	G	H
city?								
swimming pool?								
organises trips?								

Exam Advice

When you choose an answer, check the text has *all* the things the person wants.

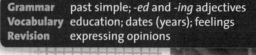

What did you do at school today?

Grammar	past simple; -ed and -ing adjectives
Vocabulary	education; dates (years); feelings
Revision	expressing opinions

Introduction

1   Look at the photographs. How do you think these students feel about their classes?

Which class would you like to attend? Why?

2   Work in a group. Look at this student message board on a school website.

Do you agree with these teenagers' opinions?

3   What opinion would you add to the message board?

Vocabulary spot

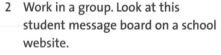

False friends are words which look the same in different languages but have different meanings.

Be careful how you use the word *education* in English.

Match this sentence to the correct meaning, a or b.

I had a good education.

a   I went to a good school.
b   I had a good home.

Make a note when you find any *false friends* between English and your language.

Messages

School uniform is a good idea.

Sport is important for everybody.

Boys and girls learn better in single-sex schools.

Students only work hard when they have exams.

Schools don't listen to students' opinions.

Every student needs a laptop.

Most school rules are unnecessary.

Teachers only care about exam results.

I enjoy school.

Homework is boring.

Reading

1 Look at the three photographs of people, then read the magazine article quickly. Which photograph do you think matches each paragraph?

2 Write the names above the paragraphs and below write the year you think the people started secondary school.

My first day

Mavis Carver

Anita Green   Neil Johnson

A ....

On my first day at secondary school I was very excited. My father walked to the school with me – he was very proud of me. A teacher took me into the hall with the other girls. She gave us some books and told us which rooms to go to. She used our surnames and we felt very important. My first lesson was in the science laboratory. Of course, very few schools had labs in those days. I was nervous of doing something wrong, but I was very interested and I soon stopped feeling worried. I became a scientist that day! I studied hard because I wanted to go to university to do science. And I went when I was eighteen.

Year ....

B ....

I remember my first day at secondary school very well. I was eleven years old. When I arrived at the school, the playground was full of big boys, some of them looked like men to me. I was frightened. I asked some boys where to go, but no one helped me. When I found my classroom, the teacher was angry because I was late. I was miserable. I wanted to go home. Of course, I soon made friends and began to enjoy some of the lessons. But those first days were terrible.

Year ....

C ....

My first day at secondary school was fun! I was with my friends from primary school, so I wasn't nervous. In the morning, some of the older students took us on a tour of the school. They showed us the different departments like the art rooms, the computer rooms and the sports ground. Then we met our teachers and they gave us our timetables. Everyone was very friendly and we all felt quite happy. Of course, when we started lessons, we realised that the work was difficult. I could understand the science, but I couldn't understand the maths at all. At the end of the day I was very tired! And we got lots of homework. I didn't feel so confident then.

Year ....

Language focus

Adjectives describing feelings and opinions

1 Read the texts again. Underline the adjectives which tell you about people's feelings.

2 Look at the adjectives you underlined. Which are about good feelings and which are about bad feelings? Write the adjectives in two lists. Can you add any other words to these lists?

3 Think about your first day at a school. How did you feel? Were you excited, frightened or proud?

excited, proud,

nervous, worried,

-ing and -ed adjectives

1 Look at these photographs. How do the people feel?
Complete the sentences with adjectives from the box.

> amused ~~bored~~ frightened interested
> tired worried

  a This is a *bored* teenager.
  b She's ....
  c This man is ....
  d This boy is ....
  e These boys are ....
  f They're ....

2 Look at these pictures. Complete the sentences with
adjectives from the box.

> amusing boring ~~frightening~~ interesting
> tiring worrying

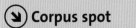

a That's a *frightening* film.

b Some people think that programme is ....

c I think this is .... news.

d Lots of my friends say this is an .... magazine.

e He's got a .... job.

f We all think that book is ....

🢃 Grammar spot   *-ing* and *-ed* adjectives

Look at Exercises 1 and 2 above and complete these sentences.

We use .... adjectives to describe the thing (or person) that *causes* the feeling.

We use .... adjectives to describe the person who *has* the feeling.

🢃 Corpus spot   *-ing* and *-ed* adjectives 👁

Choose the correct form for the adjectives in these sentences by PET students.

a I am so *bored / boring* with my room.
b My first lesson was very *interested / interesting*.
c She is *interested / interesting* in cinema and theatre.
d I felt very *relaxed / relaxing* on the beach.
e I was really *surprised / surprising* by the beautiful house.
f My parents liked it very much but I found it *bored / boring*.
g At the time, it was *embarrassed / embarrassing* for me, but now I think it's funny!
h I am very *excited / exciting* about your holiday in my city.
i It was very *surprised / surprising* news for me.
j She was *amazed / amazing* by the shops and restaurants.

🢆 GF page 207

Past simple

1 Who can write the past tense of these verbs most
quickly? (They are all in the magazine article on
page 41.)

List A		List B	
arrive	*arrived*	be	*was/were*
ask	....	become	....
help	....	begin	....
look	....	can	....
realise	....	feel	....
show	....	find	....
start	....	get	....
stop	....	give	....
study	....	go	....
use	....	make	....
walk	....	meet	....
want	....	take	....
		tell	....

2 What is the difference between the verbs in List A
and the verbs in List B?

To be		Regular verbs			Irregular verbs		
+	I **was** / we **were**	**+**	I / we	**arrived/studied** **stopped/helped**	**+**	I / she	**had/took/saw …** **had/took/saw …**
−	he **wasn't** / they **weren't**	**−**	he / they	**didn't** **arrive/study** **stop/help**	**−**	he / they	**didn't** **have/take/see …**
?	**Was** I? / **Were** you?	**?**	**Did** he / you	**arrive/study?** **stop/help?**	**?**	**Did** he / you	**have/take/see …?** **have/take/see …?**

↻ **Grammar spot**

Negatives and questions in the past simple

Look at the table above and answer these questions about the past simple.

a How do you make negatives and questions of the verb *to be* in the past simple?

b What verb do you use to make negatives and questions of other verbs in the past simple?

3 Put the words in these questions in the correct order.

a Mavis / on her first day at school / excited / was?

Was Mavis excited on her first day at school?

b any boys in the hall / there / were / ?

c did / walk / to school alone / she / ?

d the teacher / did / the girls any books / give / ?

e Mavis's first lesson / was / in the classroom / ?

4 Match these short answers to the questions you made in Exercise 3.

1 *Yes, she was.* **a**

2 *No, it wasn't.*

3 *No, there weren't.*

4 *No, she didn't.*

5 *Yes, she did.*

5 Work with two other students. Look at the texts about Neil and Anita. Write three questions, using *was*, *were* or *did* in each question. Give your questions to another student. Answer the other student's questions. Check their questions and answers and let them check yours when you finish.

6 Now ask and answer questions about people in your class.

7 Complete this interview with a historian by putting the verbs in the box into the past simple.

attend	be	become	believe	get	~~go~~	go	have
not learn	make	not need	stay	teach	work		

History online

This week Zari Ahmed talked to Dr Jim Bennett about education in England in the nineteenth century.

JB: Before 1876, many children in England never (a) _went_ to school. These children (b) .... from poor families and they (c) .... on farms or in factories. So they (d) .... to read or write.

Z: (e) .... anyone .... to evening classes?

JB: Yes, some men, who then got better jobs and (f) .... more money. Some (g) .... engineers or writers or politicians. Some (h) .... other working men in their free time.

Z: (i) .... women .... evening classes?

JB: Very few. I'm afraid that in the nineteenth century many people (j) .... that women (k) .... education. But after 1876, all children (l) .... some education. They (m) .... at school until they were at least ten years old.

Z: That's not very old.

JB: No, but it was a start.

8 Write three questions about the history of your country beginning with the words given.

a Who … ? **b** What … ? **c** Where … ?

Exchange questions with another student. Answer each other's questions.

↘ **GF page 207**

《Pronunciation》

1 Make three cards with /t/, /d/ and /ɪd/ on them.

2 **1 25** Listen to some verbs in the past simple. Raise the card which shows the sound at the end of each verb. Does everyone in the class agree?

3 Put the verbs into the correct column.

arrived /d/	helped /t/	started /ɪd/

《Activity》 Past simple bingo

Who is the first to cover a line of verbs?

《Activity》 Subjects to study

Work in a team. Which team can make the longest list of school subjects in three minutes? Which subjects can you do in your school or college? Are there any other subjects you would like to do?

Exam folder 6

Listening Part 2

1 Look at the picture. Who are the people and how do they feel?

2 🔊 **26** Listen to a taxi driver talking. Does the picture match what you hear?

3 Listen again and answer these questions.

    a What did the woman need to do at 10.30?
    b What happened at 10.15?
    c What time was the flight to New York?
    d Did the woman have the wrong plane ticket?
    e Were they at the right airport?

4 Now answer these questions. They are like the questions in the PET exam.

    1 What time did they arrive at the airport?
      A 10.15
      B 10.30
      C 12.20

    2 Why was the woman angry?
      A The taxi was very expensive.
      B Her plane ticket was wrong.
      C She was at the wrong airport.

5 If you have a recording script, underline the sentence which gives you the answer to question 1. Then underline the sentences which give you the answer to question 2.

6 Look at the picture. What is happening?

7 🔊 **27** Listen to a woman talking about her first day working in a restaurant kitchen. Choose the correct answer A, B or C.

Read the questions before you listen.

    1 How did she feel on her first morning?
      A excited
      B worried
      C frightened

    2 Why didn't she enjoy her first day?
      A She didn't feel well.
      B She didn't like the chef.
      C She was alone in the kitchen.

    3 What happened when she made mistakes?
      A The customers complained.
      B The customers were happy.
      C The waiters were angry.

Exam Advice

The questions often use different words from the recording.

Writing folder

Writing Part 3

1 Read this question. It is an example of the kind of task you will see in Part 3 of the Writing Paper.

- This is part of a letter you receive from an English friend.
  I'm coming to your school for one term. In your next letter, tell me about the school. What do you like about it?
- Now write a letter to this friend.
- Write your letter in about 100 words.

2 Read these three answers. Which one answers the question above?

a I'm coming to your school for one term and I'd like to know more about it. How big is it? What are your favourite lessons? I'd like to know how many computer rooms there are because I want to study computing after I leave school. My best subject is maths but I also like science. The science teachers in my school are very good. I hope you do lots of different sports. I enjoy rugby and athletics and I'm in my school team. I know you have lots of friends so I hope I'm in the same class.

b My school is quite small. It's in the city centre. I walk there every day. The building is old and in winter it's very cold. After school my friends and I sometimes go to the city centre. There are three cinemas and lots of coffee bars. I like playing tennis and basketball and I go to the sports hall in the city centre at weekends. I think school is boring. I want to travel round the world and I'm looking forward to leaving school soon.

c My school is in the city centre. It has 1000 students aged 12–18. We have lessons from 8.30 until 4.30 except Wednesday afternoons. On Saturdays we have lessons from 8.30 until 12. My favourite lessons are science and sport. We have very good laboratories and I enjoy those lessons. I also like sport – we play basketball, football, hockey and tennis. There's a really good swimming pool too. I often go to the computer room after school and do my homework. I've got a lot of good friends here. It's a very friendly school. We often meet after school and at weekends.

3 Make a list of the topics students A, B and C wrote about. Can you think of any other things to write about in your answer?

buildings
position
favourite subjects

4 What do you like about your school? Write some notes next to each heading like this.

buildings – new, clean, lots of windows
position – near railway station
favourite subjects – English, drama

5 Now answer the question. Write about your school. Count the words. Are there 90–110?

Exam Advice

You may lose marks if you write under 80 words.

6 How many lines of your writing is 90–110 words?

Speaking

1 Work with a partner. Look at these sentences. Say if each sentence is true for you and give your partner some extra information.

  a I've got blue eyes and short dark hair.
    Yes, that's true. My eyes are blue and my hair is short and wavy.
    OR
    No, that's not true. I've got brown eyes and my hair is shoulder length.
  b I've got brothers and sisters.
  c There are three tall girls in this class.
  d Circuses are fun.
  e My friends and I like the same kinds of music.
  f I often go to concerts.
  g I always enjoy parties.
  h I went to a great football match last weekend.
  i I caught a bus to my friend's house yesterday.
  j My friends and I like going horse riding.

Vocabulary

2 Think about the meaning of these words. Circle the odd one out in each of these lists.

  a bat (flat) net racket
  b engineer helicopter lorry tram
  c confident lazy shy slim
  d ferry nightclub theatre zoo
  e guest helmet shorts skirt
  f century flight journey tour
  g thief colleague joke person
  h diary factory magazine notebook
  i performance playground subject timetable

Reading

3 Read this email and answer the questions using short answers.

To: marco.bossi@petmail.com
From: alain.berger@petmail.com
Subject: Sorry!

Dear Marco

I hope you're not angry with me because I didn't see you at the sports club yesterday. I'm really sorry, but I had a terrible morning. I left home at nine o'clock but I didn't arrive at the club until eleven! I usually ride my bike, but my brother wanted it, so I walked to the railway station. You can usually get a bus from there to near our club. Yesterday I waited for half an hour but I didn't see any buses. I looked for a taxi and I found one quite quickly, but the motorway was busy and then, after ten minutes, the taxi stopped. I don't know why. The driver didn't phone a mechanic. He said, 'I can mend it.' But he didn't and I felt very worried because I was so late. After twenty minutes a lorry driver gave us a lift to a café. I walked from the café to the club, but it was very late and you weren't there. We need to meet and practise for our match on Saturday. I'm visiting a friend this evening, so can you phone me early?

Alain

  a Did Alain go to the club yesterday? *Yes, he did.*
  b Did Alain arrive at the club early?
  c Does Alain often cycle to the club?
  d Do buses go from the railway station to near the sports club?
  e Were there many buses near the railway station yesterday?
  f Did Alain get a taxi?
  g Were there many cars on the motorway yesterday?
  h Does Alain know why the taxi stopped?
  i Did the taxi driver mend his taxi?
  j Was Alain happy?
  k Did Alain and the taxi driver walk to the café?
  l Are Marco and Alain playing in a match this weekend?
  m Is Alain going out this evening?

Vocabulary

4 Use one word from the box to complete each space.

became	boring	describe	design	excited
exciting	finished	hard-working	helped
job	share	summer	take	~~teenagers~~	tired

Penny is twenty-one. She's a journalist on a magazine for (a) *teenagers* .

I (b) .... a journalist when I (c) .... college last (d) .... I saw an advert for this (e) .... in the local newspaper and I was really (f) .... when I got it. There's a lot to do every day, but I'm a (g) .... person, so I'm happy. I am often (h) ...., but life is never (i) .... I travel to some (j) .... places and I go clubbing in different cities. I (k) .... photographs and I (l) .... my adventures for the magazine. We are a small team on this magazine, so we (m) .... all the work with our colleagues. Last week I (n) .... my boss to (o) .... some pages. That was fun.

Grammar

5 In each group of the sentences below, only one is correct. Tick the correct sentence and put a cross by the incorrect ones.

1 A Are you like horse riding? ✗
   B Do you like horse riding? ✓
   C Would you like horse riding? ✗

2 A Does often your brother go cycling with you?
   B Does your brother often go cycling with you?
   C Does your brother go often cycling with you?

3 A We needn't book our tickets today.
   B We needn't to book our tickets today.
   C We don't need book our tickets today.

4 A How many students there are in your class?
   B How many students have your class?
   C How many students are there in your class?

5 A They didn't find any good CDs in that shop.
   B They didn't found any good CDs in that shop.
   C They weren't find any good CDs in that shop.

6 A My sister's a medical student.
   B My sister she's a medical student.
   C My sister's medical student.

6 Tick the correct word(s) to complete each sentence.

1 I want … about what's on this weekend.
   A some informations
   B some information ✓
   C an information

2 Do they serve … on the train?
   A any refreshment
   B a refreshment
   C any refreshments

3 I'm going shopping … lunchtime.
   A in   B on   C at

4 We've got … luggage in the car.
   A several   B lots of   C a couple of

5 Do you enjoy … new people?
   A meeting   B to meet   C meet

6 … any journalists at the concert?
   A Were   B Was   C Went

7 Put the verbs into the correct tense.

Vicky: Hi, Zara, (a) *you're* (you/be) late today.
Zara: Hi, Vicky. Yes, (b) .... (I/can/not) wake up this morning.
Vicky: Why? (c) .... (you/go) to bed late?
Zara: Yes, (d) .... (I/go) to a concert with my sister.
Vicky: (e) .... (it/be) good?
Zara: Oh, (f) .... (it/be) wonderful. (g) .... (we/see) a pop group called Travellers. (h) .... (I/usually/not/like) pop music, but (i) .... (I/enjoy) this. But (j) .... (the concert/begin) at nine o'clock and (k) .... (it/end) at midnight and then (l) .... (we/meet) some friends.
Vicky: Well, (m) .... (you/have) a good time. (n) .... (I/not/do) anything exciting.
Zara: What about next weekend? (o) .... (you/go) out then?
Vicky: Yeah. (p) .... (my cousin/give) a party. (q) .... (you/want) to come? (r) .... (he/always/have) good music and (s) .... (he/know) lots of interesting people. His name's Glen Jarvis.
Zara: Is Glen your cousin? (t) .... (I/not/realise) that. Yes, let's go together.

7 Around town

Introduction

Grammar prepositions of place and movement; comparative adjectives
Vocabulary places; directions; polite questions; saying you don't understand
Revision adjectives; spelling rules

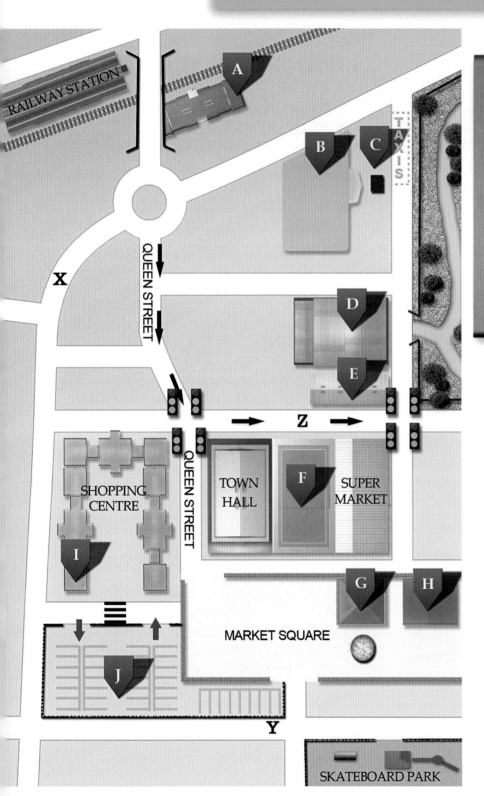

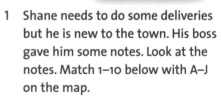

To: Shane
From: Manager
Subject: Today's deliveries

Greengrocer – on left inside Greenwood Shopping Centre. Entrance to shopping centre by pedestrian crossing. Large car park opposite entrance.
Nightclub – near railway station, entrance under the bridge
Museum – in market square (fountain in front of museum)
Library – in corner of market square next to museum
Theatre – in one-way street between supermarket and town hall
Newspaper kiosk – outside bus station (taxi rank in front of kiosk so sometimes difficult to stop)
Swimming pool – opposite park gates
Petrol station – next to swimming pool and opposite supermarket by some traffic lights

1 Shane needs to do some deliveries but he is new to the town. His boss gave him some notes. Look at the notes. Match 1–10 below with A–J on the map.

1	greengrocer	....../......
2	car park	....
3	nightclub	....
4	museum	....
5	library	....
6	theatre	....
7	bus station	....
8	newspaper kiosk	....
9	swimming pool	....
10	petrol station	....

2 Can you think of any other important buildings in your town which aren't on this map? Write them here.

....

....

Listening

1 ⟨**1 28**⟩ Find X, Y and Z on the map on page 48. Then listen to three conversations. For each one, follow on the map the directions you hear and decide where each person wants to go. For Conversation 1 start at X, for Conversation 2 start at Y and for Conversation 3 start at Z.

2 Can you guess the question each person asks to get directions? What can you say when you don't understand?

⟨**1 29**⟩ Listen to check your answers and complete the sentences below.

Polite questions

a .... help me, please? I .... a petrol station.

b Excuse me, ... the shopping centre, please?

c Excuse me, ... the skateboard park, please?

Which is more polite? *Can* or *could*?

Saying you don't understand

d I'm ....
again, please?

e I'm ...., I don't understand.

How do British people usually reply to *thank you*?

....

Language focus
Directions

Write the directions next to these diagrams.

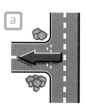

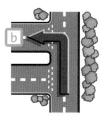

a *Turn*...... left.

b Take the .... the left.

c Go ....

d .... at the ....

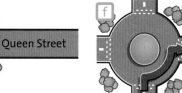

e .... right .... Queen Street.

f .... at the ....

g It's on the ....

⟪**Pronunciation**⟫

1 Say these words aloud. Can you hear the sound /aʊ/ or /ɔː/? Put the words into the correct column.

| out | or | round | sports | town | course | corner | about |
| hall | board | down | how | walk | | | |

/aʊ/	/ɔː/
out	or

2 ⟨**1 30**⟩ Listen to check your answers. Repeat the words after the recording.

3 Find the /aʊ/ or /ɔː/ sound in these sentences. Underline them in different colours.

a It's on the <u>cor</u>ner.
b Walk down the road.
c Of course.
d Turn right at the roundabout.
e Go past the town hall.
f Where's the skateboard park?
g It's outside the sports stadium.

4 ⟨**1 31**⟩ Repeat the sentences after the recording.

⟪**Activity**⟫ **Directions**

Look at the map on page 48.

You are in the market square. Write on a piece of paper the place you want your partner to go to. Don't show the paper to your partner. Give directions to your partner. At the end, your partner can tell you where he or she is. Show him or her what you wrote on the paper. Is your partner in the right place?

Prepositions of movement

Look at the pictures and complete the sentence for each one using one of these prepositions.

up ~~down~~ across off along
around through over

a He's skateboarding *down* the steps.
b She's skateboarding .... the pavement.
c He's cycling .... the hill.
d He's skateboarding .... the tunnel.
e They're cycling .... the track.
f He's skateboarding .... the road.
g He's skateboarding .... the roof.
h He's skateboarding .... the gate.

↘ GF page 207

Comparative adjectives

1 **Read these sentences about skateboards and bikes and underline the comparative adjective in each.**

  a A skateboard is <u>lighter</u> than a mountain bike.
  b A skateboard is cheaper than a mountain bike.
  c Cycling is safer than skateboarding.
  d A mountain bike is bigger than a skateboard.
  e Skateboarding is more exciting than cycling.
  f Mountain bikes are more fashionable than skateboards.
  g A skateboard is noisier than a mountain bike.
  h Skateboards are more popular than mountain bikes.
  i Skateboards are more common than mountain bikes.
  j Mountain bikes are better than skateboards for long journeys.

2 **Which of the statements above do you agree with? Put a tick (✓) or a cross (✗).**

↘ Grammar spot   Comparative adjectives

Look at the sentences in Exercise 1 and complete the rules.

Most one-syllable adjectives (e.g. *light*) add *er* ....

One-syllable adjectives ending in *e* (e.g. *safe*) add ....

Most adjectives ending in a .... and a consonant (e.g. *big*) double the consonant and add ....

Most adjectives with more than one .... (e.g. *popular*) use *more* (e.g. *more popular*).

Adjectives ending in *y* (e.g. *noisy*) usually change *y* to .... and add ....

Good and *bad* are irregular and become .... and *worse*.

3 **Write the comparative of these adjectives in the correct row of the table below.**

friendly   thin   steep   famous   popular   bad
nice   strong   old   lazy   wet   busy   rich
difficult   tidy   miserable   good   wide

Add *er*	
Add *r*	
Double the last letter and add *er*	
Use *more*	
Change *y* to *i* and add *er*	
Irregular	

4 Rewrite the sentences in Exercise 1 using *not* or *less*.

a A mountain bike _is not as light as_ (not) a skateboard.

b A skateboard is _less expensive than_ (less) a mountain bike.

c Skateboarding .... (not) cycling.

d A skateboard .... (not) a mountain bike.

e Cycling .... (less) skateboarding.

f Skateboards .... (less) mountain bikes.

g Mountain bikes .... (not) skateboards.

h Mountain bikes .... (less) skateboards.

i Mountain bikes .... (not) skateboards.

j Skateboards .... (not) mountain bikes for long journeys.

↘ **Grammar spot**   Comparing two things

Complete these sentences.

Mountain bikes are more fashionable .... skateboards.

= Skateboards are not as/so fashionable ....
mountain bikes.

= Skateboards are .... fashionable ....
mountain bikes.

↘ **Corpus spot**   Comparative adjectives

Correct these mistakes made by PET students.

a Alex is old than me by five days.   _older_

b I would like to buy a new TV that is biger than my old one.

c Hotels are more cheap here than in the city.

d My parents are not excited as I am about the holiday.

e Modern furniture is easyer to clean than old furniture.

f This supermarket is more better than the other one.

g I think he is more taller than I told you.

h I'm not as good at tennis than you are.

5 Look at each pair of pictures and write a sentence comparing them, using the words given.

Tom   Edward   Steve   John   Jack   Sue   school bus   taxi

Edward / cold   Steve / hot   Sue's homework / bad   taxi / slow

Edward isn't as/so cold as Tom.
or Edward is less cold than Tom.

The Thames   The Amazon   Liz   Jill   watch   ring   shorts   T-shirt

The Amazon / wide   Jill / sad   ring / expensive   shorts / dirty

↘ **GF page 207**

«Activity» **Comparatives Snap**

Your teacher will give you some cards.
Match the words on the cards with their endings.
The winner is the person who collects the most cards.

«Activity» **Mazes**

Work with a partner. Your teacher will give you a maze.
Find your way through it. Now join another pair of
students and tell them how to get through your maze.
Then they do the same for you.

Exam folder 7

Reading Part 3

1   Look at the photograph of Lincoln, a city in the east of England.
    What can you say about Lincoln from the photograph?

2   Read the text. Don't worry if there are some words you don't understand.
    Does it say what you expected from the photograph?

3   Mark the parts of the text which tell you about:
    a the cathedral
    b The Lawn
    c the Tourist Information Centre and St Mark's Shopping Centre
    d the Waterside Centre
    e the river
    f the railway station

4   Now look at this sentence:

    1 The cathedral is near the castle.

    Read the part of the text about the cathedral again. Is the cathedral near the
    castle? Underline the answer. Is the statement correct or incorrect? Write A for
    correct or B for incorrect.

5   Now look at these sentences. For each one, find the right part of the text.
    Decide if the text says the same as the question. Is each sentence correct or
    incorrect? Write A for correct or B for incorrect.

    2 The Lawn is a hospital.
    3 It takes an hour to walk from the Tourist Information Centre to
        the castle.
    4 The Waterside Centre is older than St Mark's Shopping Centre.
    5 The river goes through the centre of the city.
    6 You need to cross the road to go from the bus station to the
        railway station.

Exam Advice

For each question, find the right
part of the text, then read it slowly.

Lincoln

The city of Lincoln is 2,000 years old and there are a lot of interesting buildings to see. The cathedral is in the north of the city just outside the main city centre. You can walk to many of Lincoln's other attractions from the cathedral. It's not far from the castle. There is a wonderful view of the city from there. Behind the castle is The Lawn, an old hospital, which is now a museum with shops and a café. You can sit in the beautiful gardens to have lunch or a coffee. There is a car park a few metres from the café.

During the summer, walking tours leave from the Tourist Information Centre, which is next to the castle. They are not expensive, last about an hour and visit all the main attractions. There are some very interesting museums. The Toy Museum is near the Tourist Information Centre and has children's toys and games from the last century.

There are shops and a market in the old city centre. There are two shopping centres – one is the Waterside Centre opposite the market and the other is St Mark's Shopping Centre. St Mark's is newer than the Waterside Centre and is just south of the main city centre. Go straight down the High Street from the city centre and it is on the right.

In the middle of the city centre, there are some beautiful spots away from the crowds. For example, you can walk by the river or take a boat trip. Trips leave from Bayford Pool.

You can travel to Lincoln by train, bus or car. It is 216 km from London. The bus station is beside the river and the railway station is a few minutes' walk away from the bus station on the other side of St Mary's Street.

 Corpus spot

Prepositions

Correct these mistakes made by PET students. Look for similar sentences in the text to help you.
a We will meet 15 minutes before the film starts at the outside of the cinema.
b My flat isn't too far away of the town centre.
c There is a lovely view of the sea by the window.
d We saw a big tree and behind of it was a lake.
e The cinema is a few metres of the Underground station.
f In my room there is a radio next the TV.
g I live in the south of France next to Toulouse.
h I am staying in a small town besides a large forest.
i He works only one block away where I am working.

8 Let's celebrate

Grammar present perfect; *just, already, yet*
Vocabulary celebrations; giving good wishes
Revision dates; describing a picture; present tenses

Introduction

1 Look at the photograph. What is happening?

2 Do people celebrate like this on special days in your country?

Which dates do they celebrate?
What do they do?

3 Work with a partner. Look at the pictures.

What is happening? What do you think the people are saying?

4 🔊 32 Listen to the recordings. Write what the people are saying in the spaces. Did they say what you thought?

Repeat the words after the recording.

5 Can you use any of these phrases at other times?

Reading

1 Look at these photographs. They tell us something about the weddings of four different couples. What can you guess about them?

2 Read the newspaper article and match the photographs to the couples.

What style of wedding do people in the UK want these days?

Our reporter Suzy Hill talked to four couples who have some very different wedding plans.

We're getting married ...

... in the Caribbean

Anna We're having a romantic wedding on the beach at sunset. I've bought a new bikini and some sunscreen.
Jay I've just been to the travel agent to book our plane tickets and our hotel. We've told our family and friends and they're organising a barbecue to celebrate with us when we come back.

... in our local church

Nigel We got engaged last year and we're having a family wedding in the village where we live. We've invited all our friends and our parents and all our relations.
Fiona My parents have organised a big party. It's taken months! They've booked a band to play in the evening and they've hired a special car to take me to the church. We've planned our honeymoon, but we haven't told anyone where we're going because some people aren't good at keeping a secret – we'll tell them on our wedding day.

... in secret

Lorne Do you promise you aren't printing this until next week? OK. We're both very famous, so we often have problems with our fans. We've bought the rings and we've rented a cottage in the mountains for our honeymoon. No one can disturb us there.
Esmerelda We're very much in love and want to be alone together. We haven't planned a party. We haven't even told our families or friends. We haven't told our secretaries or our agents, and we certainly haven't told any journalists except you. I hope we're not making a mistake now. Please don't tell anyone before next week!

... in our lunch hour

Dawn We're both very busy people. We run a successful business. Our secretaries have organised everything and they've sent invitations to our friends. I don't know who's accepted or who's refused.
Gary My secretary has made the appointment at the registry office and she's already booked a table at a good restaurant for lunch – we're taking an extra long lunch break. Then we're going back to work! We haven't planned a honeymoon yet because we're too busy to go away. Perhaps next year …

3 Work with a partner. Read the article again and answer these questions together.

a Where are Anna and Jay getting married?
   in the Caribbean
b What has Anna bought?
c Who have they told?
d When are they having a party?
e Why do Lorne and Esmerelda have problems?
f What have they bought?
g Why have they rented a cottage in the mountains?
h Who have Nigel and Fiona invited to the wedding?

i Who has organised a party for them?
j Who is doing the music?
k Why haven't they told anyone where they're going for their honeymoon?
l Why doesn't Dawn know who is coming to her wedding?
m Where are Dawn and Gary going after the wedding? And then where?
n Why haven't they planned their honeymoon?

4 Can you match these words from the newspaper article? Check your answers in the text.

a	take	**1**	an appointment
b	keep	**2**	a band
c	book	**3**	a barbecue
d	organise	**4**	a break
e	refuse	**5**	a car
f	make	**6**	a cottage
g	rent	**7**	an invitation
h	hire	**8**	a mistake
i	make	**9**	a secret

5 Which couple has made the best wedding plans, in your opinion? Why?
Are weddings in your country like any of these weddings?

Language focus

Present perfect; *just, already* and *yet*

1 Put the verbs into the present perfect, then look at the article on page 55 to check your answers.

a I *'ve bought* (buy) a new bikini and some sunscreen.

b We .... (tell) our family and friends.

c We .... (rent) a cottage in the mountains for our honeymoon.

d We .... (not plan) a party.

e We .... (not tell) our secretaries or our agents.

f They .... (book) a band to play in the evening.

g They .... (send) invitations to our friends.

h I don't know who .... (accept) or who .... (refuse).

i My secretary .... (make) the appointment at the registry office.

We form the present perfect with *has/have* + a past participle.			
+	I She	**have** **has**	finished. eaten.
−	You It	**haven't / have not** **hasn't / has not**	eaten. finished.
?	**Have** **Has**	we she	finished? eaten?

⬎ Grammar spot   **Present perfect**

Formation

Complete this table.

Regular verbs have the same form for the past simple and the past participle:

verb	past simple	past participle
open	opened	....
plan	....	planned
organise	organised	....

Some irregular verbs have the same form for the past simple and the past participle:

send	....	sent
tell	told	
make	....	made

Some irregular verbs have a different form for the past simple and the past participle:

take	....	taken
eat	ate	....
be	was/were	....
go	....	gone

Meaning

Complete the explanations with the names of tenses: *past simple* or *present perfect*.

a If we say when something happened we use the
....
(*I lost my key on Monday.*)

b The .... describes what happened some time before now, but we do not say when it happened because we are thinking about the present result of the action.
(*I've lost my key and I don't know where it is now.*)

2 Look at the pictures below. It's Wednesday. Jeff and Paul are having a party, but there have been a few problems.

Make sentences about the pictures using the present perfect. Use page 216 to check the past participles if necessary.

a burn / pizza

They've burnt the pizza.

b break / chair

c drop / glass

d lose / key

e eat / food

f spill / juice

g drink / fizzy drinks

h make / terrible mess

3 It's Thursday. Jeff has gone to work, so Paul is clearing up. Jeff wants to be sure that Paul remembers everything. Write the questions Jeff asks when he phones Paul, and then write Paul's answers.

a clean / floor   *Have you cleaned the floor yet?*
                   Yes, I've just cleaned it.

b wash / glasses   e throw away / rubbish
c tidy / living room   f buy / food
d find / key   g mend / chair

«Activity» Planning a party

Make a list of all the things you need to do to plan a party. Then play the memory game. Your teacher will give you the instructions.

↘ Grammar spot

just, already and ***yet*** + present perfect

Complete the sentences with *just*, *already* and *yet* so that they match the ideas in brackets.

a She's .... booked the tickets.
  (She did it a few minutes ago.)
b She's .... booked a table.
  (She did it some time before now.)
c She hasn't arrived ....
  (She's not here, but she'll probably come soon.)
d Has she finished her work ....?
  (That's a nice surprise!)
e Has she arrived ....? (I want to know.)
f Hasn't she arrived ....? (She's late!)

4 Complete the conversation with *already* or *yet*.

Paul: Have you planned your weekend
        (a) *yet*?

Jeff: Oh, yes. I'm taking Samantha to see *Golden Boy*. I've (b) .... booked the tickets.

Paul: Oh, right, the new film. Have you invited her (c) ....?

Jeff: Well, I haven't phoned her (d) .... But she said last week she wants to see it.

Paul: It's very good.

Jeff: Have you (e) .... seen it? That's quick!

Paul: Yes, I have. And Samantha's (f) .... seen it, too.

Jeff: How do you know?

Paul: We went together last night.

↘ GF page 208

«Pronunciation»

1 How do you say these dates?

  3 July   1 January   25 March
  24 October   2 February

2 🔊1.33 Listen to the recording and repeat them.

3 🔊1.34 Write down the dates you hear.

4 Work in a group. Think about important events in your country, your school and your own lives. Can you find one event for each of the dates below (they can be in any month)? Which group finishes first?

  1st 2nd 6th 15th 25th 31st

Exam folder 8

Speaking Part 3

1 Here are some festivals that people celebrate in the UK. Can you match the photographs to the festivals?

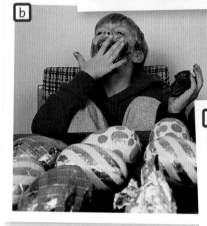

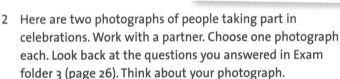

1 Christmas – on 25th December
2 St Valentine's Day – on 14th February
3 Easter – in March or April
4 Notting Hill Carnival – at the end of August

2 Here are two photographs of people taking part in celebrations. Work with a partner. Choose one photograph each. Look back at the questions you answered in Exam folder 3 (page 26). Think about your photograph.

3 Tell your partner about your photograph. While you are listening to your partner, think about the questions from Exam folder 3. At the end, tell your partner if he/she has answered all the questions. Are there any questions you can add to the ones on page 26?

Exam Advice

Learn expressions you can use when you don't know the word for something.

I don't know the word in English. It's a kind of X.

Speaking Part 4

Do you have any festivals in your country like the ones in the photographs?

Work with a partner. Ask and answer these questions about festivals in your country.

What / do?	How / prepare?
What / celebrate?	Wear / special clothes?
When / happen?	Eat / special food?
Go out / friends / family?	

Writing folder

Writing Part 2

Exam Advice

In Writing Part 2 you need to understand the following verbs – *apologise, ask, describe, explain, invite, say, suggest, tell, thank.*

1 Read these questions. Underline the three things you must do in each task. Check that you understand the verbs in the Exam Advice box.

1 You are having a birthday party next Friday.
Write a card to your English friend Matthew. In your card, you should
- invite him to the party
- tell him who is coming
- suggest how to get there

2 Your English friend, Catherine, has invited you to her birthday party next week but you can't go. Write a card to Catherine. In your card, you should
- thank her
- apologise
- explain why you can't go

3 It was your birthday last week. Your English friend Ben sent you a present. Write a card to Ben. In your card, you should
- thank him for the present
- describe what you did on your birthday
- ask him when his birthday is

⤵ Corpus spot 👁

Come or go?

We use *come* + *here* or *to me, to you, to my/your house*, etc.

but *go* + *there* or *to him, to her, to another place*, etc.

Complete these sentences by PET students with *come* or *go*.

a He asked me to visit him in Rio and I would really like to ....

b I hope I can .... to visit you when I am in your town.

2 Put the correct name at the beginning of each card.

a Dear ....
I'm having a birthday party next Friday. Would you like to come? All our friends from school are coming and some of my family. I live in the city centre. Take a bus to the bus station, then you can walk from there.

b Dear ....
Thank you very much for the book you sent me for my birthday. I spent the day with my family and I went to a nightclub in the evening with my friends. Can you tell me when your birthday is?

c Dear ....
Thank you for inviting me to your birthday party next week. I'm sorry but I can't come because my brother and his wife are visiting us with their new baby. I hope you enjoy the party.

3 Look at card a. Underline *Would you like to come?* These words invite Matthew to the party. Now underline in different colours the words which tell him who is coming and the words which suggest how to get there.

4 Do the same with cards b and c.

5 Write the answers to these questions. Write 35–45 words.

Your English friend called Emily has invited you to go to a concert next Saturday but you can't go.
Write a card to send to Emily. In your card, you should
- thank her
- apologise
- explain why you can't go

You spent last Saturday in the city centre with some friends.
Write an email to your English friend called Tim. In your email, you should
- tell him how you got there
- describe what you did
- invite him to go with you next time

9 How do you feel?

Grammar short answers
Vocabulary parts of the body; illnesses; giving advice; *at*
Revision present tenses; past simple; present perfect

Introduction

1 What are these people doing? Which parts of their bodies are they exercising?

2 Label the parts of the body (a–s) in the photographs and drawing.

These are the words you need but all the vowels are missing.

l_p	_y_br_w	br_ _n
th_mb	f_r_h_ _d	ch_st
sh_ _ld_r	l_ng	ch_ _k
ch_n	n_ck	wr_st
f_ng_r	_lb_w	h_ _rt
nkl	kn_ _	st_m_ch
t_ _		

a ....
b ....
c ....
d ....
e ....
f ....

g ....
h ....
i ....
j ....

k ....
l ....
m ....
n ....

o ....

p ....

q ....

r ....

s ....

3 The three people in the photos are in a gym. When we exercise we use calories. Which of the people in the photos is using the most calories, do you think?

Do you go to a gym? Do you use any of the machines in the pictures? What do you do to keep fit?

4 Exercising helps you keep fit but some everyday jobs keep you fit too. Match the number of calories to the activities.

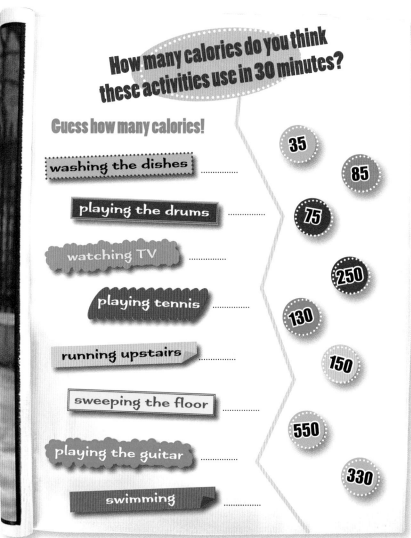

How many calories do you think these activities use in 30 minutes?

Guess how many calories!

washing the dishes ....

playing the drums ....

watching TV ....

playing tennis ....

running upstairs ....

sweeping the floor ....

playing the guitar ....

swimming ....

35 85 75 250 130 150 550 330

Listening

1 **1 35** In some places, when people feel ill they can phone a medical helpline and talk to a nurse. Listen to some people talking to a nurse. Why are they phoning?

2 Listen again. What advice do you think the nurse gives each one?

- go to the hospital • go to the doctor's • call an ambulance • stay at home

3 Work in a group. Compare your answers with other students. If you disagree, decide which answer is the best.

4 **1 36** Listen to the nurse's answers.

Compare her answers with your group's answers. Were they the same or different?

Language focus
Illnesses and advice

1 How do you say what is wrong with you? Complete these sentences and write them under the pictures.

My arm ....   I've got ....   I've got a ....   I've got a ....
I've got a .... in my chest.   I feel ....   I've got a .... eye.   I've got a ....

 a

 b

 c

 d

I've got a temperature.

 e

 f

 g

 h

2 🎧 **37** Listen to the nurse's answers again. Write down what she says when she gives advice.

  a You *should take* him to the hospital.
  b Why .... some cough mixture?
  c You .... an ambulance.
  d She .... any more food today.
  e Why .... your eyes in warm water?
  f You'd .... the doctor.

3 Give the people in the pictures some advice. You can use some of these expressions.

  • take some cough mixture / antibiotics / paracetamol / aspirin
  • have a warm drink
  • stay in bed
  • call an ambulance
  • go to the doctor's

Expressions with *at*

Complete these sentences from the listening on page 61. They all contain expressions with *at*.

night	home	~~school~~	last	least
the moment	all	lunchtime	once	
the weekend				

  a My son fell over at *school* .
  b He can't move his fingers at ....
  c I cough at ....
  d Have you got a cold at ....?
  e She had a burger and chips at ....
  f I'm relaxing at ....
  g He's just stopped at ....
  h I don't want to ring the doctor at ....
  i Sleep with at .... two pillows.
  j You'd better dial 999 at ....

> ↘ **Corpus spot**   Expressions with *at* and *in*
>
> These sentences written by PET students all have an expression with *in*. Two are correct. Tick (✓) them and correct the others.
>
> a The weather is cold in night.
> b I get bored staying in home doing nothing.
> c I suggest you come here in summer.
> d That's all I have to tell you in the moment.
> e We usually go to the beach in the weekend.
> f The film starts at eight o'clock in the evening.

Short answers

1 Match these questions and answers.

a Did he hit his head?
b Have you got a cold?
c Does he feel sick?
d Does she have a headache?
e Has she eaten a lot today?
f Are you tired?
g Do you wear glasses or contact lenses?
h Is he hot?
i Has he taken any aspirin?

1 Yes, he has.
2 Yes, she does.
3 No, I'm not.
4 No, he didn't.
5 Yes, he is.
6 No, I don't.
7 No, she hasn't.
8 Yes, he does.
9 No, I haven't.

↘ Grammar spot   Short answers

Complete this table about short answers. Use the words in the box.

did ~~does~~ haven't don't have hasn't do didn't doesn't has

Question	Short answer
Present simple	*does* , ... or .... , ... ,
Past simple	.... or ....
Present perfect	.... , ... or .... , ...

2 Write short answers for these questions. Exchange answers with a partner and check your partner's work.

a Have you completed the exercise above?
   Yes, I have.
b Do you understand it?
c Is your teacher in the room?
d Are your friends working?
e Are you working?
f Is this exercise easy?
g Have you finished it yet?
h Has your partner checked your answers?
i Do you want to take a break soon?

↘ GF page 208

«Activity» Illnesses

Work in a group. Your teacher will give you a card. Mime what it says on the card. The other students guess what's wrong with you and give you advice.

«Activity» Giving and receiving advice

Read the problem your teacher gives you. Below the problem is some advice, but it isn't the right advice for your problem. Someone else has the right advice for you. Listen to other students' problems and tell your problem to other students. Give your advice to the right person.

«Pronunciation»

1 Which letters – a, ay, ai, e, ie or ea – complete the words? You need to use some of the letters more than once.

a My son f_e_ll over.
b Can I h......lp you?
c My fr......nd t......kes the tr......n to college.
d I eat a h......lthy br......kfast every d........
e I hit my h......d and now I've got a p......n.
f Don't br......k that glass.
g I saw a gr......t pl...... tod........

2 Look at the letters you have filled in. Which make the sound /eɪ/ (as in *say*)? Underline them in a colour. Which make the sound /e/ (as in *tell*)? Underline them in a different colour.

3 **1 38** Listen and repeat the sentences. Were you correct? Make any corrections.

4 Which letters spell the sound /eɪ/? Which letters spell the sound /e/?

«Activity» How healthy are you?

1 Answer these questions about yourself.

a Do you and your friends enjoy dancing? YES/NO
b Are you keen on computer games? YES/NO
c Do you love chocolate? YES/NO
d Have you got a bicycle? YES/NO
e Are you a member of a sports club? YES/NO
f Have you got more than one TV in your house? YES/NO
g Do you and your family go for walks together? YES/NO
h Do you put extra salt on your food? YES/NO
i Did you eat any vegetables yesterday? YES/NO
j Have you got a car? YES/NO
k Did you eat two or more burgers last week? YES/NO
l Do you eat fresh fruit every day? YES/NO
m Do you sleep at least seven hours every night? YES/NO
n Do you exercise three times a week? YES/NO

2 Your teacher will give you a board with the questions on it. You can use your answers above as you play.

3 Can you think of other things you can do to stay healthy and keep fit?

Exam folder 9

Reading Part 4

1 In Reading Part 4, the first question always asks you what the writer is trying to do. Read these four texts and match them to A, B, C and D below. Underline the words in each text which helped you to find the answers.

> What is the writer trying to do?
> A advise someone
> B apologise to someone
> C advertise something
> D complain about something

2 There is always a question asking you about the writer's opinion. Match the texts opposite to A, B, C and D below. Underline the words in each text which helped you to find the answers.

> Which of the following opinions does the writer have?
> A The equipment in the club isn't very good.
> B The club is the best in town.
> C The pool in the club is better than the gym.
> D The club needs more staff.

3 There are always two questions about the details in the text. This may be about something very small. Match the texts opposite to A, B, C and D below. Underline the words in each text which helped you to find the answers.

> Which of the following is stated in the text?
> A The writer works at the club.
> B The writer is a new member of the club.
> C The writer always goes to the club on the same day.
> D The writer goes to the club several times a week.

Exam Advice

For some questions you need to read part of the text. For other questions you need to read all of the text.

---

1 I joined your health club last week. The equipment is up-to-date and easy to use but when I came in for the first time on Thursday I was very surprised that there were no instructors in the gym. Nobody checked my heart before I started using the equipment. I am not happy about this because it is very dangerous. I am coming back next week to use your pool and I hope you have a lifeguard there.

2 You know I go to the health club at least twice a week and I use the pool there because it's brilliant. You should try it. The gym is OK too and I sometimes go there. When I saw you last week you were very stressed. You really shouldn't work hard all the time. Why don't you join the health club? We can go together then.

3 **Blacks Health Club is opening next week and we are offering a special discount to the first 100 members. You can join the club for half the normal price. Just come along or phone me, Mick Smith, the manager, on 983546.**

Don't miss the chance to join and use our gym and pool. There is no other club in town which is as good as this one.

4 I was very surprised to see you in the health club last week because you always say that you hate doing exercise. It was very rude of me to laugh at you when you tried to ride the exercise bike in the gym. I'm really sorry. The equipment in the gym is old and is sometimes difficult to use, so it wasn't your fault. But the club is cheap! I hope we can be friends again. I go to the club every Sunday afternoon – shall we meet there?

Speaking Part 2

1 Look at the boy in the picture, Josh. What is wrong with him? How does he feel?

2 You want to visit Josh and take him a present. Look at the things in the pictures. Think about which ones Josh can use and which ones he can't use. Which things does he need? Which would he like to have?

3 Work with a partner. Discuss which present to take Josh. Explain why you think some things are better than others. Try to agree on what to take.

4 See if the rest of the class agrees with you.

Say what you think:
I think …
In my opinion …

Make suggestions:
We'd better take him X because …
Why don't we take him X?

Agree and disagree:
I (don't) agree (that) …
That's (not) a good idea.
I don't think that's a very good idea.
I've got a better idea.

Exam Advice

If you don't understand what to do, ask the examiner to repeat what he or she said. You can say *Please can you repeat that?*

10 I look forward to hearing from you

Grammar present perfect / past simple; *ago, for, since, in; ever*
Vocabulary letters and emails, etc.
Revision verb tenses

Introduction

1 Look at the pictures 1–8. What do they show?

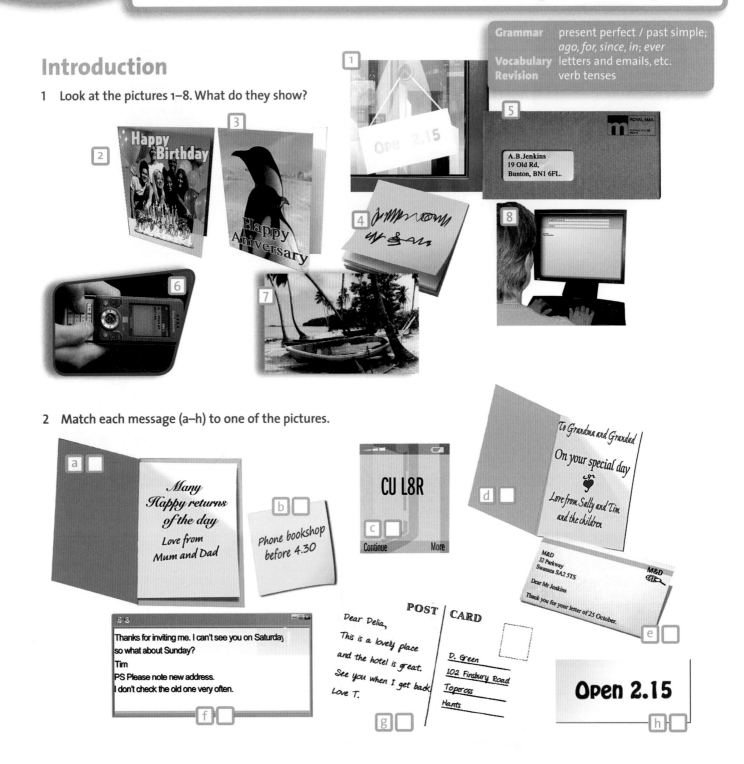

2 Match each message (a–h) to one of the pictures.

a Many Happy returns of the day Love from Mum and Dad

b Phone bookshop before 4.30

c CU L8R   Continue   More

d To Grandma and Grandad On your special day Love from Sally and Tim and the children

e M&D 32 Parkway Swansea SA2 5TS Dear Mr Jenkins Thank you for your letter of 25 October.

f Thanks for inviting me. I can't see you on Saturday so what about Sunday? Tim PS Please note new address. I don't check the old one very often.

g POST CARD Dear Delia, This is a lovely place and the hotel is great. See you when I get back Love T. D. Green 102 Finsbury Road Topeross Hants

h Open 2.15

3 Do you write letters or cards? Which of **a–h** have you written or read recently?

4 Do you send texts and emails? What do these shortcuts mean?

:) :(:{ :o CU 4U 2U CUL8R RUOK? YRUX? 2b/nt2b=?
Do you know any others?

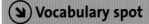

Vocabulary spot

Beginning and ending letters and emails
How do you begin letters (or emails) in English?
How do you end a letter (or email) to a close friend?
How do you end a letter (or email) to a stranger?

Reading

1 Work with a partner. Read letter **a** (to Mike) and letter **b** (to Maria). Then quickly read the other letters and emails (**c–h**). Decide which three belong with the letter to Mike and which three belong with the letter to Maria.

2 Put Mike's and Maria's letters/emails in the correct order. Label them *Mike 2*, *Mike 3*, *Mike 4* and *Maria 2*, *Maria 3*, *Maria 4*.

[a]
Dear Mike,

Do you remember me? I was in your class five years ago. We had a lot of fun and I learnt a lot of English. And you see I haven't forgotten it. Isn't that good?

I hope everything is OK with you and the other teachers at The Edge School.

I'm writing now for my cousin, Thomas. He is coming to your school next month. He's twenty-two. He hasn't studied English since secondary school so he isn't very confident.

Have there been many changes to the school since I was there? I stayed with a very friendly family five years ago – the Gibsons. Do they still take students?

You can email me on phil298@haupt.org

With many thanks for your help,

All the best,

Philippe Haupt

[b]
The Edge School of English
105 Redcoats Road, Birmingham B15 4LB UK

Ms Maria Schmidt
Landhutstr. 384
3427 Utzenstorf
Switzerland

Dear Ms Schmidt,

Thank you for your application form for our summer course (15th–30th July).

I have arranged accommodation for you with Mrs Susan Miller at Lime Trees, 15 The Grove, Birmingham B14 2AJ. Please can you write to her and tell her the date and time of your arrival.

We look forward to seeing you in July.

Yours sincerely,

J H Elling

John Elling
Office Manager

[c]
Dear Thomas Haupt

Mike spoke to me yesterday. I have reserved a room in the hostel for you.

Have a good journey.

Best wishes

Lynn Brady
Accommodation manager

[d]
Dear Mrs Miller,

I am attending a course at The Edge School from 15th to 30th July. The school has given me your name and address. I plan to arrive in Birmingham on Saturday, 13th July and leave on the 31st. Is that convenient for you? Please can you tell me how to get from the airport to your house by public transport? I've never been to Birmingham before. You can email me on marscheschmidt.org
I look forward to meeting you.
Yours sincerely,
Maria
Maria Schmidt

[e]
Dear Susan
Are you sure? It's very kind of you. My flight arrives at 11.30 am. It's Swallow Air flight no. SWA25. Thank you very much indeed.
Yours
Maria

[f]
Dear Philippe

It was great to get your letter. Yes, I remember you well. We all enjoyed that course. And you learnt some English!

I'm very well, thank you. The Edge School has grown bigger. Last year we started a new Business English course. It's been very successful.

Unfortunately, the Gibsons have moved to another town. I haven't seen them for two years. But we opened a student hostel three years ago. Would Thomas like a room there?

With best wishes

Mike Churchfield

[g]
Dear Maria
Thank you for your letter. Those dates are fine. You don't need to use public transport because I can meet you in the car. What time does your flight arrive?
And please call me Susan.

Best wishes

Susan

[h]
Dear Mr Churchfield
My cousin Philippe wrote to you last week. Please can you reserve a room for me in the hostel?
I haven't been to England since I was a child. I came with my parents ten years ago and I've wanted to come again since then.
I look forward to meeting you. Philippe has told me lots of stories about his time at your school.
Yours
Thomas Haupt

3 Answer these questions.

a How has The Edge School changed?
   It's grown bigger.
b Why hasn't Mike seen the Gibsons for two years?
c Why isn't Thomas very confident?
d Has Thomas been to England before?
e What has Lynn done for Thomas?

f When did Mike teach Philippe?
   Five years ago.
g When did the Business English course start?
h When did the school open a student hostel?
i Who did Philippe stay with in England?
j When did Thomas first visit England?

Language focus
Present perfect and past simple; *ago, for, since, in*

Grammar spot

Present perfect and past simple + *ago, for, since, in/on/at*

1 Complete the sentences below with *ago, for, since, in* and a number where necessary.

I've worked here .... 2007.
I've worked here .... years.

2007 ═══════════ **NOW**

I started this job .... 2007.
I started this job .... years ....

2 Complete these rules.
  a We use the .... tense with *since* + a point in the past (e.g. *2008*).
  b We use the .... tense with *for* + a length of time (e.g. *two years*).
  c We use the .... tense with a point in the past (e.g. *in 2008*, *on Monday*, *at five o'clock*).
  d We use the .... tense with a length of time (e.g. *two years*) + *ago*.

1 Choose the correct tense: present perfect or past simple. When you have finished, check your answers with a partner.

Thomas: Hi. I'm Thomas. Are you a new student?
Maria: Yes. (**a**) *I arrived/I've arrived* on Saturday. My name's Maria.
Thomas: (**b**) *Did you have / Have you had* a good journey?
Maria: Yes, it (**c**) *was / has been* very easy. My landlady (**d**) *met / has met* me at the airport. (**e**) *Were you / Have you been* here long?
Thomas: (**f**) *I was / I've been* here for two weeks. (**g**) *I learnt / I've learnt* quite a lot of English.
Maria: (**h**) *Did you go / Have you been* to England before?
Thomas: Yes, (**i**) *I did / I have*. But that (**j**) *was / has been* ten years ago. What about you?
Maria: (**k**) *I visited / I've visited* London last year. But (**l**) *I didn't come / I haven't come* to Birmingham.
Thomas: (**m**) *I found / I've found* some good shops and cafés since (**n**) *I arrived / I've arrived*. Would you like to look round the city centre with me later?
Maria: Yes, sure. But we'd better go to our classes now.
Thomas: OK. See you later.

2 After her language course, Maria got a job. She wrote this email to Thomas. Put the verbs into the present perfect or past simple.

3 Complete the second sentence in each pair of sentences so that it means the same as the first. Use *ago, for, in* or *since*.

  a My boyfriend has been away since January.
    My boyfriend went away ....*in*.... January.
  b This restaurant has been here for six months.
    This restaurant opened six months ....
  c I started this job in June.
    I've worked here .... June.
  d We bought this car five months ago.
    We've had this car .... five months.
  e Ali left here on Tuesday.
    I haven't seen Ali .... Tuesday.
  f I haven't lived in that flat for two years.
    I left that flat two years ....

Corpus spot

For, since or ago?

Complete these PET students' sentences with *for, since* or *ago*.

  a We've been great friends .... college.
  b Some years .... I travelled to England with a friend called Bruno.
  c I haven't seen Michael .... he moved to Vancouver.
  d Two weeks .... I finished school and I wanted to do some sport.
  e He's from Manchester but he's lived in Zurich .... two years.

GF page 208

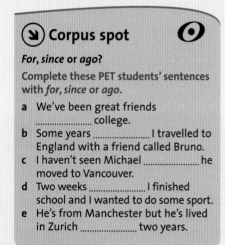

Dear Thomas
I'm having my lunch break and I want to tell you about my summer job at the telephone sales office.
I (a) *'ve been* .... here for one week and I (b) .... (already earn) £200! When I (c) .... (begin), the manager (d) .... (give) me a list of people to phone. I (e) .... (tell) them about our cheap holidays but they (f) .... (not want) to buy one. Then I (g) .... (get) a new list of people to phone. I (h) .... (sell) fifteen holidays since Wednesday. Yesterday I (i) .... (buy) two new CDs, a coat and some shoes. In fact I (j) .... (spend) £180 since the manager paid me. I'd better start work again!
Love,
Maria

⊗ Corpus spot   *Been* and *gone*

He's gone to Acapulco. = He's there, not here.

He's been to Acapulco. = He went there, but he isn't there now.

He's never been to Acapulco. = He hasn't visited Acapulco in his life.

Choose the correct verb in these PET students' sentences.

a We've *gone / been* to the cinema to see a new film. It was great.

b She's *gone / been* to the USA and I haven't heard from her since she got there.

c He's *gone / been* on holiday and he's having a great time.

d I've already *gone / been* to that beach and I like it very much.

e He's never *gone / been* to that restaurant.

f Now he's *gone / been* back to Canada and I really miss him.

g They need some advice because they've never *gone / been* on a cycling holiday before.

⬎ GF page 208

Have you ever ...?

Work with a partner. Ask your partner some questions about the pictures using *Have you ever* and the words below. Answer your partner's questions truthfully, saying *Yes, I have* or *No, I haven't*. If you say *Yes*, tell your partner when you did it.

EXAMPLE: *Have you ever played volleyball?*
            Yes, I have. I played in a match last year.

a play volleyball

b buy something online

c go to Bangkok

d go to a pop concert

e ride a bike

f go to a wedding

1 Underline the words below ending in /ɪz/.

🔊 39 Listen to the recording and check your answers.

a He needs new <u>glasses</u>.

b There are ten bridges in the city.

c I bought two new hairbrushes.

d There are three football matches tomorrow.

Copy the underlined words into the /ɪz/ column.

/ɪz/	/s/	/z/
glasses	books	schools

2 🔊 40 Listen to the recording and put the underlined words into the correct column above: /s/ or /z/.

a Those are my <u>books</u>.

b There are three <u>schools</u> in this street.

c Where are the <u>shops</u>?

d She's got really long <u>legs</u>.

e Her <u>shoes</u> are uncomfortable.

f We had <u>chips</u> for lunch.

g I like <u>cakes</u>.

h The <u>lessons</u> were boring.

i Her <u>boots</u> are black.

3 🔊 41 Mark the final sounds /s/, /z/ and /ɪz/ in different colours in these sentences. Listen and repeat.

a My father plays tennis very well.

b My back aches.

c He never catches the ball.

d She swims every day.

e He likes travelling.

f She stays at home on Sundays.

g He never finishes work early.

h He eats salad every day.

i She always watches him when he plays football.

j He hopes to be a scientist.

k The hotel arranges everything.

«Activity» Did you ...?

Your teacher will give you the name of a famous person. Don't show it to anybody. Answer the questions other people ask you and ask questions to find out who the other people are. Ask and answer questions like these:

Did you live in England? – No, I didn't.

Did you die in the last century? – Yes, I did.

Did you paint pictures? – Yes, I did.

Have I seen any of your pictures? – Yes, you have.

Were you Picasso? – Yes, I was!

If you don't know the answer, say *I can't remember*.

Exam folder 10

Listening Part 1

1 Look at the question and pictures for question 1 in Exercise 3. What is the question about? Think of some vocabulary which is useful before you listen.

2 Work with a partner. Look at questions 2–5 in Exercise 3. Write down some useful vocabulary.

3 **1 42** Listen to the recordings.

For each question there are three pictures and a short recording.
Choose the correct picture and put a tick (✓) in the box below it.

1 How did the woman travel?

A ☐   B ☐   C ☐

2 Where did the man stay?

A ☐   B ☐   C ☐

3 Which is the girl's brother?

A ☐   B ☐   C ☐

4 Which job is Alice doing now?

A ☐   B ☐   C ☐

5 What has the boy bought his mother?

A ☐   B ☐   C ☐

Exam Advice

The answer is sometimes at the beginning, sometimes in the middle and sometimes at the end of the recording.

Writing folder

Writing Part 3

1 Look at the task below and think about these questions.

a What does *What about you?* mean here?

b What kind of places can you write about?

c What kind of things can you do to keep fit?

> • This is part of a letter you receive from an English penfriend.
>
> Dear Alice,
> I've just joined a fitness centre. What about you? Is there a place where you can do sport near your home? Tell me how you keep fit.
>
> • Now write a letter to your penfriend.
> • Write your **letter** in about 100 words.

2 Look at this answer. Does it answer the questions in the task? Is it a good answer?

> I don't go to a fitness centre. I prefer to do sport outdoors.
> There's a sports ground near our house.
> I go swimming quite often.
>
> All the best,
> Mirza

Exam Advice

In Writing Part 3, it is important to answer the question and to give extra information to make your answer interesting.

3 Which of these sentences can you use to improve Mirza's letter? Decide where to put them. Why can't you use the other sentences?

a Thanks for your letter.

b I live near the station.

c There's one near our house and my brother joined it last year. He says it's good.

d I often go to the cinema with my brother.

e I go there on Saturdays and play football with my friends.

f On Sundays we have matches against other teams.

g I usually go to the big pool in the city centre, but sometimes we go surfing in the sea.

h Do you go to a fitness centre?

i I really like that and I think it's a great way to keep fit.

⤵ Grammar spot   Asking for a reply

When we write a letter, we often want to say that we would like a reply. How do we say this in English? Mark the correct words in each column, then write the sentence in the space.

I	wait look forward like look	hearing to hear for hearing to hearing	from of by	you.

I .... you.

4 Now look at this answer. Make up some sentences to add to it. Compare your ideas with those of other students.

> I go to our local fitness centre every week. There's also a tennis club near our house, but I don't go there. I sometimes play volleyball after school.
>
> Love,
> Liz

5 Write your own answer to the task in about 100 words.

Facts and figures

Grammar superlative adjectives; present passive
Vocabulary countries, nationalities, languages; number; measurements; what to say when you're not sure
Revision comparative adjectives

Introduction

a 8
Japan

b
....

c
....

d
....

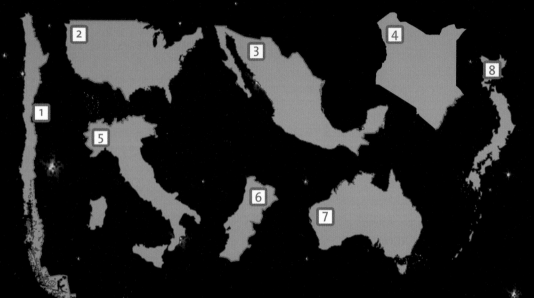

e
....

f
....

g
....

h
....

1 Work in a group. Match the flags of the countries to their shapes and write the names underneath.

> Chile ~~Japan~~ the USA Portugal
> Australia Kenya Mexico Italy

2 In your group, complete these sentences about the countries above.

a _Kenya_ is in Africa.
b _____ is in the same continent as Portugal.
c _____ and _____ share a border.
d _____ is on the equator.
e _____ and _____ are islands.
f The Atacama Desert is in _____.
g Off the west coast of _____ is the Atlantic Ocean.

Who finished first? Who got them all correct?

3 In your group, choose one country and write three facts about it, using the sentences in Exercise 2 and/ or the expressions in the box below. If you know the country's flag, draw it.

Each group takes turns to read their sentences. The rest of the class tries to guess the country.

> It has a border with …
> It has a mountain/mountain range/lake called …
> It's near/next to …
> It's large/small/long and thin.
> It's to the north/south/east/west of … ·

EXAMPLE: *It's long and thin, it's to the east of Norway and it has several large lakes.*
(Answer: Sweden)

Listening

1 Look at these questions from a radio quiz. Do you know any of the answers? Tick what you think is the correct answer.

2 **2 02** Listen to the quiz. Mark the answers that Rory gives in a different colour. Does he choose the same answers as you?

3 Work in a group. Three of Rory's answers are wrong. Which are they?

4 **2 03** Now listen to the answers and check which ones Rory got right. Did you find his three wrong answers in Exercise 3?

5 Can you remember what Rory says when he wants to think about his answer? Complete the expressions below. Listen again if you need to.

Oh, just a ....
Er, I'm sorry, could you
.... that, please?
Er, I'm not ....
Let me .... again.
Let me ....
I'm sorry, I don't ....

1 Which is the smallest ocean in the world?
A the Atlantic Ocean
B the Indian Ocean
C the Arctic Ocean

2 Which is the longest border in the world?
A between the USA and Canada
B between the USA and Mexico
C between Argentina and Chile

3 Where is the wettest place in the world?
A in India
B in Colombia
C in Nigeria

4 Which planet is the largest?
A Earth
B Venus
C Jupiter

5 In which country is the busiest airport in the world?
A in the USA
B in Japan
C in Greece

6 Which island is the biggest?
A Great Britain
B Greenland
C Cuba

7 Which continent has the most people?
A Asia
B Australasia
C Africa

8 Which city is the most expensive to live in?
A Geneva in Switzerland
B Paris in France
C Tokyo in Japan

9 Where is the deepest valley in the world?
A in the USA
B in China
C in Kenya

10 Which country is the farthest from the equator?
A Portugal
B Australia
C Peru

Language focus

Superlative adjectives

1 Use the quiz to help you complete this table.

Adjective	Comparative	Superlative
small	....	....
long	....	....
wet	....	....
....	larger	....
....	....	the busiest
big	....	....
expensive	....	....
....	deeper	....
....	farther or further	....
good	....	the best
....	worse	the worst

Grammar spot

Superlative adjectives

Look at the words in the table on the left and complete the rules for making superlative adjectives.

Most one-syllable adjectives (e.g. *small*) **add** ....

One-syllable adjectives ending in *e* (e.g. *large*) **add** ....

Most adjectives ending in a .... and a consonant (e.g. *wet*) **double the consonant and add** ....

Most adjectives with more than one .... (e.g. *expensive*) **use the** ....

Adjectives ending in *y* (e.g. *busy*) **usually change *y* to** .... **and add** ....

Far, ... and .... are irregular **and become *the farthest/furthest,*** .... **and** ....

William

Charlie

Michael

....
....
....

2 Look at the people above and write three sentences about each person using the superlative form of the words in the box to help you.

happy confident interesting friendly
angry kind serious hard-working shy

EXAMPLE: *William is the happiest.*

Compare your sentences with a partner.

⬇ Corpus spot

Superlative adjectives

The following sentences were written by PET students and the superlative adjectives are incorrect. Correct them.

a Vilnius is the bigest town in my country.
b That's the worse joke I've ever heard.
c The most cheapest hotels are near the railway station.
d Those four days were the happier in my life.

↘ **GF pages 208–9**

Numbers and measurements

1 Write these abbreviations in words.

mm .... cm .... m ....
km .... km² ....

2 Listen to some numbers your teacher will read to you. Write them down (in figures, not words).

3 Now listen to the answers to the radio quiz again and write the answers to these questions in figures.

a How large is the smallest ocean? *14,351,000km²*
b How long is the longest border?
c How much rain falls every year in the wettest place?
d How wide is the largest planet?
e How many people go through Atlanta airport every year?
f What is the area of Greenland?

Countries, nationalities, languages

1 **2 04** Listen to six different students say 'I'm a student and I like all kinds of sports' in their own language. Do you know which languages they are speaking? Choose from the box below.

German Greek Italian Japanese
Polish Portuguese Russian French

Check your answers and complete the table.

	Language	Nationality	Country
a			
b			
c			
d			
e			
f			

2 Now complete this table for other countries.

Language	Nationality	Country
		Spain
	Mexican	
French		
	Brazilian	
		Australia

3 How many languages do you speak? How many languages do you think there are in the whole world?

A 69
B 691
C 6,912
D 69,120

Present passive

1 Look at these sentences, then make some similar sentences about three other languages.

Australians **speak** English.

English **is spoken by** Australians.

> **Present passive**
> *to be* + past participle
> + English **is spoken by** Australians.
> + Many different languages **are spoken** in the world.
> − Coffee **isn't grown** in England.
> − Pineapples **aren't grown** in Canada.
> ? **Is** tea **grown** in Italy?
> ? **Are** bananas **grown** in Peru?

2 Write the past participles of these verbs.

hold *held* ....   carry ....

invent ....   keep ....

lead ....   light ....

make ....   play ....

3 Read this paragraph about the Olympic Games. For each gap, choose one verb from the list above and write it in the present passive.

The Olympic Games first took place in Olympia in Greece over 2,000 years ago. They **(a)** *are held* every four years. The Olympic torch **(b)** .... using a mirror and the sun at the ancient site of Olympia. It **(c)** .... by runners from Olympia to the location of the Games and it **(d)** .... there until the end of the Games. Each year a new design **(e)** .... for the medals, which are bronze, silver and gold. The gold medals **(f)** .... (not) from pure gold now. Every Games has an opening parade but, wherever it is, the athletes **(g)** .... (always) by the Greek team. Some sports like golf, cricket and rugby **(h)** .... (not) any more at the Games.

4 Look at this example.

oranges / Spain / England ? (grow)
Are oranges grown in Spain or England?
They're grown in Spain. They aren't grown in England.

Work in pairs.
Student A: Write two questions in the passive using these words.

cars on the left / Italy / Australia ? (drive)
baseball / the United States / Russia ? (play)

Student B: Write two questions in the passive using these words.

kilometres / Canada / Mexico ? (use)
rice / China / Switzerland ? (produce)

Ask your partner your questions and then answer their questions using the example above to help you.

↘ **GF page 209**

«Pronunciation»

1 What sounds are at the beginning of these two words?

c͟heese   s͟hampoo

2 Look at the underlined letters in these words. How do you say them? Which sound do you hear? Some words are in the wrong column. Which are they?

c͟heese	s͟hampoo
C͟hinese	s͟hy
teac͟her	spec͟ial
muc͟h	informat͟ion
c͟heap	oc͟ean
bru͟sh	lunc͟h
ques͟tion	pic͟ture
temperat͟ure	mac͟hine

3 **2 05** Listen and repeat the words. Were you right?

«Activity» Quiz

Look again at the quiz on page 73. Work in two or three teams. Write six similar questions about your town, school, region or country. Read your questions to the other team(s). Who gets the highest score?

«Activity» Numbers

Your teacher will give you a card with a number on it. Think how to say it in English and try to remember it. Listen to other students say their numbers and decide which order they come in.

Exam folder 11

Reading Part 5

In this part of the exam, you have to choose the correct word to go in each space in a text.

1 In some questions, the answer is correct because of its meaning.

Look at these four words and fit each one into the correct sentence below.

A birthday   **B** wedding   **C** celebration   **D** anniversary
1 Yesterday was the .... of when we first met.
2 I was 19 on my last ....
3 After the .... they went on their honeymoon.
4 They had a huge .... when he arrived home.

2 In some questions, both the meaning and the grammar are important.

Look at these four words and fit each one into the correct sentence below.

A realised   **B** watched   **C** looked   **D** saw
1 She .... at the painting for a long time.
2 When I .... my friend, I shouted to her.
3 I .... the football match until the end.
4 The man .... the bus was late.

How did you decide for sentence 1?
How did you decide for sentences 2, 3 and 4?

3 Some questions just test grammar.

Look at these four words and fit each one into the correct sentence below.

A Did   **B** Have   **C** Was   **D** Has

1 .... Carmen invited me to her house at the weekend?
2 .... Carmen invite you to her house last weekend?
3 .... Carmen working when you visited her?
4 .... you ever been to Carmen's house?

4 In some questions, you need to choose the correct word to join two parts of the sentence.

Look at these four words and fit each one into the correct sentence below.

A because   **B** so   **C** but   **D** although
1 The food was disgusting .... he didn't eat it.
2 The food was disgusting .... my sister isn't a good cook.
3 The food was disgusting .... everyone ate it.
4 .... the food was disgusting, everyone ate it.

5 Look at the photograph opposite and answer these questions.

a Where are these people?
b What are they doing?
c What is in the background?
d What's the weather like?
e What are they wearing?
f How do they feel?

6 Now read the text opposite and answer these questions. Don't look at Exercise 7 yet.

a Where did Alan Chambers and Charlie Paton go?
b How did they get there?
c Where did they spend one day? Why?
d How did they get home?
e What did Alan give Charlie?

Exam Advice

Read the text before you answer the questions so you have an idea of what it says.

TO THE TOP OF THE WORLD

The coldest walk in the **(0)** ....*A*........ is probably the one Alan Chambers and Charlie Paton did a few years **(1)** .... when they walked to the North Pole. To prepare for the trip they **(2)** .... a day in a freezer at a temperature of –30°C. But they were more comfortable there than at the North Pole **(3)** .... they weren't tired or hungry!

They began their 1,126 km walk **(4)** .... 8 March 2000 and **(5)** .... at the North Pole 70 days later. A plane took them straight home from there.

Charlie had his 30th **(6)** .... during the trip and he was amazed when Alan gave him **(7)** .... small cake with a candle on it. Alan said the **(8)** .... moment for him was Charlie's face when he **(9)** .... that cake.

The strange thing is that more men **(10)** .... walked on the moon than to the North Pole.

7   You now know what the text is about. Look at the questions below. Read the text again and choose the correct word for each space. Look carefully at the words around the space.

0	**A** world	**B**	country	**C**	planet	**D**	earth
1	**A** then	**B**	ago	**C**	since	**D**	after
2	**A** passed	**B**	stayed	**C**	spent	**D**	put
3	**A** because	**B**	but	**C**	therefore	**D**	so
4	**A** in	**B**	at	**C**	on	**D**	for
5	**A** got	**B**	reached	**C**	went	**D**	arrived
6	**A** celebration	**B**	anniversary	**C**	wedding	**D**	birthday
7	**A** the	**B**	a	**C**	much	**D**	some
8	**A** greater	**B**	good	**C**	best	**D**	better
9	**A** saw	**B**	looked	**C**	watched	**D**	realised
10	**A** did	**B**	have	**C**	was	**D**	has

A good read

Grammar past continuous / past simple; *while/when*
Vocabulary books; reviews
Revision giving opinions

Introduction

1 **2·06** Listen to the recording. At the end, say what you think happened.

2 Which of these books do you think the story comes from?

3 Here are some kinds of books. Match them to the pictures of covers above.

   1 a modern novel   *f*
   2 a horror story   5 a thriller
   3 a biography   6 a love story
   4 a science fiction novel

4 Which of the books are fiction and which are non-fiction?

5 What kinds of books do you like reading?

Reading

1 Here is part of a book called *The Double Bass Mystery* by Jeremy Harmer.

Penny is a double bass player. She and her boyfriend Simon play in an English orchestra. They are in Barcelona. Last night they gave their first concert there. Penny was tired after the concert and fell asleep quickly.

Read on and find out what happened next.

Chapter 5
Screams in the night

I was asleep, but my head was full of pictures and stories. I was dreaming about double basses and violinists and parties on the beach. Simon was in my dream. Our conductor was in it. So was my old teacher, playing a double bass on the sand. Then I heard a different sound. Somebody was shouting. No, it was worse than that. Somebody was screaming, screaming very loudly. I opened my eyes. I woke up. It was five o'clock in the morning.

Somebody screamed again. And again. And again. This time I wasn't dreaming. I got out of bed. I put on a T-shirt and some jeans and went out of my room. Doors were opening on the left and the right. Adriana came out of her room. She ran up to me. She was half asleep, still in her night-dress. 'What is it?' she asked sleepily. 'What's going on?'
'I don't know,' I answered.
Martin Audley (a trumpet player) came up to us.

'Who screamed?' he asked.
'Nobody knows,' I told him. 'But it sounded terrible.'
There was another scream. It came from outside.
We ran back into my room and looked out of the window, down at the street. There was a police car there, some people, more and more people. And something else.
'Come on,' I said. We got the lift to the ground floor. When it stopped we ran out of the hotel and pushed to the front of all the people.
Marilyn Whittle, the harp player, was already there. Her face was white and her eyes were large and round.
'Look! Look!' she said. She was pointing in front of her. She screamed again.
We looked. She was pointing at the person at her feet. It was Frank Shepherd. His mouth was open. There was blood all over his head.
Martin spoke first. 'My God!' he said. 'He's dead!'

2 Now answer these questions.

a Why did Penny wake up?
b What did she do next?
c Who did she talk to?
d What did they see out of the window?
e Why was Marilyn screaming?

3 Work in a group. What do you think happened next?

CAMBRIDGE

THE DOUBLE BASS MYSTERY

Jeremy Harmer

Language focus

Past continuous and past simple

1 What was happening? Match the sentences a–c with the sentences 1–3.

a Penny woke up.
b Penny went out of her room.
c Marilyn said, 'Look! Look!'

1 She was pointing at Frank.
2 Doors were opening.
3 Somebody was screaming very loudly.

⬇ Grammar spot   Past continuous and past simple meaning

Look at the sentences in the exercise above. Write *a, b, c* or *1, 2, 3* in the spaces below.

Sentences .... tell us about events that happened.

Sentences .... tell us *what was happening around the time* of those events.

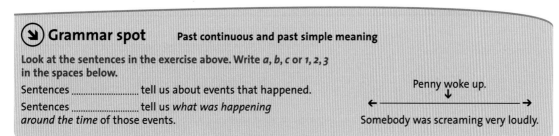

Penny woke up.
↓
←————————————————→
Somebody was screaming very loudly.

2 Look at the table and put the verbs in the story below into the past continuous.

+	I We	was were	screaming.
–	He They	wasn't / was not weren't / were not	screaming.
?	Was Were	she they	screaming.

The spy

When I left the nightclub it **(a)** _was raining_ (rain). When I reached the underground station, a lot of people **(b)** .... (wait) for trains. While I **(c)** .... (walk) along the platform, I noticed a girl with long hair. She **(d)** .... (stand) beside a chocolate machine. She looked worried. Suddenly, she screamed and fell to the ground. A man came forward. He **(e)** .... (carry) a bag. 'I'm a doctor,' he said. I watched her carefully while the doctor **(f)** .... (help) her.

A train came into the station. While the passengers **(g)** .... (get) onto the train, I saw the girl give the doctor a piece of paper. I thought she was ill. The doctor **(h)** .... (read) something on the paper. I watched his face.

Then I looked for the girl. She **(i)** .... (not lie) on the ground. She **(j)** .... (sit) in the train. The doors closed. When the train started to move, I saw that she **(k)** .... (laugh).

3 What do you think was happening? Answer these questions.

a Who was the spy?
b What was wrong with the girl?
c What was the doctor reading?
d Why was the girl laughing?

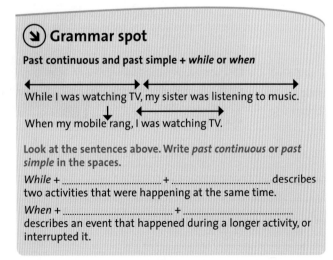

⬇ Grammar spot

Past continuous and past simple + *while* or *when*

⟵──────⟶ ⟵──────────⟶

While I was watching TV, my sister was listening to music.
⬇ ⟵──⟶
When my mobile rang, I was watching TV.

Look at the sentences above. Write *past continuous* or *past simple* in the spaces.

While + ... + ... describes two activities that were happening at the same time.
When + ... + ...
describes an event that happened during a longer activity, or interrupted it.

4 Georg is a university student. His twin brother Kurt is a disc jockey. Write sentences about what they were both doing last Saturday.

	Time	Georg	Kurt
a	6.30	get up	drive home from work
b	7.00	cook breakfast	have shower
c	11.00	play basketball	sleep
d	1.30	have lunch	still sleep
e	3.00	work in library	buy some new CDs
f	7.00	walk home	listen to music
g	9.00	watch television	still listen to music
h	11.00	go to bed	drive to work

a *While Georg was getting up, Kurt was driving home from work.*

5 What were Georg and Kurt doing when the phone rang? Complete the sentences using the past continuous.

When the phone rang, Georg _was listening to music_ .

When the phone rang, Georg and Kurt
....

When the phone rang, Kurt
....

When the phone rang, Georg and Kurt
....

When the phone rang, Kurt
....

6 Now look again at pictures a–e with a partner. Take turns to ask and answer questions about them, using the words given:

a study grammar
   Was Georg studying grammar when the phone rang?
   No, he wasn't studying, he was listening to music!
b watch football on television
c have a shower
d sit in a café
e write an email

7 Think about the recording you listened to in the Introduction. Choose the correct verb form.

Dyson (**a**) ~~was entering~~ / entered the office very quietly and (**b**) *was shutting* / shut the door carefully. First, he (**c**) *was pulling* / pulled down the blind. Next, he (**d**) *was switching* / switched on his torch. Then he (**e**) *was taking* / took some papers out of the desk. While he (**f**) *was reading* / read them, he (**g**) *was hearing* / heard a car door outside the building. The police? No, not yet. Kelly – it must be Kelly!

Quickly, Dyson (**h**) *was switching* / switched off his torch and (**i**) *was listening* / listened. What (**j**) *was happening* / happened? He heard doors banging. Kelly (**k**) *was looking* / looked in other rooms. Then he heard footsteps. She (**l**) *was walking* / walked along the corridor. Dyson was ready. He (**m**) *was standing* / stood behind the door with his gun in his hand when Kelly (**n**) *was coming* / came into the room.

8 Put the verbs into the past simple or past continuous.

Kelly (**a**) *hit* (hit) Dyson's arm and (**b**) .... (try) to take the gun. A bullet (**c**) .... (hit) Dyson's foot and he (**d**) .... (fall) to the floor. Kelly (**e**) .... (try) to decide what to do when she (**f**) .... (hear) the police car. She (**g**) .... (run) out of the building, (**h**) .... (jump) into her car and (**i**) .... (drive) away.

Dyson (**j**) .... (still lie) on the floor of the office when the police (**k**) .... (arrive).

> ↘ **GF page 209**

≪Pronunciation≫

1 Practise the sounds /uː/ as in *two* and /ʊ/ as in *took*. Can you find them in these two sentences?

Don't shoot! Put the gun down!

2 (**2 07**) Listen and repeat these sentences. Which words have the sound /uː/? Which words have the sound /ʊ/? Mark them in different colours.

a The p<u>oo</u>l is t<u>oo</u> f<u>u</u>ll.
b Would you like to come too?
c The school rules are in this blue book.
d Look at that cool suit.
e It's true he's a good cook.
f Put your hand on the rope and pull.
g You stood on my foot.

3 Check your answers and put the words into the table.

/uː/	/ʊ/
pool, too	full

4 Say the sentences again with a partner.

≪Activity≫ What can you say about a book?

Work in a group and put these sentences into four lists. Use the headings your teacher gives you. Some sentences can go with more than one heading.

a These stories are really fantastic.

b This book has had great reviews.

c These are my favourite poems.

d This thick book is expensive, but it has lots of up-to-date diagrams.

e My friends have enjoyed this book.

f The descriptions are terrible.

g Everybody wants to borrow this book from the library.

h It's a stupid story.

i It's a perfect book for a long journey.

j I think this is a brilliant and original book.

k This story is similar to others in the same series.

l The characters aren't believable.

m This book is very popular in America.

n This book is depressing.

o This amusing story takes place in Athens.

p This is an amazing story with wonderful descriptions.

q This book is a translation.

r This book has had an astonishing success.

s The writer tells a traditional story in simple language.

≪Activity≫ Write a review

Think of a book you have read. Write a short review of it for the other people in your class. Write 50–60 words. Use the Activity above to help you. Try to answer these questions:

What is the book called and who is it by?
Is the book fiction or non-fiction?
If it's non-fiction, what is it about?
If it's fiction, what kind is it and where does the story take place?
What is your opinion of it?

Exam folder 12

Speaking Part 1

In this part of the exam, the examiner talks to each student and asks a few questions. The students spell a word for the examiner.

1 **2 08** Listen to the recording. The students are taking PET in England. What kind of information does the examiner want to know?

2 Listen again and complete the questions.

Examiner: Good afternoon. (a) *Can I have your mark sheets, please* ? I'm Janet and this is Celia. She's going to listen to us. Now, what's your name?

Luca: I'm Luca.

Examiner: And what's your name?

Paulina: Paulina.

Examiner: And (b) ...., Luca?

Luca: Maragna.

Examiner: (c) .... ?

Luca: M-A-R-A-G-N-A

Examiner: And what's yours, Paulina?

Paulina: Josefowski.

Examiner: And how do you spell that?

Paulina: J-O-S-E-F-O-W-S-K-I

Examiner: Thank you. So, Luca, (d) .... ?

Luca: The north of Italy, near Brescia. Have you heard of it?

Examiner: Yes, I think so. And (e) .... in Brescia?

Luca: I'm a student at the university.

Examiner: (f) .... ?

Luca: Science. I'm interested in chemistry.

Examiner: Thank you. Now, Paulina, (g) .... ?

Paulina: I'm living in London now. I come from Poland.

Examiner: (h) .... ?

Paulina: I'm working now. I'm going to university next month.

Examiner: Thank you. Do you think English will be useful for you in the future?

Paulina: (i) .... ?

Examiner: Do you think English will be useful for you in the future?

Paulina: Oh, yes. It'll be useful when I am at university. And later, when I want to find a good job, it will be an advantage for me.

Examiner: And Luca, (j) .... ?

Luca: Er, sometimes.

Examiner: What do you enjoy doing in your free time?

Luca: (k) .... ?

Examiner: What do you enjoy doing in your free time?

Luca: Oh, I like dancing and, er, spending time with my friends.

Examiner: Thank you.

Exam Advice

Learn these useful questions. You can use them in the exam. *Could you repeat that, please? Could you speak more slowly, please?*

3 Can you spell your name and your surname?

4 Work with a partner. Take turns asking questions like the examiner and answering them about yourself.

Writing folder

Writing Part 3

1 Read these titles of stories.

   1 The unwanted present
   2 A wonderful surprise
   3 The lost key
   4 The wrong house
   5 A dangerous plan
   6 A difficult journey

2 Below are the beginnings and endings of the stories. Match each one to its title.

3 Work in a group. Write the middle of one of the stories on a piece of paper.

4 When you have finished, pass your piece of paper to another group. They decide which story it belongs to.

5 Choose one of the titles and write your own story. Write about 100 words.

Exam Advice

Make sure your story has a good beginning and ending.

a Last Friday the weather was good so I walked to school. While I was going across the park I saw something metal on the ground.

....

The businessman gave me €100. I was really amazed. He said, 'I was looking for it all round town. Thank you for finding it.'

b Last summer, we moved to a big city. A few days later, I went to the city centre on my own.

....

I phoned home. I said, 'I know we live in Oxford Road, but what number is it?'
When I arrived, all my family were laughing about me. I've been careful not to forget our address since then.

c When we looked out of the tent, it was snowing hard. We packed our rucksacks and put on our coats.

....

At last we saw the lights of the city. An hour later we were sitting in a café with a hot drink in front of us.

d It was John's birthday, but he was sitting alone in his room. He usually met his friends on Saturday evenings, but this week they were all busy. He was miserable.

....

'It's been a great evening,' he said.

e I work in a café on Saturdays. One man who often comes in is a journalist. A fortnight ago, when I brought him his coffee, he said, 'I'm going to meet someone.'
'Who?' I asked.

....

'I hope you'll return safely,' I said.
'I hope so, too!' he answered.

f I like my cat. Her name is Sheba and she is black, beautiful and very intelligent. At night she explores the garden.

....

I wrapped it in newspaper and put it in the dustbin before Sheba woke up. I don't think she knows.

↘ Corpus spot   *search / search for / look for*

We *search* *somewhere* when we want to find something.
We *search for* or *look for* something or someone that we want to find.
Choose the correct verb in these PET students' sentences.

a It's no good *looking for / searching* your watch now, it's lost!
b We *searched for / searched* the whole town until almost nine o'clock in the evening but we didn't find him.
c I know that you are *looking for / searching* a job in your holidays.
d When it suddenly started to rain, we left the beach and *looked for / searched* a hotel.
e I've *looked for / searched* everywhere but haven't found it.

Units 7–12 Revision

Speaking

1 Work with a partner. Look at these sentences.

Say if each sentence is true for you and give your partner some extra information.

a In my city the cinemas are opposite the shopping mall. *Yes, that's true. The cinemas are near the bus station opposite the shopping mall.* OR *No, that's not true. The cinemas are opposite the supermarket.*

b The weather this week is colder than last week.

c Skateboarding is more popular than football.

d I am older than my partner.

e I often have a sore throat after a football match.

f I've never been to a barbecue.

g My friends often have parties in winter.

h I visited New Zealand six months ago.

i My country has lots of lakes.

j I like reading love stories.

Grammar

2 Complete this email with words from the box.

| already | yet | for | since | ~~ago~~ |
| in | ever | while | on | never |

○○○

🚫 ↩ ↩ → 🖨
Delete Reply Reply All Forward Print

Dear Fiona,

Nick and I arrived in London two days **(a)** *ago* . Have you **(b)** .... been to London? I've **(c)** .... been before but Nick came here **(d)** .... 2008. I've wanted to come **(e)** .... I was a little boy. We've **(f)** .... been on a river trip and on a bus around the city – I enjoyed them both. I haven't been to any museums **(g)** .... but Nick went to one yesterday **(h)** .... I was looking round the Tower of London. We're staying in London **(i)** .... a week and we're going to Edinburgh **(j)** .... Friday. See you soon.

Mark

Reading

3 Read these reviews of four books, then look at the sentences below. Decide which book each sentence matches.

A

I have read several books by Darren McGough and this novel is as good as all his others. Most of McGough's stories happen in Australia because that is where he comes from. This one starts on a beach in Spain and finishes up a mountain in China. It is very exciting and the ending is a surprise.

B

Like all Sergio Sanchez's books, this one is very popular in South America and Spain. I've wanted to read it for a long time and now I can because it is available in English. It is about a journey which a group of people made across Argentina at the beginning of the last century.

C

This is the third book Colin Wesley has written about animals but I enjoyed this one the most. It is easier to read than the others and the photographs are beautiful. Wesley spent a year living in Australia taking photos and writing about Australian animals. It costs a lot (€30).

D

Ruth Rawlings takes 400 pages to write about the life of Maria Cornwell. She was an opera singer in the 1920s and she travelled all over the world. The book is very long but is not expensive at €10. Rawlings has not written a book before and I hope this is not the last one, as it is very good.

	A	B	C	D
1 The story takes place in South America.				
2 It is the writer's first book.				
3 It is expensive.				
4 It is fiction.				
5 It is translated from another language.				
6 The writer is Australian.				
7 It is a biography.				
8 It is a thriller.				
9 It is already successful in some countries.				
10 It is better than the last book by this writer.				

Grammar

4 There is one mistake in each of these sentences. Correct it.

a I lived in this road since 2000.
   I've lived in this road since 2000.
b This is the funnyest book I've ever read.
c Portuguese is spoke in Brazil.
d This cinema is less modern as the one in my town.
e The café is in corner of the park.
f Why you don't phone the doctor?
g The weather here is hotest in July.
h This is the worse painting I've ever done.
i Could you to speak more slowly, please?
j My racket wasn't as expensive than my teacher's.
k Natalya is from Russian.

Vocabulary

5 Look at the map on page 48 and complete these directions.

> To get from the skateboard park to the railway station by car, (a) _turn_ left when you come out of the skateboard park, go (b) .... on past the car park until you get to a (c) .... Turn right here and go (d) .... this road until you get to a (e) .... Turn left and go (f) .... a bridge. The railway station is (g) .... the left.

> To get from the skateboard park to the park on foot, walk to the square. This is a (h) .... area. Walk (i) .... the square to Queen Street. Go (j) .... the town hall and turn (k) .... at the crossroads. This is a (l) .... street for cars. When you get to the supermarket, turn (m) .... and the park gates are (n) .... the right (o) .... the swimming pool.

6 Think about the meaning of these nouns. Divide them into four groups.

~~roundabout~~ ~~wedding~~ ~~cough~~ ~~border~~ ankle carnival desert entrance anniversary continent birthday corner honeymoon island stadium thermometer neck ocean throat tongue turning valley festival fountain

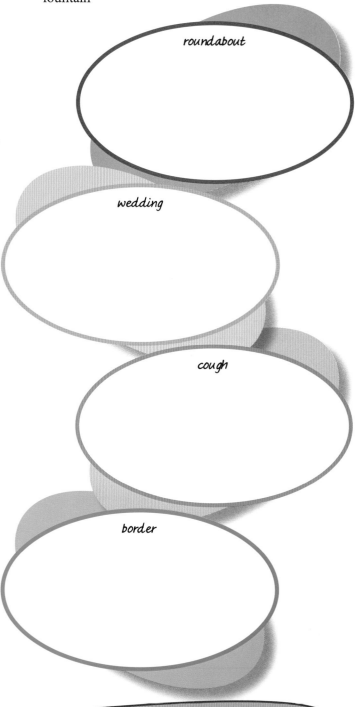

⬇ Vocabulary spot

When you are learning new vocabulary from a reading text, write it down in groups of related words.

A place of my own

Grammar	modals (probability, possibility); prepositions of place
Vocabulary	rooms and furniture; saying what you prefer
Revision	present and past tenses; advice

Introduction

1 Look at the photographs. What are these things called? Which of the words in the box can you use to describe each of them?

antique	beautiful
cheap	comfortable
crazy	expensive
glass	modern
ugly	plastic
useful	old-fashioned
unusual	traditional
wooden	

2 Read what people say about their things and match them to the photos.

> **1** I think this is great because I like unusual furniture. Some people say it's not very comfortable in hot weather but I don't mind.

> **2** This is useful, it's modern and it was cheap. It's not beautiful, but it's not ugly and I can keep a lot of my clothes in it.

> **3** I was walking down a side street when I saw this in a shop window, and I decided to buy it that day. I don't have any other antiques, but this is the kind of thing which looks good in any big room.

> **4** I've had it for two years now. It was expensive, but in my opinion, it was worth it because it's the most useful thing in the kitchen.

> **5** I don't really like it at all because it's old-fashioned, and I prefer modern furniture. But I can't afford to change it and it's quite useful – I can keep lots of things in it.

> **6** This matches the other furniture in the room because it's traditional – we've had it since we got married. We all like it because it's very comfortable.

> **7** My parents gave it to me for my birthday. I know it was expensive, but I love modern design, and really beautiful things are always fashionable.

> **8** It's crazy, isn't it? Everyone laughs when they see it, but it works OK, and it makes me happy.

3 Work with a partner. Tell each other what kind of furniture you like.

⤵ Vocabulary spot

Talking about the price of things

Complete these sentences with a word from the box.

afford	is	cost	worth

a How much does/did it .... ?
b I can/can't .... it.
c It .... cheap/expensive.
d It's (not) .... £100.

Listening

1  Listen to four people called Neil, Ian, Adam and Patricia talking about where they live. Write the name of the speaker next to each photograph.

2 Listen again. Who talks about these things? Mark your answers in the table.

	Ian	Patricia	Adam	Neil
dining room				
bathroom	✓			
shower				
roof				
towers				
windows				
curtains				
carpets				
hi-fi				
central heating				
solar power				

3 Answer these questions.

a How does Ian save money?
  He doesn't pay rent.

b What does Ian do when he gets bored with the view?

c What were Patricia and her husband doing when they found their unusual home?

d Where is Patricia's sitting room?

e What did Adam use to make his house?

f Why isn't Adam worried about his house?

g Why doesn't Neil mind the noise?

h Why is Neil's house perfect for him?

Language focus

could/might/must/can't + be

⬆ Grammar spot　　　Modals

Read this dialogue and complete the table with the words underlined.

Dad: You've passed all your exams and I've bought you a present.
Sara: What is it?
Dad: Guess! It's something you want.
Sara: Well, it's very small. It <u>can't be</u> a handbag. I'm sure about that.
Dad: Correct.
Sara: It <u>could be</u> an MP3 player. That's one possibility.
Dad: Yes, it <u>might be</u>, it's the right size. But you've already got one.
Sara: Yes. Well. I really want a camera. It <u>must be</u> a camera! I'm sure it is.
Dad: Open it and see.

I'm sure it is	I'm sure it's not	Perhaps it's
It .... (1)	It .... (2)	It .... (3)
		It .... (4)

⬇ GF page 209

1 Work with a partner. Talk about the things in the pictures. Can you guess what they are? Use the language in the Grammar spot.

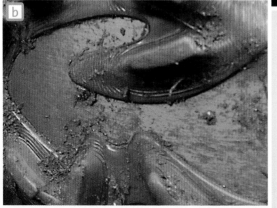

2 **Choose the correct verb.**

1 **A:** Who's that man? Isn't he a well-known actor?
 B: I don't know, but he <u>*could*</u> / *must* be. He's very handsome.

2 **A:** I've just tried to phone Toni at her aunt's house, but she's not there.
 B: But she *must* / *might* be there. She's babysitting her cousins.

3 **A:** I want to buy a computer like your brother's. Do you know how much they cost?
 B: No, but they *can't* / *must* be very expensive because I know he hasn't got much money.

4 **A:** Where's the orange juice?
 B: I'm not sure. Probably in the fridge, or it *must* / *might* be on the table in the other room.

5 **A:** Are your neighbours on holiday?
 B: They *can't* / *could* be. The car isn't outside the house.

Prepositions of place

Are these sentences true or false? Correct them if necessary.

a The basin is below the mirror.　*true*
b The toilet is opposite a cupboard.
c There's a mirror facing the basin.
d The basin is on top of a cupboard.
e There's a window behind the basin.
f There's a step between the basin and the cupboard.
g There's a low cupboard in the corner.
h There are towels on hooks on the wall opposite the mirror.
i We can see toothbrushes inside some of the drawers.
j There's a cupboard on the wall beyond the step.

1 Work with a partner. Can you name all the rooms and furniture in this flat?

2 Now decide which rooms to put these things in. Use your dictionary if necessary.

basin   chest of drawers
cooker   poster
desk   bath
wastepaper basket sink
mirror   air conditioning
sofa   bedside table
curtains   television
pillows   clock
central heating carpet
dishwasher   washing machine

3 The owners of this flat want to buy some more furniture. What advice would you give them? Use these expressions from Unit 9:

You should …
You'd better …
Why don't you …?

> **⬎ Vocabulary spot**
>
> Learning the names of things on a picture can help you to remember them. Remember the picture and the names of the things together.

«Pronunciation»

1 Think about the sounds /ʒ/ and /dʒ/. Can you find them in this sentence?

I heard a great joke on television yesterday.

2 **2 10** Listen and repeat these sentences. Which words have the sound /ʒ/? Which words have the sound /dʒ/? Mark them in different colours.

a Can you <u>measure</u> these <u>jeans</u>, please?
b We keep the fridge in the kitchen and the TV in the lounge.
c I'm doing revision for my college exams.
d Do you go jogging for pleasure?
e She usually pays generous wages.
f The Bridge Hotel has excellent leisure facilities.
g We've just made an important decision.
h A giraffe is an unusual pet.

3 When you have checked your answers, put the words into the table.

/ʒ/	/dʒ/
television	joke

4 Work with a partner. Take turns to repeat the sentences in Exercise 2 again. Listen to each other's pronunciation.

«Activity» Comparing pictures

Work with a partner. Your teacher will give each of you a picture. Don't look at each other's pictures.

Tell each other what you can see in your picture and where everything is. Can you find ten differences? Make sentences like this:

In Picture A the TV is on the table, but in Picture B it's on the desk.

Exam folder 13

Reading Part 2

In this part of the exam, you read five descriptions of people. For each one, you choose one text to match it.

1   Here are five texts about people who all want to do a language course at a college in England and eight advertisements for colleges. Underline the important information in 1–5 below.

1   Alma doesn't like cities and wants to live somewhere quiet with an English family. She wants to do a full-time course.

2   Kostas enjoys city life. He wants to do a part-time course and have a part-time job as well. He is not interested in going on trips or doing activities with the college after his classes. He wants to rent his own flat.

3   Margarita would like to live in a hostel with other students. She wants to do a full-time course. She likes to play sport in her free time.

4   Tomek is looking for a full-time four-week course at a college which organises social activities for students. He doesn't mind living in the city or the country but he wants to stay with a family.

5   Hiroki wants to do a part-time course at a college which can arrange his accommodation. He loves walking, so he wants to be near the countryside. He doesn't enjoy organised trips and activities.

2   Look at the description of Alma again. Quickly look through the advertisements on the opposite page.

   a Find the colleges which aren't in the city. Are they in quiet places?
   b Which of these colleges have accommodation with a family?
   c Which of these colleges have full-time courses?
   d Which college is suitable for Alma?

Exam Advice

No text can be the answer to two questions.

3 Decide which college would be the most suitable for the other people.

A

Langdale College is on the edge of a small town surrounded by hills, twenty kilometres from the city. It offers English lessons in the mornings with activities, sports and trips to other towns and places of interest in the afternoons and at weekends. Courses last six or twelve weeks. All students live with local families.

B

Anderson College is in the centre of the city. Students can choose from a range of part-time courses – either mornings only, afternoons only or three mornings/afternoons and two evenings. The college has sports facilities, a drama centre, library and club which students can use if they wish. The college does not arrange accommodation.

C

The Park School is ten kilometres from the city. It is surrounded by woods and there are lots of footpaths through attractive countryside. All students live in a hostel next to the school. There are classes in the mornings and the rest of the time students are free for private study.

D

Highcliff College is in the city near the university. It runs four-week and eight-week full-time courses. Students live with families. They spend evenings and weekends with their families learning about English family life and practising their English.

E

The Milburn Academy is in the city centre. It offers full-time twelve-week courses. Students are also expected to join in the social and sports events organised for evenings and weekends. The college owns several large houses nearby where students live and prepare their own meals.

F

The Waterside College is a large city college which has part-time English courses all year round. All students live in college hostels in different parts of the city. The college has its own sports hall and swimming pool and at weekends there are trips to other cities.

G

The Marlowe School offers two-week and four-week courses all year, full-time. It is situated in a quiet part of the city but there are buses both into the centre and to the nearby countryside. Students stay with local families if they wish. Every evening during the week there is a social event for students and there are trips at weekends.

H

The Beechwood Academy is in a village about 15 km from the city. It offers full-time courses. Students live with families in the village and are encouraged to join in family life as much as possible. The village has a leisure centre.

 Corpus spot *Do and take*

We use *do* or *take* + a course of study.

1 **These PET students have all used the wrong verb. Replace them with the correct form of *do* or *take*.**
   a I want to follow a course here in England.
   b We're going to make the same course.
   c Last year I visited an English course in Bristol.

2 **Now complete these sentences with the correct form of *do* or *take*.**
   a Zoë's French is quite good because she .... a course in Paris last summer.
   b My brother failed his science exam, so he .... an extra course at the college this term.
   c This cake is delicious. .... you .... a cookery course?

14 What's in fashion?

Grammar *used to*; *too* and *enough* + adjs; adj order
Vocabulary clothes; colours; centuries and decades
Revision describing things

A   B   C   D

Introduction

1   Look at the picture. What is happening?

2   **2 11** Listen to some people in the audience. Decide which model each speaker is talking about. Circle A, B, C or D.

    1 A   B   C   D   7 A   B   C   D
    2 A   B   C   D   8 A   B   C   D
    3 A   B   C   D   9 A   B   C   D
    4 A   B   C   D   10 A   B   C   D
    5 A   B   C   D   11 A   B   C   D
    6 A   B   C   D   12 A   B   C   D

3   Listen again for these adjectives. Write down the nouns they describe.

high	*heels*	fashionable	....
leather	....	striped	....
enormous	....	comfortable	....
grey	....	dark blue	....
awful	....	sleeveless	....
silk	....	orange	....

4   What kind of clothes do you like to wear?

Reading

1 Read this magazine article about fashion in Britain during the last century. Match each paragraph to one of the photographs. Then work in a group and decide which decade each paragraph is describing (1920s, 1950s, 1960s or 1990s).

Do you think you're
fashionable?

What did your granny or your dad use to wear?

19............s

Fashion went mad in Britain at this time. Clothes were made from exciting new materials like shiny plastic and even paper. Women used to wear very short skirts and long shiny black plastic boots. Sometimes the boots went over their knees. Young men used to wear bright colours. They wore wonderful patterned shirts with wide collars and big ties. Their hair was quite long.

19............s

In this period women used to wear long straight dresses. They ended just below the knee and didn't have a waist. The dresses often used to have a belt around the hips. Women liked wearing scarves and beads round their necks. Their hair was very short and they always used to wear hats when they went out. Men used to wear trousers with very wide legs. They often wore sweaters and flat caps.

19............s

Very full skirts were in fashion for young women at this time. They often used to wear gloves, sometimes even indoors. Teenage girls sometimes used to wear short white cotton socks and flat shoes. Some young men, who were known as 'teddy boys', used to wear very narrow ties and narrow trousers. Their shoes or boots sometimes had high heels and pointed toes.

19............s

Very short tops or T-shirts were the latest fashion in this decade. Girls used to wear them with jeans. Everyone wore trainers. Teenagers used to wear a lot of jewellery – in their ears, noses and even tongues – and they painted their nails in crazy colours. Young men used to have very short hair and they used to wear baseball caps and loose trousers. Sweatshirts and jogging pants were also very popular.

2 Read the text again. Underline any words you don't know.

Work in a group. Talk about the meaning of the words you underlined.

⬇ Vocabulary spot

Use the pictures and photographs to help you understand and learn words you don't know. Cut out pictures from magazines and label the clothes.

3 Which of the clothes look comfortable/ uncomfortable? Which are the most uncomfortable? Which look cool/warm? Which look exciting/boring? Which do you think are made from wool? cotton? leather? silk? Which would you like to wear?

Language focus
Used to

1 What did people use to wear? Make two sentences with *used to* about men, women or teenagers in each decade, using the words in the box and the article on page 93 to help you.

EXAMPLE: In the 1920s women *didn't use to* wear jewellery in their noses.
In the 1950s teenagers *used to* wear white socks.

very short skirts	flat caps
baseball caps	narrow trousers
gloves	shiny black boots
jewellery in their noses	white socks
big ties	beads

⬇ Grammar spot   Used to

Used to (verb) shows something was true in the past but not now.

I used to	I stopped	now
◄- - - - - - - - - - - - - - - ▶↓		↓

Write the correct form of *used to*.

+	In the 1920s, women .... wear hats.
−	In the 1950s, women .... have short skirts.
?	In the 1970s, did men .... wear ties?

≪Activity≫ Colours

How do these colours make you feel? Choose some words from the middle and write them on the colour you think they belong with.

Compare your wheel with your partner's. Have you chosen the same words for each colour?

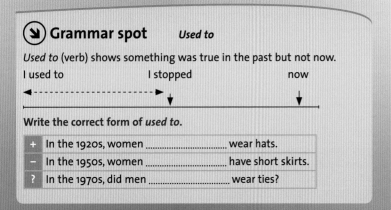

happy, cheerful, sad, miserable, bored, tired, quiet, peaceful, thoughtful, energetic, hot, warm, angry, cool

2 Ask your partner what he/she used to do when he/she was seven years old.

a What / wear? *What did you use to wear?*
b What time / get up?
c What time / bed?
d What / do / weekends?
e What / enjoy doing?

3 Now write three sentences about what your partner used to do.

↘ GF page 209

≪Activity≫ Used to

1 Work in pairs.

Student A, look at the picture on page 200. It is a picture of a street 100 years ago.
Student B, look at the picture on page 202. It is a picture of the same street now.
Student B, ask Student A questions beginning *Did there use to be …?*
Student A, reply *Yes, there did* or *No, there didn't*. Give Student B some extra information by saying *There used to be …*

2 Write down at least five things which have and haven't changed.

≪Pronunciation≫

1 Look at these lists of words. Think about the sound /f/. Which is the odd word out in each list?

a bright   light   cough   through
b enough   photograph   telephone   alphabet
c paragraph   fashion   geography   physics

2 ❷12 Listen and repeat the words. Do you want to change your odd word out?

3 What are the different ways of spelling the sound /f/?

What are the different ways of pronouncing the letters *gh*?

Too and enough

1 Look at the pictures on page 92 and choose one answer in the sentences below.

a The red hat *is too big / isn't big enough* for her.
b The green shorts *are too big / aren't big enough* for him.
c The grey trousers *are too long / aren't long enough* for him.
d The red and purple dress *is too bright / isn't bright enough*.
e The sunglasses *are too dark / aren't dark enough*.

> **↘ Grammar spot** **Too and enough**
>
> Choose *too* or *enough* to complete the rules below.
> We use *not* with *too/enough*.
> *Too/Enough* goes before an adjective.
> *Too/Enough* goes after an adjective.

2 Match the adjectives in Box A with their opposites in Box B.

A		B	
bright		thick	
short		tight	
thin		high	
loose		wide	
large		patterned	
low		dull	
narrow		long	
plain		small	

3 Look at these pairs of sentences. Finish the second one so that it means the same as the first one.

a Her skirt is too short for her.
Her skirt isn't _long enough_ for her.
b The tunnel is too narrow for us to drive through.
The tunnel isn't .... for us to drive through.
c The bridge is too low for the bus to go under.
The bridge isn't .... for the bus to go under.
d The suitcase isn't large enough for all our things.
The suitcase .... small for all our things.
e The material isn't thick enough to keep you warm.
The material .... thin to keep you warm.

4 Which of the clothes on page 93 don't you like? Write some sentences with *too* and *enough*. Use the adjectives in the box to help you.

> short warm large wide bright long colourful

EXAMPLE: *In **a**, the man's trousers are too wide.*
*In **c**, the girl's skirt isn't long enough.*

Adjective order

1 Here are some descriptions from the magazine article on page 93. What do these adjectives tell us about the nouns? Put them in the correct column.

> shiny cotton ~~wonderful~~ plastic
> white ~~long~~ black patterned short

Opinion	Size	Description	Colour	Material	Noun
	long				boots
wonderful					shirts
					socks

2 Look back at the first and second paragraphs of the magazine article and find the words from the exercise above. Are the columns in the correct order?

3 Now put these adjectives in the correct order.

a a blue/large sofa *a large blue sofa*
b a brown/warm coat
c a(n) wooden/old/beautiful desk
d a(n) amazing/silk/short dress
e a new/brilliant film
f some cotton/black/fashionable shorts
g a glass/shiny table

> ↘ **GF page 209**

《Activity》 **Clothes**

Think about what you were wearing yesterday. Write a description on a piece of paper without your name on it. Give it to your teacher. Listen to everyone's description. Can you guess who they all are?

Exam folder 14

Listening Part 4

1   Read this instruction. What does it tell you about the people? What does it tell you about their conversation?

You will hear a conversation between a boy, Sandy, and a girl, Megan, about their jobs.

> **Exam Advice**
>
> Read the instructions. They tell you who the speakers are and what they will talk about.

2   Work with a partner. Read the six sentences in Exercise 6. What subjects do you think Sandy and Megan talk about? Can you guess what their jobs are?

3   When you listen, you decide if each sentence is correct or incorrect. If it is correct, put a tick (✓) in the box under A for YES. If it is not correct, put a tick (✓) in the box under B for NO.

Practise with these sentences. Are they correct or incorrect?

		A YES	B NO
1	I've finished this course.	☐	☐
2	We are living in the twentieth century.	☐	☐
3	A baseball cap is a kind of hat.	☐	☐
4	The Arctic Ocean is the smallest ocean in the world.	☐	☐
5	Earth is the largest planet.	☐	☐

4   Questions 1 and 4 in Exercise 6 ask if Sandy and Megan are happy in their jobs. They use these adjectives in their conversation. Put them into two groups: *like* and *dislike*.

> awful   not interesting enough   miserable
> depressing   interesting   great   brilliant
> exciting   boring

like
....
....
....
....
....

dislike
....
....
....
....
....

5   Question 3 in Exercise 6 asks if Megan agrees with Sandy. They use these expressions in their conversation. Put them in two groups: *agree* and *disagree*.

> Of course.   You're wrong there.
> I don't think so.   That's not a good idea.
> Exactly.

6   **2 13** Do the task below.

> You will hear a conversation between a boy, Sandy, and a girl, Megan, about their jobs.
> Decide if each sentence is correct or incorrect.
> If it is correct, put a tick (✓) in the box under A for YES. If it is not correct, put a tick (✓) in the box under B for NO.

		A YES	B NO
1	Megan thinks her new job is perfect.	☐	☐
2	Megan takes photographs of models.	☐	☐
3	Megan agrees that bookshops are depressing.	☐	☐
4	Sandy is looking for a job in a different bookshop.	☐	☐
5	Sandy has studied photography.	☐	☐
6	Megan agrees to ask about a job for Sandy at the magazine.	☐	☐

7   Listen again and check your answers.

Which words helped you to answer the questions?

Writing folder

Writing Parts 2 and 3

1 Read this question. What kind of things are you going to write about?

- This is part of a letter you receive from an English friend.

  I'm really looking forward to hearing about your new flat. Did you find the furniture you wanted?

- Now write a letter to this friend.
- Write your **letter** in about 100 words.

2 Now read this answer. How many different things did the writer buy?

  Dear Nicholas,
  I went shopping this morning and I bought some things for my flat. I got a lamp in that new shop near the station. Then I found some cushions to match my sofa. They look nice. Then I bought a mirror, which I've put on my chest of drawers. It was cheap. I'd like to buy a bed but I can't afford it, so I bought a cover instead. The bed I've got is old. When I was coming home I walked through the market and I saw some posters, so I bought three.
  All the best,
  Dan

3 There aren't many adjectives in the letter. Add some of these adjectives to the letter to make it more interesting.

modern	large	shiny	crazy
tiny	blue	plastic	big
comfortable	red	amazing	green
colourful	cotton	leather	small
soft	wooden	new	lovely

4 Read this question.

  You are on holiday at the seaside and you buy a postcard.
  Write the postcard to your English friend called Sarah. In your card, you should
  - tell her about your journey
  - describe the place where you are staying
  - say what you like best

5 Here is an answer. Put a different adjective into each space.

  Dear Sarah,
  We had a very ....
  journey here because the weather was
  .... , so the ferry was
  late. We are staying in a ....
  town. We have a ....
  room with a .... view.
  I like the sea best. The water is
  ....

  Love,
  Rosie

6 Now do this question.

- This is part of a letter you receive from an English friend.

  In your next letter, tell me what kind of clothes you like wearing. Tell me what you have bought recently.

- Now write a letter to this friend.
- Write your **letter** in about 100 words.

Exam Advice

Use adjectives to make your writing more interesting.

Grammar modals (permission, obligation); adverbs
Vocabulary phrasal verbs with *get*; activities
Revision adjectives

Introduction

1 In the UK, the law says you can do some things when you are 16 but you can't do others. Guess which things you can do in the UK when you are 16.

When you are 16 ...	UK	
you can buy a pet.	✓	
you can vote in elections.	✗	
you can get a tattoo.		
you can work full-time.		
you can buy fireworks.		
you can buy lottery tickets.		
you can get a pilot's licence.		
you can ride a scooter.		
you can learn to drive a car.		
you can give blood.		
you can get married (if your parents agree).		

2 Complete the other column for your country. Put ? if you aren't sure.

3 Compare your answers with a partner.

4 Can you add any more things you can or can't do at age 16 in your country? Write them down.

5 Which things are different in your country from Britain? Do you agree with the laws in your country about what you can do at age 16? Which would you like to change?

I think 16 is the right age to ... / is too young to ... / isn't old enough to ...

Listening

2 **14** Listen to Ryan talking to his friend Martha, who did the Marathon of the Sands last year.

Decide if these sentences are true or false.

a Ryan enjoyed skydiving. *true*

b You have to be over a certain age to do the race.

c Martha thought that running on sand was the most difficult thing about the race.

d The runners have to share tents.

e The average daytime temperature is 40°.

Language focus

Can, can't; have to, don't have to

1 Martha says these things about the competition.

Listen again and put them into the correct column.

a finish in seven days
b carry your own food
c carry water for seven days
d take other drinks to mix with the water
e carry your own tent
f bring your own sleeping bag
g stay in your tent after sunrise
h go into the organisers' camp
i take an MP3 player

You have to	You can't	You can	You don't have to
a			

⬎ Grammar spot   Modal verbs: permission and obligation

Write *can*, *can't*, *have to* and *don't have to* in the spaces below next to the meanings.

It is a rule   ....

If you want   ....

We also use *must* and *mustn't* for rules.

2 Using the box below to help you, choose *can*, *can't*, *have to* or *don't have to* for each gap.

Modal verbs						
Permission: *Can*			**Obligation: *Have to***			
+	I She	can	vote.	+	You She	have to has to	take a tent.
−	You We	can't	vote.	−	You He	don't have to doesn't have to	take a tent.
?	Can	he they	vote?	?	Do Does	I she	have to	take a tent?

a Our teacher is really strict and we *can't*............... give her our homework late.
b What time .... (we) be at football practice?
c In most places, it is possible to use a credit card so you .... carry lots of cash around with you.
d You .... eat as much as you like as I've cooked lots.
e You .... have a picnic here because it's private land.
f I .... do the washing up three times a week or I don't get any pocket money.
g How much .... (students) pay for a lost library card?
h I live in the city centre so I .... wait for the bus because I walk to school.

⬎ GF page 209–210

 **Jobs**

Work in a group. Your teacher will give you some cards with the names of jobs on them. Take turns to take a card. Don't tell the other students your job.

They ask you: *Do you have to ...?*

You can give them one clue: *You don't have to ...* or *You have to ....*

Which group guesses the jobs first?

Possible questions

get up early?
wear a uniform?
work regular hours?
travel around in a car?
walk a lot?
wear a costume?
stand up most of the day?
work in the evening?
get dirty?
talk a lot?
write lots of emails?

Phrasal verbs with *get*

Can you remember what Ryan and Martha said in the recording?

Complete the sentences with the words in the box.

off ~~on~~ on with on with up

a How did you get _on_............. ?
b You have to get .... quickly when the organisers call everyone.
c You need to get .... the other people.
d When you get .... the plane you can't believe how hot it is.
e I have some work that I need to get ....

⬎ Vocabulary spot

Write down phrasal verbs as you learn them. Write them in a sentence so you have an example of the meaning. Keep them in one place in your notebook so you can look at them when you need to.

Had to, didn't have to

1 Read the beginning of this email Ryan wrote after he tried skydiving.

What did he have to do? What didn't he have to do? Underline the answers.

Dear Sergio,

I went skydiving today. Someone told me about a place where you could do it and I decided to try. I had to arrive several hours before the jump so I could fill in some forms and they could give me instructions on how to jump. I didn't have to take any special clothes with me because they gave me a skysuit.

2 Look at some more photographs of people doing activities which might be risky. Have you ever done any of the things in the photos? Would you like to try?

3 Have you ever done anything risky? What did you have to do? What didn't you have to do? Did you enjoy it? Write three sentences using the box below.

+	I/you/he/she/we/they **had to** take a tent.
–	I/you/he/she/we/they **didn't have to** take a tent.
?	Did I/you/he/she/we/they **have to** take a tent?

4 Complete the gaps in these sentences with the correct form of *have to*.

a My friend was scared, so I __had to__ hold her hand.

b There weren't many people at the fair, so we .... wait long to go on the ride.

c .... (you) wear a helmet when you went skydiving?

d I have my own wetsuit so I .... borrow one when I went into the cave.

e The weather was bad so we .... come back the next day to go skydiving.

f A truck took us to the top of the mountain so I .... walk there.

g .... (they) wear special clothes for the bungee-jump?

h The cave was very dark so I .... shine my torch to see the way.

> ↘ GF page 210

《Pronunciation》

1 Say these four words. They each contain the letters *ou*, but *ou* is pronounced differently in each word.

ner<u>v<u>ou</u>s</u>   <u>y<u>ou</u>ng</u>   <u>b<u>ou</u>ght</u>   h<u>ou</u>se

2 🔊2 15 Listen and repeat the words after the recording.

3 🔊2 16 Put the words below into the correct column. Listen and check your answers.

dangerous   thought   shout   enough
ought   out   touch   flavour

/ə/ nervous	/ʌ/ young	/ɔ:/ bought	/aʊ/ house

4 Can you think of any other words to add to the columns?

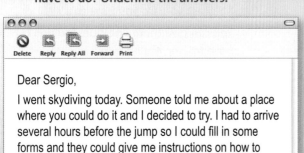

Adverbs

1 Martha gave Ryan some information about the Marathon of the Sands. Look at the sentences below. The underlined words are adverbs. Can you make adjectives from them?

   a You have to behave <u>sensibly</u>. *sensible*
   b The organisers travel more <u>comfortably</u>.
   c They wake everyone up very <u>noisily</u>.

Grammar spot

Making adverbs from adjectives

Complete the rules below.

Add .... (*perfect → perfectly*)

Change *y* to .... and add .... (*noisy → noisily*)

For adjectives ending in *le*, take off .... and add .... (*comfortable → comfortably*)

Some adjectives don't change when they become adverbs: *fast, early, hard, late*.

The adverb from *good* is *well*: He was a *good* instructor. He taught me *well*.

2 Now make adverbs from these adjectives.

anxious	*anxiously*
cheerful	....
heavy	....
perfect	....
confident	....
loud	....
quick	....
gentle	....

3 Here is the rest of Ryan's email. Put the adverbs from Exercise 2 in the spaces.

I was joined by a special belt to an instructor. There were three of us who did the jump with our instructors. We sat in the plane waiting
(a) *anxiously*...... for our turn. The instructors chatted (b) .... the whole time. When the plane got to the right height, my instructor turned to me and shouted very (c) .... 'Are you ready?' If you don't answer (d) .... , they don't allow you to jump. Then I jumped and it was brilliant. You fall very (e) .... for about 40 seconds, then you pull the cord to open your parachute. And you float down very
(f) .... I landed (g) .... on the ground with a bump but I didn't hurt myself. I was very pleased because I did everything
(h) ....
I'll write again soon.
All the best,
Ryan

 Corpus spot   Spelling of adverbs

Correct the spelling mistakes in these sentences.
a I can understand my teacher easilly.
b Luckly, it was a sunny day so I was able to swim in the lake.
c My bedroom is completly white.

«Activity» Adverbs

1 Make these adjectives into adverbs.

angry   quick   quiet   nervous   miserable   lazy
happy   secret   serious   slow   loud   sleepy   excited

2 Your teacher will give each of you an adverb. To get a point for your team, you must say the sentence below so that the other team can guess your adverb. For example, if your adverb is *anxiously*, you should say your sentence anxiously.

When I was on my way here today, something strange happened to me.

↘ GF page 210

«Activity» Taking risks

1 Answer this questionnaire.

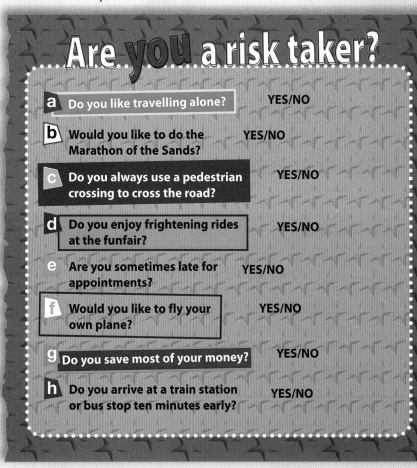

Are you a risk taker?

a	Do you like travelling alone?	YES/NO
b	Would you like to do the Marathon of the Sands?	YES/NO
c	Do you always use a pedestrian crossing to cross the road?	YES/NO
d	Do you enjoy frightening rides at the funfair?	YES/NO
e	Are you sometimes late for appointments?	YES/NO
f	Would you like to fly your own plane?	YES/NO
g	Do you save most of your money?	YES/NO
h	Do you arrive at a train station or bus stop ten minutes early?	YES/NO

2 Check your answers on page 103. Are you a risk-taker? How many people in your class got 6 or more marks?

Exam folder 15

Reading Part 1

In this part of the exam, you look at short texts. There are three possible explanations – A, B or C. You have to decide which one says the same as the text.

1 Look at this sign and answer the questions.

   a Where is the sign?
   b What does *children under five* mean?
   c Which children can go on the ride without an adult?

2 Read the three possible explanations. Which explanation – A, B or C – means the same as the sign? Why are the other explanations wrong?

   A Children less than five years old cannot go on this ride alone.
   B Children in groups of five or more must have an adult with them.
   C Adults are not allowed on this ride.

Children under five must have an adult with them on this ride

3 Now look at another sign and answer the questions.

   a Signs often have words missing to make them shorter. Add the missing words to the sign.
   b Where in the park is this sign?
   c How many entrances are open before 11 am today?
   d How many entrances are open after 11 am today?

4 Read the three possible explanations of the sign then answer the questions.

   A There will only be one entrance to the park after today.
   B This entrance cannot be used before 11 am today.
   C The park opens at 11 am today.

   a Does *cannot be used* mean the same as *closed* in the sign?
   b Does *until 11 am today* mean the same as *after today*?
   c Which is the correct explanation – A, B or C?
   d Why are the other explanations wrong?

ADVENTURE PARK
THIS ENTRANCE IS CLOSED
UNTIL 11AM TODAY
USE OTHER ENTRANCE
BESIDE CAFÉ

5 Which words can you add to this sign?

6 Read the three possible explanations of the sign and decide which is the correct explanation – A, B or C. Why are the other explanations wrong?

   A The ride starts when all the seats are full.
   B Do not stand up when the ride is moving.
   C If the ride stops, wait until it begins again.

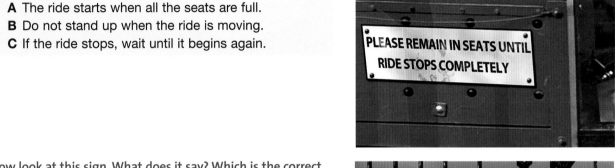

7 Now look at this sign. What does it say? Which is the correct explanation – A, B or C?

   A The park shuts earlier than 6 pm on some days.
   B The park stays open later for one month of the year.
   C The park is open all year except in December.

8 Now look at this sign. What does it say? Which is the correct explanation – A, B or C?

   A You can buy a hot meal in two different places.
   B The restaurant near the lake serves hot food in the middle of the day.
   C Sandwiches and drinks are only available at lunchtime.

16 Free time

Grammar *going to*; present after *when*, *until* and *after*
Vocabulary study/leisure; the time; making arrangements
Revision invitations; present continuous for plans

Introduction

1 Do you make good use of your free time? Try this flowchart to find out.

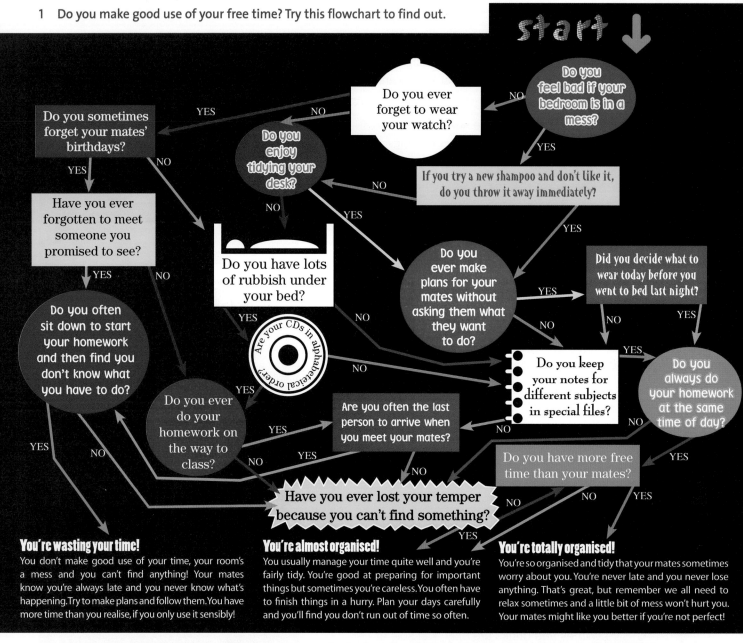

start ↓

Do you feel bad if your bedroom is in a mess? — NO → Do you ever forget to wear your watch?

Do you feel bad if your bedroom is in a mess? — YES → If you try a new shampoo and don't like it, do you throw it away immediately?

Do you ever forget to wear your watch? — YES → Do you sometimes forget your mates' birthdays?

Do you ever forget to wear your watch? — NO → Do you enjoy tidying your desk?

Do you sometimes forget your mates' birthdays? — YES → Have you ever forgotten to meet someone you promised to see?

Do you sometimes forget your mates' birthdays? — NO →

Do you enjoy tidying your desk? — NO → Do you have lots of rubbish under your bed?

If you try a new shampoo and don't like it, do you throw it away immediately? — NO → Do you enjoy tidying your desk?

If you try a new shampoo and don't like it, do you throw it away immediately? — YES → Did you decide what to wear today before you went to bed last night?

Have you ever forgotten to meet someone you promised to see? — YES → Do you often sit down to start your homework and then find you don't know what you have to do?

Have you ever forgotten to meet someone you promised to see? — NO →

Do you ever make plans for your mates without asking them what they want to do? — YES → Did you decide what to wear today before you went to bed last night?

Do you ever make plans for your mates without asking them what they want to do? — NO →

Are your CDs in alphabetical order?

Did you decide what to wear today before you went to bed last night? — NO →

Did you decide what to wear today before you went to bed last night? — YES → Do you always do your homework at the same time of day?

Do you have lots of rubbish under your bed? — YES → Do you ever do your homework on the way to class?

Do you have lots of rubbish under your bed? — NO →

Do you keep your notes for different subjects in special files? — YES → Do you always do your homework at the same time of day?

Do you keep your notes for different subjects in special files? — NO →

Do you often sit down to start your homework and then find you don't know what you have to do?

Do you ever do your homework on the way to class? — YES → Are you often the last person to arrive when you meet your mates?

Do you ever do your homework on the way to class? — NO →

Are you often the last person to arrive when you meet your mates? — YES →

Are you often the last person to arrive when you meet your mates? — NO →

Do you have more free time than your mates? — YES →

Do you have more free time than your mates? — NO →

Do you always do your homework at the same time of day? — NO →

Do you always do your homework at the same time of day? — YES →

Have you ever lost your temper because you can't find something? — NO → Do you have more free time than your mates?

Have you ever lost your temper because you can't find something? — YES →

You're wasting your time!
You don't make good use of your time, your room's a mess and you can't find anything! Your mates know you're always late and you never know what's happening. Try to make plans and follow them. You have more time than you realise, if you only use it sensibly!

You're almost organised!
You usually manage your time quite well and you're fairly tidy. You're good at preparing for important things but sometimes you're careless. You often have to finish things in a hurry. Plan your days carefully and you'll find you don't run out of time so often.

You're totally organised!
You're so organised and tidy that your mates sometimes worry about you. You're never late and you never lose anything. That's great, but remember we all need to relax sometimes and a little bit of mess won't hurt you. Your mates might like you better if you're not perfect!

2 Do you agree with the result? Tell other people your result. Do they agree?

3 Look at the pictures. These students have an English test tomorrow. What are they doing now? Are these good ways to use your time the day before an English test?

🔽 Corpus spot 👁

Which verb do we use with *homework*?
Complete these PET students' sentences.

a We .... some homework for an hour, then we went out.
b My room has a nice chair and a table where I .... my homework.

What other noun + verb pairs can you remember? (Look back to Unit 8.)

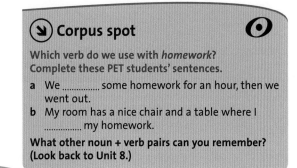

Reading

1   Look at this message board from a website. What is it about?

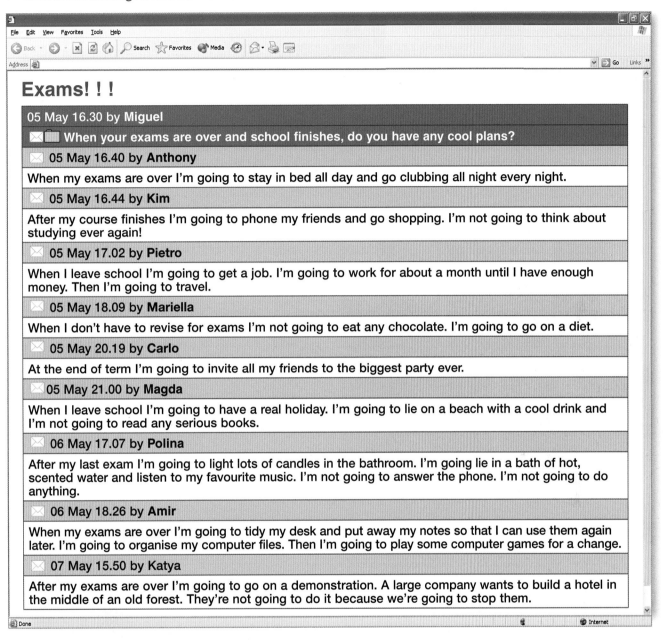

Exams! ! !

05 May 16.30 by Miguel

✉ When your exams are over and school finishes, do you have any cool plans?

05 May 16.40 by Anthony

When my exams are over I'm going to stay in bed all day and go clubbing all night every night.

05 May 16.44 by Kim

After my course finishes I'm going to phone my friends and go shopping. I'm not going to think about studying ever again!

05 May 17.02 by Pietro

When I leave school I'm going to get a job. I'm going to work for about a month until I have enough money. Then I'm going to travel.

05 May 18.09 by Mariella

When I don't have to revise for exams I'm not going to eat any chocolate. I'm going to go on a diet.

05 May 20.19 by Carlo

At the end of term I'm going to invite all my friends to the biggest party ever.

05 May 21.00 by Magda

When I leave school I'm going to have a real holiday. I'm going to lie on a beach with a cool drink and I'm not going to read any serious books.

06 May 17.07 by Polina

After my last exam I'm going to light lots of candles in the bathroom. I'm going lie in a bath of hot, scented water and listen to my favourite music. I'm not going to answer the phone. I'm not going to do anything.

06 May 18.26 by Amir

When my exams are over I'm going to tidy my desk and put away my notes so that I can use them again later. I'm going to organise my computer files. Then I'm going to play some computer games for a change.

07 May 15.50 by Katya

After my exams are over I'm going to go on a demonstration. A large company wants to build a hotel in the middle of an old forest. They're not going to do it because we're going to stop them.

2   Work with a partner. Match these questions and answers.

1   What is Anthony going to do all day when his exams are over?   *d*

2   When is Kim going to phone her friends?

3   How is Pietro going to get money?

4   Why isn't Mariella going to eat chocolate?

5   Where is Katya going to go?

6   What isn't Magda going to do?

7   Who is Carlo going to invite to his party?

8   Why is Amir going to tidy his desk and put away his notes?

a   After her course finishes.

b   On a demonstration.

c   She's going to go on a diet.

d   He's going to stay in bed.

e   Read any serious books.

f   So that he can use them again later.

g   He's going to get a job.

h   All his friends.

3   Who has the best idea? Who has the worst?

Language focus
Going to

We use *going to* for plans and when we can already see what is going to happen.

I am you/we/they **are** he/she/it **is**	**(not) going to**	go to the beach. fall over.
Am I **Are** you/we/they **Is** he/she/it	**going to**	go to the beach? fall over?

1 What are these people going to do? Look at the table above and make sentences.

a *She's going to jump out of the plane.*

b ....

c ....

d ....

e ....

2 Work with a partner. Ask and answer questions using these phrases with *going to*. When you finish, tell the class some of the things your partner is going to do.

a after this lesson

A: *What are you going to do after this lesson, Brigitte?*

B: *I'm going to have a coffee.*

b this evening

c tomorrow morning

d next weekend

e when you finish this course

f after you complete this exercise

3 Who gave the funniest or most interesting answers? Write down three of them.

4 Work with a partner. Use the sentences a–h below to complete the conversation.

Liz: Hi, Sam. What are you doing?

Sam: **1** *I'm making a poster. Do you want to help me?*

Liz: I'm afraid I can't. I'm going to watch the football on television. Aren't you going to watch it?

Sam: **2** ....

Liz: Why?

Sam: **3** ....

Liz: So what's wrong with that?

Sam: **4** ....

Liz: Another time perhaps. Anyway, I think the car park's a good idea. There isn't enough parking in the town.

Sam: **5** ....

Liz: Why not?

Sam: **6** ....

Liz: OK, but what are you and your friends going to do to stop it?

Sam: **7** ....

Liz: Well, good luck. Now I'm going to watch the match.

Sam: **8** ....

a Because the council is going to build a new car park.

b But it's a really bad idea. It isn't going to make things better for teenagers.

c Because they're going to put it by the market, you know where Space Party is? The club we went to last week. That's where they're going to build it. Would you like to come on the demonstration?

d ~~I'm making a poster. Do you want to help me?~~

e We're going to stand in the shopping centre and we're going to tell people what's happening.

f Because they're going to knock down Space Party. So what are we going to do at weekends? Space Party's the only place to go to in this town.

g OK. You can tell me about it when I get home.

h No, not this time. I'm going to join a demonstration in the city centre.

5 **2 17** Listen to the recording and check your answers.

↘ GF page 210

«Activity» I'm going to . . .

Your teacher will give you a card with an activity on it. You have to mime the preparation for the activity. Do not mime the activity. You can mime alone or with a partner. The class has to guess what you are going to do.

Present tense following *when, until, after*

⬇ Grammar spot

When, until, after + present tense

Read these sentences and complete the rule below using the words in the box.

After this course ends we're going to have a party.

I'm going to work hard until I have lots of money, then I'm going on holiday.

When I find my mobile, I'm going to phone home.

| present | future |

When we talk about .... time, a .... tense follows the adverbs *when, until* and *after*.

Complete the sentences with a verb in the present simple.

a When I ....*see*...... my brother, I'm going to ask him for some money.

b When my sister .... home from university, we're going to have a party.

c Our neighbours are going to move when their son .... a new job.

d I'm not going to do any more work until you .... me.

e I'm going to listen to some music after we .... this exercise.

f We're going to play tennis until it .... dark.

g I'm going to have a shower when I .... home.

⬇ GF page 210

The time

ten to one

1 **2 18** Listen to the recording. In column A below, write down the times you hear, using figures.

A The clock shows	B We say
a *12.50*	a *ten to one*
b	b ....
c	c ....
d	d ....
e	e ....
f	f ....

2 Listen again and check your answers in column A.

3 Now write the times in words in column B.

⬇ GF page 210

⬇ Vocabulary spot   Asking the time

How many ways of asking the time do you know? Complete this table using the words in the box.

| it | tell | know | what's |

Excuse me,
a .... the time of the next train, please?
b can you .... me the time, please?
c do you .... the time of the next bus?
d what time is ...., please?

«Pronunciation»

1 Practise asking the time and answering.

2 Work with a partner. Ask and answer questions about time, using these words, then invent one or two more questions.

a get up / last Friday *What time did you get up last Friday? – At ten to seven.*

b be / now   d arrive / today

c get up / next Sunday   e be / now in New York

«Activity» Making plans

1 **2 19** Listen to three short conversations between Marco and three of his friends. Look at his personal organiser and write down his plans for Sunday.

2 What is Marco going to do on the day before his English test? Do you think this is a good plan?

3 Write down three things (real or imaginary) that you are going to do this weekend. Write down the exact time for each activity.

4 Go round the class. Tell other people what you are going to do and invite them to join you. Accept and refuse invitations to do things with them. You can't change the times you have chosen. Do not show your notes to other people.

5 When you finish, find out who is going to have the busiest weekend.

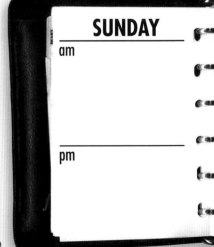

SUNDAY

am

pm

Exam folder 16

Listening Part 2

In this part of the exam, you listen to a recording of one person speaking or an interview and answer six questions by choosing A, B or C. You hear the recording twice.

1 Look at the instructions at the top of the exam task on the right. What can you learn about the recording?

   a What kind of conversation is it?
   b How many people do you hear?
   c What is the conversation about?

2 Look at question 1 in the exam task. Question 1 tells us that we are going to hear about a woman called Philippa. What else does it tell us?

   Now look at questions 2–6 in the exam task and make guesses about what you are going to hear. When you have finished, compare your guesses with the answers in the box at the foot of this page.

Exam Advice

Before you hear the recording, you have some time to read through the instructions and questions. You should use these to help you understand what you are going to hear.

3 Now read the options for each question in the exam task. Remember that the words you read in the questions are often different from the words you hear, although they have a similar meaning. Can you match the words from the questions (1–6) with the words which have a similar meaning (a–f)?

   1 some poetry
   2 with a group of tourists
   3 two weeks
   4 travelling by air
   5 crossing the States by bus
   6 an exhibition

   a a show
   b travelling by bus across the States
   c a poem
   d flying
   e a tour organised by a travel agent
   f a fortnight

4 **2 20** Now do the exam task.

You will hear a radio interview with a woman called Philippa about a trip she is going to make.
For each question, put a tick (✓) in the correct box.

1 How did Philippa win her prize?
   A by writing some poetry ☐
   B by writing a novel ☐
   C by describing a journey ☐

2 Philippa is going to travel with
   A a group of tourists. ☐
   B two friends. ☐
   C her brother. ☐

3 When are they going to leave the UK?
   A immediately ☐
   B in two weeks ☐
   C at the end of the year ☐

4 Where are they going to stay first?
   A Amsterdam ☐
   B New York ☐
   C California ☐

5 Which part of the trip is Philippa most excited about?
   A travelling by air ☐
   B visiting famous cities ☐
   C crossing the States by bus ☐

6 When Philippa returns she is going to
   A have an exhibition. ☐
   B get a job. ☐
   C study. ☐

5 Listen again. Use the second listening to answer any questions you were unsure about.

Writing folder

Writing Part 1

1 Look at the two sentences below. Which word do you need to write in the space so that the second sentence means the same as the first? Below are three students' answers. Which one is correct?

1 We have a new swimming pool in our town.
There .... a new swimming pool in our town.

Student A: *have*
Student B: *has*
Student C: *is*

2 Read this question and look at three students' answers. Which one is correct?

2 The new pool opened two days ago.
The new pool has been open .... days.

Student A: *for two*
Student B: *since two*
Student C: *after two*

Exam Advice

Write only the missing words.

3 Now do these questions. Complete the second sentence so that it means the same as the first, using no more than three words.

3 The old swimming pool wasn't as big as the new one.
The new swimming pool is .... the old one.

4 The new pool is closed on Monday mornings.
The new pool isn't .... on Monday mornings.

5 Young children are not allowed to go in the deep end.
Young children must .... in the deep end.

6 This is the first time I've been to the new pool.
I .... to the new pool before.

7 I went to the old pool every week.
I used .... to the old pool every week.

8 My old swimming costume isn't big enough for me.
My old swimming costume is too .... for me.

9 I borrowed a swimming costume from my friend.
My friend .... a swimming costume.

10 We stayed in the pool for three hours.
We .... three hours in the pool.

1 Philippa won a prize.
2 She's going to travel with some other people.
3 They are going away from the UK.
4 They are going to visit more than one place.
5 Philippa is most excited about one part of her trip.
6 She talks about what she plans to do after her trip.

Next week's episode

Grammar   *will/going to*; *everyone/someone* etc.
Vocabulary TV and radio
Revision   *need*; present continuous

Introduction

1 **2 21** Listen to the theme music of four TV programmes. Which kinds of programmes do the pieces of music introduce? Choose from the box.

2 Look at this page from a TV guide. Label the columns using the words in the box. Which programmes would you choose to watch?

> Documentary   News
> Costume drama
> Children's programmes   Sport
> Soaps   Game shows   Police drama

1 *News*	2	3	4	5	6	7	8 ....
6.00 **Early evening news** *BBC1*	**5.00** **Playschool** Art games and exciting things to make and do *Channel 6*	**7.30** **Choices** Who makes your T-shirts and how much are they paid? Get the facts. *ITV3*	**5.00** **Wordplay** Can you beat tonight's team at their own game? *BBC2*	**8.30** **Pamela** *Episode 2* Will Pamela escape from her wicked admirer in 18th century London? *BBC4*	**7.30** **The Man** Can the new detective find the kidnappers before he loses his job? Last episode in the series. Starring Lee Young. *Channel 8*	**5.00** **Morning Square** Charlene isn't pleased with Gary. Why? *BBC3*	**9.30** **Matchplay** A look at the names and games that are going to be in the news next season. *Channel 24*
6.30 **Local news and weather forecast** *BBC1*	**5.30** **Kidscene** What will Kim and Rob find in the old house? *Channel 8*	**6.15** **You're out!** Which contestant is going to win the £1000 holiday? Presenter Joelle Patel *Channel 20*				**7.30** **My guys** Another episode, another broken heart. *Channel 20*	**11.30** **Tennis** Highlights from today's matches in Australia. *Sports Channel*
7.00 **News** *Channel 4*							
10.30 **Newsnight** *BBC2*		**11.30** **Coast Watch** Sea levels will rise. What will happen to people in coastal regions? *Channel 24*		**9.00** **Love and Death** The prizewinning serial of murder, money and love in the time of Napoleon. *ITV1*			

3 Do this crossword. The answers are all in Exercise 2.

Across
2 It's good to have lots of TV ... to choose from. (8)
6 Each part of 5 down (7)
7 see 12
11 Will it rain tomorrow? Check the ... . (7, 8)
12, 7 We enjoy the clothes as well as the story in a ... . (7, 5)

Down
1 If you like answering questions, why not enter a ... show? (4)
3 A number of programmes about the same subject with a new story each time (6)
4 A story about a group of people which continues for years (4)
5 A story that continues through several programmes (6)
8 How can we find out what is happening in the world? Watch the ... . (4)
9 The person who introduces a programme (9)
10 A programme which gives us true information (11)

Adam
Karim's flatmate

Karim
works as a waiter

Claudia
a student, works as a waitress

Nathalie
Claudia's flatmate, a student

Mario
the owner

Meet the people at Café Europe

Listening

1 *Café Europe* is a radio soap. Look at the photographs and talk about the characters. Would you like to meet any of them? Who?

2 Look at what happened last week in *Café Europe*.

> LAST WEEK   First, Mario had a quarrel with the chef and the chef left. Next, Claudia decided to sell her car and Karim wanted to buy it. Then, Adam, an old friend, arrived to share Karim's flat. Nathalie wanted to borrow Claudia's car. Claudia wasn't happy about the idea, but in the end she agreed.

What will happen this week? Look at these predictions.

a The chef will come back.
b Nathalie will get a job in the café.
c Adam will meet Nathalie.

Do you think they are right? Discuss your predictions. Write some down.

3 **2 22** Listen to the first part of this week's episode and answer these questions.

a What does Mario need?   *A new chef.*
b What does Nathalie need?
c Why will Nathalie go to see Mario later?

4 **2 23** Listen to the second part of this week's episode and answer these questions.

a Where are Karim and Adam?   *In Karim's flat.*
b What does Karim show Adam?
c What did Adam see yesterday?

5 **2 24** Listen to the rest of this week's episode. Check these facts. Write *true* or *false*, then compare your answers with another student.

a Karim is going to pay Claudia next week. *false*
b Claudia believes her car is in good condition.
c Claudia thinks Mario will offer Nathalie a job as a waitress.
d Nathalie is a good cook.
e Nathalie knows Adam well.
f Adam knows something about Nathalie.

Language focus

Will future

1   Look at the predictions you wrote down in Listening Exercise 2. Were your predictions right? Are you usually good at guessing what will happen when you watch soap operas?

+		**will**	
	I, you, he, she, we, they		go.
–		**won't / will not**	
?	**Will**	I, you, he, she, we, they	go?

2   Listen to the whole episode again if you need to. Refer to the tense table and say what you think will happen in the next episode. Discuss these questions.

   a Why does Nathalie need money?
   b Will Mario find out about Nathalie's cooking?
   c Will Claudia find out about her car?
   d What will happen at the beginning of the next episode?

3   Complete the sentences about the future. Use *will*.

   a Next month, the weather *will be colder.*
   b Next year, some of my friends ....
   c In the next century, the weather ....
   d Next week, our teacher ....
   e In 2018, I ....

4   Use your own ideas to make sentences using *won't*.

   a Next month, *we won't have lunch in the garden.*
   b Next year, ...
   c In the next century, ...
   d Next week, ...
   e In 2018, ...

Talking about the future

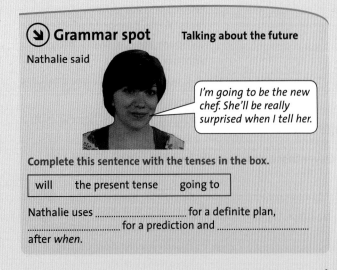

⊙ Grammar spot   **Talking about the future**

Nathalie said

I'm going to be the new chef. She'll be really surprised when I tell her.

Complete this sentence with the tenses in the box.

will   the present tense   going to

Nathalie uses .... for a definite plan, ... for a prediction and .... after *when*.

1   Work with a partner. Look at the Grammar spot and complete these sentences.

   a I *'m going to buy* (buy) some flowers for my mum. She *'ll be* (be) very happy when I *give* (give) them to her.
   b My brother .... (leave) college. My dad .... (get) very angry when he .... (hear) the news.
   c I .... (not join) my friends' demonstration. They .... (be) disappointed when I .... (tell) them.
   d Our teacher .... (give) us a test. We .... (not enjoy) it when she .... (give) it to us but it .... (help) us to check our progress.

2   Now write similar sentences using your own ideas.

What are you going to do at the weekend / next year? What will your friends/parents say?

What is your family / your class going to do next summer / next week? What will they / other people think about that?

↘ **GF page 210**

Everyone/everybody, no one/nobody, someone/somebody or *anyone/anybody*

1   Look back at the photograph of the people in *Café Europe* and answer these questions.

   a Who is looking at the camera?
   b Who is wearing a hat?
   c Is anyone wearing a tie?

⊙ Grammar spot   *Anyone/anybody, etc.*

Fill the spaces in this table with one of these words and choose the correct word in the sentence below:

anyone   anyone   anyone   no one   someone

+	–	?
Today, everyone wants coffee.	(a) .... wants tea.	Does (b) .... want a biscuit?
There is (c) .... in the room.	There isn't (d) .... in the room.	Is there (e) .... in the house?

We use a *singular / plural* verb with these words.

Note: *everybody, nobody, somebody* and *anybody* mean the same as *everyone, no one, someone* and *anyone*.

↘ **GF page 210**

2 Write some sentences like these about the people in your classroom.

Everyone is writing.
No one is shouting.
There isn't anyone who enjoys homework.

«Activity» Everyone has something

1 Look at the pictures. What are these things?

2 Work in a group.

Which of these things does everyone have in their bedroom?

Which does no one have?

Ask about other things.

Ask: *Does anyone have ... in their bedroom?*

«Pronunciation»

1 ♦2 25 Look at these three sentences and listen to the recording. Each sentence has two words with the same vowel sound. Underline the words. Say the sounds, then the words, then the sentences.

a She's got a large car.
b My toes were all sore.
c Take the third turning.

2 Work with a partner. Look at these sentences and underline any words containing one of the three sounds. Then copy the words into the table below.

a My head hurts when I talk too much.
b I saw the shirt this morning.
c I need to earn more money.
d I can't see in the dark.
e These doors aren't dirty.
f You must learn to work harder.
g I only heard half the story.

/ɑː/	/ɔː/	/ɜː/
can't	talk	hurts

3 ♦2 26 Listen to the recording and check your answers. Repeat the sentences.

«Activity» A script for a soap

Work in a group. Do one or more of the following activities.

a Decide on a story for next week's episode of *Café Europe*.
b Write some dialogue for next week's episode and learn it.
c Act out your episode for the rest of the class.
d Write a summary of one of the episodes your class acted.

«Activity» Predictions

a On a piece of paper, write four sentences about what someone in the class will and won't do in the future. Don't say who you are writing about.
b Read out your sentences and see if the class can guess who you have written about.

Exam folder 17

Reading Part 4

In this part of the exam, you read a text and answer five questions about it by choosing A, B, C or D.

1   On the opposite page, there is a text and some questions. Don't look at the text yet. Here is question 1. What can you learn from it about the text?

> **1** Why has Class 10 written this letter?

2   Now look at questions 2–5 below and make guesses about what you are going to read.

> **2** Why is Parson's Place particularly important, in their opinion?
> **3** What will cause traffic jams?
> **4** Class 10 believe that ordinary people who live in the town will probably soon …
> **5** Which of these posters has Class 10 made?

3   Now read the text. If you don't know the meaning of a word or phrase, don't stop. Read on to the end and try to understand the text as a whole.

4   Follow these instructions.

  a Look at question 1 on the opposite page. Find clues in the text which tell you why Class 10 have written the letter. Quickly read the whole text again and answer question 1.

  b Look at question 2 on the opposite page. Find the two sentences which give Class 10's opinion about Parson's Place and underline them. Now answer question 2.

  c Look at question 3 on the opposite page. Find the paragraph in the text which talks about traffic. Read this paragraph carefully and answer question 3.

  d Look at question 4 on the opposite page. Find words in the text which mean the same as *ordinary people*. Read the whole paragraph and answer question 4.

  e Look at question 5 on the opposite page. Can you answer it without reading the text again?

> **Exam Advice**
>
> Some of the questions ask about facts and some ask about opinions.

We students of Class 10 have learnt of a plan to build three hundred houses on the land called Parson's Place which is behind our college! Few people know about this new plan to increase the size of our town. We all feel Parson's Place is special because we've visited it with our families since we were small children and we still like going there. It is a beautiful natural area – the small wood has many unusual trees and the stream is a great place for children to play. It's very quiet and safe because there are few houses or roads nearby. We think that losing this area will be terrible because there are no other similar facilities in the neighbourhood.

We are also against this plan because it will cause traffic problems. How will the people from the new houses travel to work? The motorway and the railway station are on the other side of town. Therefore, these people will have to drive through the town centre every time they go anywhere. The roads will always be full of traffic, and the tourists who come to see the lovely old buildings will leave. Shops and hotels will lose business. If the town really needs more homes, the empty ground beside the railway station is a more suitable place.

No doubt the builders will make a lot of money by selling these houses. But, in our opinion, the average family will quickly be made poorer by this plan, and we will lose a very special place.

We're going to the local government offices on Monday afternoon to protest about this plan and we hope that the rest of the college will join us there.

Read the text and questions below.
For each question, circle the letter next to the correct answer – **A**, **B**, **C** or **D**.

1 Why have the students written this letter?
 A to persuade the government to build new houses
 B to protest about a new motorway near the town
 C to encourage more people in the town to use Parson's Place
 D to inform other people about the builders' plans

2 Why is Parson's Place particularly important, in the students' opinion?
 A because it is near the football ground
 B because lots of people live near it
 C because it is a place near the town where people can enjoy nature
 D because local people can get there easily by car from the town centre

3 What will cause traffic jams?
 A building on Parson's Place
 B building near the railway station
 C tourists in the narrow streets
 D people going to the shops and hotels

4 The students say that ordinary people who live in the town will probably soon
 A open new shops and hotels.
 B choose to live near the station.
 C be able to buy new homes.
 D have less money.

5 Which of these posters have the students made?
 A
 SAVE OUR SPORTS GROUND

 B
 SAY NO TO HOUSES ON PARSON'S PLACE

 C
 WE NEED HOMES NOT HOTELS

 D
 USE THE TRAIN NOT THE ROAD

18 Shooting a film

Grammar past perfect
Vocabulary films; telling a story
Revision past simple; opinions

a ....

b ....

c ....

d ....

e ....

f ....

g ....

h ....

Introduction

1 What kind of film is each one? Use the words in the box below and write them next to the films.

> action film   cartoon/animation   comedy   historical film
> horror film   love story   musical   science fiction film

Do you know the names of any of the films?

2 Work in a group. Tell the other students the story of a film you saw recently. Can they tell you the name of the film? Use the words in the box to help you.

> At the beginning   At first   Suddenly
> Then   Next   At the end

3 What kind of film did you talk about?

4 Tell the other students what kinds of film you like best. Who is your favourite film star?

Reading

1 Before a day's filming begins, what do the actors have to do? What do the film crew have to do? Use these words to help you:

actor   director   costumes   lighting
microphone   camera crew
dressing room   make-up

2 Quickly read this newspaper article. How much of the film did they shoot during one day?

A Day's Work at the Seaside

Do you know how many hours' preparation are needed to make a very short piece of film? Our reporter went down to the beach to find out.

Five o'clock was very early in the morning for me but I wanted to get there to see all the preparations. The beach looked a bit different from usual and not just because the tourists were all missing at that time in the morning. But there were plenty of people around. I noticed several caravans in the car park with men and women going in and out of them. I soon realised that one caravan was the make-up room. The actors went in as one person and came out looking like someone else. In fact they looked completely different when they came out – some older, some younger, some more handsome. One actress spent a whole hour with the make-up artist. When she went in she was 25 and when she came out she was 65!

Another caravan was the dressing room and the actors went in dressed in ordinary jeans and T-shirts and came out in the clothes of the 1920s. They all looked very relaxed, sitting on picnic chairs on the beach, chatting and drinking coffee – they were obviously well prepared.

The camera crew were very busy – they were moving the cameras into the right positions. The rest of the film crew were setting up the lights and checking microphones. I had a chat with a man called Ted – he was very keen to tell me about his job, which was to clear all the rubbish from the beach. The beach needed to be completely clean and he had to make sure there was nothing modern in sight because the film is about the 1920s. He even had to move some notices.

The director told everyone what to do. I looked for the star of the film, Alexia Harris, but I couldn't see her anywhere. She finally arrived at about 10 o'clock and looked rather annoyed because she had to wait for a technician to check the microphones.

I got the answer to my question – how long does it take to shoot a film? They shot only ten minutes of film in one whole day and the film crew were there for ten hours. I think I prefer my job – at least I don't usually have to get up at 5 am! But it was fun to be a visitor for a day.

3 Read the article again. What did the actors do? What did the film crew do? Put a tick or cross next to the following:

The actors ...	The film crew ...
went to the make-up room	set up the lights
went to the dressing room	moved the cameras
read the scripts	checked the microphones

4 Without reading the text again, say if these sentences are true or false.

a It was too early for holidaymakers. *true*
b The actors slept in the caravans.
c In her make-up, one of the actresses looked older than she really was.
d The actors wore their normal clothes in the film.
e The star of the film was angry because other people were late.

5 Would you like to work for a film company? Which of these jobs would you like to have – director, actor, make-up artist, costume designer, camera operator, lighting technician, sound technician? Which job is the most popular?

⬇ Vocabulary spot

When you read, underline words that you can use to talk about yourself and your interests. For example, you may want to talk about films in a Speaking test.

Language focus

Past perfect

We form the past perfect with *had* + a past participle.

+	I She	had	arrived.
–	You It	hadn't / had not	arrived.
?	Had	they she	arrived?

(point of time in the past)

When Alexia **arrived** at the beach,
they **had moved** the cameras.

1 Work with a partner. Look back at the article on page 117 and complete the sentences below. Use the box above to help you.

When Alexia arrived, …

a the actors *had changed their clothes.*
(change / clothes)

b the actors ....
(visit / make-up artist)

c the rest of the film crew ....
(set up / lights)

d a man called Ted ....
(clear / rubbish)

e the director ....
(tell / everyone what to do)

f the technician ....
(not / check / microphones)

When the reporter left, …

g they ....
(shoot / ten minutes of the film)

h the film crew ....
(be / ten hours)

2 Write down the age you first did these things. Guess if you can't remember. Put X if you haven't done something.

travel abroad	move house or flat
fly in an aeroplane	start school
learn to read	see a film at the cinema
learn to swim	play a computer game

Then make two sentences like these.

By the time I was six, I'd started school but I hadn't learnt to read.

Ask a partner questions like these.

By the time you were seven, had you travelled abroad?

Past perfect and past simple

1 Answer the questions about the two sentences below. Then complete the Grammar spot.

  A *When Alexia arrived, the film crew had set up the lights.*

  B *When Alexia arrived, the film crew set up the lights.*

In which sentence did two things happen at almost the same time? *Sentence A / Sentence B*
In which sentence did one thing happen before another? *Sentence A / Sentence B*

⤵ Grammar spot

Past perfect and past simple

Write the correct tense in the gaps – *past perfect* or *past simple*.

When two things happen almost at the same time, we use the .... tense in both sentences.

When one event happens before another, we use the .... tense for the first event and the .... tense for the second event.

2 Put the past simple or the past perfect in these sentences.

a When the actress came out of the make-up room, she *waved* .... (wave) to me.

b When they stopped filming, they all .... (have) a drink.

c When Alexia arrived, they .... (not finish) checking the microphones.

d When I got there, the director .... (welcome) me.

e When I arrived at the beach, the film crew .... (be) there for hours.

f When Alexia arrived, she .... (be) annoyed.

g When the actor came out of the dressing room, he .... (change) his clothes.

h When I saw the film star, I .... (not recognise) her.

⤷ GF pages 210–211

3 Complete this part of the story of a film. The film company were shooting it on the beach (see page 117). Use verbs from the box in the correct tense – past simple or past perfect.

| decide live be take remind not know cover not see put |
| write find start write be meet dig read ~~return~~ |

In 1921, a woman (a) _returned_ to the town where she
(b) .... as a teenager. She was walking along the beach
when she (c) .... a friend who she (d) ....
for ten years. He (e) .... her that one day when they were
seventeen, they (f) .... a hole in the sand, they
(g) .... a bottle in it with some poems inside that they
(h) .... to each other and then they (i) .... it
up. They (j) .... to find the bottle. After an hour, they
(k) .... the place and they (l) .... to
dig. The bottle (m) .... still there.
They (n) .... it out of the hole and
(o) .... the letters they (p) ....
to each other ten years before. They (q) ....
very embarrassed and (r) .... what to say.

↘ GF page 211

«Pronunciation»

1 Most of these words have the same vowel sound in the last syllable. What is it? Which two words have a different sound?

woman   important   holiday   camera   letter   appointment
newspaper   horror   preparation   telephone   actor   answer

2 **2 27** Listen and repeat the words after the recording. Were you right?

3 Here are some definitions. What are the words they define? Write them in the correct columns below.

a They pretend to be other people in a play or film.
b The opposite of *non-fiction*.
c The opposite of *same*.
d A v.............................. is someone who comes to your house for a short time.
e Someone aged between 13 and 19.
f You get them in the post.
g An adventure film has lots of ac.............................. .
h A shop .... helps you buy something.
i You ask this before you get an answer.
j He or she tells everyone what to do in a film.
k A violin is a musical ....
l He or she teaches you.

ending in er(s)	ending in or(s)	ending in tion	ending in ant or ent
	actors		

4 **2 28** Listen and repeat the words.

«Activity» Telling a story

1 Your teacher will give you a card which shows a scene from a film. Four other people in your class have other scenes from the same film. Find the people with the other scenes from your film.

2 Now work together in your group and invent an ending for your film.

«Activity» Films

Your teacher will give you a quiz about films. In teams, try to answer the quiz questions. Which team gets the most answers correct?

Listening Part 3

In this part of the exam, you listen to a recorded announcement or someone speaking about a particular subject. You fill in the words which are missing from some notes. You hear the recording twice.

1 Look at this advertisement outside the Victoria Cinema and complete the spaces with the correct words.

performances   discounts   a programme
box office   screens

VICTORIA CINEMA

Ask inside for (a)............... of films showing this week.

(b)................ open from 10.30 every day.
Four (c)................ every day.
Two (d)................ .
(e)................ for students and children.

2 Here are some sentences about a cinema. Complete the spaces with any suitable words.

a The film begins at ....
b There is a late performance on ....
c The cinema is next to the ....
d The film won a prize for the best ....
e The film is in .... with subtitles.
f The film is suitable for ....
g The tickets cost ....
h Phone .... for more information.

Exam Advice

You can guess what kind of words you need to listen for.

3 Look at these notes about the Victoria Cinema. Some information is missing. What kind of words will you listen for?

VICTORIA CINEMA
films showing from 7 July

One Summer Night – normally three performances but only one at 7.30 pm on (1) ....

Talk by the (2) .... of The Violinist on Wednesday.

Late-night film Dead Men's Shoes has won a prize for the (3) ....

On Saturday at 5 pm you can see the film A Dangerous Game in (4) .... with subtitles.

Children's film club:
at 10 am The Young (5) ....
at 11.30 am The Mad Professor

You can book tickets by phone between 10.30 am and (6) .... pm with a credit card.

4 **2 29** Do this exam task.

- You will hear a recorded message giving you information about films.
- For each question, fill in the missing information in the numbered space.

5 Listen again and look at the recording script to check your answers.

Writing folder

Writing Part 2

1 Complete each of these three sentences with words from the box. How do you decide?

| this weekend   tomorrow afternoon   last night |

a I'm arriving at the station at 3.15 ....
b I've done lots of shopping ....
c I had a great time at the concert ....

2 Read the three questions below, then discuss what verbs/tenses you will use in your answers. How do you decide?

1 You are spending the weekend at a friend's house. Write a postcard to your brother or sister. In your postcard, you should
- say what the house is like
- say what you have done this morning
- tell him/her your plans for the rest of the weekend

2 You are spending next weekend with some friends who live in the country. Write a postcard to them. In your postcard, you should
- say how you plan to get there
- ask about what you will all do
- tell them what time you will arrive

3 You spent last weekend at a friend's house. Write a postcard to your friend. In your postcard, you should
- say what you enjoyed most
- tell him/her about your journey home
- tell him/her your plans for next weekend

3 Work in a group. On a piece of paper, write an answer for one of the questions in Exercise 2. Write 35–45 words.

4 Pass your answer to another group. Look at the piece of paper your group is given. Which question does it answer? Has the group used the right tenses?

Exam Advice

Read the question very carefully to find out what tenses you need to use.

Units 13–18 Revision

Speaking

1 Work with a partner. Look at these sentences. Say if each sentence is true for you and give your partner some extra information.

   a I spend lots of money on shoes because I want to look really fashionable.
Yes, that's true. I go shopping every week and I buy lots of shoes. My favourite designers are …
OR *No, that's not true. I prefer comfortable, old trainers. I usually buy …*

   b There aren't enough clubs for young people in this town.

   c I used to live in the country.

   d I'd never been to another country until last year.

   e It'll probably rain tomorrow.

   f Everyone in this class likes frightening rides at funfairs.

   g In this country, you can get married when you are fifteen.

   h We have to take an exam at the end of this course.

Vocabulary

2 Use one word from the box to fill each space.

> ~~adventure~~   coast   entrance   from
> in   instructions   on   rope   square
> tower   tunnel

I saw an **(a)** _adventure_ film last week. The story wasn't very easy to believe but it was quite exciting. It was about a man and a woman who were locked in a high **(b)** .... on a mountain and they had to reach the **(c)** .... where they had left a boat. So they made a **(d)** .... out of a shirt and climbed down from the window. They decided to walk through a **(e)** .... to the other side of the mountain. They didn't know where it went but **(f)** .... the way they found a coin from their country on the ground. Then they suddenly came out in a market **(g)** .... There was nobody **(h)** .... sight apart **(i)** .... one old man who was sitting in the **(j)** .... to a museum. He gave them **(k)** .... about how to reach their boat and in the end they were safe.

3 This email contains sixteen mistakes which are often made by PET students. Can you find and correct all of them? The first one has been done for you.

Dear Hanna

How are you? I ~~hop~~ *hope* you're well.
I'm fine. I went shoping yesterday with my freind Emil becouse it was my birthday and I recived some mone
I saw a beatiful jacket in my favourit cloths shop. I tried it on an it was confortable. But I though it was to expensive. Then Emilia showed me the ticket – it was half prize! I bought it, than we decided to go to ristaurant which is near their. We had a very good da

love from
Miki

4 Think about the meaning of these words. Mark the odd one out in each of these lists.

   a leather (pattern) plastic silk

   b roof sofa stairs wall

   c belt collar curtain sleeve

   d amazing awful dull horrible

   e boots gloves socks trainers

   f anxious nervous sensible worried

   g basin cooker shower toilet

   h break damage save smash

Grammar

5 Choose the correct word, A, B or C, for each space.

1 My grandmother ..*B*.. use to wear jeans when she was young.
  A hasn't   B didn't   C wasn't

2 I .... give my friend a lift because my brother had borrowed my car.
  A couldn't   B mustn't   C shouldn't

3 Will you come to my house after .... your homework?
  A you'll finish   B you finished   C you finish

4 Do you .... school on Saturdays?
  A have to going to   B have to go to   C have go to

5 The film begins at ....
  A fifteen to six   B five past six   C six and a half

6 That .... be my handbag because I haven't got one.
  A needn't   B mustn't   C can't

6 In each group of three sentences, only one is correct. Tick the correct sentence and put a cross by the incorrect ones.

1 A This is too big house for our family.   ✗
  B This house is too big for our family.   ✓
  C This house is too much big for our family.   ✗

2 A When the food had been ready, we ate it.
  B When the food was ready, we ate it.
  C When the food was ready, we had eaten it.

3 A Excuse me, what time opens this shop?
  B Excuse me, what time does open this shop?
  C Excuse me, what time does this shop open?

4 A She has a beautiful big red car.
  B She has a red beautiful big car.
  C She has a big beautiful red car.

5 A I used to like cartoons, but now I think they're boring.
  B I use to like cartoons, but now I think they're boring.
  C I used to liking cartoons, but now I think they're boring.

6 A Are you going to wait here until the rain stopped?
  B Are you going to wait here until the rain stops?
  C Are you going to wait here until the rain will stop?

7 Look at the pairs of sentences below. Fill the spaces with words from the box so that the second sentence means the same as the first. Some words fit more than one space.

> ~~can~~   can't   could   don't have to
> has to   have to   might   mustn't
> need   used to

a It's OK to park here if you work at the hotel.
  Hotel employees ..*can*.. park here.

b I'm not sure if that's my brother's DVD.
  That DVD .... belong to my brother.

c Do not bring ice creams into this shop.
  You .... bring ice creams into this shop.

d I've never learnt Portuguese.
  I .... speak Portuguese.

e I can finish this work without your help.
  You .... help me finish this work.

f In the past, people walked more than they do now.
  People .... walk more than they do now.

g Everyone helps tidy the club after parties. It's a rule.
  Everyone .... help tidy the club after parties.

h The weather is hot, so a coat is not necessary.
  It's quite hot, so you .... bring a coat.

i In England all motorcyclists wear helmets because that's the law.
  You .... wear a helmet on a motorcycle in England.

j Perhaps that's the letter about my new job.
  That .... be the letter about my new job.

k If you want to visit Japan, it's necessary to get a visa.
  You .... a visa if you want to visit Japan.

19 Happy families

Grammar expressions + *to/-ing*; *make* and *let*
Vocabulary families; agreeing/disagreeing
Revision advice

Introduction

1 Look at Daniel's family tree. Read what he says about his family below and then fill the spaces using some of the words from the box. Two of the words don't fit anywhere.

married

 (1) Angela

 Tony

divorced

 (2) Clare

married

 Caroline

 Hugh

 Maria

married

 Nick

 Sarah

married

 Daniel

 Emily

 Joelle

 Michael

divorced

 Anna

 Leo

brother-in-law aunt daughter
ex-wife sister cousin nephew
son ~~grandmother~~ stepmother
husband niece uncle half-sister

I've moved away from the town where I grew up. When I go back it's quite easy for me to visit all my relatives because most of them live in the same part of town. In fact my **(a)** .... , Lily, lives next door to her **(b)** .... Caroline. My **(c)** .... Hugh lives in the next street to my grandma and my father lives about ten minutes away, so my grandma has all her children near her. That's good because her **(d)** .... , Bob, died a few years ago, so she's alone now in the house. My parents got divorced about ten years ago and my father remarried. My **(e)** .... Sarah and I weren't sure about our new **(f)** .... , Clare, at first but now we like her a lot. She and my father have one child, so I have a **(g)** .... She's called Emily. Emily is only six and I have a **(h)** .... , Leo, who is the same age. I also have a **(i)** .... called Anna. I get on really well with my **(j)** .... Nick. Sarah, Nick, Leo and Anna live in Scotland and I often visit them. I have one **(k)** .... called Michael. We used to play together a lot when we were small. Michael married young and he's divorced now but we still see his **(l)** .... , Joelle, because she's my sister's best friend.

2 Work with a partner. Tell your partner about your family or another family. Your partner draws the family tree for you. Now do the same for your partner's family.

Listening

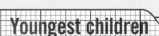

1   **2** 30 Listen to four people speaking. What position
are they in their families (oldest, middle, youngest,
or only child)? What disadvantage does each person
talk about?

Speaker	Position in family	Disadvantage
Rebecca		
George		
Charlotte		
Peter		

2   Read these descriptions. Write Rebecca, George,
Charlotte and Peter against the correct heading. Add
your name to one of the headings.

Oldest children

★ expect to do well
★ are good at looking after other people
★ need to keep everything tidy
★ like keeping rules

Youngest children

★ love taking risks
★ have a good sense of humour
★ often refuse to do what other people tell them
★ are interested in studying artistic subjects

Middle children

★ are good at solving arguments
★ enjoy being with other people
★ are good managers and leaders
★ don't mind changing their plans

Only children

★ prefer being with adults
★ are quite serious
★ are afraid of failing
★ are hard-working

3   Listen again and look at the descriptions above. For
each person, put a tick (✓) next to the things they do
or did.

4   Find other people in the class who are in the same
position as you in their family. Discuss how you feel
about your position in your family. Do you agree with
what the descriptions say? Use language like this to
help you.

I agree that …
I don't agree that …
It's true that …
It's not true that …

EXAMPLE: *I agree that middle children enjoy
being with other people.*

5   Are there any other things your group wants to add
to the list? Use language like this to help you.

We think …
In our opinion, …

Tell the rest of the class about what you discussed.
What is the best position in a family?

 Corpus spot   *Agree*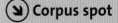

Correct these mistakes made by PET students.

a   I am agree with you about the new restaurant.
b   Are you agree about that?
c   I hope she will be agree to come with us tomorrow.
d   My friend was agree to meet me at 7.30.

Language focus
Words followed by *to* or -*ing*

1 The words in the box are from the descriptions on page 125. Are they followed by *to* or -*ing*? Put them into the correct column below.

> ~~expect~~   ~~be good at~~   need like   enjoy   don't mind   love refuse   be interested in be afraid of

Verbs and expressions followed by *to*	Verbs and expressions followed by -*ing*
expect	be good at

2 Add these words from the recording to the table above. Your teacher will give you the recording scripts.

> look forward to be fed up with   would like begin   start   stop   continue try   seem   arrange   want learn   prefer

Which words are in both columns? Write them here.

Verbs followed by *to* or -*ing*

3 Are these words followed by *to* or -*ing*? Write them in one of the columns above.

> hope   agree   promise plan   decide   offer

4 Look at these two sentences. What is unusual about *make* and *let*?

Rebecca says *My parents didn't make me look after my little brother.* George says *They never let you grow up.*

Write down one thing your parents let you do when you were five years old and one thing they made you do. What about when you were ten? Compare with other people.

⭳ Vocabulary spot

Use sentences from a listening or reading to help you learn words and expressions. For example, it is easier to remember which words are followed by *to* and -*ing* if they are in a sentence: *I got fed up with reading stories. I try to be nice to them.*

⭳ Corpus spot   *to* and -*ing*   ◉

Correct these mistakes made by PET students.

a   Don't forget write to me.
b   I am enjoying to be here on holiday.
c   I am looking forward to hear from you soon.
d   We decided catch the train back.
e   My parents didn't let me to stay in the hotel alone.
f   When we finished to eat, I went to my house.
g   I would like to met you and your family.
h   I am interested in to join this club.

5 Read these letters on a problem page in a magazine. Write the correct form of the verb in brackets. Use either *to* or -*ing*.

 Ask **Anna**

Dear Anna,

I'm 17 and my sister is 14 and she's really annoying. When my friends come round to my house and we want **(a)** *to go* (go) to my room and be on our own, she expects **(b)** .... (be) with us and she refuses **(c)** .... (go) away when I ask her. She always promises **(d)** .... (sit) quietly but she loves **(e)** .... (be) the centre of attention. She always spoils everything. Why doesn't she understand that I prefer **(f)** .... (be) with my friends without her?

David

Dear Anna,

My brother and I are twins. We always got on very well until we left school last year. We enjoyed **(g)** .... (do) the same kinds of things – music, sport, and we had the same friends. But my brother's now at university and lives in a hall of residence and I have continued **(h)** .... (live) at home. I really look forward to **(i)** .... (see) him at weekends when we arrange **(j)** .... (meet). But he often decides **(k)** .... (do) something with his new friends and isn't interested in **(l)** .... (see) me. What shall I do? I'm not very good at **(m)** .... (say) how I feel about things so he probably doesn't know.

Martin

⭳ GF page 211

Giving advice

1 Read the magazine's answer to one of the problems. Do you agree with it?

Dear Martin,

You should try to have a group of friends of your own so you are busy sometimes too. Why don't you join a sports club and make some new friends or ask some of your old friends to go out with you? You ought to tell your brother how you feel. I'm sure he wants to see you too but you shouldn't expect him to spend all his free time with you. You'd better learn to do things without your brother because you both have your own separate lives now. Good luck.

Anna

2 Underline five expressions used to give advice in Anna's letter. Write them here.

Giving advice
You ....
Why .... you
You .... to
You ....n't
You ....

3 Work in a group. Write an answer to the other letter using the expressions above. Read your answer to the class. Do other students agree with you?

«Pronunciation»

1 **2 31** Listen and repeat these words. Which two are the odd ones out?

this   the   think
there   then   mother
thing   father   other

2 **2 32** Now listen to these words. For each word, decide if *th* is pronounced /ð/ as in *their* or /θ/ as in *thirsty* and write it in the correct column. Then listen, repeat and check your answers.

their   thirsty   thank   that   both
birthday   thirty   they   bath   although
teeth   Thursday   weather   mouth   thousand

/ð/	/θ/
their	*thirsty*

3 **2 33** Listen to these sentences and repeat them.

a They're both thirsty on Thursdays.
b I think his birthday is on the fourth Thursday of the month.
c The weather is better in the north these days.
d This thing is worth one thousand and thirteen pounds.
e Their mother had healthy teeth then.

4 Work with a partner. Try saying the sentences as fast as you can.

«Activity» Families

Look at this family tree. All the names are missing. You are a member of the family. Your teacher will give you a card telling you who you are. Ask other students who they are and write the names in the correct place on the family tree.

Fill in these names on the family tree.

Female:	Julia	Emma	Rosa	Jane	
Male:	Simon	Tom	Sam	Robert	John
	Ben	Paul	Jack		

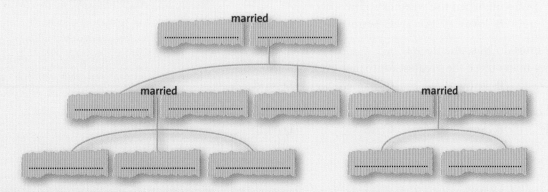

Exam folder 19

In this part of the exam, you have to choose the correct word to go in each space in a text.

Reading Part 5

CHECK!
a What will you do before you look at the questions?
b Which is the example?
c Before you choose your answer, what will you do?
d If you don't know the answer, what will you do?
e Where will you mark your answers?

1 Here are some words which are often tested in this part of the exam. Choose the correct answer, A, B, C or D.

1 Only a .... people were able to come to the concert.
  A few   **B** couple   **C** lot   **D** several

2 We .... that our house had once been a hotel.
  A reported   **B** invented   **C** discovered   **D** reminded

3 The journey to Bristol .... two hours longer than usual.
  A spent   **B** took   **C** passed   **D** made

4 This desk is narrower .... my old one and the computer doesn't fit very well on it.
  A as   **B** than   **C** from   **D** to

5 She .... to wear glasses – she really can't see well enough to drive.
  A should   **B** can   **C** must   **D** ought

6 They .... off two hours earlier than usual to drive to Manchester because of the fog.
  A got   **B** took   **C** set   **D** put

7 While her brother was .... school Sarah used his computer.
  A to   **B** by   **C** on   **D** at

8 I .... walking when the weather is fine.
  A agree   **B** love   **C** want   **D** decide

9 Edson Arantes do Nascimento was .... as 'Pelé' and is thought by many to be the greatest footballer ever.
  A called   **B** known   **C** named   **D** said

10 We don't need to book seats as there are .... plenty left.
  A already   **B** just   **C** yet   **D** still

128 EXAM FOLDER 19

2 Look at the photograph and the title of the text below. What are you going to read about?

3 Do the exam task.

Read the text below and choose the correct word for each space.
For each question, circle the letter next to the correct word – **A**, **B**, **C** or **D**.

FATHERS AND SONS

Harry Redknapp and Frank Lampard played football together for West Ham football club (**0**) ....*A*.... the 1960s. They were best friends and married two sisters, so their sons, Frank Lampard junior and Jamie Redknapp, are (**1**) .... Their fathers used to take them to the football field after school and make them (**2**) .... All the hard work meant that they were soon very good (**3**) .... football and they both (**4**) .... to be professional footballers. In the (**5**) .... they both played for England like their fathers. Harry and Frank (**6**) .... playing football for West Ham in the 1980s. Later, Harry became the manager of West Ham and Frank senior took the job of assistant manager. Frank junior (**7**) .... them and played for West Ham and then Chelsea in London (**8**) .... Jamie went to the other side of the country and played for Liverpool for eleven years. Jamie and Frank aren't married to two sisters like their fathers. Jamie's wife is (**9**) .... singer who hasn't got (**10**) .... sisters.

0	A	during	B	on	C	by	D	for
1	A	cousins	B	nephews	C	brothers-in-law	D	uncles
2	A	train	B	training	C	trained	D	trains
3	A	to	B	at	C	with	D	on
4	A	wanted	B	preferred	C	enjoyed	D	liked
5	A	final	B	end	C	conclusion	D	finish
6	A	continued	B	missed	C	began	D	stopped
7	A	attended	B	joined	C	shared	D	added
8	A	but	B	so	C	because	D	also
9	A	the	B	one	C	a	D	that
10	A	some	B	no	C	few	D	any

20 So you think you've got talent?

Grammar   comparison of adverbs; *so* and *such*; connectives
Vocabulary   music; congratulating; saying what you like/prefer
Revision   comparative adjectives

Introduction

1 **2 34** Listen to six different musical instruments and say what they are.

keyboard   trumpet   drum   violin   flute   guitar

a ....   b ....   c ....

d ....   e ....   f ....

2 Do you play an instrument? What instrument would you like to play? Do you sing?

3 Listen to the different musical instruments again and compare them. You can use the following words:

fast/slow   loud/quiet   happy, cheerful / sad
beautiful   boring, dull / exciting, crazy
modern/traditional

EXAMPLE: *The trumpet was the loudest.*
The violin sounded sadder than the drums.

4 Which instruments might you hear in a classical concert, a jazz concert and a rock concert? Write the names of the instruments.

....

5 What kind of music do you like listening to? Write the names of different kinds of music here.

....

6 A person who plays a guitar is a guitarist. What do we call people who play the trumpet, the piano, the violin and the drums? Write them in the table below.

-er	-or	-r	-ist
			guitarist

Add *er, or, r* or *ist* to these words to make the names of jobs. Write the jobs in the correct column of the table.

act   employ   photograph   art   farm   report
dance   journal   teach   direct   manage   dive   novel

🡖 Vocabulary spot

We often add *er, or* or *r* to nouns or verbs to make a word which is a job. Sometimes we add *ist*. Keep a list of the different jobs you learn. Add these to the jobs you learnt in Unit 3.

Reading

1 A TV station has had a competition to find a new band. The three judges had to choose one of the bands below to go into the final. Look at page 131 and quickly read the notes they made when they were watching the bands. Write the name of each band next to their picture.

a

b

c

d

2 Which bands do you think came first, second, third and fourth? You will find out later.

Patrick McLaurie

Texas Team
The violinist didn't play as loudly as the other musicians so I couldn't tell how good he was – the drums and the guitar were very loud.

Eastside
Their music wasn't as good as their dancing. The guitarist played too loudly and they didn't have a bass guitar or any drums. I couldn't hear the keyboard player.

Third Avenue
The guitarist, Jason, played much better than the other guitarists. He's the best young guitarist I've heard for a long time. The keyboard player was quite good but the drummer needs a lot of practice.

The Storm
The two guitarists sounded very good. The drummer played much more quietly than the other drummers but she did very well.

BEST BAND

Maurice Moreno

Texas Team
Mara sang more confidently than the other singers but she wasn't always in tune.

Third Avenue
The singer didn't look very happy. That was a shame because he's got a good voice.

Eastside
The singers didn't sing as well as the singers in the other bands.

The Storm
The singer sang beautifully. The songs were much more traditional than the other songs we heard but they performed them perfectly.

BEST BAND

Clara Howlett

Texas Team
They danced less professionally than the other bands but they made a lot of effort.

Third Avenue
They didn't dance as well as the other bands.

Eastside
They are excellent dancers, especially Sadie. Every step was perfect.

The Storm
The dancing was quite good.

Language focus

Comparison of adverbs

1 Read the judges' notes again and answer these questions, choosing one of the bands.

   a Which drummer played loudly? *Texas Team*
   b Which drummer played badly?
   c Which violinist played more quietly than the others in the band?
   d Which band sang the most beautifully?
   e Which band danced the best?
   f Which band danced the worst?
   g Which band played better than all the others?

2 Now look at the judges' notes about Texas Team. Underline the answers to these questions.

   a How did Mara sing?
   b How did Texas Team dance?
   c How did the violinist in Texas Team play?

↘ GF page 211

> **⤵ Grammar spot**   **Comparison of adverbs**
>
> Look at these three sentences. Do they have the same meaning? Yes / No
> Mara sang **more** confidently **than** the other singers.
> The other singers sang **less** confidently **than** Mara.
> The other singers did**n't** sing **as** confidently **as** Mara.

3 Copy the other sentences you have underlined and then write them in two different ways.

   a Texas Team danced less professionally ....

      ....

      Texas Team didn't ....

      ....

      The other bands danced ....

      ....

   b The violinist in Texas Team didn't play ...
      The ...
      The ...

4 Now write sentences to compare these people.

   a The Storm's drummer with the other drummers.
   b Jason and the other guitarists.
   c The Eastside singers with the other singers.

So and *such*

1 **2 35** The judges announce the winner to go through to the final. Listen to their decision. Who came first, second, third and fourth? Did you guess correctly?

2 Listen again to the judge's speech and complete the spaces in these sentences.

    a The violinist played _so quietly_ that we couldn't hear him.

    b They are .... they should enter for a dance competition.

    c The singer looked .... we thought maybe he didn't want to win!

    d The singer had .... that we had to give them first place.

Grammar spot   *So*, *such* and *such a*

Look at Exercise 2 and complete the rules using these words.

an adjective   an adverb   an adjective + noun

So is used before .... or ....

Such is used before .... or a noun.

Put these words in the correct column.

good dancers   great voice   loud drums   nice food
difficult decision

Such + (adjective) + plural or uncountable noun	*Such a* + (adjective) + singular noun
good dancers	

Corpus spot   *So* and *such*

Correct these mistakes made by PET students.

a She is so kind woman.
b My grandparents are always such happy together.
c She has a so pretty face.

---

3 Make six sentences from this table.

EXAMPLE: *The fans were so excited they were jumping up and down.*

    a The fans were so   well   (that) we couldn't afford to go.
    b They danced so   excited   I wanted to watch them for ever.
    c The concert was in such   good seats   we couldn't hear the band.
    d The seats were so   a small room   there wasn't space for everyone.
    e The fans made such   expensive   we could see very well.
    f We had such   a terrible noise   they were jumping up and down.

↘ GF page 211

Congratulating and choosing

1 Look at the recording script. What does the judge say to the people who won and to the people who didn't win? Write the expressions he uses here.

Expressions to use when someone has won:

....

Expressions to use when someone has lost:

....

2 **2 36** The winner goes through to the final with two other bands. Listen to the bands who play in the final. Decide who is first, second and third. Write some notes. Have a vote. Use these expressions:

I prefer … to …   *I don't like …*
My favourite is …   *The worst band is …*
I like … best.

«Pronunciation»

1 **2 37** Listen to some words and write them down. If you can think of more than one way to spell the word, write them both down.

2 Write the words you heard in these pairs of sentences.

    a The best band _won_ the competition.
        Only _one_ group can win.
    b .... do the winning band come from?
        What shall I .... tonight?
    c Come ....
        I can't .... the violinist.
    d I really like .... music.
        The winning band is over ....
    e I swam in the ....
        Can you .... that boat over there?
    f They .... like to win.
        My desk is made of ....
    g Their .... is called Harry.
        The .... is shining.
    h .... mother is 50 tomorrow.
        The bus comes once an ....

Connectives

1 Here is an interview with a band who recently won the 'New Band on the Block' competition. Read it through quickly. Then complete the script with the words in the box.

| although | as | as soon as | because | but | either | or | so | ~~so~~ |

How did you feel when you knew you'd won?

Mark: We were really surprised. We'd heard all the groups (a) *so* .... we knew they were brilliant.

Michelle: I cried. I'd really hoped to win (b) .... I still couldn't believe it.

Do you all get on well?

Anika: Yes. (c) .... we have arguments like any band, we like doing the same things and we care about each other. We've been together for two years now (d) .... we know each other really well.

Tanya: I hope we'll be together forever.

Michelle: Yes, we go out together in the evenings (e) .... we like doing the same things.

What are you all going to do now?

Jamie: Well, (f) .... we've won the competition, we're going to appear on the *Pop in the Park* programme on Saturday.

Anika: And then we're going to record a CD (g) .... we can.

Mark: After this interview, I'm (h) .... going to go out dancing (i) .... lie on the sofa. I can't decide.

2 The band were asked another question. Join their sentences together using the words in the box. Use each word once only.

| because | ~~but~~ | although | or | so |

What do you do in your spare time?

Jamie:
I play football a lot. I won't have much time to do that in future.
I play football a lot but I won't have much time to do that in future.

Michelle:
I try to go to the gym three times a week. I like to keep fit.

Anika:
I go shopping. I go swimming.

Mark:
I go racing on my motorbike. I'm not very good at it.

Tanya:
I'm busy writing songs for the band. I don't have much spare time at the moment.

↘ GF page 211

↘ Grammar spot   Connectives

Use the words in the box to complete the rules and the examples.

| although | as | because | but | either | or | so |

a We use .... or .... when we give a reason for something.
I didn't go swimming .... I had a cold.

b We use .... to give the result of something.
The bus didn't come .... I walked to the city centre.

c We use .... and .... in the same sentence to give two different choices.
We can .... stay at home .... go for a walk.

d We use .... or .... to contrast or compare two ideas.
The film was funny .... it was too long.
.... the film was funny, it was too long.

≪Activity≫ Music quiz

1 Write five questions about pop music (or another kind of music) and give them to your teacher with the answers. Here are some ideas.

What is ...'s real name?

Where was ... born?

Who sang ... ?

Which country does the band ... come from?

Who is the singer in ... ?

How old is ... ?

What was ...'s first hit?

Which band has a musician called ... ?

2 Work in teams and answer as many questions as you can.

Exam folder 20

Listening Part 1

In this part of the exam, you listen to seven short recordings and decide which of three pictures answers the question. You hear the recording twice.

2 38 Do the exam task.

CHECK!

a What will you look at before you listen?

b What will you think about before you listen?

c What will you do if you can't answer a question the first time?

d What will you do if you can't answer a question the second time?

e How many times will you hear the recording?

For each question, there are three pictures and a short recording.
Choose the correct picture and put a tick (✓) in the box below it.

1 Where will they meet?

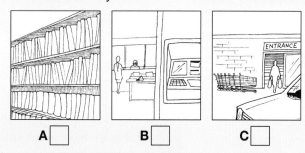

A ☐   B ☐   C ☐

2 What time will the boy catch the bus?

A ☐   B ☐   C ☐

3 Which band does Robert play in?

A ☐   B ☐   C ☐

4 Which is Lisa's new T-shirt?

A ☐   B ☐   C ☐

5 What will the weather be like tomorrow?

A ☐   B ☐   C ☐

Exam Advice

Sometimes you need to listen for a lot of information, sometimes only one small detail.

Writing folder

Writing Part 3

1 Read the exam question below and discuss what different kinds of story you could write. For example, could it be a story about

a visit?
a crime?
a journey?
a party?
a ghost?
a spy?

- Your English teacher has asked you to write a story.
- Your story must begin with this sentence:
  It was dark when I entered the house.
- Write your **story** in about 100 words.

2 Work in a group. Think about one kind of story from Exercise 1. Talk about what will happen in your story.

3 Write down five words which you need to tell your story. Are there any important words which you need that you don't know? Can you change the story to use words you know? Tell other people what you decide.

4 How can you make a story more interesting? Look at this paragraph.

I went into town to buy a CD. There was a man outside the shop. He was worried. He had a piece of paper. He asked my name. I told him. He smiled. He gave me a prize.

5 Now look at the paragraph below.

Yesterday, I went into town to buy a CD. A tall man with a long white beard was standing outside the shop. He seemed rather worried and he was looking nervously at a piece of paper. When he saw me, he asked, 'What's your name?' Although I didn't know him, I told him. Suddenly he smiled. 'You've won a prize!' he announced, and gave me a large brown envelope with my name on it.

a What adjectives has the writer added? Mark them in a colour.
b What adverbs has the writer added? Mark them in a different colour.
c The writer has added the words which the man said. Mark them in a different colour.
d Underline the other changes the writer has made.

Exam Advice

- Don't tell a story which doesn't fit the sentence you are given.
- Don't plan to write a story which needs words you don't know.
- Think about the words you will use.
- Try to make your story interesting by using different kinds of words.

6 Choose one of the sentences below to begin a story. Don't write the story, but write some notes, including some useful words.

When I reached the station, the train had left.

I found the book on my way home from school.

We took the wrong turning off the main road.

When we arrived at the hotel, the owner looked very worried.

7 Work with a partner. Tell your story to your partner.

8 Write your story in about 100 words.

21 Keep in touch!

Grammar *have sth done; tell/ask sb to do sth; possessive pronouns/adjectives*
Vocabulary making phone calls
Revision commands; present simple; plans

Introduction

1 Are you a good communicator? Do this quiz to find out.

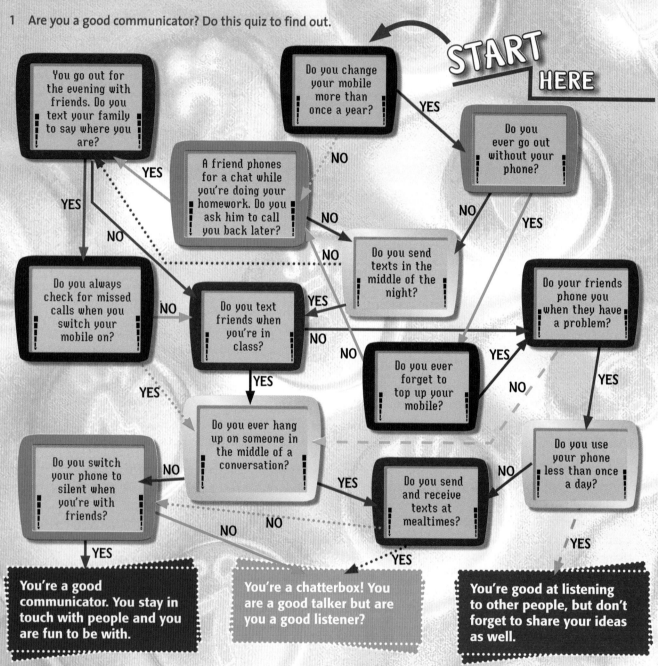

START HERE

Do you change your mobile more than once a year?

You go out for the evening with friends. Do you text your family to say where you are?

A friend phones for a chat while you're doing your homework. Do you ask him to call you back later?

Do you ever go out without your phone?

Do you send texts in the middle of the night?

Do you always check for missed calls when you switch your mobile on?

Do you text friends when you're in class?

Do your friends phone you when they have a problem?

Do you ever forget to top up your mobile?

Do you ever hang up on someone in the middle of a conversation?

Do you switch your phone to silent when you're with friends?

Do you send and receive texts at mealtimes?

Do you use your phone less than once a day?

You're a good communicator. You stay in touch with people and you are fun to be with.

You're a chatterbox! You are a good talker but are you a good listener?

You're good at listening to other people, but don't forget to share your ideas as well.

2 Do you agree with your result? Why? / Why not?

3 Find expressions in the quiz which mean

   a to pay money to a mobile phone company so that you can continue to make calls
   b to turn on
   c a phone call someone made to your mobile when it was off
   d to end a phone call
   e to phone someone again

4 When should people *not* use their mobiles? Why?

Listening

1　**3 02** You are going to hear a student called Ivan make four phone calls. Which conversations are with a friend and which are with strangers?

2　Put the conversations in the correct order.

....

3　**3 03** Listen to the first three conversations again in the correct order. Here are some of the things the people talk about. Write down the words they use.

Conversation 1
a　Say who you are when you make a phone call.
b　Tell someone the reason why you are phoning.
c　Ask for another person's phone number.
d　Ask a friend to wait.

a　*This is Ivan.*

Conversation 2
a　Ask to speak to someone.
b　Tell the caller that the person they want cannot speak to them.
c　Ask the caller to phone again at another time.

Conversation 3
a　Ask for the caller's name.
b　Ask the caller to wait.
c　Ask the caller what he/she wants.

«Pronunciation» Phone numbers

1　**3 04** Listen to the end of Conversation 1 again. What is Mrs Lee's telephone number? How does Helen say it?

2　Say these telephone numbers, then write them in words.

a　357798　　*three five double seven nine eight*
b　01223 277203
c　020 7584 3304
d　44 1273 509672

3　**3 05** Listen and check your answers.

Language focus
Making phone calls

1　Complete the spaces in these telephone conversations with the expressions from the box.

> a friend　a friend of　ask for　I'm ringing
> to ring you　may I speak　let me know
> give me the number　hang on　one moment
> how can I　how about　~~this is~~　told me
> meeting you　very kind of　would you like to

Conversation 1

Harry:　Hello?

Chloe:　Hello, Harry. (**a**) *This is* .... Chloe.

Harry:　Oh, hi, Chloe. How are you?

Chloe:　Fine, thanks. (**b**) .... to ask for your advice.

Harry:　Oh, really?

Chloe:　You told me (**c**) .... if I have problems with my laptop.

Harry:　Oh, of course.

Chloe:　Well, can you (**d**) .... of that company you use?

Harry:　Oh, yes. I've got it here somewhere. (**e**) .... a minute. Here it is. It's 474747. (**f**) .... Gareth Holmes. And say you're (**g**) .... of Harry's.

Chloe:　OK. Thanks very much.

Harry:　That's OK. (**h**) .... how you get on.

Conversation 2

Secretary:　PC Solutions.

Chloe:　(**i**) .... to Gareth Holmes, please?

Secretary:　May I have your name?

Chloe:　Oh, yes. It's Chloe Parsons. I'm (**j**) .... Harry Black's.

Secretary:　(**k**) .... , please.

Gareth:　Hello, Chloe? (**l**) .... help you?

Chloe:　I need to get my laptop mended. Harry (**m**) .... to contact you.

Gareth:　Oh, right. (**n**) .... bring it in today? (**o**) .... this afternoon at half past four?

Chloe:　Oh, thanks very much. It's (**p**) .... you to help me.

Gareth:　Not at all. I look forward to (**q**) ....

2 Practise these telephone conversations. Work in groups of four.

1 **Student A**
You want to buy a motorbike. Your friend knows a good motorbike shop.
Phone him/her and ask for the phone number.

Student B
You know someone who sells motorbikes. This is his business card.

2 **Student A**
Phone the motorbike shop. Ask to speak to Steve Ellis. When you speak to him, explain why you are phoning him.

Student C
You are Steve's assistant. Answer the phone and pass the call to Steve.

Student D
You are Steve. Suggest a time to meet.

STEVE ELLIS MOTORBIKES
new and second-hand

Phone 503498
for excellent service
and good prices

Have something done

Mrs Lee said *I'm having my office painted.*

I, you, we, they he, she, it	+ has/have + am/is/are having + had	+ something	done

1 Alexi is an international football star. He has a busy training schedule and an even busier social life. He has lots of jobs done for him by other people.

Look at the table above and complete the sentences below to show what he has done. Use a present tense.

a boots / clean **b** car / wash **c** hair / style

d contract / check **e** autobiography / write

a He *has his boots cleaned* after every match.
b He .... twice a week.
c He .... before each match.
d He .... at the end of every season.
e He .... at the moment.

2 Last year Alexi got married to his girlfriend Lucilla. They bought a beautiful new house, but Lucilla wanted to make a lot of changes to it. She spent £1,000,000. What did she have done? Complete these sentences

a every room / paint **b** indoor swimming pool / build

c garden / redesign **d** all the carpets / change

a She *had every room painted*.
b She ....
c She ....
d She ....

But that wasn't all. Can you suggest two other things Lucilla had done to their house?

e ....
f ....

↘ GF page 212

Reported commands and requests

Ivan said: *Helen told me to contact you.*
Commands

| Do it! | tell someone to do something |
| Don't do it! | tell someone not to do something |

Ivan said: *The teacher's asked me to write about a journalist.*
Requests

| Please* do it. | ask someone to do something |
| Please* don't do it. | ask someone not to do something |

*Remember that *please* is an important word in English requests.

1 Alexi's team have just lost a match. He is phoning the manager. What does he want the manager to tell these people? Make sentences using *Tell* + the ideas in the box below.

> don't go clubbing every night
> learn the rules of the game
> have his eyes tested
> leave the club and don't come back
> buy some good players

a the club owner
Tell the club owner to buy some good players.

b the coach   d the goalkeeper

c the rest of the team   e the ref

Possessive pronouns and adjectives

↘ Corpus spot   Reported speech ◉

Now look at these PET students' sentences. Do they report commands or requests? Write the words these people said.

a Peter asked me to read some of my poems.
b Rodrigo told us to go to the hospital immediately.
c I asked my friends to help me.
d He told me not to lose the stone.
e Shusha told them to call her at nine o'clock.

2 Report these requests and commands.

a Please help me, Julie.
She asked Julie to help her.

b Don't forget your wallet, Michael.
He told ....

c Please phone your dad from the airport, Angela.
Angela's mum ....

d Please don't use my shampoo, Mandy.
She ....

e Phone the doctor immediately, Ronnie!
He ....

Ivan said to Helen: *A friend of yours is a journalist.*

This is another way of saying *One of your friends is a journalist.*

Rewrite these sentences using *a __ of __* .

a One of my classmates is a dentist.
A classmate of mine is a dentist.

b One of Clara's aunts works in this office.
An aunt of Clara's works in this office.

c One of your classmates said you were ill.

d She saw one of her friends on TV last week.

e Kamran's lucky because one of his cousins owns a hotel in London.

f One of Pedro's colleagues lives in our road.

g I didn't realise that one of their friends played football for England.

h I heard that one of my students met the Prime Minister last week.

i I believe one of our neighbours has won the lottery.

↘ **GF page 212**

≪Activity≫ Tell me about your life

1 Group A: You are journalists. You are going to interview Alexi and write a magazine article about him. Discuss the questions you will ask.

Group B: You are Alexi. Think about your life. What do you do every day? What's good and bad about your life? What are your plans for the future?

2 Each student in A now interviews a student in B and makes notes.

3 Group A: You are now Lucilla. Think about your life. What do you do every day? What's good and bad about your life? What are your plans for the future?

Group B: You are now journalists. You are going to interview Lucilla and write an article about her. Discuss the questions you will ask.

4 Each student in B now interviews a student in A and makes notes.

5 Write your articles.

≪Activity≫ Mobile messages

3 06 Helen has a message on her mobile which plays when she doesn't answer. Listen and write it down.

Do you have a message like this on your mobile? Write one in English.

Exam folder 21

Reading Part 3

In this part of the exam, you read a text and decide if ten sentences are correct or incorrect.

1   You have to decide if the words in the question mean the same as the words in the text. Complete the words in the expressions on the right so they match the expressions on the left.

   a our busiest day   the m_ _ _ people
   b reduced   pay l_ _ _
   c up to six   m_ _ _ _ _ _ of six
   d forbidden   not a_ _ _ _ _ _
   e beyond the park   out_ _ _ _ the park

2   The text opposite is about a shopping mall. Look at the sentences (1–10) in Exercise 4. What will you read about in the text?

3   Read the text quickly. As you read, underline the parts of the text which contain the answers to the questions.

4   Read the question and the part of the text carefully. Is each sentence correct or incorrect?

If it is correct, write A. If it is not correct, write B.

> **1** The park stays open later than the shops every day in summer.
>
> **2** There are the most people at the mall on Fridays.
>
> **3** There is an information centre on the same floor as the cinema.
>
> **4** The nightclubs are next to the swimming pool.
>
> **5** Students pay less for afternoon performances at the cinema than evening performances.
>
> **6** The mall has its own hotel.
>
> **7** The maximum number of people in a boat is six.
>
> **8** It is forbidden to ride hired bicycles outside the park.
>
> **9** Each level of a car park has different coloured signs.
>
> **10** The bus journey from the railway station takes 15 minutes.

Exam Advice

The questions are in the same order as the information in the text. Some parts of the text are not tested.

THE SOUTH LAKES MALL

The South Lakes Mall offers 200 shops, a swimming pool, restaurants, a bowling alley and two nightclubs as well as 30 acres of parkland with three lakes.

Outside the mall

Opening hours

Shops	Mon–Fri	10 am–9 pm
	Sat	9 am–8 pm
	Sun	10 am–5 pm
Park	9 am–5 pm in winter	
	9 am–8 pm in summer	

We have thousands of visitors every day, our busiest day of the week being Friday. To avoid the crowds, come on a Monday or Tuesday.

Inside the mall

When you arrive, go to one of our information offices to get a map. There is one by the main bus stop and another at the bottom of the escalator which goes up to the cinema.

The shops are all on the ground floor and you will find everything from specialised furniture stores to clothes shops and department stores as well as restaurants, a bowling alley and a swimming pool. On the first floor above the pool you will find a 12-screen cinema and two nightclubs. If you wish, you can buy entrance tickets for any of these facilities except the nightclubs from the information centres. Before 5 pm, entrance tickets to all facilities are reduced for students and the over-sixties.

If you wish to stay overnight, the information centres can give you a list of accommodation in the area, ranging from grand hotels to Bed and Breakfast accommodation.

Make time to visit the 30 acres of parkland which surround the mall. Boats for up to six people can be hired and taken out onto one of the lakes for £12 an hour.

Bicycles can be hired every day for £6 an hour. There are 4 kms of paths but you are not allowed to take hired bicycles beyond the park.

Travel

The mall is located one mile from the M49. Just follow the signs from Junction 13. There is free parking for 10,000 cars and there are six car parks. Car parking spaces are never more than five minutes' walk away from an entrance. Remember where your car is parked by looking at the coloured signs – no car park uses the same colour and each level in the car parks is numbered.

It is just as easy to visit the mall by train. There is a rail service every 15 minutes from Central London. When you reach Barnwell station, jump on a number 19 bus to the mall. It's a five-minute journey and there's a bus every 15 minutes.

⬎ Corpus spot **A different kind of false friend!** 👁

There are some English words which are also used in other languages, but in different ways.

Correct the mistakes in these PET students' sentences. Replace the underlined words with the correct English forms.

a There are lots of <u>campings</u> that we like.
b There aren't any <u>shoppings</u> or cinemas here.
c I went quickly to the <u>police office</u> to tell them what happened.
d I'll see you in the cinema <u>parking</u> at half past eight.

22 Strange but true?

Grammar   reported speech
Vocabulary reporting verbs; science fiction
Revision   modals; present/past tenses; agreeing/disagreeing

Introduction

1   Look at the photographs. Discuss what you think
    they could be. Which ones show real things?
    Which ones show tricks, in your opinion?

    Use words like these:
    It could be …
    It might be …
    It can't be …
    It must be …
    I think someone made it.
    I don't think it's real.
    It's a trick photograph / a computer-generated
        picture.

2   Have you ever seen anything strange like this?

    Do you know anyone who has?

    Why do you think science fiction and UFO stories
    are so popular?

What did they say?!?

Mac Brazel had a farm in New Mexico, USA. One day in 1947, he found some strange silvery pieces of material in a field. Not far away a man called Grady Barnett found a large disc-shaped object which had crashed to the ground. They also found some bodies. Barnett and Brazel said that the bodies looked like humans but they were not humans. The US army has a base at Roswell near Brazel's farm. Soldiers arrived at the farm. They ordered everyone to go away. They collected everything the people had seen. Later they announced that a weather balloon had crashed there. They showed journalists some material. They said it was part of a weather balloon. Mac Brazel said that he had seen a different kind of material. He told the journalists that he would never believe the soldiers.

In early 1958, the Brazilian ship *Almirante Saldhana* was in the South Atlantic near Trinidade Island. Many of the crew said that on 16th January they had seen a strange UFO above the island. They said that it had had a ring around it like the planet Saturn. Although it moved away very quickly, a photographer on the ship had time to take a picture of it.

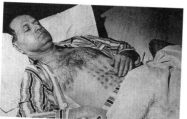

Canadian Stephan Michalak described what happened to him in 1967. He said he had gone to search for gold in a lake. Suddenly he saw two UFOs in the sky. He told people one of them had landed near him and he explained that he had approached it. Although it was very hot, he touched it. His shirt caught fire. Three weeks later he said he was still feeling ill, with strange burns on his chest and stomach.

Reading

1 Look at the black and white photographs above. What do they show?

2 Read the reports in the magazine above. Which ones match the photographs?

Language focus

Reported speech

1 Look at the sentences in the direct speech column. Write the names of the speakers.

Who?	Direct speech	Reported speech
a *Barnett and Brazel*	The bodies look like humans.	They said that the bodies _looked_ like humans.
b	A weather balloon crashed here.	Later they announced that a weather balloon _had crashed_ there.
c	It's part of a weather balloon.	They said it .... part of a weather balloon.
d	I saw a different kind of material.	Brazel said that he .... a different kind of material.
e	I will never believe the soldiers.	He told the journalists that he ...
f	On 16th January we saw a strange UFO.	Many of the crew said that on 16th January ...
g	It had a ring around it.	They said that it ...
h	I went to search for gold in a lake.	He said ...
i	One of them landed near me.	He told people ...
j	I approached it.	He explained that ...
k	I'm still feeling ill.	He said ...

2 Work with a partner. Look at the sentences in the direct speech column again. Find the words in the magazine article which report them and mark them. Copy the missing words into the spaces in the reported speech column.

3 Now underline anything in the reported speech column which is different from the direct speech column.

EXAMPLE: *The bodies look like humans.*
They said that the bodies looked like humans.

Grammar spot　　　Reported speech

Complete this table with the names of the tenses.

What people say →	Reporting what people said
(a) .... → I see aliens quite often.	Past simple She said she saw aliens quite often.
Present continuous → I'm feeling ill.	(b) .... She said she was feeling ill.
(c) .... → We'll meet you later.	would + verb They said they'd (would) meet us later.
(d) .... → I've seen lots of aliens here.	Past perfect She said she'd (had) seen lots of aliens there.
Past simple → I saw some aliens last week.	(e) .... She said she'd (had) seen some aliens last week.

4　Look at this report from the magazine. Write the sentences which report what people said on the right and the words they actually said on the left, as in the example below. Then underline the differences.

Franck Fontaine told a lot of people that aliens had kidnapped him. Two of his friends said that on 6th November 1979, at Cergy-Pontoise in France, they had seen a light all round Franck's car and then Franck had disappeared. Franck said aliens had taken him to their spacecraft and he had woken up a week later in the middle of a field. He said the aliens would return in August 1980 and he was meeting them in the field. Two hundred people said they believed him and went to meet the aliens but they did not arrive.

EXAMPLE:

Aliens kidnapped me.	Franck Fontaine told a lot of people that aliens had kidnapped him.

5　Discuss the four stories from the magazine. Do you believe them? Can you explain any of them? Look at page 147 for some explanations.

6　Work with a partner. Tell each other what these people said. Use the present simple or the past simple. Write your answers in the spaces when you finish.

a　He said he knew Lily Allen.

I know Lily Allen. ....

b　She said she worked in London.

(....)

c　They told us they lived in New York.

(....)

d　We explained that we didn't have any money.

(....)

e　He told me he had visited Paris last year.

(....)

7　Work with a partner. Tell each other what these people said. Use the present simple or the present perfect. Write your answers in the spaces when you finish.

a　I explained that I'd already had lunch.

I've already had lunch. ....

b　They told her they had lost the keys and didn't know what to do.

(....)

c　He said he hadn't seen a UFO yet but he hoped to see one soon.

(....)

d　She told me she had already met some aliens and that they spoke good English.

(....)

e　I told him I'd never eaten Martian food before.

(....)

8 Report what these people said. Write your answers.

a I enjoy films about space travel.
He said *he enjoyed films about space travel.*

b I don't enjoy cartoons.
She said ....

c We're both fans of Manchester United.
They said ....

d I haven't seen my brother for three weeks.
She said ....

e My mum is making me a great birthday cake.
He said ....

f My friend didn't invite me to her party.
She said ....

↘ **GF page 212**

《**Pronunciation**》

1 Cross out the consonants which are silent in these words. Practise saying the words.

comb   whcn   honcst

2 Work with a partner. How many words with a silent consonant can you find in each sentence? Mark each word.

a Do you <u>know</u> <u>what</u> the <u>answer</u> is?   *Three*
b The knives might be in the high cupboard.
c I've broken my wrist, my thumb, my knee and my foot.
d That foreigner could be a scientist.
e You need a bright light to write the receipt.
f Let's meet in half an hour.

3 Look at the words you found in Exercise 2. Are the silent consonants at the beginning, middle or end of the words? Write the words in three columns, as below. Cross out the silent letters. Are any of these letters always silent?

Beginning	Middle	End
know	what, answer	high

4 **3** 07 Listen and repeat the sentences in Exercise 2.

《**Activity**》 **Who am I?**

Work in a group. Your teacher is a famous person. The first group to guess who he/she is wins the game.

- Your group sends one person to ask the teacher for a clue. That person goes back to the group and reports what the teacher said.
  EXAMPLE: *She said she lived in the USA.*
  Then the group sends a different student for another clue.
- If your group thinks you know who the famous person is, you can write the name on a piece of paper and show it to the teacher. If you are wrong, your group must miss a turn of hearing the clues.

↘ **Corpus spot**   *Said or told?*

Choose the correct verb in these PET students' sentences.

a My girlfriend *said / told* me that she had found a new flat.
b She *said / told* that there would be a great party the next weekend.
c Someone *said / told* me that it was a good place to spend the day.
d Anabel *said / told* that she was fifteen years old.
e Yesterday you *said / told* me that you wanted to come to the cinema.

《**Activity**》 **UFO survey**

1 Work with a partner. Find out what other people think about UFOs. Ask as many people as possible and write the number of people who agree with each statement.

UFO SURVEY

Which of these statements is true for you?

1 I believe in UFOs.
I'm not sure about UFOs.
I don't believe in UFOs.

2 I believe there's life on other planets.
I think life on other planets is a possibility.
I'm sure that there is no life on other planets.

3 I enjoy science fiction films.
I like reading science fiction novels.
I don't like science fiction.

4 I've seen a UFO.
I've never seen a UFO.
I'm hoping to see a UFO soon.

5 I've met an alien.
I've never met an alien.
I'll meet an alien one day.

6 I know someone who has seen a UFO.
I don't know anyone who has seen a UFO.

7 I know someone who has met an alien.
I don't know anyone who has met an alien.

2 When you have finished, write a report about your most interesting results. Use numbers (or percentages, if you like).

EXAMPLE:
We spoke to twenty people.
Five people said they believed in UFOs.
Ten people said they weren't sure about UFOs.
25% said they believed in UFOs.
50% said they weren't sure about UFOs.

Exam folder 22

Listening Part 4

1 In this part of the exam, the speakers usually express opinions, beliefs and feelings. Look at the words in the box. Can you fit them into the sentences below?

anxious astonished ~~certain~~ cheerful cross embarrassed grateful unsure

a Are you absolutely ....*certain*........ where Rebecca lives? You've never visited her before.

b We're rather .... about our cat. We haven't seen him for two days.

c Lennox was .... when he saw me at school. He thought I was away on holiday.

d They wanted to give her a present, but were .... what to buy.

e How do you stay so .... when everyone else is sad?

f Giles was .... when he met his boss at the football match. He had told her he was ill.

g I'm very .... for all your help. You've been very kind.

h I'm very .... with my brother because he borrowed my new CD without asking.

In this part of the exam, you listen to a conversation between two people and decide whether six sentences are correct or incorrect. You hear the recording twice.

2 Can you match each statement on the left with the one on the right which means the same?

a I approve of that.
b I respect you.
c I disagree with you.
d I doubt whether it will happen.
e I expect something to happen.
f I dislike that.
g I intend to do that.
h I prefer one thing to another.

1 I'm not sure that it will happen.
2 I have a good opinion of you.
3 I like this better than that.
4 I don't like that.
5 That's a good idea.
6 I don't agree with your idea.
7 I think something will probably happen.
8 I plan to do that.

3 Before you listen, look at the instructions for the exam task. What do you learn about the people and their conversation?

● You will hear a conversation between a girl, Dina, and a boy, Jason, about Dina's sister, Jessica.

Exam Advice

Listen carefully to what both speakers say. They will give their opinions and agree or disagree with each other.

4 **3** 08 Now do this exam task.

Look at the six sentences for this part.
You will hear a conversation between a girl, Dina, and a boy, Jason, about Dina's sister, Jessica.
Decide if each sentence is correct or incorrect.
If it is correct, put a tick (✓) in the box under **A** for **YES**.
If it is not correct, put a tick (✓) in the box under **B** for **NO**.

	A YES	B NO
1 Jason is surprised to see Dina near his work.	☐	☐
2 Dina is going on holiday soon.	☐	☐
3 Jason respects Jessica's attitude to work.	☐	☐
4 Dina feels sorry for Jessica.	☐	☐
5 Dina believes Jessica saw a ghost.	☐	☐
6 Jason intends to visit Jessica soon.	☐	☐

Writing folder

Writing Part 1

Here are some sentences about going to a cinema.

For each question, complete the second sentence so that it means the same as the first. Use no more than three words.

1 The Regent Cinema is near my house.
The Regent Cinema is not _far from_ my house.

2 The cinema has seven screens.
There .... seven screens in the cinema.

3 I go there every Saturday with my friend.
I go there .... Saturdays with my friend.

4 We pay £7 each for the tickets.
The tickets .... £7 each.

5 Last week my brother said he wanted to come with us.
Last week my brother said, 'I .... to come with you.'

6 My sister is too young to come with us.
My sister isn't .... to come with us.

7 The film was so long that I fell asleep.
It was such .... that I fell asleep.

8 I found the film boring.
I was .... by the film.

9 The title of the film was *The Last Man*.
The film was .... *The Last Man*.

10 My brother said it was the worst film he'd ever seen.
My brother said, '............................... the worst film I've ever seen.'

11 'We're all going to the cinema,' they said.
They said they .... to the cinema.

12 'I won't go with you,' she said.
She said she .... with them.

SAMPLE

For Writing (Parts 1 and 2)

Write your answers clearly in the spaces provided

Part 1: Write your answers below.		
1		1 1 0
2		1 2 0
3		1 3 0
4		1 4 0
5		1 5 0

Part 2: (Question 6) Write your answers below.

Put your answer to writing part 3 on Answer sheet 2 ⟶

DO NOT WRITE BELOW (Examiner use only)				
1	2	3	4	5

Explanations of news stories (see pages 143 and 144)

1 Many years later, one of the soldiers told journalists that the army had deceived people. Some people now say that scientists were testing secret materials.

2 There has been no explanation. Perhaps it was a trick of the light. Perhaps it was an alien spacecraft.

3 Perhaps he was telling the truth! Some psychologists think that people remember dreams about UFOs and think they are real.

4 Later, a friend of Franck's said he knew that it had been a joke.

Grammar	relative clauses; adjs + prepositions
Vocabulary	friendship; introducing people
Revision	personality adjs

Introduction

1 We can't choose our family but we can choose our friends. Look at the following list. Which of these are important to you? Mark this list 1–10 (1 is the most important, 10 is the least important).

A best friend should ...
   be honest.
   be fun to be with.
   like the same music as me.
   like my other friends.
   live near me.
   have lots of money.
   share my sense of humour.
   be kind when I'm unhappy.
   support the same football team as me.
   like doing the same things as me.

2 Work in a group. Compare your answers. What did most people put first, second and third? What wasn't important?

3 Can your group think of other things you would like to add to the list?

4 Look at the photographs of people on this page. Which person would you like to make friends with? Think about why.

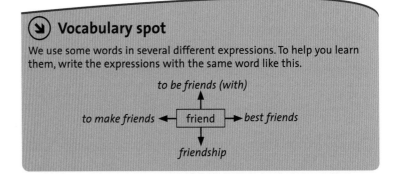

(↘) Vocabulary spot

We use some words in several different expressions. To help you learn them, write the expressions with the same word like this.

$$to\ be\ friends\ (with)$$
$$to\ make\ friends \longleftarrow \boxed{friend} \longrightarrow best\ friends$$
$$friendship$$

(↘) Corpus spot   *Meet* and *make*

Here are some sentences by PET students which contain one wrong verb. Use the correct form of *meet* or *make* to correct them.

a In the first lesson I knew a girl from Valencia and now she's my best friend.
b I did many new friends but I missed my old ones.
c The film begins at seven, so join me at ten to seven outside the cinema.

Listening

1 **3 09** Listen to three conversations between people who have just met. Look at these questions and choose pair 1, pair 2 or pair 3. Put a tick (✓) in the correct box.

Which pair do you think:	1	2	3
will probably become friends?			
might become friends?			
won't get on with each other?			

2 Listen again. Decide if these statements are true or false.

Pair 1 (Monica and Alex)

a Alex has been to parties at the college before. *true*

b Monica and Alex agree about the music at the party.

c Alex apologises for what he says about the people at the party.

d In the end, Monica gets tired of talking to Alex.

Pair 2 (Francis and Neil)

e Francis finds the work in the restaurant easier than on the building site.

f Francis and Neil have similar interests to the other waiters.

g Francis and Neil support the same football team.

h Francis and Neil arrange to go to the match together.

Pair 3 (Carla and Kate)

i Peter told Carla about Kate's flat.

j There will be three people living in the flat.

k Carla plays more than one musical instrument.

l Kate and Carla agree that they are both untidy.

3 How does Peter introduce Kate to Carla? Fill the gaps.

Peter: Carla, ... Kate. Kate, ... Carla.

Carla: Hi, Kate.

Here is another way of introducing someone:

Peter: Carla, I'd like to introduce you to Kate.

Carla: Pleased to meet you.

Which way of introducing someone is more formal?

Language focus

Relative clauses

1 Look at these pairs of sentences. Join each pair using *who* or *which* to make one new sentence.

a He's got a friend. He sometimes gets free tickets.
He's got a friend who sometimes gets free tickets.

b There's a match on Wednesday evening. It'll be really good.
There's a match on Wednesday evening which will be really good.

c There are some customers over there. They're waiting for a table.

d There's one other person. He's studying biology.

e I play an electric guitar. It has a volume control.

f I saw a flat. It's very near the university.

2 Now choose *who* or *which* for each of these sentences.

a They usually play the kind of music **who/which** I hate.
They usually play the kind of music which I hate.

b What about that girl **who/which** I saw you with just now?

c I'll introduce you to some people **who/which** you'll like.

d I'm just a bit nervous of people **who/which** I don't know.

e It's very different from the job **who/which** I had last summer.

3 Answer these questions.

a Can you put *that* instead of *who/which* in the sentences in Exercise 1? What about in the sentences in Exercise 2?

b In which sentences can you leave out *who* and *which*?

4 When do we use *where* and *whose* to join two sentences? Put *where* or *whose* in these sentences.

EXAMPLE: Let's go over there. It's less crowded.
Let's go over there where it's less crowded.
I have a friend. Her hobby is rock climbing.
I have a friend whose hobby is rock climbing.

a I want to find a place ..*where*.. I can have parties.

b I know a café .... you can get really good ice cream.

c I work in a restaurant .... owner is Italian.

d That's the shop .... I lost my wallet.

e I met a girl .... mother used to be my teacher.

Grammar spot   Relative clauses

Look at the words in italics and choose the correct one.

Subject relative clauses

a I saw a **flat**. **It** is very near the university.
I saw a flat *who / which* is very near the university.

b There are some **customers**. **They** are waiting.
There are some customers *who / which* are waiting.

Object relative clauses

c I saw a **flat**. I liked **it**.
I saw a flat *who / which* I liked. OR I saw a flat I liked.

d We met a **girl**. We knew **her**.
We met a girl *who / which* we knew. OR We met a girl we knew.

Relative clauses with *where* and *whose*

e I've found a **flat**. We can live **there**.
I've found a flat *where / whose* we can live.

f Kate is the **person**. I share **her** flat.
Kate is the person *where / whose* flat I share.

---

5 Read this poem. It was written by a girl. What is the poem about? Do you think she was writing about another girl or a boy? Has this ever happened to you?

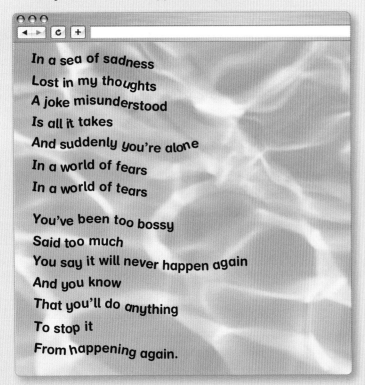

In a sea of sadness
Lost in my thoughts
A joke misunderstood
Is all it takes
And suddenly you're alone
In a world of fears
In a world of tears

You've been too bossy
Said too much
You say it will never happen again
And you know
That you'll do anything
To stop it
From happening again.

---

6 Other people wrote to the website to give their opinions about the poem. Complete the sentences with *who*, *which* or *whose*.

a I had a friend **who** did this to me but I forgave him.

b I often say things .... I think are a joke but my friend doesn't.

c I have a friend .... jokes always upset me.

d I don't think before I speak, so I often say things .... upset my friends.

e This poem was written by someone .... friend is angry.

f I have a friend .... I can't trust any more.

g This poem reminded me of something .... happened to me.

h I had a friend .... was very bossy and I got tired of him.

7 In which sentences can you put *that*? Which sentences need nothing in the space?

8 Now write some sentences using *who*, *which*, *whose* or *where*.

I have a friend …
I like music …
I enjoy watching films …
I live in a town …

➘ GF page 212

«Activity» Relative clauses

Work in a group. Your teacher will give your group a list of nouns which all begin with the same letter. Write a definition for each of the nouns and then pass them to another group. Do not write the nouns. The other group will guess the nouns and decide which letter they all begin with.

EXAMPLE: [artist] *someone who paints pictures*
[airport] *a place where you catch a plane*
[apple] *something which is red or green and grows on trees*

Adjectives + prepositions

1 Match the beginnings and endings of these sentences from the conversations you heard earlier. Which preposition (e.g. *of, from, about*) follows which word?

EXAMPLE: *It's kind of Samantha to ask me.*

a	It's kind	**of**	interesting people.
b	I'll never get tired	**from**	the job I had last summer.
c	I'm not very keen	**of**	people I don't know.
d	This room is full	**of**	listening to it.
e	I'm nervous	**about**	the match.
f	It's very different	**of**	Samantha to ask me.
g	They aren't really interested	**at**	it.
h	I'm quite excited	**with**	me.
i	I'm quite good	**on**	the music.
j	My parents are always getting angry	**in**	the same kind of things as students.

2 Write three sentences using the words in the table.

EXAMPLE: *I'm not keen on going to classical concerts.*
My mum gets tired of tidying everyone's rooms.

I		keen	
My best friend		tired	on
My parents		nervous	of
Some of my friends		bad	at
Young children	am/is/are (not)	excited	about ....
Men	get(s)	good	in
Women		angry	with
My teacher		afraid	
My mum		interested	
		fed up	

3 Write three questions using the words in the table and ask your partner.

Do you get ...?   *Have you ever got ...?*   *Are you ...?*

↘ GF page 212

«Activity» Friendship

1 Read these quotations from a website. Do you agree with them?

2 Write your own quotation: *A real friend is someone who ...*

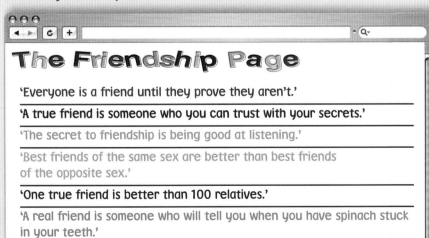

The Friendship Page

'Everyone is a friend until they prove they aren't.'

'A true friend is someone who you can trust with your secrets.'

'The secret to friendship is being good at listening.'

'Best friends of the same sex are better than best friends of the opposite sex.'

'One true friend is better than 100 relatives.'

'A real friend is someone who will tell you when you have spinach stuck in your teeth.'

«Pronunciation»

1 Look at the expressions below. When do we join a word to the word which follows when we speak?

kind‿of you
full‿of people
nervous‿of people
tired‿of school
good‿at football
bad‿at history
fed‿up with school
keen‿on music
interested‿in people

2 **3 10** Listen and repeat the expressions above.

3 Now look at these sentences. Mark all the words which you will join when you say the sentences.

a It's kind‿of Samantha.
b This room is full of interesting people.
c I'm quite good at it.
d She's bad at playing the guitar.
e I'm not very keen on this kind of music.
f I'll never get tired of this song.
g I'm not interested in talking.

4 **3 11** Listen and repeat.

⬇ Corpus spot

Adjectives + prepositions
Correct these mistakes made by PET students. Use a dictionary if you need to check which is the correct preposition.

a I began to run because I was afraid to miss the bus.
b I was very worried for the weather before I came to England.
c He was disappointed of his car.
d I am very happy of your idea.
e He is very bad in explaining things.
f I am very pleased of the present you sent.

Exam folder 23

Reading Part 1

In this part of the exam, you look at five short texts. There are three possible explanations – A, B or C. You have to decide which one says the same as the text.

CHECK!

a What kind of texts will you read?
b What kinds of words are sometimes missing from signs?
c What should you do if you don't know the answer?

Exam Advice

Check that the answer you choose means exactly the same as the text.

Look at the text in each question.
What does it say?
Mark the letter **A**, **B** or **C** next to the correct explanation.

1

> BUY THREE BOOKS,
> GET CHEAPEST ONE FREE.
> OFFER AVAILABLE ONE WEEK ONLY FROM TODAY

A You can get three books at half their normal price after today.
B You only get a discount this week when you buy two books.
C You don't pay for one book if you buy two others as well today.

2

> Jan
> If Peter rings, tell him I have posted the book to him because I didn't have time to go to his house. Michael

A Jan should tell Peter to bring the book back.
B Michael has gone to Peter's house.
C Peter will receive the book in the post.

3

> Carlos
> We have to be at college by 9 tomorrow instead of 9.15. I'll pick you up by the crossroads as usual, but at 8.30. Jack

Jack is asking Carlos to

A meet him earlier than usual.
B take him to college by car.
C see him in a different place from usual.

4

> MAKE SURE THIS DOOR IS SHUT
> WHEN YOU LEAVE THE BUILDING

A Use another exit when this door is shut.
B Do not leave this door open when you go out.
C This door is the only exit from this building.

5

> Dear Mariana,
> The hotel is wonderful – just as you described it. Thank you for recommending it. We've already booked for next year! Karin

A Mariana has visited the hotel Karin is staying in.
B Karin has stayed in the hotel before.
C Karin and Mariana are going to the hotel together next year.

Corpus spot   *Stay* and *live*

You *live* where your home is.
You *stay* somewhere for a short time.

Look at these sentences written by PET students. Tick (✓) the sentences where *live* is correct. Correct the sentences which are wrong.

a My new friend lives near my house.
b At the moment they are living in a wonderful hotel.
c My family used to live in a small village.
d We lived in the city for one week.
e We lived in a nice cottage in the forest on our holiday.

Speaking Part 2

1 You are going to spend the day in the city centre with another student. You will travel there by bus. Look at these pictures. They show the things you want to do.

2 Think about these questions.

   a What do you want to buy?
   b Which shops will you visit?
   c Are any of the things you need to buy heavy?
   d When will you go to the bank?
   e When will you go to the café?

3 Write down different ways of:

   a making suggestions
   b agreeing and disagreeing
   c giving your opinion

(Look back at Exam folder 9 to check.)

4 Work with a partner and talk about where you need to go and in which order. You have three minutes to agree.

Exam Advice

Try to agree with your partner but don't worry if you don't.

I've got an idea

Grammar	past and future passive
Vocabulary	shapes, materials and objects
Revision	present simple passive

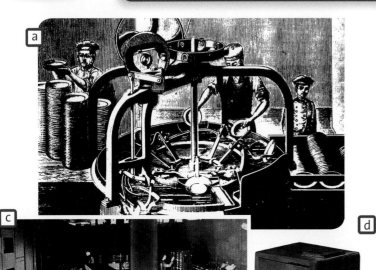

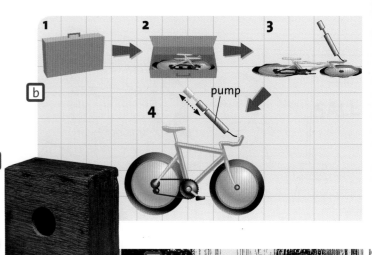

pump

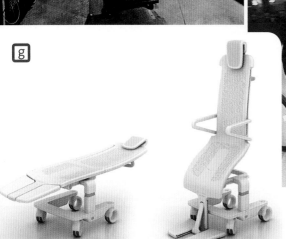

Introduction

1   Look at the pictures of inventions. Can you guess what they are used for?

2   **3** 🔢 Listen to someone talking about two of the inventions. Which ones are they? What are they used for? Were you right?

3   Work with a partner to write a description of one of the inventions (or another one you can think of) and read it out to the class. Use the language in the box to help you. Can other students guess what it is?

> It's round/square.   It's a kind of …   It's like a …
> It's used for …ing.   It's made of …   It must be …   It can't be …
> It might be …   It could be …

4   Which of these inventions have been successful?

5   Which invention from the last hundred years is the most important in your life?

Reading

1 Read the first paragraph of a text opposite. What is it about?

2 Now read the first paragraphs of two other texts below. What inventions are they about?

Ben and Jerry's invention

Ben and Jerry's famous products are sold in a range of delicious flavours with unusual names such as Rainforest Crunch and Peanut Butter Cup. Two childhood friends, Ben Cohen and Jerry Greenfield, started the company. They had the idea of working together when they were at school and *The Homemade Ice Cream Parlour* was opened by Ben and Jerry in May 1978.

Charles D. Seeberger's invention

Moving chains were used by people in ancient Egypt to transport water in and out of the fields. But it wasn't until the 1890s that moving stairs were invented by Charles D. Seeberger. His stairs could transport people.

Hubert Cecil Booth's invention

One day Hubert Cecil Booth went to see an inventor demonstrate his new dust-removing machine at a London railway station. A huge air blower was placed over the open door of a train. The idea was to blow dirt into a bag which was put over another door. A lot of dust was pushed up into the air but then came down again inside the train instead of inside the bag. Booth didn't think it was a very good idea.

3 Each text has three more paragraphs but they are mixed up. Work in three groups: Ben and Jerry, Charles D. Seeberger or Hubert Cecil Booth. Find the paragraphs which finish your text and put them in the correct order.

a The station hired a man who had a wooden leg to demonstrate how easy it was to use the escalator. Some people went up and down several times before going to catch their train just because they enjoyed the experience. After that, escalators were put in shops and other public buildings.

b Because of this, local restaurants and shops asked them to make ice cream and deliver it. A year after the parlour opened, a special day was held. As a thank you to customers, they weren't charged for their ice cream cones on that day.

c People complained about the number of stairs they had to climb up and down so the first escalator was opened in London in an underground station on 4 October 1911. Notices were displayed at the top and bottom of the escalator: 'Please do not sit on the moving stairs. Step off with the left foot first.'

d He had a better idea. He was in a restaurant one day and he decided to demonstrate. He placed a handkerchief over the back of his seat, put his lips to it and the dirt was sucked into the handkerchief. A ring of black spots appeared on the handkerchief.

e Now a worldwide business, the company produces new flavours all the time. Each flavour is tested for at least six months before it is sold in shops. Sometimes the company holds competitions and asks for suggestions. About 275,000 tourists visit the factory each year.

f It was so noisy that it frightened horses in the streets. After a while, rich people had their houses cleaned by the machine and the King and Queen invited Booth to Buckingham Palace to demonstrate it.

g They made the ice cream themselves and each flavour was given a crazy name. People could listen to live music while they ate ice cream and the parlour became very popular.

h He was sure this was the answer so a machine was built. The first model was named 'The Puffing Billy' and a whole team of men was needed to operate it. One man worked the machine while another man guided a long hose inside offices or houses to clean them.

i The first escalators were built in shops and railway stations in the USA at the end of the nineteenth century. More and more people were using the underground trains in Britain especially after clean electric trains replaced dirty steam trains in 1906.

4 Check with other people who read the same text. Do you have the same order? Underline new vocabulary.

5 Tell the rest of the class what order you decided on and what your text is about. Then read the other two texts to check which order they are in.

6 Each of these words is connected with one invention. Put them under the correct heading.

dust   a flavour   a public building
to transport   to clean   a cone   a machine
a factory   moving stairs   dirt   a spot
a handkerchief   an underground station
a customer   to step on/off   a product

ice cream	escalator	vacuum cleaner

Language focus

Past passive

1. Underline the verb in this sentence. What tense is it?

   Ben and Jerry's famous products are sold in a range of delicious flavours.

   Look again at the first paragraph of the Ben and Jerry text on page 155. Find a verb in the past passive and underline it.

2. Look at the two texts in Exercise 2 on page 155 again and underline five verbs in the past passive. Check with a partner. Did you underline the same verbs? How many verbs can you find in the passive in the rest of the texts on page 155?

> ### ⬎ Grammar spot   Passive (past simple)
>
> **was/were + past participle**
> Write the passive verbs in the sentences below.
> + The vacuum cleaner .... by Hubert Cecil Booth. [*passive*]
>   Hubert Cecil Booth **invented** the vacuum cleaner. [*active*]
>
> – Customers .... by Ben and Jerry for their ice cream on one special day. [*passive*]
>   Ben and Jerry **didn't charge** customers for their ice cream on one special day. [*active*]
>
> ? What .... by Charles D. Seeberger? [*passive*]
>   What **did** Charles D. Seeberger **invent**? [*active*]
>
> Revise irregular past participles, e.g. *give* → *given, tell* → *told*, because you need them to make the passive. See page 216.

3. Rewrite these sentences so they have the same meaning. Change the verbs from passive to active.

   a. The aeroplane was flown to Miami.
      The pilot *flew the aeroplane* to Miami.

   b. The passengers were shown the emergency exits by the steward.
      The steward .... the emergency exits.

   c. Lunch was served during the journey.
      The stewards .... during the journey.

   d. The passengers weren't told where to wait for their luggage.
      The airport staff .... where to wait for their luggage.

   e. My passport wasn't stamped.
      The immigration officer .... my passport.

   f. When the luggage arrived, one man was ordered to open his suitcase by the customs officer.
      When the luggage arrived, the customs officer .... his suitcase.

4. Here are some sentences about the inventions in the texts. Write each sentence in the present or past passive.

   a. About 275,000 tourists visit the factory each year.
      The factory *is visited by about 275,000 tourists each year.*

   b. Ben and Jerry don't make the ice cream themselves now.
      The ice cream *isn't made by Ben and Jerry themselves now.*

   c. The station manager hired a man with a wooden leg.
      A man with a wooden leg ....

   d. The company holds competitions.
      Competitions ....

   e. 'The Puffing Billy' frightened horses.
      Horses ....

   f. The British didn't build the first escalators.
      The first escalators ....

   g. The King and Queen invited Booth to Buckingham Palace.
      Booth ....

   h. Clean electric trains replaced dirty steam trains.
      Dirty steam trains ....

   i. The company produces new flavours all the time.
      New flavours ....

⬎ GF page 213

> ### ⬎ Corpus spot   Do and make
>
> Ben and Jerry *made* ice cream. Choose the correct verb in these sentences written by PET students.
>
> a. You can *do / make* a lot of different activities at the sports centre.
> b. I couldn't *make / do* a decision about which English course to choose.
> c. I've just *done / made* a big cake.
> d. We *did / made* a sightseeing tour around the city centre.
> e. I have to *do / make* some exercises.
> f. Before we have dinner we'll *do / make* some shopping.

156 UNIT 24

«Activity» Past passive

1 Work in a group. Your teacher will give you a list of inventions. Decide when they were invented and where. Make guesses.

2 When you have finished, you ask the other group six questions. They have the answers. Choose the things you are most unsure of so you can make as many true sentences as possible.

Future passive

1 Read what someone predicts about the future and underline the verbs in the future passive.

I think a special car will be invented which will be driven by a computer so a human driver won't be needed. It will be made of plastic and it will be programmed to go on the road or fly through the air. A fee will be paid by car owners at the end of the year to the government. They will be charged according to how many kilometres they have travelled by air and on the road.

(↘) Grammar spot — Future passive

Will be + past participle

Complete the sentences with the future passive verbs from Exercise 1.

+ The car .... by a computer. [*passive*]

A computer **will drive** the car. [*active*]

− A human driver .... [*passive*]

The car **won't need** a human driver. [*active*]

? How much .... by each car owner? [*passive*]

How much **will** each car owner **pay**? [*active*]

2 What do you think will be invented in the next fifty years? Can you think of something which will make life easier at home or at work or for travel? Who will it be used by? What will it be made of? How will it work? Write a few sentences.

↘ GF page 213

«Pronunciation»

1 Look at these sentences. Find words ending in *r* or *re*. If they are followed by a word beginning with a vowel, join them together.

a Sugar‿and salt are‿added.
b Shops asked them to deliver ice cream.
c The mixture is frozen.
d There are four escalators in the station near my house.
e He had a better idea.
f Where is Ben and Jerry's ice cream sold?

2 **3** [13] Listen and repeat.

3 Look at these sentences. Which words will you join when you say them?

a Television was‿invented‿in the 1920s.
b Where are escalators used?
c Ben and Jerry's ice cream is sold in many places.
d Many shops have escalators.
e Some inventions aren't successful.
f I met him at four o'clock.
g Some people went up and down all day.
h I've lost your address.

4 **3** [14] Listen and repeat. Were you right?

«Activity» Describing objects

1 What is this everyday thing?

They are used all over the world, in both hot and cold countries. Today they are made of material and metal or plastic. They can be used instead of a coat to keep you dry. They can be folded up and put in a bag or pocket when they are not needed.

2 Work in a group. Write a description of an object to read to the class. Try to answer these questions in your description:

What is it made of?   What is it used for? What does it look like?

3 Read your description. Other students may interrupt if they can guess what it is. Can you get to the end of your description before they guess?

Exam folder 24

Listening Part 3

In this part of the exam, you listen to a recorded announcement or someone speaking about a particular subject. You fill in the words which are missing from some notes. You hear the recording twice.

CHECK!
a What do the instructions tell you?
b What should you do before you listen?
c Are the words you write down the same as the ones you hear?
d How many times do you hear the recording?

1 Look at the instructions in the task below. What is the man going to talk about?

2 Look at the exam task and answer questions a and b.

 a What is the name of the museum?
 b What kinds of words will you listen for?

You will hear a man talking on the radio about a museum.
For each question, fill in the missing information in the numbered space.

The Weston Museum of Science

First opened: in the year (**1**) .... in the Market Square.

Museum opening hours: every day from 9 am to 5 pm except (**2**) .... from 9 am to 9 pm

Exhibition in new gallery: learn about the (**3**) ....

Children's activity this week: (**4**) ....

Café: open all day on the (**5**) .... floor.

Until 24 July: the (**6**) .... is closed.

3 ③ 15 Listen to the recording and fill in the missing information.

4 Listen again and check your answers.

5 Look at the script and listen again.

6 Mark the answers on your script and check them.

Exam Advice

You usually have to write one word but sometimes you have to write two.

Writing folder

Writing Part 3

1 Can you match the halves of these sentences? Underline the words which help you.

a I really like that band
b I was listening to music
c While I was watching the band
d Although I like music
e The music was so loud
f I used to like folk music
g I enjoy listening to music
h You can have this CD

1 I don't own many CDs.
2 but I don't play an instrument.
3 when I fell asleep.
4 because I don't like it.
5 but now I prefer rock music.
6 that we couldn't talk.
7 my phone was stolen.
8 so get me a ticket too.

2 Read the beginning of a letter which Alessia wrote to her English friend, Sophie. Can you join any of the sentences? Use some of the words you underlined in Exercise 1.

Dear Sophie,
I went to a concert last week. My friend bought the tickets. She couldn't go. She was ill. My brother came instead. The band was good. I didn't want the music to stop. My brother doesn't like listening to their CDs. He enjoyed the concert. The concert finished at 11 o'clock. We went backstage to meet the band.

3 Look at the words in the box and put each one under the most suitable heading.

awful enjoyable enormous excellent exciting extraordinary fantastic
great hopeless large strange terrible tiny unexpected useless
well-known wonderful

good	bad	big	small	unusual	famous

4 Read the next part of Alessia's letter. Use some of the words from Exercise 3 to replace the words which are underlined.

It took a long time to get out of the hall because there was such a big crowd. We saw a famous actor and his girlfriend. She was wearing unusual clothes. She looks good, but my brother says she's a bad actress. We had a good evening. See you soon.
Love, Alessia

5 Imagine you went to a concert last week. Write a letter to an English friend and tell him/her who you went with, who was playing and what you thought of the concert. Write about 100 words.

Exam Advice

Remember to join some of your sentences to make your writing more interesting.

Units 19–24 Revision

Speaking

1 Work with a partner. Look at these sentences. Say if you agree with them and why. Find out your partner's opinion.

   a It's good to have lots of brothers and sisters.
     Yes, I agree. You can play with them when you are younger. What do you think?
     OR No, I don't agree. In my opinion that's not true because …

   b Most children are spoilt by their grandparents.

   c It isn't good to be famous when you are a teenager.

   d Most pop singers have an easy life.

   e Everyone should learn a musical instrument.

   f It's a good idea to make friends with people who have different interests from you.

   g Cars are the worst things that were ever invented.

Telephoning

2 Complete these phone conversations. Use the sentences in the box.

> This is Regina.
> Can you hang on a minute?
> I'll call you back in twenty minutes.
> May I have your name?
> I can't speak to you just now.
> I'm afraid he's not available at the moment.
> ~~I'm ringing to find out about a necklace I ordered.~~
> Can you call back in about an hour?
> Can you give me their number?

> **Shop assistant:** The Jewellery Store.
> **Regina:** Oh, yes, hello. (a) *I'm ringing to find out about a necklace I ordered.*
> **Shop assistant:** (b) ....
> **Regina:** Regina Hopper.
> **Shop assistant:** (c) ....
>   I'll just look. Oh, no, it hasn't arrived yet.
> **Regina:** Oh. Well, thanks anyway.

> **Receptionist:** Emsworth and Company.
> **Regina:** May I speak to John Hopper, please?
> **Receptionist:** (d) ....
> **Regina:** Oh. I need to speak to him this afternoon.
> **Receptionist:** (e) ....
> **Regina:** OK, thanks.

> **Regina:** Hello, Dad? (f) .... I want to tell you –
> **Dad:** Oh, I'm sorry, (g) .... Someone's just arrived for a meeting.
> **Regina:** But I need to talk to you.
> **Dad:** (h) ....
> **Regina:** Well, don't forget.
> **Dad:** No, I won't.

> **Regina:** Hello.
> **Dad:** Regina? Sorry, what did you want to tell me?
> **Regina:** That necklace we wanted for Mum's birthday present. I phoned the shop but it hasn't come yet.
> **Dad:** Right, I'll call them. (i) ....
> **Regina:** 226012.
> **Dad:** Thanks. I'll find out what's happening.
> **Regina:** Thanks, Dad. See you later.
> **Dad:** Bye.

Vocabulary

3 Look at the words 1–9. Think about which ones are nouns and which are adjectives, then match them with their definitions, a–i.

   1 battery   4 judge   7 employer
   2 bossy   5 vacuum cleaner   8 honest
   3 confident   6 niece   9 inventor

   a someone you work for
   b someone who decides the winner in a competition
   c someone who designs new machines
   d a word describing someone who feels certain about what they are doing
   e a word describing someone you can trust
   f your brother or sister's daughter
   g something you need to make your torch work
   h a machine you use in your house
   i a word describing someone who always tells other people what to do

Grammar

4 In each group of three sentences, only one is correct. Tick the correct sentence and put a cross by the incorrect ones.

1 **A** Our team prepared more carefully than the others. ✓

B Our team prepared the most carefully than the others. ✗

C Our team prepared less carefully as the others. ✗

2 **A** Can you explain me this sentence?

B Can you explain this sentence to me?

C Can you explain this sentence mean?

3 **A** What the spaceship looks like?

B What does the spaceship looks like?

C What does the spaceship look like?

4 **A** I've read the magazine you recommended.

B I've read the magazine that you recommended it.

C I've read the magazine you recommended it.

5 **A** She asked me not to phone in the evening.

B She asked me don't phone in the evening.

C She asked me to not phone in the evening.

5 Choose the correct word(s) to complete each sentence below.

1 We're very excited _B_ winning the match.
A for **B** about **C** of

2 I don't mind .... while you get ready.
A waiting **B** wait **C** to wait

3 You really ought .... this new shampoo.
A try **B** to try **C** trying

4 He agreed .... me at the bus station.
A meeting **B** to meet **C** meet

5 The team captain made them .... on Saturday afternoon.
A to practise **B** practising **C** practise

6 Look at the pairs of sentences below. Complete the second sentence in each pair so that it means the same as the first.

a He told her to leave the room.
'*Leave the room,*' he said.

b These machines were invented many centuries ago.
People .... many centuries ago.

c Jill asked Ali to phone her after his exam.
'Please .... after your exam,' said Jill.

d The building will be opened by the president.
The president .... the building.

e Mary told her grandson not to play football in the sitting room.
'.. in the sitting room,' said Mary to her grandson.

f My brothers are given more money than me.
My parents .... more money than me.

g My boyfriend said he'd rung me but I hadn't answered the phone.
My boyfriend said 'I .... the phone.'

h The police examined the strange vehicle very carefully.
The strange vehicle .... very carefully by the police.

i Our neighbours feed our dog when we're away.
Our dog .... when we're away.

j 'I've won the lottery!' shouted Annie.
Annie shouted that .... the lottery.

k My best friend will give me a lift home.
I .... home by my best friend.

7 Choose one of the words in the box to fill each space in this newspaper article. If no word is necessary, mark –.

who	which	where	whose

THIEVES MAKE A MISTAKE

The car of the pop star Saskia Labelle, **(a)** _who_ arrived in town yesterday, was damaged by two young men **(b)** .... broke a window and took a jacket **(c)** .... was on the back seat. Saskia's secretary, **(d)** .... jacket it was, said the thieves probably believed it was Saskia's.

The men, **(e)** .... were both tall with fair hair, were described by a security guard **(f)** .... had seen them in the hotel **(g)** .... Saskia was staying.

The concert **(h)** .... Saskia is giving tonight will start at nine o'clock at the City Hall. She will sing songs from her new CD **(i)** .... is called *Girltalk*.

25

Shop till you drop

Grammar reported questions; verbs + two objects; *too much/many, not enough*
Vocabulary shops and shopping
Revision reported speech; clothes

Introduction

1 Look at the photographs. What do they show?

2 Work with a partner. Look at one of the photographs. Check this list of advantages and disadvantages. Which are correct for your picture? Are there any other advantages or disadvantages of shopping this way?

You can do this at any time.
You have to go out in bad weather.
It's a good place to meet friends.
These shops are often expensive.
You meet local people.
You know the people who sell things to you.
You have to give information about yourself to people you don't know.
You can buy things without leaving your home.
You can touch and try the things before you buy.
You have to wait for days or weeks before you get what you've bought.

3 Compare your list with some other students.

4 Discuss which ways of shopping are most suitable for the following people and give reasons why.

a busy parents
b teenagers
c people who live a long way from a city
d old people

Listening

 **3** **16** Listen to Andy phoning his older brother Darren. Decide whether these statements are true or false.

a Andy wants Darren to collect him from the city centre. *true*
b Darren complains that Andy spends too much money on clothes.
c Andy saw some shirts he liked in the market.
d A woman spoke to Andy when he was leaving a store called Tempo.
e The manager thought that Andy had stolen a pullover.
f Andy was questioned by a police officer.
g The shop assistant agreed with Andy's story.
h Andy apologised to the manager for the trouble he had caused.

Language focus

Reported speech

1 Write these statements as you heard them on the recording.

   a 'They're selling some quite cool ones in the market.'
   A friend told me *they were selling some quite cool ones in the market.*

   b 'I've sold them all already.'
   The man who runs the stall said ....

   c 'I want to try them on.'
   I said to the assistant ....

   d 'That's OK.'
   He said ....

   e 'They don't fit.'
   I told the assistant ....

   f 'Yes, I am.'
   I said ....

2 Look at these statements from the conversation. Write down the exact words the people said.

   a I said I had.
   Andy said, ' *Yes, I have.* ....'

   b I agreed, although I added that I wasn't very happy about it.
   I said, '...................................'

   c I told him I'd bought a pullover at about 9.30.
   I told him, '...................................'

   d I tried to explain I'd thrown away the Tempo bag and had put the pullover in the shoe shop bag.
   I tried to explain. I said, '...................................
   ....'

   e I said I didn't remember who had served me.
   I said, '...................................'

   f He said he was sorry for troubling me and he told me I was welcome to use his phone.
   He said, '...................................'

3 Write down the exact questions the people asked.
   Think about the changes you make. Underline the words which are different in each pair of sentences. What do you notice about the word order?

   a She asked me <u>if I was</u> leaving the shop.
   '<u>Are you</u> leaving the shop?'

   b She asked me if I'd paid for everything in my bag.
   '...................................'

   c She asked me if I would come to the manager's office with her.
   '...................................'

   d The manager asked me how long I'd been in the shop and how many things I had bought.
   '...................................'

   e I asked what was going on.
   '...................................'

   f He asked me whether I had a receipt for the pullover.
   '...................................'

   g They asked which assistant had served me.
   '...................................'

   h Then the store detective asked the manager if he wanted her to call the police.
   '...................................'

   i I asked her if she remembered me.
   '...................................'

> ### ⟲ Grammar spot   Reported questions
>
> Complete the sentences with verbs in the correct tenses.
>
> **Yes/no questions + *if* or *whether***
>
> Do you like this? → I asked her if she .... it.
>
> Do you have a laptop? → He asked me whether I .... a laptop.
>
> Will you come shopping with me? → She asked me if I .... shopping with her.
>
> **Wh- questions**
>
> What's happening? → I asked what ....
>
> Which assistant spoke to you? → They asked which assistant .... to me.

4 Rhiannon wants to get a job in a shop. The manager interviews her and asks her some questions. After the interview, Rhiannon tells her friend Frederika what she was asked. Complete the spaces.

Have you ever worked in a shop before?

Why do you want to work in this shop?

Do you speak any foreign languages?

How will you travel to work every morning?

How old are you?

Can you start immediately?

She wanted to know (a) _how old I was_. Next she asked if (b) .... any foreign languages and whether (c) .... in a shop before and (d) .... Then she wanted to know (e) .... to work every morning. And then she asked if (f) .... immediately!

5 Would you like to work in a shop? Why? / Why not?

6 Complete this email with the reported forms of the questions below.

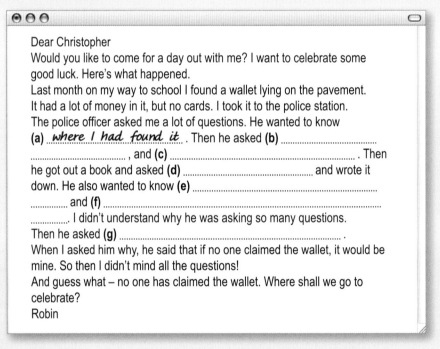

a Where did you find it?
b What time did you find it?
c Were you alone?
d Where do you live?
e How long have you lived there?
f Will you be at that address for the next month?
g Do you have an email address?

➥ GF page 213

Dear Christopher
Would you like to come for a day out with me? I want to celebrate some good luck. Here's what happened.
Last month on my way to school I found a wallet lying on the pavement. It had a lot of money in it, but no cards. I took it to the police station. The police officer asked me a lot of questions. He wanted to know
(a) _where I had found it_ . Then he asked **(b)** ....
.... , and **(c)** .... Then he got out a book and asked **(d)** .... and wrote it down. He also wanted to know **(e)** ....
.... and **(f)** ....
.... I didn't understand why he was asking so many questions.
Then he asked **(g)** ....
When I asked him why, he said that if no one claimed the wallet, it would be mine. So then I didn't mind all the questions!
And guess what – no one has claimed the wallet. Where shall we go to celebrate?
Robin

Too much, too many, not enough

🔽 Grammar spot   *Too much, too many, not enough*

Look at these sentences.
There are too many people at the bus stop.
There aren't enough buses.
I haven't got enough money for a taxi.
There is too much traffic on the road.

Choose the correct words – *too many*, *too much* or *enough* – to complete the rules.

When we talk about quantities, we use
a .... before a countable noun.
b .... before an uncountable noun.
c .... before either a countable or an uncountable noun.

Complete the sentences with *enough*, *too much* or *too many*.

a Our cities have .... traffic, so you can't relax.
b My bedroom is very untidy and there isn't .... furniture.
c There's .... noise in her flat.
d I asked for a new wardrobe because I've got .... clothes. I haven't got .... room for everything.
e We're not going to have .... time to go to the beach.
f If you don't want to spend .... money, you can get student accommodation.
g The spring is the best time because there aren't .... tourists.

➥ GF page 213

1 **3** **17** Listen to the recording. Underline the stressed word in each answer.

   1 A Did you say ten o'clock?
     B No, I said <u>two</u> o'clock.
   2 A Did you say there were five guests?
     B No, I said there were nine guests.
   3 A Did you say we had a spelling test?
     B No, I said we had a reading test.
   4 A Did you say you came by air?
     B No, I said I came by car.
   5 A Did you say she was a doctor?
     B No, I said she was a teacher.
   6 A Did you say you came from France?
     B No, I said I came from Greece.

2 Listen again and repeat.

3 Work with a partner. Take turns to ask questions and give answers like the ones in Exercise 1. Use the words below. Be careful of the stress in the answers.

   a Did you say / live / Bonn? (Rome)
     Did you say you lived in Bonn? No, I said I lived in <u>Rome</u>.
   b Did you say there / be / fifteen students? (sixteen)
   c Did you say we / want / ham sandwiches? (jam)
   d Did you say she / be / model? (actress)
   e Did you say it / be / quarter to eleven? (quarter to seven)

«Activity» **Whispers**

You are going to play a whispering game in groups of three.

Student A whispers a question to Student B, e.g. *What's the time?*
Student B whispers what Student A said to Student C, e.g. *He/She asked what the time was.*
Student C whispers the answer to Student B, e.g. *It's half past ten.*
Student B reports the answer aloud, e.g. *He/ She said it was half past ten.*

Take turns to ask, report and answer. Do the answers match the questions?

Verbs with two objects

give + **person** + object	= *give* + object + **to person**
*Dad gave **me** some money.*	= *Dad gave some money **to me**.*
The store detective showed **the manager** *the pullover.*	= *The store detective showed the pullover **to the manager**.*

1 Rewrite each of these sentences without *to*, so that it means the same as the one before.

   a The passengers gave their tickets to the driver when they got on the bus.
     The passengers gave *the driver their tickets when they got on the bus.*
   b I sent a postcard to my parents from London.
     I sent ....
   c Will you send the bill to my boss?
     Will you send ....
   d He wrote a long letter to me when he arrived in India.
     He wrote ....
   e On my birthday, the children brought my breakfast to me in bed.
     On my birthday, the children brought ....
   f Can you bring some more bread to us, please?
     Can you bring ....

2 Rewrite these sentences, adding *to*.

   a Take the headteacher this note, please.
     Take ....
   b Show the immigration officer your passport.
     Show ....
   c We took our classmate some fruit when he was ill.
     We took ....

⬎ GF page 213

«Activity» **A new jacket**

Where are these people?

Your teacher will give you some cards.
Match the two parts of the conversations.
Practise the shopping language with a partner.

Reading Part 3

In this part of the exam, you read a text and decide if ten sentences are correct or incorrect.

CHECK!

Read these sentences about Reading Part 3.
If a sentence is correct, write A. If it is incorrect, write B.

a The instructions tell you what the text is about.
b The sentences are in the same order as the information in the text.
c You need to understand every word in the text to answer the questions.

Look at the sentences below about a supermarket called Sainsbury's.

Read the text on the opposite page to decide if each sentence is correct or incorrect.

If it is correct, write **A**.

If it is incorrect, write **B**.

1 When the first Sainsbury's shop opened, it sold meat as well as milk, butter and eggs.
2 Shoppers paid more at Sainsbury's shop because of the quality of the food.
3 Sainsbury's second shop was in central London.
4 In the nineteenth century, some Sainsbury's shops were open until 2 am.
5 After 1900, some of the food sold came from other countries.
6 In 1900, people spent more of their income on food than they do now.
7 In the 1920s, Sainsbury's gave shoppers more choice than other shops.
8 It was possible to have your food delivered by Sainsbury's in the 1970s.
9 English people enjoyed self-service shopping when it was first introduced.
10 It took more than 30 years for every Sainsbury's shop to become self-service.

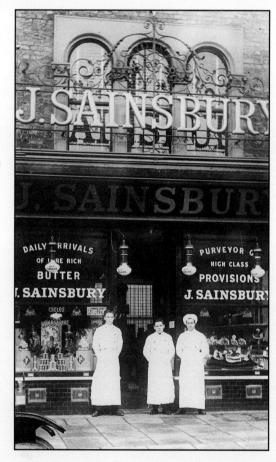

Exam Advice

Don't spend too long reading the text. Read it quickly and find the parts of the text which answer the questions.

SAINSBURY'S SUPERMARKETS

One of the most successful supermarkets in Britain is Sainsbury's. The first shop was opened nearly 150 years ago. In 1869, John James Sainsbury and his wife, Mary Ann, opened a small shop selling fresh milk, butter and eggs in Drury Lane, London. Other products like meat and vegetables weren't introduced until later. The shop became well known because, in spite of the food being of higher quality than at other shops, the prices were not higher. The business was so successful that by 1882, John James Sainsbury had opened three more shops in London, followed by a shop just outside London in Croydon.

Working conditions in nineteenth-century shops would seem hard to us but Sainsbury's workers were well looked after. In return, they had to work long hours. In fact, Saturday evening was often the busiest time. After closing, the shop had to be cleaned and tidied and it could be after 2 am before the workers were able to leave.

By 1900, Sainsbury's was importing food from abroad. People have always complained about how much they have to pay for their food, but it is worth noticing that food is much cheaper now, compared to average wages, than it was in 1900.

By the 1920s, the design of many of the shops had changed and a typical Sainsbury's shop had six departments offering a much wider range of products than other food shops. Each shop offered home delivery throughout the surrounding area, an important service in the days before most people had cars. This service came to an end during the 1960s as people had their own transport but has come into fashion again with the twenty-first century since people started ordering their food on the internet and having it delivered.

By 1939, there were 244 shops around the country and everything sold was stored in London before being delivered to each shop around the country. This system didn't change until the 1960s.

The first self-service shop opened in June 1950 in Croydon. The long counters, long queues and chairs for customers were replaced with checkouts. It was expected that people would miss what they were used to but there was no need to worry because people welcomed the change. However, it was nearly thirty years before all Sainsbury's traditional shops had been replaced with modern supermarkets.

In 1974, Sainsbury's first out-of-town supermarket opened on the edge of Cambridge and today most towns in Britain have a Sainsbury's nearby, some having one just outside the town and one in the town centre.

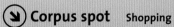 **Corpus spot**   Shopping

Choose the correct words in these PET students' sentences.
a We're going to *do / make* some shopping in the town centre.
b It's a big city with many *shoppings / malls* and cinemas.
c I don't often buy clothes at that shop because of the *expensive / high* prices.
d In the city you can *do / go* shopping if you get bored.
e I was in the *shop / shopping* buying shoes when I saw him.

26 Persuading people

Grammar first conditional; *if* and *when*; *unless*
Vocabulary advertising; reporting verbs
Revision telling a story

a b c d

Introduction

1 Here are parts of some famous logos. Do you recognise them?

2 Look around the room. How many logos can you see? How important are logos to you? Do you buy clothes with logos on them?

3 Look at these adverts. What are they advertising? Which advert is the most successful? Which advert is the least successful?

4 How important are adverts in your life? Do you take any notice of them? What is your favourite advert on TV at the moment?

THANK GOODNESS FOR Kleenex

PACK A POCKET P...

Ariel serves up Championship whites.

That's another load off your mind

www.ariel-info.co.uk

FREE LIMO SERVICE
along with all the refined luxuries that await you
in our First Class direct flight from Heathrow – Los Angeles
to MAKE THE SKY THE BEST PLACE ON EARTH.

AIR FRANCE

Reading

1 Read the photo story and answer these questions.

a What does Robert say he wants to do on his birthday?

b When is he planning to celebrate his birthday?

c What are the boys planning?

d Do they all think the plan is a good idea?

e How does Carolina know about the party?

f Does she think Robert will enjoy it?

g What does she think will happen if a lot of people are invited?

h What does she decide to do? Do you agree with her decision?

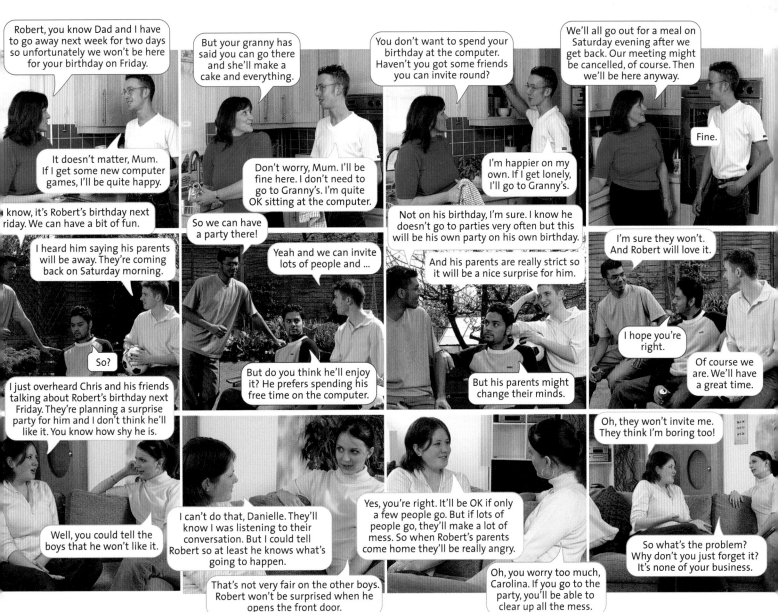

2 Read these questions. Look at the underlined verbs. What do they mean? Can you guess?

Then answer the questions.

1 What does Robert's mother do?
   A persuade him to spend his birthday with someone else
   B explain to Robert why she has to go to the meeting
   C complain about how much time he spends on the computer
   D promise to celebrate with him

2 What do the boys want to do?
   A organise a party at Robert's house
   B spoil Robert's birthday plans
   C influence the way Robert spends his free time
   D find out what Robert's parents are really like

3 What does Carolina want to do?
   A suggest the boys tell Robert about the party
   B apologise for listening to the boys' conversation
   C inform Robert's parents about the party
   D warn Robert about the party

4 What does Danielle do?
   A encourage Carolina to tell Robert's parents
   B recommend that Carolina tells Robert
   C persuade Carolina not to do anything
   D prevent Carolina from going to the party

(↓) **Vocabulary spot**

Verbs like *suggest*, *inform*, *warn*, etc. are often used in multiple-choice questions, especially in PET Reading Part 4. Make sure you know what the verbs in this exercise mean.

3 Complete the sentences with a verb from the box in the correct form.

apologise	encrouage
~~explain~~	influence
prevent	recommend
warn	

a We __explained__ the problem to the receptionist.
b Our volleyball captain .... the team to practise every day.
c Do advertisements .... your decisions about where to shop?
d My doctor .... that I should try a new skin cream.
e The tour guide .... the tourists about pickpockets in the area.
f The police .... the crowd from entering the square.
g Did the girls .... for making such a mess?

⊻ Corpus spot

Correct the mistakes.

a I want to warn you from the cold weather here.
b This will encourage me study harder.
c I explained her how it was made.
d My illness prevented me to go out.

Language focus

First conditional

⊻ Grammar spot   First conditional

A conditional sentence has two halves – a condition and a result.

Look at the two conditional sentences below and write either *the present tense* or *will* in the gaps.

condition	result
IF + ... ,	....

*If only a few people **go** to the party, **it won't be** a problem.*

result	condition
....	IF + ...

*He'll have a really good time if the boys **organise** a party for him.*

Complete the sentences below with the correct tense.

a The boys will know Carolina was listening to their conversation if she ......__tells__...... (tell) them what she thinks.
b If lots of people go to the party, the house .... (be) a mess.
c If the house is a mess, Robert's parents .... (get) angry.
d If Robert goes to his granny's house, the party .... (not happen).
e If the meeting is cancelled, Robert's parents .... (stay) at home.
f Robert will go to his granny's house if he .... (feel) lonely.
g If Carolina tells Robert about the party, Robert .... (not have) a surprise.
h If Robert gets some computer games for his birthday, he .... (be) happy.

↘ GF page 213

Unless

⊻ Grammar spot   Unless

Unless = if not
Write the verb in the 'unless' sentence so it means the same as the 'if' sentence.

If Robert doesn**'t** go to his granny's house, he will be at home.
Unless Robert .... *to his granny's house, he will be at home.*

1 Rewrite these sentences using *unless*.

a If the meeting isn't cancelled, Robert's parents will be away. *Unless the meeting is cancelled, ...*
b If Carolina doesn't tell Robert about the party, it will be a surprise.
c Robert will enjoy the party if the boys don't ask too many people.
d If the boys don't organise a party for Robert, he won't have one.
e Robert's parents won't know about the party if Carolina doesn't tell them.

2 Finish the sentences with *if* or *unless* and an ending from the box.

EXAMPLE: *You'll miss the bus unless you leave now.*

a You'll miss the bus
b I can come shopping with you
c I won't tell anyone   + *if* or
d I won't pass my exam   *unless*
e The letter will get there tomorrow

you post it by five o'clock.
you help me with my revision.
you leave now.
you tell me the secret.
you lend me some money.

If and *when*

➲ Grammar spot   *If* and *when*

1 Look at these two sentences.
   A ***When*** Robert's parents come home, they'll take him out for a meal.
   B ***If*** Robert's parents are at home, there won't be a party.
   In which sentence does the speaker know something definite about Robert's parents? A/B
   In which sentence is the speaker not sure about where Robert's parents are? A/B

2 Sometimes you can use *if* or *when* in the same sentence but the meaning changes. Look at these two sentences.
   A ***If*** Robert answers the door, he'll be surprised.
   B ***When*** Robert answers the door, he'll be surprised.
   In which sentence will Robert definitely answer the door (the speaker is sure)? A/B
   In which sentence will Robert possibly answer the door (the speaker isn't sure)? A/B

Choose *if* or *when*. In two of the sentences you can use either. What is the difference in meaning?

a Everyone will be hungry *if* / *when* we arrive late, so we'd better hurry!

b I'll eat that sandwich *if* / *when* you don't want it.

c I'll go to university *if* / *when* I pass this exam.

d *If* / *When* those shoes are still in the shop, I'll buy them.

e *If* / *When* we get to the town centre, we'll ask for directions to the theatre.

f I'll record the football match for you *if* / *when* I get home in time.

g I'll learn to drive *if* / *when* I'm seventeen.

h *If* / *When* I buy a new computer, I'll give you my old one.

i I'll be very disappointed *if* / *when* there are no tickets left.

> **↘ GF page 213**

《Activity》 Finishing a story

Work in a group. What happened next in the photo story on page 169? Write a fourth conversation and act it out.

《Pronunciation》

1 **3 18** Listen to this conversation and underline the words (or parts of words) which are stressed.

Joanna:	<u>What's</u> the <u>time</u>?
Michael:	Five to nine.
Joanna:	Oh dear.
Michael:	What's the problem?
Joanna:	It doesn't matter.
Michael:	Tell me.
Joanna:	I'm late for college. Can you give me a lift?
Michael:	Of course I can.
Joanna:	Thank you.
Michael:	You're welcome.

2 Listen again and then practise the conversation.

《Activity》 Adverts

Look at these adverts. Write some slogans for them. Use *if*, *when* and *unless*.

《Activity》 Superstitions

Do you believe in superstitions? Look at these pictures. Do these things mean bad luck, good luck or nothing in your country?

Write some sentences.

EXAMPLE: *If you open an umbrella indoors, you will have bad luck.*

Compare your answers in a group.
Add some more superstitions.

Exam folder 26

Speaking Part 1

In this part of the exam, the examiner talks to each student and asks a few questions. The students say a number and also spell a word for the examiner.

CHECK!
a How many people are in the room for the speaking test?

In Part 1:
b Who do you speak to?
c What subjects will the examiner probably ask you about?
d What can you say if you don't understand?
e How long does this part last?

1 Spell your name when your teacher asks you.

2 Think about your answers to these questions.

Where do you come from?
Do you work or are you a student?
What subjects do you study? / What job do you do?
Do you enjoy studying English? Why (not)?
Do you think that English will be useful for you in the future?
What did you do last weekend?
What do you enjoy doing in your free time?

3 Ask your partner the questions in Exercise 2 and listen to his/her answers. Then your partner asks you the questions. Can you make any suggestions to improve each other's answers?

Exam Advice
Don't answer the examiner's questions with just *yes* or *no*.

Speaking Part 2

In this part of the exam, you are given some pictures. You work in pairs and try to arrive at a decision together about a situation which the examiner describes to you.

CHECK!
a What will the examiner give you?
b Who will you talk to?
c What can you say if you don't understand?
d How long do you and your partner need to talk?
e What will happen if you can't think of anything to say?

1 A small town is planning to improve its facilities for young people. Look at the pictures of different suggestions on page 201. Think about which of the places you use or would like to use.

2 Decide which facility you think is the most important for young people. Which is the next most important? Put them in order.

3 Look at each place and think about these questions.
How expensive is it to build?
How many young people would use it?
How expensive is it to spend time there?

4 Work with a partner. You are going to decide how the town should spend its money. Talk about the different suggestions and decide which are the most important.

Look at Exam folder 9 to remind you of useful expressions.

Exam Advice
Learn ways of making suggestions, giving your opinion, agreeing and disagreeing.

Writing folder

Writing Part 3

1 Here is part of a story. Can you use these four words to fill the spaces?

| after | when | while | next |

I went into my hotel room and (**a**) .... I had locked the door, I opened the envelope from my bank. There was a letter and some money in it. First, I counted the money. (**b**) .... , I looked at the letter. (**c**) .... I was reading it, I heard a sound in the bathroom. I put the letter in my pocket and went to the bathroom door. Somebody was having a shower – in my bathroom! What should I do? I was still trying to decide (**d**) .... I heard the shower stop.

2 Work with a partner. Put these sentences in the correct order to tell the rest of the story. Which words help you to understand the order in which things happened?

  a 'What are you doing here?' we said at the same time.
  b In the evening, the hotel gave us a free meal.
  c Then he looked at the key which was still in my hand.
  d When he saw me he looked angry.
  e A man came out wearing a towel.
  f After he had put his clothes on, we went to see the receptionist.
  g Suddenly the bathroom door opened.
  h She apologised and gave him a different room.
  i We've been friends ever since.
  j 'I suppose they've given one of us the wrong key,' he said and began to laugh.

3 Write a story called *The surprise*. Write about 100 words. How many of the words in the box below can you use in your story?

| after | already | ever since | in the morning | next | still | when | while |

Exam Advice

A story can be about an everyday event.

27 Travellers' tales

Grammar reflexives; adverbs; *each, every, all*
Vocabulary travel; word building
Revision guessing unknown words; the passive

Introduction

1 **3** 19 Listen to a song and say which of the photographs you think it fits best.

2 Look at the words of the song below. Some of them are missing. Can you guess what sort of word (noun, adjective, verb, preposition) you need for any of the spaces?

3 Listen to the song again and write down the missing words.

4 Why is the singer travelling, do you think?

5 Look again at the photographs. Why are the people in them travelling?

Can you think of other reasons why people travel?

6 What is the best way to travel, in your opinion?

Somewhere the sun is (a) _____
Somewhere the (b) _____ is blue
Somewhere the (c) _____ lining is (d) _____ for me and you.
And I know that the (e) _____ is a (f) _____ one to travel on
over (g) _____ mountains and by the sea strand,
(h) _____ of the valley the sun (i) _____ shines upon
to the (j) _____ glades of that sweet promised (k) _____ .

↘ Vocabulary spot

Reasons for travelling
We can talk about reasons for travelling using nouns or verbs:
*on holiday, **on business**, but **for pleasure***
*travelling **to meet** new people, travelling **to see** the world*
*We **go on a** trip, **on a** tour but **on** holiday.*

Listening

1 If you don't know the meaning of a word, think about the answers to these questions.

   a Does it look like a word in your own language?
   b Can you say whether the word is a person or a thing?
   c Is it made of other words you already know?
   d Can you guess the meaning of the word from the words around it?

2 Look at these words and think about their meanings.

   a accordion   b nanny   c volunteer
   d boardwalk   e archaeologist   f campfire
   g basement

3 **3 20** Listen to a radio programme and write down what you think the words in Exercise 2 mean.

4 Say how you guessed each word.

5 Listen to the radio programme again and complete these notes using between one and three words in each space.

   a Joe helped to look after ___cows___ on a farm.
   b The farmer's wife made excellent _____ .
   c Natasha was paid £ _____ a week.
   d A friend helped Natasha to write _____ .
   e Owen worked on an island in _____ .
   f The weather was often _____ .
   g Jennifer's hands and _____ hurt while she was working in the desert.
   h She liked the desert because it was beautiful and _____ .
   i Martin was introduced to the old man by _____ .
   j The old man's _____ asked Martin to paint her basement.

6 Would you like to do any of the work described in the programme? Why? Which work would you definitely not want to do? Why not?

 **Word-building** *Snap*

Play *Word-building Snap* with one or two other students. Your teacher will give you the cards.

Language focus

Adverbs at the beginning of sentences

1 Look at these sentences from the radio programme. Can you remember which adverb was at the beginning of each sentence?

   a *Luckily / Surprisingly / Actually*, a Finnish friend helped me to write a little notice.
   b *Obviously / In fact / Unfortunately*, I liked helping to save the forest.
   c *Unluckily / Surprisingly / Of course*, the sun was really hot during the day, but it was very cold at night.
   d *In fact / Luckily / Unfortunately*, digging is very hard work.
   e *Fortunately / Actually / Obviously*, we needed to be quite fit.
   f *Of course / Surprisingly / Luckily*, his landlady was so satisfied with the job I did that she asked me to paint her basement.
   g *Unfortunately / Obviously / In fact*, I had a letter from someone last week offering me work there next summer.

2 Which of the adverbs in Exercise 1 have the same meaning?

3 Now complete these sentences using your own ideas.

   a I went to bed very late last night. Surprisingly, *I wasn't tired this morning.*
   b Some people say that English weather is always bad. Actually, _____
   c My sister bought several lottery tickets last week. Unfortunately, _____
   d The film star said he hadn't got any money. Of course, _____
   e I thought his jacket looked really expensive. In fact, _____
   f My friend suggested we should have a party the night before my exam. Obviously, _____

4 Choose two adverbs from Exercise 1 and write sentences with each one like the sentences in Exercise 3.

Reflexive pronouns

myself, yourself, himself, herself, itself, ourselves, yourselves, themselves

Look at these sentences from the radio programme:
You obviously enjoyed **yourself** there.
We needed to know how to look after **ourselves**.
She helped **me** to write a little notice about **myself**.

1 Complete these sentences using the correct form of the verb and a reflexive pronoun.

   a Does your brother need a babysitter when your parents go out? No, he
   looks after himself. (look after)

   b Were you listening to the radio in your room or were you .... ? (talk to)

   c Susan mustn't carry that heavy box. She might .... (hurt)

   d Hello, everyone! Please .... (help) to drinks.

   e It rained every day when we went camping so we .... (not enjoy)

   f Sometimes I .... (ask) why I work so hard.

   g Don't worry about them. They can ....
   .... (look after)

2 Choose some verbs from the sentences in Exercise 1 and write three sentences using reflexive pronouns.

   EXAMPLE: *I don't like people who help themselves to my things without asking me.*

⏎ Grammar spot

Each other / themselves

Check that you understand the difference between these sentences. Match each sentence to the correct picture.

a *They're looking at each other.* Picture ....
b *They're looking at themselves.* Picture ....

3 Can you draw or describe a pair of cartoons to show the difference between these two sentences?

   a They hurt themselves.
   b They hurt each other.

↘ GF page 213

Every, each, all

⏎ Grammar spot   *Every, each, all*

Look at these sentences.
*It rained nearly **every** day.*
***Every** evening the old farmer played his accordion.*
***Each of** the workers had a small tent.*
***Each** person told their friends about me.*
*I liked **all** the people there.*
*I kept **all** the money.*
*I looked after the little one **all** day.*

a Complete these notes with the words *singular* or *plural*.
   We use *each* and *every* + a .... countable noun.
   We use *each of* + a .... countable noun.
   We use *all* + a .... noun or an uncountable noun.

b When we talk about time, *every* and *all* have different meanings. Complete these sentences with *every* or *all*.
   .... *day* means *a complete day*.
   .... *day* means *more than one day*.

Use *every, each* or *all* to complete these sentences.

a I asked ...*all*...... the boys to look for my ring.

b In the first lesson, ... of the students told the class about his or her holiday.

c This restaurant has .... kind of food – Italian, Mexican and many more.

d .... the furniture in my room is old.

e I'll show you .... the best places to eat.

f Our house is big enough for .... of you to have your own room.

g This year, I'll be here .... summer.

h Joe ordered a drink for .... of his friends.

↘ GF page 213

≪Pronunciation≫

1 Practise the sounds /eə/ and /ɪə/.
   Can you find them in the sentence *Here's your chair*?

2 **3 21** Listen and repeat these sentences, then mark the sounds /eə/ or /ɪə/ in different colours. When you have checked your answers, put the words into the columns below.

   a He r̲a̲rely feels f̲ea̲r.
   b He's got fair hair and a beard.
   c Take care on the stairs, dear.
   d There's a box of pears near the door.
   e Where did they appear from?
   f The volunteers worked in pairs.
   g The engineer steered the old car carefully.

/eə/	/ɪə/
rarely	*fear*

3 Work with a partner. Take turns to repeat the sentences again. Listen to each other's pronunciation.

Using the passive

1 Look at these sentences from the radio programme, which have passive verbs, then look at the sentences with the same meaning, which have active verbs.

*Some students **are helped by** their parents (passive). = Some parents **help** students (active).*
*I **was given** a room (passive). = The farmer **gave** me a room (active).*

Rewrite the sentences below with an active verb.

a I was employed as a nanny.
A Finnish family *employed me as a nanny.*

b I wasn't paid.
No one ....

c The buildings were buried for hundreds of years.
Sand ....

d I was employed by lots of people.
Lots of people ....

e Our listeners will be encouraged by those stories.
Those stories ....

2 Look at this email which a volunteer sent to a friend. What does Chris feel about his summer job?

○ ○ ○

🚫 Delete   ↩ Reply   ↩ Reply All   ➡ Forward   🖨 Print

Hi Eddy
You said you wanted to hear what I did this summer. Actually, I was working as a volunteer on our local beach. It looks a real mess sometimes. When I was a child, people didn't drop their rubbish on the beach but they do now, and tourists start fires sometimes. So this summer volunteers cleaned the beach every evening. They collected thousands of empty bottles. Next year the government will employ someone to organise the volunteers. Pollution damages lots of beaches but I hope it won't spoil this one. So you see, I was doing something useful for once. I'll probably do it again next year. What about you?
Chris

---

3 Chris wrote a report about his work for the local paper. Rewrite the sentences from the email using passive verbs. Decide when you want to use *by*.

Young volunteers clean up town beach

By Chris Appleton

This summer I joined other volunteers to help clean up the local beach. In the past, rubbish **(a)** *wasn't dropped on the beach* but nowadays you see it everywhere and sometimes fires **(b)** .... But this summer the beach **(c)** .... every evening and thousands of empty bottles **(d)**................ . Next year someone **(e)** .... to organise the volunteers. Every year lots of beaches **(f)** .... but I hope our local beach **(g)** ....
I will probably work on our beach again next year and I hope some of my friends will volunteer with me.

«Activity» Eco-questionnaire

1 Read the questionnaire on page 203. In small groups, discuss the questions.

2 Use the questionnaire to find out who is the most earth-friendly person in your class (or family). Score the answers using the key. What advice would you give to someone who gets a low score?

3 In your group, write about three different people:

a an earth-friendly person who would get a high score on the questionnaire

b someone who would get an average score

c the kind of person who doesn't worry about the earth and who would get a low score.

Exam folder 27

Reading Part 2

In this part of the exam, you read five descriptions of people. For each one, you choose one text to match it.

CHECK!

a How many questions are there?
b How many texts are there?
c How many texts are not used?
d Can the same text be the answer to two questions?
e What should you do after you have read the questions?
f What should you check before you choose an answer?

The people below all want to travel in Europe.
On the opposite page there are eight advertisements.
Decide which advertisement would be the most suitable for each person.
For questions **1–5**, write the correct letter (**A–H**).

1  Cassie spent some time last summer travelling around Europe by bus and train. Next month she wants to visit a friend she met in Italy but she can't afford the fare.

2  Andy wants to travel alone around Europe for two months in the summer making his own decisions about how long he spends in each place.

3  Rachel wants to travel in Europe but she has very little money. She is free for nine months before she goes to university.

4  The Roberts family want to see as much as possible in Europe but have only two weeks. They want someone else to make all the hotel and travel arrangements for them.

5  The Graham family want to spend their holiday in the countryside, away from crowds and traffic. They would like to get some exercise while they are away.

Exam Advice

When you think you have found the answer, read the text carefully. There may be one or two details which make it wrong.

A

SPECIAL OFFER on rail tickets.
Unlimited travel through ten European countries
during June, July and August for only £450.
Family discounts. No minimum stop between journeys.
Apply at least one month before travelling.

B

Express coaches London to Switzerland or Italy.
Special discounts this month on one-way tickets.
Air-conditioned coach with toilet. Two stops for meals.
Sandwiches and drinks on sale during the journey.
Phone now for details of departure times and unbelievable
prices.

C

Do you have experience of travelling around Europe?
Do you want to visit Italy?
Responsible young adult required to look after six
teenagers travelling from London to Rome by train.
Ticket and meals paid during journey.
Depart in two weeks.

D

Take the worry out of your holiday in France, Italy or Spain and save money on hotels and petrol.
On our ten-day holidays, you cycle on paths between
campsites. When you arrive, everything is ready for you:
tent, barbecue and swimming pool! You can organise dates
to suit your family. And you'll get fit in beautiful countryside.

E

Would you like to spend six months travelling in southern Europe?
American family requires nanny to help with their children.
We will pay for all meals, travel costs and give you £30
pocket money a week. The right attitude is more important
than qualifications or experience. Interviews next week.
Phone for further information.

F

Our business is your pleasure.
See the best of southern Europe in a fortnight.
Air-conditioned coach tours visit the most beautiful and
historic cities in Spain, Southern France and Italy. Spend each
night in a comfortable hotel with a swimming pool and
enjoy the local food in a carefully chosen restaurant. Special
prices for families and single travellers.

G

Leave everything to us. If you are a business traveller
and frequently need to travel to France or Italy but
don't have time to spend booking tickets, call Quick-
ticket now. We store all your details on our computer:
how you prefer to travel, usual destinations, etc.
All you do is call or email one day before your journey.

H

Planning to travel in Europe this summer?
We are three students looking for a fourth to share
costs travelling by car and camping for about six weeks.
We have planned our route through five countries but would
be prepared to make some changes.

⬇ Corpus spot   *Travel, trip and journey*

Complete these PET students' sentences with the correct word from the box.

| travel   trip   journey |

a   The first prize is a .... to New York.
b   The .... was boring, and took ten hours, but we
    arrived safely.
c   I love .... and I want to visit England next year.

28 What would you do?

Grammar	second conditional
Vocabulary	jobs; expressions with prepositions
Revision	opinions; agreeing/disagreeing; first conditional; and *if/when*

Introduction

1 Do you recognise any of the people in the photographs? Why are they famous?

2 Match the adults to the photographs of them when they were children. Use the words in the box to help you.

I think that ...	I agree that ...	X used to ...
I don't agree that ...	It might be ...	X still has ...
It could be ...	I think it's ...	X has the same ...

3 Compare your answers with other students and talk about how you made your choice.

4 Choose one of the children and imagine what he/she was thinking.

When If	I	grow up become famous earn lots of money become a ...	I will won't	be ... work ... live ... have ...

EXAMPLE: When I grow up, I'll be a famous ...

Reading

1   Read this web page about jobs you can have working with celebrities. Match paragraphs A–F
    with the jobs. If you don't know what all the jobs are, try to guess while you are reading.
    Don't worry about any words you don't understand.

A .... B .... C .... D .... E .... F ....

---

www.mychat.com

Do you fancy being a star but know you never will be? Then working for a star could
be the job for you. With plenty of cash and no journalists looking through your rubbish
bins, it could be perfect. Here are just some of the jobs you could choose.

personal trainer fashion designer bodyguard celebrity chef stylist personal assistant

A Stars take a lot of interest in what they eat so what do they
do when they feel hungry but don't want to get their hands
dirty? Employ me, of course. I have to be very good at my job
because I'm responsible for preparing meals not just for my
boss but for all his famous friends. Would you like my job?
Yes? In that case you should get good qualifications and then
work in one of the best restaurants for at least a couple of
years. And of course your own TV show will help too.

B Who do you think makes those stars look 100% perfect? It
doesn't just happen by accident. It's my job to make sure
my celebrity looks wonderful at all times. Imagine if you had
someone to shop and choose clothes for you! You too would
look like a star all the time. The best thing about my job is that
I go everywhere with my boss because famous people can't
afford to make any mistakes in public, can they? I'm with her
nearly all the time, whether she's at home or on holiday.

C At present I have celebrities knocking at my door because
they like my clothes. And if I'm lucky they invite me to events
where everyone can see the clothes I've designed. I have
to keep my ideas up-to-date because no star wants to be
seen in something that looks old-fashioned. Of course, in the
end if they decide they don't like my clothes any more, I'll be
famous one day and unknown the next.

D I get the chance to experience the life of the rich and famous
without actually being famous myself. I take phone calls and
look at all the fan mail, plan parties and do all the jobs the
star doesn't want to do. I travel first class with the star, make
sure she arrives everywhere on time and meet lots of famous
people. I have to stay very calm and not mind being shouted
at even when I've done nothing wrong. In my job you can
earn lots of money like a star but I'm never on the front page
of the newspaper just because I've got a new boyfriend.

E I'm essential to a star who wants to look good. I'm the only
person who tells a celebrity what to do and they listen to me.
I watch and shout instructions while they cycle, run and lift
weights. There's also a chance of someone famous falling in
love with me – it has happened before.

F My job is to make sure the boss is never in danger and I need
to be strong, both physically and mentally, to do that. I have to
see problems in advance before they happen and, if there is
any trouble, I have to be there at once. I'm closer to the star
than anyone. And I have to do what she does and keep her
in sight all the time. So don't forget that if the boss wants to
spend every night dancing in a nightclub, I'll be there too. In
fact I sometimes spend 24 hours at work without a break.

---

2   Work in a group. Read the web page again and think about the answers to these
    questions. Underline any words you don't know and talk about them in your group.

Job A
1   What is meant by *to get their hands dirty*?
2   What does *I'm responsible for* mean?

Job B
3   What does a stylist do?
4   Why is he/she so important?

Job C
5   What does *knocking at my door* mean in the
    text?
6   What does *up-to-date* mean?
7   What might happen?

Job D
8   What kind of jobs does a personal assistant do?
9   Why might he/she get shouted at?

Job E
10 Why can a personal trainer tell a star what to do?
11 What might happen?

Job F
12 Why does a bodyguard have to be strong both
    physically and mentally?
13 What might be a disadvantage of the job?

3   Think of four advantages and four disadvantages of
    being famous. Would you like to be famous? Why? /
    Why not?

⊙ Vocabulary spot

Sometimes the words in an expression do not mean exactly what
they say, e.g. *to get their hands dirty*. Look at the words in the
sentences around them to try to understand what they mean.

Language focus
Second conditional

> ### 🔁 Grammar spot   Second conditional
>
> Put the verbs *have* and *look* into the correct form in these sentences.
>
> | condition | result |
> |---|---|
> | *If* + past tense | *would* + infinitive |
> | If I .... a stylist, I .... good all the time. |
>
> | result | condition |
> |---|---|
> | *would* + infinitive | *if* + past |
> | I .... good all the time if I .... a stylist. |

1 You read about some people who work with celebrities on page 181. Would you like that kind of job? Who would you like to work for? Make some conditional sentences.

EXAMPLE: *If I was/were X's bodyguard, I'd …*

2 Put the verbs in brackets into the correct tense. Use the second conditional.

  a If we *lived* .... (live) near the sea, we*'d go* .... (go) to the beach every weekend.

  b If I .... (not have) so much homework to do, I .... (go) out with my friends.

  c I .... (buy) a new computer if I .... (have) plenty of money.

  d If I .... (own) a plane, I .... (fly) in it every day.

  e If Andrea .... (get up) earlier, she .... (not be) late every day.

  f If my neighbours .... (be) friendly, I .... (invite) them to my party.

  g If Suzi .... (be) old enough, she .... (learn) to drive.

  h My brother .... (teach) you the guitar if he .... (have) time.

3 Complete these sentences using your own ideas. Use the first or second conditional.

  a If I was a pop star, *I'd write amazing songs.*

  b If you lose your purse, *I'll lend you some money.*

  c If I had a helicopter, ...

  d If you spoke perfect English, ...

  e If I go to bed late tonight, ...

  f If you don't help me with this work, ...

  g If you were a beautiful model, ...

  h If I didn't do any homework, ...

↘ GF page 214

Expressions with prepositions

1 Read these sentences from the article on page 181. Fill in the prepositions without looking at the texts.

at	by	in	on

  a You should work in one of the best restaurants for *at* .... **least** a couple of years.

  b It doesn't just happen .... **accident**.

  c Famous people can't afford to make any mistakes .... **public**.

  d I'm with her nearly all the time, whether she's .... **home** or .... **holiday**.

  e My job is to make sure the boss is never .... **danger**.

  f I have to see problems .... **advance** before they happen.

  g If there is any trouble I have to be there .... **once**.

  h I have to keep her .... **sight** all the time.

  i I sometimes spend 24 hours .... **work** without a break.

  j I make sure she arrives everywhere .... **time**.

  k There's also a chance of someone famous falling .... **love** with me.

  l .... **present** I have celebrities knocking at my door.

  m Of course, ... **the end** if they decide they don't like my clothes any more, I'll be famous one day and unknown the next.

2 Which preposition goes before each of these words? Write them in the correct circle below.

breakfast bus business car first
foot   last mistake   post school
stock   town

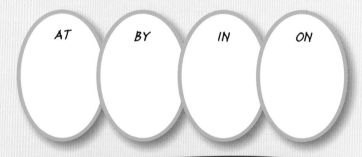

AT   BY   IN   ON

> ### 🔁 Vocabulary spot
>
> Learn these expressions as they are very common. People may not understand you if you use the wrong preposition, e.g. *The train arrived on time* (at the correct time) or *I got to the cinema in time* (just before the film started).

«Pronunciation»

1 Decide what is missing from these sentences. Use the box to help you. Write the whole word at the end of each line.

's	've	'll	'd	're

a If I had a car, I _'d_ lend it to you. *would*

b Wait for me – I .... almost finished watching this programme.

c They .... be late if they don't hurry.

d They .... already arrived when I got there.

e If she lived near her friends, she .... be happier.

f You .... not listening to me, are you?

g This is the first time he .... played the trumpet in public.

h We .... ring you if we go swimming next weekend.

i She .... coming home late tonight.

2 **3 22** Listen and check your answers.

3 **3 23** Listen and repeat.

4 **3 24** Look at these sentences and listen to the recording. If what you hear is exactly the same as what you see, mark ✓. If it is different, circle the letters which are different and write what you heard.

a They(ve)already left. *They'd*

b He'd help you.

c The pop star's leaving.

d It'd be too dark to see anything.

e I've seen the programme before.

f She'd got plenty of money.

«Activity» Quiz

1 Answer these quiz questions about yourself.

«Activity» A desert island

1 Look at what some people said they would take to a desert island.

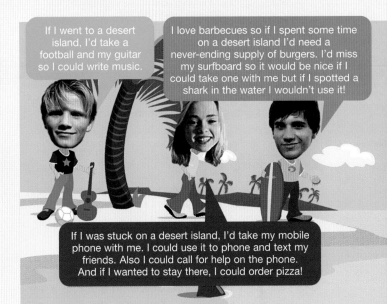

If I went to a desert island, I'd take a football and my guitar so I could write music.

I love barbecues so if I spent some time on a desert island I'd need a never-ending supply of burgers. I'd miss my surfboard so it would be nice if I could take one with me but if I spotted a shark in the water I wouldn't use it!

If I was stuck on a desert island, I'd take my mobile phone with me. I could use it to phone and text my friends. Also I could call for help on the phone. And if I wanted to stay there, I could order pizza!

2 Think of two things you would take to a desert island and why. Think of two things you would miss. Write the sentences on a piece of paper without your name on it and give it to your teacher.

3 Work in a group. Your teacher will give you some pieces of paper. Decide who wrote them.

4 Think about one of your favourite stars and imagine how they would answer.

2 Exchange quizzes. Look at the scores on page 184 and tell your partner what kind of person he/she is.

WHAT ARE YOU LIKE?

1 If a shop assistant was rude to you but then forgot to charge you for something, would you:
a) go back and tell her?
b) run away as fast as possible?
c) go home, then feel bad and phone the shop?

2 If you saw an old lady stealing food from the supermarket, would you:
a) take no notice?
b) offer to help the old lady to carry the food to the checkout?
c) call an assistant?

3 If you went shopping with your friend and he/she decided to buy some clothes which looked terrible, would you:
a) tell him/her the truth?
b) suggest something else which suited him/her better?
c) let him/her buy them because he/she liked them?

4 If you saw your favourite star when you were out shopping, would you:
a) scream and point at him/her?
b) just walk past?
c) ask him/her for an autograph?

5 If you found out that your best friend had two boyfriends/girlfriends at the same time, would you:
a) ask your friend how he/she would feel in the same situation?
b) tell one of the boyfriends/girlfriends?
c) say nothing – it's not your problem?

6 If your friend invited you to go on holiday with her family but you didn't like her mum, would you:
a) explain how you feel about her mum and refuse the invitation?
b) say nothing and go on the holiday?
c) invent an excuse not to go?

Exam folder 28

Listening Part 2

In this part of the exam, you listen to a recording of one person speaking or an interview and answer six questions by choosing A, B or C. You hear the recording twice.

Exam Advice

If you don't hear the answer to a question, don't spend time worrying about it. You will miss the answer to the next question too!

1 **3 25** Do the exam task.

You will hear a radio interview with a young actor called Paul.
For each question, put a tick (✓) in the correct box.

1 Paul first appeared on TV in a
  A soap opera. ☐
  B children's drama. ☐
  C quiz show. ☐

2 What does Paul say about playing Frank?
  A He didn't like Frank's personality. ☐
  B He wanted to have a bigger part. ☐
  C He did it for too long. ☐

3 What problem did Paul have when he was in the soap opera?
  A He couldn't trust anyone. ☐
  B He got very tired. ☐
  C He didn't like people recognising him. ☐

4 What did Paul realise when he was in a theatre play?
  A He preferred acting in theatres to TV programmes. ☐
  B He enjoyed performing to an audience. ☐
  C He didn't know how to act on stage. ☐

5 In the future, what does Paul want to act in?
  A TV programmes ☐
  B theatre plays ☐
  C films ☐

6 How do Paul's parents feel about his choice of career?
  A worried ☐
  B disappointed ☐
  C surprised ☐

2 Look at the script and listen again. Underline the words in the script which give you the answer to each question.

3 Now circle the words in the script which tell you why the other options are wrong in each question.

Scores for quiz on page 183

1	a) 3	b) 1	c) 2	4	a) 1	b) 3	c) 2
2	a) 3	b) 2	c) 1	5	a) 2	b) 3	c) 1
3	a) 1	b) 2	c) 3	6	a) 1	b) 2	c) 3

Score 15–18 ...
You are very kind and you think about other people's feelings. Remember to think about yourself too, and don't let other people walk all over you!

Score 10–14 ...
Congratulations! You think about other people's feelings and try to do the best thing. You are a good friend.

Score 6–9 ...
You need to be careful or you won't have many friends. You are very honest but you need to consider other people's feelings too. Remember to think before you speak.

Writing folder

Writing Part 1

Here are some sentences about going shopping. For each question, complete the second sentence so that it means the same as the first, using no more than three words.

1 My friend and I took the bus to town last week.
My friend and I went to town *by bus* .... last week.

2 My friend forgot to bring her purse.
My friend didn't .... bring her purse.

3 She asked me how much money I had in my purse.
She asked me, 'How much money .... in your purse?'

4 She borrowed some money from me.
I .... her some money.

5 The town has got lots of shops.
There .... lots of shops in the town.

6 First we went into a shop called *Stella's*.
First we went into a shop .... name was *Stella's*.

7 We couldn't afford the clothes in *Stella's*.
The clothes in *Stella's* were .... for us.

8 We bought nothing in *Stella's*.
We didn't .... in *Stella's*.

9 The shop next door is owned by my mother's friend.
My mother's friend .... the shop next door.

10 Although she showed me lots of clothes, I couldn't choose.
She showed me lots of clothes .... I couldn't choose.

11 We said, 'If we don't hurry, we'll miss the bus.'
We said, 'Unless .... , we'll miss the bus.'

12 We had such a tiring day we fell asleep on the bus.
We were so .... we fell asleep on the bus.

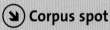

Corpus spot

Borrow* and *lend

In some of these sentences *borrow* is correct. Put a tick against them. Write the correct form of *lend* in the other sentences.

a Could you borrow me that book for two weeks?
b I would like to borrow your camera, please.
c I borrowed Tom my bicycle.
d I've asked to borrow my father's car.
e When I got home, I didn't have the beautiful scarf my mother had borrowed me.

Corpus spot

There is/are

Correct these sentences written by PET students.

a There do a lot of interesting historic buildings.
b There have three films to choose from.
c In the centre there a new club.
d There is a lot of things to do in my town.
e You could go to the National Museum where it is a painting by Michelangelo.
f Sometimes there comes a special guest on the show.
g There is two cupboards in my room.
h We will go to a big park where is a roller coaster.

What's on the menu?

Grammar	so/nor do I; polite questions
Vocabulary	food; restaurants; apologies
Revision	reported questions

Introduction

1   Write the names of all the things in the photograph in the correct columns under their first letter.

B	C	E/F/G	K/L	O/T	P	S
bananas						

2   Work in a group. You are going to have a picnic together. Look at the food in the photograph and decide what you will take. Write a list on a piece of paper.

3   Pass your list around the class. Look at each group's list. Is anyone taking too much or too little? Decide which group has the healthiest picnic and which group has the most unhealthy picnic.

4   The words below are all names of food but the letters are in the wrong order. What are the words?

a   bruger   *burger*
b   iol
c   schip
d   eefcof
e   crame
f   sifh
g   hotgdo
h   maj
i   limk
j   rugas
k   cagabbe
l   apenut
m   tals
n   spachin
o   roommush

5   Work in a group. Divide the words into two lists.

Healthy foods: ....

Unhealthy foods: ....

⮯ Vocabulary spot

Adjective opposites

Many adjectives make their opposite with *un*, like *healthy/unhealthy*; for example: *able, grateful, happy, lucky, important, necessary, sure, true, usual.*

Make a note of any others you meet.

⮯ Corpus spot   *Have + food and drink*

Correct the mistakes in these PET students' sentences using the correct form of *have*.

a   We decided to take our dinner in a pizzeria.
b   What about drinking a cup of coffee together?
c   That restaurant is the best place to spend a romantic meal.
d   After the film we'll take a drink in the bar.
e   We went to the beach and took an ice cream there.

Listening

1 Look at the pictures. Which place would you prefer to eat in?

2 **3 26** Listen to five conversations and match them to the pictures.

a ☐

b ☐

c ☐

d ☐

e ☐

Language focus

So do I and *neither/nor do I*

1 Try to remember what the people said in conversations 1 and 2 and fill the spaces.

Conversation 1

Alison: So, let's go and eat. I'm hungry.

Daniel: So (**a**) *am I* . Where shall we go?

Alison: There are plenty of restaurants round here. Do you like Mexican food? Or what about Thai?

Beata: Can you tell me what Thai food tastes like? I've never tried it.

Daniel: No, nor (**b**) ....

Alison: Well, I love it. It's quite spicy.

Beata: Oh, is it? I'm not very keen on hot spices.

Daniel: No, neither (**c**) ....

Alison: OK. Er, so not Thai or Mexican. There's a good Italian restaurant further up the road.

Daniel: Oh, I love Italian food.

Beata: Really? So (**d**) ....

Alison: Right, let's go there then.

Conversation 2

Graham: Good evening. Table for two?

Greta: For three, please. We're meeting a friend.

Graham: Certainly. Inside or outside?

Greta: I don't like sitting outside.

Brigitte: Neither (**e**) .... , so inside, please.

Graham: Thank you. There's a table just there, near the window.

Brigitte: That'll be all right.

Greta: Yes, it's fine.

Graham: Would you like to order any drinks before your friend arrives?

Brigitte: Er, yes. I'm really thirsty. I can't wait.

Greta: Neither (**f**) ....

Brigitte: I'd like an orange juice, please.

Tina: Hi! Sorry I'm late. I got lost.

Brigitte: So (**g**) .... It's hard to find, isn't it? Never mind. Come and sit down. We're just getting some drinks.

Tina: I'll have a mineral water, I think.

Greta: So (**h**) ....

Graham: Still or sparkling?

Tina: Still, please.

Graham: Thank you. I'll bring the menu in a moment.

Greta: Thank you.

2 Listen again and check your answers.

Grammar spot   *So/nor/neither*

We use *So ..... I* or *Neither/Nor ..... I* when we agree with what someone says.

Agree with these sentences.

I'm a vegetarian.	*So am I.*
We're not hungry now.	*Nor am I.*
She often cooks Indian dishes.	*So do I.*
I don't like this ice cream.	*Neither do I.*
I've really enjoyed this evening.	
I've never tried this before.	
They enjoyed the main course.	
We didn't want a big meal.	
I'll come here again.	
I won't finish all this.	
He's going to give the waiter a tip.	
I can't eat any more.	
We'd like to come here again.	

◥ GF page 214

«Activity» Agreeing and disagreeing

Your teacher will give you a card. Tell other people what you think about the subject on your card. Respond to what they say about theirs. If you and another student both agree with each other's statements, swap cards and talk to someone new. Say things like these:

I love spicy food.	*So do I.*	or	*Really? I don't!*
I'm not afraid of spiders.	*Nor am I.*	or	*Really? I am!*
I've got a motorbike.	*So have I.*	or	*Really? I haven't!*

Polite question forms

1 Look at conversations 3, 4 and 5 and listen to them again. Underline what is different from what you hear.

Conversation 3

Bob: Now, what are we going to have?

Carl: What do you recommend?

Bob: They do home-made soup, that's usually very nice. And there's always a hot dish.

Carl: Oh, yeah. I see. 'Today's special', it says on the board. <u>What is that?</u>

Bob: It says underneath, look. Lancashire Hotpot.

Carl: It sounds a bit funny. Has it got meat in it?

Bob: It's made of lamb with potatoes and onions, cooked for a long time. A traditional dish from the north of England. Very good on a cold day like today.

Carl: Oh, right. I'm a vegetarian, so I won't have that.

Bob: OK. We'll ask for a menu. Would you like a starter?

Carl: No, thanks. I'll just have a main course. I don't want to fall asleep this afternoon.

Bob: No, neither do I. OK, now, where's the waiter?

Conversation 4

Gary: Yes?

Tammy: One burger, one milkshake, one vegeburger and one cappuccino, please.

Gary: What flavour milkshake?

Tammy: Oh, sorry. Rosie, what flavour milkshake does your friend want?

Rosie: Oh, she didn't say.

Tammy: Oh, typical.

Rosie: What flavours have you got?

Gary: Chocolate, strawberry, banana and vanilla.

Rosie: She'd like strawberry, I think.

Gary: OK. Now do you want to eat in or take away?

Tammy: Take away. Oh, and one portion of chips.

Gary: OK. That's thirteen pounds twenty.

Tammy: Here you are.

Gary: Enjoy your meal.

Rosie: Thank you.

Conversation 5

Nigel: Excuse me!

Marco: Yes? Can I help you?

Nigel: I hope so. You see, we ordered a tuna salad and a baked potato with cheese fifteen minutes ago! Is there a problem?

Marco: I'm sorry, we are very busy, as you see.

Nigel: But we said we were in a hurry and the waitress promised to be quick.

Laura: Are we going to get our food soon? We have to catch a train at one fifty-five.

Marco: OK. What did your waitress look like?

Nigel: Oh, here she comes now.

Anna: I'm ever so sorry. Someone else took your order by mistake.

Nigel: All right. Thank you. Now we can eat.

Laura: This potato isn't properly cooked. Part of it is almost raw!

Nigel: Oh, no. Well, that's it. I'm going to see the manager.

🔄 Grammar spot   Polite question forms

Write the questions you underlined in Conversations 3, 4 and 5. Listen again and write down the questions you heard.

What is that? ⟶ *Can you explain what that is?*

What kind of questions use *if* when they are reported?

---

2 You want to ask a tour guide some questions. Ask politely, using the words in the box below, adding *if* when necessary. Write down your polite questions.

> Can you tell me … ?
> Can you remember … ?
> Do you know … ?
> I'd like to know ….
> Can you find out … ?

a How much does a burger cost?
  Can you tell me how much a burger costs?

b Is the service included?
  Do you know if the service is included?

c Where is the toilet?

d Do they serve vegetarian dishes?

e What flavour ice cream have they got?

f Can we sit outside?

g When does this café close?

h What is the name of this dish?

↘ GF page 214

《Pronunciation》

1 **3 27** Listen to the recording. Underline the sound /ə/. Listen again and repeat.

a cup of coffee

2 **3 28** Now do the same with these sentences. Listen again and repeat.

a glass of milk and some pieces of cake
some ice cream but no burgers

3 **3 29** Work with a partner. Underline the sound /ə/ in these sentences. Then listen to the recording and check what you underlined. Listen again and repeat.

It's made of eggs and sugar.
He wants a cup of tea and a sandwich.
I'd like a slice of meat and some potatoes.
You can have a bag of crisps but not a packet of biscuits.
They've got fish and chips and meat and rice but no bread and cheese.

《Activity》 Eating out

1 Work in a small group.
   Plan a short menu with your group and write it out. Include a variety of dishes that you like.

2 You are a group of tourists visiting a restaurant. Each person must politely ask the waiter to explain something on the menu, then order a meal.

3 Take turns to be the waiter.
   When you are the waiter, you take a customer's order and answer his/her questions.
   One of the dishes he/she orders is not available. Apologise.

Asking politely for information	Ordering food	Apologising
Can you tell me	I'll have	I'm so sorry, but
Can you explain	Can I have	I do apologise, but
I'd like to know	I'd like	

WHAT'S ON THE MENU?   **189**

Exam folder 29

Reading Part 4

In this part of the exam, you read a text and answer five questions about it by choosing A, B, C or D.

CHECK!

a Do all the questions ask about one part of the text?

b Do you need to read all of the text carefully?

Read the text and questions below.
For each question, circle the letter next to the correct answer – **A**, **B**, **C** or **D**.

I've read and heard so many good reports of the Thai restaurant *The Golden Spoon* that I decided to try it myself. The menu appeared to be all in Thai but then we noticed the English translations. When the waitress realised it was our first visit, she came across as she knew it would take us a long time to choose. In the end we ordered what she recommended because we didn't know where to start – there was so much choice. Because it was early on a Monday evening (they are open from midday to midnight without a day off), it wasn't too busy but it got busier later and in fact they recommend that you book, even on Mondays.

The Golden Spoon offers a wide range of extremely tasty food, mostly quite spicy, but that was fine with me. Even the vegetarian among us had plenty of choice. Everything was cooked quickly and perfectly. The first course looked rather small, but there were six more courses to follow and we couldn't finish all of them.

The entrance to the restaurant is rather dark and the inside isn't much better. The Thai family who run it (the father and grandfather do all the cooking) have been there since 1975 and haven't really changed it since then. There are some Thai paintings on the wall which are probably rather beautiful but they are very dusty so it's difficult to tell. But none of that is important because I didn't go there to look at the walls. What I did look at was our meal being prepared in the kitchen, which is in one corner of the restaurant, and that was a wonderful sight. The meal cost more than I had expected but was worth it.

1 What is the writer trying to do?
 A suggest changes a restaurant could make
 B recommend the food in a restaurant
 C describe what he ate in a restaurant
 D complain about the service in a restaurant

2 What does the writer say about the waitress?
 A It was impossible for her to serve so many customers.
 B It was difficult to choose from the menu without her help.
 C She translated the menu from Thai for them.
 D She took a long time to take their order.

3 What did the writer think of the food?
 A It was too spicy for him.
 B There weren't enough vegetarian dishes.
 C There was too much of it.
 D It was not cooked properly.

4 What did the writer particularly like about the restaurant?
 A the paintings on the walls
 B the entrance
 C the prices
 D the position of the kitchen

5 Which of the following is an advertisement for the restaurant?

A

THE GOLDEN SPOON

Run by the same Thai family for more
than 25 years.

Recommended in local guidebooks.

Booking advised. Open 12–12 every day.

C

THE GOLDEN SPOON

New chef from Bangkok Restaurant.
Meals available to eat in the restaurant
every day from 12–12 or take away.

B

THE GOLDEN SPOON

Local restaurant recently improved –
more space available.

Run by same Thai family since 1975.

Book early so you are not disappointed.

Open 12–12 every day.

D

THE GOLDEN SPOON

Compare our prices with other Thai
restaurants and you will be pleasantly
surprised.

Open every day except Monday from 12–12.

Speaking Part 3

In this part of the exam, you and your partner are each given a photograph of a similar topic. You take turns to tell the examiner about your photograph.

1 Look at page 204. Work with a partner. Choose one photograph each.
Before you talk to your partner, think about what you will say.

What kind of restaurant is it?
What are the people doing?
What are they wearing?
Are the people enjoying themselves?
What else can you see?

2 Describe your photograph to your partner.

Exam Advice

Describe the people, what they are doing and the place.

Speaking Part 4

In this part of the exam, you and your partner have a discussion about the topic of the photographs in Part 3.

1 Work with a partner. Can you remember ways of giving your opinion?
Can you remember ways of agreeing and disagreeing?

2 Discuss these questions with your partner.

Which of the restaurants in Speaking Part 3 would you like to eat in?
Do you often go to restaurants?
What kind of restaurant is your favourite?
Do you prefer to sit down to a three-course meal or eat fast food?

Exam Advice

If you have no opinions on the subject, invent some!

Blue for a boy, pink for a girl?

Grammar	*hardly; before/after + -ing*
Vocabulary	informal language; saying goodbye
Revision	tenses/vocabulary in Units 1–29

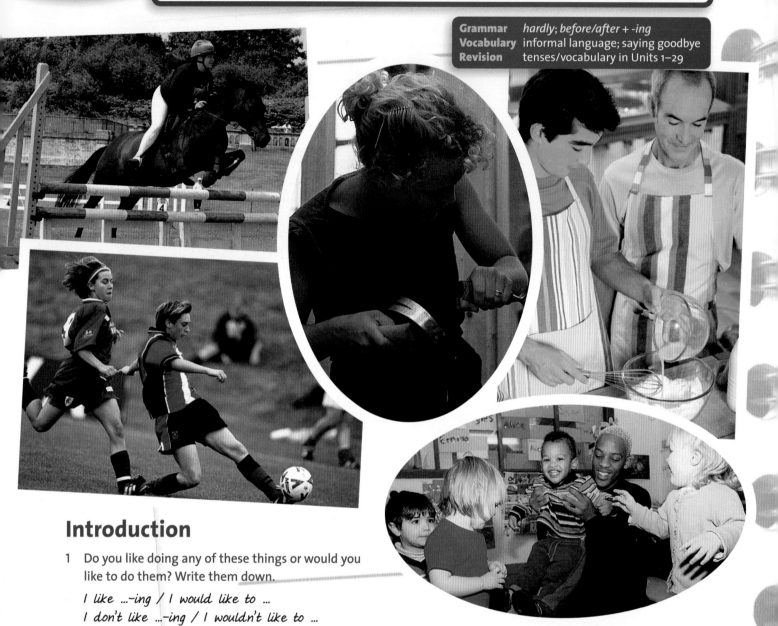

Introduction

1   Do you like doing any of these things or would you like to do them? Write them down.

I like ...-ing / I would like to ...
I don't like ...-ing / I wouldn't like to ...

2   What are your three favourite school subjects?

3   Do you agree with any of the following statements? Look at page 125 if you need to.

   a   Men and women should earn the same salary for the same job.
   b   Boys find it easier than girls to use computers.
   c   Boys and girls should study the same subjects at school.
   d   Boys are physically stronger than girls.
   e   In a government, there should be the same number of men and women.
   f   A girl can ask a boy to go out with her.
   g   Mixed football teams are a good idea.
   h   Girls find it easier than boys to talk about their feelings.
   i   Girls study harder than boys.
   j   Boys are braver than girls.

⤵ Corpus spot

Like and *would like*

Some of these sentences written by PET students are correct. Put a tick (✓) against them. Correct the mistakes in the other sentences.

   a   I like to hear from you soon.
   b   You will have a great time because you like visiting museums.
   c   I like you to join me and my friends on Saturday.
   d   I asked her what she would like to do on Sunday.
   e   Would you like go to the cinema with me?
   f   I hope you like cycling as much as I do.

Reading and Language focus

Revision of tenses

1 Here are two diaries. Work in pairs. Student A reads Monday from Jake's diary (A) and Student B reads Monday from Lucy's diary (F). Choose the correct verbs. Compare your answers to these questions.

What does Jake think about Lucy?

What does Lucy think about Jake?

2 Student A: Read what Jake wrote in his diary on Tuesday, Wednesday, Thursday and Friday. They are in the wrong order. Put them in order and write the day at the top. Put the verbs in brackets into the correct form.

Student B: Read what Lucy wrote in her diary on Tuesday, Wednesday, Thursday and Friday. They are in the wrong order. Put them in order and write the day at the top. Put the verbs in brackets into the correct form.

A Monday

I'm ordinary, I suppose – nothing special. Most important of all, not special enough for Lucy. Lucy is great – really pretty and always smiling. In class I sit / am sitting as close to her as I can but she never speaks / is speaking to me. I will sit there until she notices / will notice me. This term I am asking / am going to ask Lucy to go out with me, but I expect she says / will say no. I'm pleased I chose / was chosen for the school football team. I'm looking forward to play / playing tomorrow.

B ....

This morning after coming out of the English class, I .... (look) for Lucy when I .... (see) her with Gary Smart. He was really close to her and he .... (have) his hand on her arm, so I was right. I'm sure they're going out together. I just .... (run) out of the building.

C ....

What a surprise! Lucy and her mate, Sophie, ... (come) to watch tonight's game! I .... (score) a goal but Lucy hardly noticed me. I think she was just there to see Gary Smart. I .... (chat) to Lucy and Sophie after the match. I still want .... (ask) her to go out with me but I'm afraid of .... (say) the wrong thing, so maybe I .... (write) her a note instead.

D ....

Changed my mind about writing to Lucy. I .... (see) her with her friends this morning, and they all .... (laugh) when I went past. I must be one big joke to them. I heard Gary Smart talking about Lucy while we .... (change) for football training. Lots of girls .... (like) him. I can't see why myself – unless muscles, cool clothes and a great haircut are your thing.

E ....

Great. She's going out with Gary Smart, but she .... (want) me to do her homework for her. I must be the class idiot. But perhaps if she .... (think) I'm clever, she .... (ask) me for help again and we can become friends.

F Monday

I'm fed up with boys. Honestly, when they whistle / will whistle at you, they think / are thinking they're really cool but they're just embarrassing. The only nice boy in our class is Jake, but I hardly know him. I always am smiling / smile at him when I will see / see him but I'm worried that he isn't liking / doesn't like me. Anyway, my mate, Sophie, told me that Jake picked / was picked for the school football team last week, so maybe I go / 'll go and support the team tomorrow.

G ....

Finally found the courage to ask Jake about the maths homework. He .... (not seem) too pleased but he agreed .... (help) me. We .... (meet) in the library on Monday night so I'll ask Sophie to do my hair and make-up.

H ....

I'm sorry we laughed at Jake yesterday. If I .... (ask) him for his help with the maths homework, I .... (have) a chance to spend more time with him. I .... (bump) into Gary Smart. He .... (just have) a swim and he looked really pleased with himself. He even .... (put) his hand on my arm. He's really not my type.

I ....

Sophie and I .... (watch) Jake play football tonight and he .... (score) a goal. Before going home we .... (chat) to him. He said he .... (never play) for the team before. I told Sophie I might ask Jake to go out with me. But what .... (do) if he .... (not be) interested in .... (go) out with me? I .... (be) so embarrassed.

J ....

I .... (talk) about Jake with Sophie and the others today at school when he .... (walk) past. We all started .... (laugh) because we were embarrassed. I hope Jake isn't mad with me.

---

3 Student A: Compare with other students who read Jake's diary. Do you have the same order?

Student B: Compare with other students who read Lucy's diary. Do you have the same order?

4 Work in pairs again.

A: Ask your partner the Student A questions below.

B: Ask your partner the Student B questions below.

a Student A: Why did Lucy go to watch the football match?

b Student B: Why did Jake think Lucy was at the football match?

c Student B: Why did Jake decide to write a note?

d Student A: Why was Lucy worried about asking Jake to go out with her?

e Student A: Why were the girls laughing?

f Student B: What did Jake think when he heard the girls laughing?

g Student B: What did Jake think about Lucy and Gary Smart?

h Student A: What did Lucy think of Gary Smart?

i Student A: Why did Lucy ask Jake for help with her maths?

j Student B: Why wasn't Jake pleased when Lucy asked for help with her maths?

5 **3 30** Listen to Jake and Lucy reading their diaries. Did you have the correct order? Did you write the correct verbs?

6 **3 31** What will Jake and Lucy do next? Listen to what they wrote next and answer these questions.

a Why was Lucy confused at first when she met Jake in the library?

b Why did Jake write Lucy a note instead of asking her to go out with him?

c Where did Lucy find the note?

d How did Lucy feel when she read the note?

e Was the bowling trip successful?

f Do you think this is a true story?

⬎ Vocabulary spot

Some words are used mainly by young people (or older people in very informal conversations).
Match these words from the diaries on the left with their meanings on the right. Can you find any more words like these?

mad	guy		good	clever
smart	mate		friend	angry
cool	my type		boy/man	
			the kind of boy/girl I like	

Hardly

⬎ Grammar spot   *Hardly*

Hardly + verb
Look at these sentences.
*I **hardly** know Jake.*   *She **hardly** noticed me.*
Does *hardly* go before or after the verb?

Hardly + noun
Look at these sentences.
*We did **hardly any** maths.*   ***Hardly anybody** likes Jake.*
Which words go after *hardly*?

1 Rewrite the underlined words using *hardly*.

a I hadn't seen Monica for ten years and <u>it was difficult for me to recognise her</u>. *I hardly recognised her.*

b Now my friend is at university <u>I don't see her very often</u> during term time.

c There was a noisy party next door last night so <u>I slept very little.</u>

d My cousin has hurt her foot so <u>she only danced once or twice</u> at the disco.

e I was only four when my family moved from Scotland so <u>I only just remember it.</u>

2 Now complete the sentences below using *hardly*. Add any other words you need.

a The weather was fine nearly every day last week – there was *hardly any*................... rain.

b .... came to my party because lots of my friends were busy that day.

c I bought a very expensive pair of trainers yesterday so I have .... money left now.

d .... in Britain speaks Japanese.

e The sale was a great success – at the end there was .... left.

f It's difficult travelling on Sundays because there are .... buses.

3 Write some sentences using *hardly*.

a I hardly ever …

b I have hardly any …

c Hardly anyone I know …

⬎ GF page 214

Before and *after -ing*

> ### ⬇ Grammar spot — *Before* and *after -ing*
>
> Here are some sentences from the diaries.
> *Before **going** home, we chatted to Jake.*
> *After **coming** out of the English class, I looked for Lucy.*
> What do you notice about the verbs which follow *after* and *before*?

1 Rewrite these sentences using *before* or *after*.

  a Lucy heard that Jake was playing in the match, then she went to watch it.
    After *hearing that Jake was playing in the match, Lucy went to watch it.*

  b Jake played in the match, then he talked to Lucy. After ....

  c Lucy asked Jake for help with her maths, then she met him in the library. Before ....

  d Jake saw Lucy with Gary, then he felt sad. After ....

  e Lucy asked Sophie to do her hair, then she went out with Jake. Before ....

  f Jake met Lucy in the library, then he decided to write her a letter. After ....

  g Lucy got a letter from Jake, then she told him she liked him. After ....

2 Write three true sentences about yourself using *before* or *after*. Use these ideas if you wish.

  go to cinema in the evening / eat dinner
  I go to the cinema in the evening after eating dinner.
  have breakfast / clean teeth
  do homework / watch TV
  set alarm / get into bed
  check bank account / buy new clothes

≪Activity≫ After doing that . . .

Your teacher will give you a set of cards. Use the cards to practise *before* and *after doing* ... + the past simple.

↘ GF page 214

≪Pronunciation≫

Your teacher will give you a card with some words on it. Listen to the words your teacher reads out. Do they have the same vowel sound as any of the words on your card?

≪Activity≫ Different topics

Work in teams. Your teacher will hold up two cards – one has a letter on it, e.g. P, and the other card has an area of vocabulary, e.g. food. Your team must quickly write down as many food words as possible beginning with P. You only get a point if the words are spelled correctly. You get two points if you have a word that no other team has.

Saying goodbye

Look at these different ways of saying goodbye (1–7) and match them to the situations (a–g).

  1 Goodbye.
  2 See you later.
  3 Hope to see you again.
  4 Thank you for everything.
  5 See you soon.
  6 I've enjoyed meeting you.
  7 Have a good journey.

  a When you're not sure if you'll see someone again.
  b When you'll see someone again the same day.
  c When you say goodbye to someone you've only just met.
  d When someone is setting off on a trip.
  e When you have been someone's guest or they have helped you a lot.
  f When you expect to see someone again.
  g Any time!

Exam folder 30

In this part of the exam, you listen to a conversation between two people and decide whether six sentences are correct or incorrect. You hear the recording twice.

Listening Part 4

3 32

Look at the six sentences for this part.
You will hear a conversation between a boy, Andy, and a girl, Sarah, about dancing.
Decide if each sentence is correct or incorrect.
If it is correct, put a tick (✓) in the box under **A** for
YES. If it is not correct, put a tick (✓) in the box under **B** for **NO**.

CHECK!
a How many speakers are there?
b What should you do before you listen?

	A YES	B NO
1 Andy is doing dancing classes instead of computer classes.	☐	☐
2 Andy has told few people about his love of dancing.	☐	☐
3 Sarah thinks Andy should tell his friends about his dancing.	☐	☐
4 Andy's aunt persuaded him to learn to dance.	☐	☐
5 Andy feels happier when there are other boys in his dancing class.	☐	☐
6 Sarah agrees with Andy's parents about his plans for the future.	☐	☐

Speaking Part 3

In this part of the exam, you and your partner are each given a photograph of a similar topic. You take turns to tell the examiner about your photograph.

Look at the two photographs on page 205. Work with a partner. One of you will describe photograph A and the other will describe photograph B. Take turns to tell each other about your photograph.

CHECK!
a What will you talk about?
b What will you say if you don't know the English word for something?
c How long will you try to speak for?

Exam Advice

Don't worry if you don't know what is happening in the photograph. Just describe what you can see.

Speaking Part 4

Work with a partner and discuss these questions.

a Which kind of dancing would you prefer to watch?
b Do you like dancing?
c Do you think it is important to learn to dance?
d Do boys learn to dance in your country? What kind of dancing?
e Why do you think fewer boys enjoy dancing than girls?
f Do you think boys should be encouraged to learn to dance?
g What other activities do you think boys should be encouraged to do?
h What activities should girls be encouraged to do?

In this part of the exam, you and your partner have a discussion about the topic of the photographs in Part 3.

CHECK!
a Who will you speak to?
b What will you do if you have no opinions?
c How long will you speak for?

Exam Advice

Speak clearly so the other student can understand you.

Writing folder

Writing Part 1

In this part of the exam, you are given a sentence. You have to complete a second sentence so that it means the same as the first.

- Here are some sentences about going to a restaurant.
- For each question, complete the second sentence so that it means the same as the first. **Use no more than three words.**
- Write only the missing words.

  Example: Last week all the students in my class went to a restaurant together.

  Last week _everyone_ in my class went to a restaurant together.

1 The restaurant is usually crowded because it's so good.

It's usually crowded because it's .... good restaurant.

2 It's less crowded on weekdays.

It isn't .... on weekdays.

3 Before choosing our food, we asked the waiter's advice.

We asked the waiter's advice, then .... our food.

4 The waiter recommended a fish dish.

The waiter said, 'If I .... you, I'd have the fish dish.'

5 The service charge wasn't included in the bill.

The bill .... the service charge.

Writing Part 2

In this part of the exam, you have to write a note, email, card or postcard in 35–45 words. There are three points which you have to write about.

You and some friends are planning to go to the cinema. Write a note to an English friend called Jerry.

In your note, you should

- tell him which film you are going to see
- invite him to come with you
- say when and where you are meeting your friends

Write 35–45 words.

Writing Part 3

In this part of the exam, you have to write a letter or a story in about 100 words. There are two questions to choose from.

- This is part of a letter you receive from an English friend.

  I always spend my holidays with my family in the mountains. But this year my friend has invited me to go to the seaside with her family. What do you think I should do?

- Now write a letter to your friend giving your advice.
- Write your **letter** in about 100 words.

OR

- Your English teacher has asked you to write a story.
- Your story must begin with this sentence:

  When we set out, the sky was blue and the sun was shining.

- Write your **story** in about 100 words.

Units 25–30 Revision

Speaking

1 Work with a partner. Look at these sentences. Say if each sentence is true for you and give your partner some extra information.

a Our town has good shops.
Yes, I agree. There are two shopping centres and a market.
OR *No, I don't agree. In my opinion, that's not true because most of the shops sell the same things.*

b I find adverts on TV annoying.

c I enjoy travelling.

d I saw a famous person in the street once.

e I look for bargains when I go shopping.

f I like eating food from other countries.

g It's important for families to eat together.

h I use the internet for shopping.

Vocabulary

2 Think about the meaning of these words. Mark the odd one out in each list.

a chicken (tuna) sausage lamb beef

b cucumber peanut lettuce tomato celery

c fork dessert knife plate cup

d biscuit cake chocolate jam egg

e pepper pear strawberry grape banana

f lemonade juice glass cola water

g cream bread cheese milk butter

h cabbage spinach onion orange carrot

Grammar

3 A journalist interviewed a famous football manager. Later, the journalist met her friend and told her about the interview. Report what she said to her friend.

a What do you like best about your job?
I asked him *what he liked best about his job.*

b Did you always want to be a football manager?
I wanted to know *if he had always wanted to be a football manager.*

c When did you decide to be a football manager?
I wanted to know ....

d What other jobs have you done?
I asked him ....

e Will you always work as a football manager?
I asked him ....

f Which countries have you visited?
I wanted to know ....

g Do you work hard?
I asked him ....

h How much money do you earn?
I wanted to know ....

i Do you have any hobbies?
I asked him ....

j What will happen to your job if the team loses again?
I asked him ....

4 Here are the manager's answers. Use the words in the box to complete the spaces.

| all enough every hardly if if ~~too many~~ |
| too many too much when unless |

a There are *too many* things to tell you.

b No, but .... my brothers are teachers and I wanted to do something different.

c I was working indoors and I was spending .... time sitting at a desk.

d I've done .... jobs to tell you about them all.

e .... I'm 50, I'll look for a quieter job.

f There are .... any countries that I haven't visited.

g I work .... day of the week.

h Well, I'll never be a millionaire .... I win the lottery.

i I don't have .... time for hobbies.

j .... the team wins their next match, I'll continue working here. .... they don't win, I'll look for a new club.

Grammar

5 Read this email and put the verbs in brackets into the correct tense.

Dear Rosalyn

We're staying on a campsite which is quite nice but if we come here again we **(a)** _will stay_ (stay) at the campsite in the town. If we **(b)** .... (have) a car it would be better. If I **(c)** .... (be) rich, I **(d)** .... (stay) at a luxury hotel! It rained this morning but the weather's better now. If it **(e)** .... (be) fine this evening, we **(f)** .... (have) a barbecue. Unless it rains tomorrow, we **(g)** .... (catch) the bus to the beach which has wonderful white sand. If the campsite **(h)** .... (be) nearer the coast, we **(i)** .... (go) there every day.

The area is famous for silk clothes. If we **(j)** .... (visit) a market, I **(k)** .... (buy) you a silk scarf. There are no other English people on the campsite. If we **(l)** .... (speak) the language, it **(m)** .... (be) easier to make friends. I've taken lots of photos. When I **(n)** .... (get) home, I **(o)** .... (show) them to you.

See you soon.
Lewis

Vocabulary

6 Read these conversations and use the words in the box to complete the spaces.

| afford | bring | change | fit | fitting | ~~help~~ | matches | receipt | refund | size | stock | store | try |

Assistant 1: Can I **(a)** _help_ .... you?
Girl: Oh, yes please. Where are the long skirts?
Assistant 1: Over there.
Girl: I can't **(b)** .... those. Have you got any cheaper ones?
Assistant 1: Most of the cheaper ones are in our other **(c)** .... in the shopping mall, but we have a few here. What **(d)** .... are you?
Girl: I'm not sure. Can I **(e)** .... these on? A black one and a red one?
Assistant 1: Certainly. The **(f)** .... room is over there.
Girl: Thanks.

Girl: This red skirt **(g)** .... my jacket but it doesn't **(h)** ....
Have you got a smaller one?
Assistant 2: Sorry. We only have a few of those in **(i)** ....
Girl: Oh, well, I'll take the black one then. Can I **(j)** .... it back if I **(k)** .... my mind?
Assistant 2: Of course. You can have a **(l)** .... if you keep the **(m)** ....

Common mistakes

7 This note contains fourteen mistakes which are often made by PET students. Can you find and correct all of them?

Dear Lizzie,

Thanks for the beatiful scarf. Its perfect. I had a great birthday with Emily an Paul. On lunchtime we've tried the Mexican restorant in the shoping mall. Have you ever gone their? The food were delicios but it was terrible crowded.

I look forward to hear from you.

friendly,

Cornelia

Visual materials

Unit 4, Activity: Diary

Student A

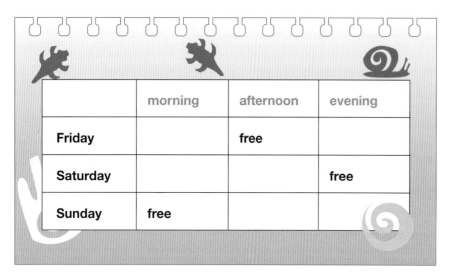

	morning	afternoon	evening
Friday		free	
Saturday			free
Sunday	free		

Unit 14, Activity: *Used to*

Student A

Unit 4, Activity: Diary

Student B

	morning	afternoon	evening
Friday			free
Saturday	free		free
Sunday			

Unit 14, Activity: *Used to*

Student B

How earth-friendly are you?

1 When you travel to school or work, you

A are driven there by someone else who then returns home. ○

B drive yourself. ○

C walk or ride a bicycle. ○

D use public transport. ○

2 At home, you

A always have the central heating or air conditioning on in the whole house. ○

B only heat or cool the rooms you are using. ○

C only use air conditioning on unusually hot days. ○

D put on an extra pullover before you turn up the heating. ○

3 When you go shopping, you

A usually buy things which are produced locally. ○

B often ask yourself if you really need something before you buy it. ○

C buy the cheapest things and don't worry about how and where they were made. ○

D buy what you like when you like. ○

4 The main reason for having a job is

A to save money for the future. ○

B to do something useful in society. ○

C to make use of your education and training. ○

D to earn money and buy things you want. ○

5 You get most of your food from

A your own garden. ○

B a local producer. ○

C a supermarket. ○

D a fast food restaurant. ○

6 You choose your food because it is

A produced by people who take care of the environment. ○

B good for your health. ○

C cheap and tasty. ○

D quick and convenient. ○

7 You normally eat because

A you are hungry. ○

B you want to reward yourself. ○

C it's a mealtime. ○

D you feel bored. ○

8 You choose leisure activities

A that require a lot of special equipment and clothes. ○

B you can do at or near your home. ○

C that do not require any effort. ○

D to keep fit. ○

9 For you, the people who really matter

A are your family. ○

B live near you. ○

C are you and your best friend. ○

D can be any human beings. ○

10 You feel that the future of the earth

A is the responsibility of governments. ○

B is the responsibility of us all. ○

C is not something one individual can help to change. ○

D is not something to worry about. ○

Key to questionnaire

1 A0 B1 C4 D3   2 A0 B3 C3 D4   3 A3 B3 C1 D0   4 A3 B4 C1 D1   5 A4 B3 C1 D0

6 A4 B3 C2 D1   7 A4 B2 C3 D0   8 A1 B4 C4 D4   9 A3 B3 C1 D4   10 A2 B4 C1 D0

Grammar folder

Unit 1

Present simple

All verbs except *to be*	
+	I/you/we/they **like** chocolate. He/she/it **likes** chocolate.
–	I/you/we/they **do not (don't) like** chocolate. He/she/it **does not (doesn't) like** chocolate.
?	**Do** I/you/we/they **like** chocolate? **Does** he/she/it **like** chocolate?

to be	
+	I **am ('m)** happy. You/we/they **are ('re)** happy. He/she/it **is ('s)** happy.
–	I **am ('m) not** happy. You /we/they **are not (aren't)** happy. He/she/it **is not (isn't)** happy.
?	**Am** I happy? **Are** you/we/they happy? **Is** he/she/it happy?

Frequency adverbs

always	usually	often	sometimes	never

- ... go **before** a one-word verb:
  *I **always eat** chocolate after lunch.*
- ... go **before** the second word of a two-word verb:
  *You **don't always eat** chocolate after lunch.*
- ... go **after** the verb *to be*:
  *He **is always** happy.*

We use the present simple with frequency adverbs.

Unit 2

like, enjoy, want, would like

- We use a **noun** or **-ing** after *like* and *enjoy*:
  *I **like/enjoy** tennis.*
  *I **like/enjoy playing** tennis.*
- We use a **noun** or *to* after *want* and *would like*:
  *I **want / would ('d) like** a new racket.*
  *I **want / would ('d) like to buy** a new racket.*

have got

We do not use *do* for questions and negatives with *have got*.

+	I/you/we/they **have ('ve) got** blue eyes. He/she/it **has ('s) got** blue eyes.
–	I/you /we/they **have not (haven't) got** blue eyes. He/she/it **has not (hasn't) got** blue eyes.
?	**Have** I/you/we/they **got** blue eyes? **Has** he/she/it **got** blue eyes?

to be + *a* + occupation

*I'm/you're/he's etc. **a** student/teacher etc.*

to be + adjective

I'm/you're/he's etc. tall/short/thin etc.

Unit 3

Present continuous

+	I **am ('m)** working. You/we/they **are ('re)** working. He/she/it **is ('s)** working.
–	I **am ('m) not** working. You /we/they **are not (aren't)** working. He/she/it **is not (isn't)** working.
?	**Am** I working? **Are** you/we/they working? **Is** he/she/it working?

Spelling the *-ing* form

- Verbs ending in one vowel + one consonant:
  double the consonant and add *ing* (e.g. *put* → *putting*)
  [exception: *deliver* → *delivering*]
- Verbs ending in two or more consonants or *y*:
  add *ing* (e.g. *paint* → *painting* or *tidy* → *tidying*)
- Verbs ending in *e*:
  drop *e* and add *ing* (e.g. *prepare* → *preparing*)
  ! Remember **ski** → **skiing**

State verbs

... are not usually used in continuous tenses. Examples of state verbs are:
believe, hate, know, like, love, prefer, think (=believe), **understand, want**

Unit 4

Prepositions of time

- **No preposition before**
  today, tomorrow, tonight, yesterday (morning, evening etc.)
  this/next/last (afternoon, week, month, year)

at	9.15, midnight, etc. the weekend, the end of the day, the moment
in	January, February, March, April, May, June, July, August, September, October, November, December the spring, the summer, the autumn, the winter 1848, 1963, 2010 *etc.*
on	Monday, Tuesday, Wednesday, Thursday, Friday, Saturday, Sunday 1st August, 30th September, etc.

Future plans

We use the *present continuous*:
I'm meeting Sally on Wednesday.
They're arriving next week.
We're not using the car at the weekend.
He's leaving tomorrow morning.

Unit 5

need + noun

+	I/you/we/they **need** a drink. He/she/it **needs** a drink.
–	I/you/we/they **don't need** any food. He/she/it **doesn't need** any food.
?	**Do** I/you/we/they **need** a ticket? **Does** he/she/it **need** a ticket?

need + verb

+	I/you/we/they **need** to go out. He/she/it **needs** to go out.
–	I/you/we/they **don't need** to go out. He/she/it **doesn't need** to go out. OR I/you/he/she/it/we/they **needn't** go out.
?	**Do** I/you/we/they **need** to go out? **Does** he/she/it **need** to go out?

Countable/uncountable nouns

Use **a/an, one/two/three** etc., **a lot of, a few, a couple of, several, (not) many** + *countable* nouns (singular or plural).

Use **a lot of, a little, (not) much, a bottle/piece of** etc. + *uncountable* nouns (singular only).

Unit 6

Adjectives ending in -ing and -ed

-ing adjectives describe a thing/person which gives you a feeling:
*This is an **amusing** film.*
*He was an **interesting** teacher.*
*The lessons were **interesting**.*

-ed adjectives describe the person who has the feeling:
*A **tired** student needs a holiday.*
*The girls were **interested** in the story.*

Past simple
Regular verbs

+	I/he/she/it/you/we/they **wanted** a bike.
–	I/he/she/it/you/we/they **did not (didn't) want** a bike.
?	**Did** I/he/she/it/you/we/they **want** a bike?

Spelling

- Verbs ending in *e* (e.g. *arrive*):
  add *d* (*arrived*).
- Verbs ending in one consonant (e.g. *stop*):
  double the consonant and add *ed* (e.g. *stopped*).
- Verbs ending in consonant + *y* (e.g. *study*):
  change *y* to *i* and add *ed* (e.g. *studied*).
- Verbs ending in two or more consonants (e.g. *help*) or
  vowel + *y* (e.g. *stay*):
  add *ed* (e.g. *helped, stayed*).

Irregular verbs
These verbs have different forms, e.g.
buy → *bought, go* → *went, make* → *made*
(See irregular verb list on page 216.)

+	I/he/she/it/you/we/they **bought** a bike.
–	I/he/she/it/you/we/they **did not (didn't) buy** a bike.
?	**Did** I/he/she/it/you/we/they **buy** a bike?

to be

+	I/he/she/it **was** there. You/we/they **were** there.
–	I/he/she/it **was not (wasn't)** there. You/we/they **were not (weren't)** there.
?	**Was** I/he/she/it there? **Were** you/we/they there?

Unit 7

Prepositions of place

inside   outside   opposite   near   under
in   next to   in front of   between   by
in the corner of   behind   beside

Prepositions of movement

up   down   across   off   along   around
through   over

Comparative adjectives
Regular adjectives
- One-syllable adjective:
  add *er* (e.g. *kind* → *kinder*)
- One-syllable adjective ending in *e*:
  add *r* (e.g. *nice* → *nicer*)
- One-syllable adjective ending in vowel + consonant:
  double consonant and add *er* (e.g. *hot* → *hotter*)
- Adjective ending in consonant+*y*:
  change *y* to *i* and add *er* (e.g. *funny* → *funnier*)
- Adjective with more than one syllable:
  more + adjective (e.g. *polite* → *more polite, confident* → *more confident*)

Irregular adjectives
good → better   bad → worse

Unit 8

Present perfect

has/have + past participle

+	I/you/we/they **have ('ve) eaten** the chocolate. He/she/it **has ('s) eaten** the chocolate.
–	I/you /we/they **have not (haven't) eaten** the chocolate. He/she/it **has not (hasn't) eaten** the chocolate.
?	**Have** I/you/we/they **eaten** the chocolate? **Has** he/she/it **eaten** the chocolate?

Past participle
Regular verbs

past participle = past simple, e.g.

like → *liked, liked*   *play* → *played, played*

Irregular verbs

Most have a different form for past participle and past simple:

do → *did, done*   *write* → *wrote, written*

know → *knew, known*

But for some irregular verbs, past participle and past simple are the same:

make → *made, made*   *buy* → *bought, bought*

just, already

… go before the past participle:

*We've **just bought** a box of chocolates.*

*I've **already opened** it.*

yet

… goes at the end of a negative sentence:

*We haven't eaten them all **yet**.*

Unit 9

Short answers

Present simple

*Do I/you/we/they/the students **like** chocolate?*
   *Yes, I/you/we/they **do**.*
   *No, I/you/we/they **don't**.*
*Does he/she/it/the class **like** chocolate?*
   *Yes, he/she/it **does**.*
   *No, he/she/it **doesn't**.*

Present continuous

*Am I **working** hard?*
   *Yes, you **are**.*
   *No, you **aren't**.*
*Are you **working** hard?*
   *Yes, I **am**.*
   *No, I'm **not**.*
*Is he/she/it/the class **working** hard?*
   *Yes, he/she/it **is**.*
   *No, he/she/it **isn't**.*
*Are we/they/the students **working** hard?*
   *Yes, you/they **are**.*
   *No, you/they **aren't**.*

Past simple

*Did I/you/he/she/it/we/they/the students/the class **work** hard?*
   *Yes, I/you/he/she/it/we/they **did**.*
   *No, I/you/he/she/it/we/they **didn't**.*

Present perfect

*Have I/you/we/they/the students **eaten** the chocolate?*
   *Yes, I/you/he/she/it/we/they **have**.*
   *No, I/you/he/she/it/we/they **haven't**.*
*Has he/she/it/the class **eaten** the chocolate?*
   *Yes, he/she/it **has**.*
   *No, he/she/it **hasn't**.*

Unit 10

Present perfect and past simple

Present perfect NOT past simple

- Past actions/events when the result is interesting now, but the exact time of the event is not important:
  She's/has bought some chocolate. [She's got some now.]
  They've/have eaten the chocolate. [There's no chocolate now.]
- A period of time beginning in the past and continuing to now:
  You've/have worked very hard. [You can take a break now.]
- Questions asking **How long?**
  *How long **have you known** Maria?*
- With **for** + length of time to now:
  *I've **known** her **for** two months.*
- With **since** + exact time before now:
  *I've **known** her **since** April.*
- Questions with **ever**:
  ***Have** you **ever played** basketball?*

Past simple NOT present perfect

- Actions/events at a particular time in the past:
  *She **bought** some chocolate **last week**.*
  *They **ate** the chocolate on **Sunday**.*
- Actions/events for a period beginning and ending in the past:
  *You **worked** very hard last year.*
  *We **played** bossaball in the summer.* [It's not summer now.]
- Questions asking **When?**
  ***When did** you **meet** Maria?*
- With **ago** for actions/events which are finished at some time before now:
  *I **met** her two days **ago**.*

to go in the present perfect
have/has gone

*They've **gone** out.* [They're not at home.]
*She's **gone** to Africa.* [She went there and she's there now.]
*She **hasn't gone** to Africa.* [She's not there now.]
OR
have/has been

*They've **been** out.* [They went out and then came home.]
*She's **been** to Africa.* [She went there and then returned here.]
*She **hasn't been** to Africa.* [She didn't go there.]
*She's **never been** to Africa.* [She has never visited Africa.]

Unit 11

Superlative adjectives
Regular adjectives

- One-syllable adjective:
  add **est** (e.g. **kind** → **kindest**)
- One-syllable adjective ending in **e**:
  add **st** (e.g. **nice** → **nicest**)

- One-syllable adjective ending in vowel + consonant: double consonant and add *est* (e.g. *hot* ⟶ *hottest*)
- Adjective ending in consonant+*y*: change *y* to *i* and add *est* (e.g. *funny* ⟶ *funniest*)
- Adjective with more than one syllable: *the most* + adjective (e.g. *polite* ⟶ *the most polite*, *confident* ⟶ *the most confident*)

Irregular adjectives

good ⟶ the best
bad ⟶ the worst
far ⟶ the farthest/furthest

Present passive

to be + past participle

The passive uses the same past participles as the present perfect. (For past participles see Unit 8 and irregular verb list on page 216.)

Active   *The students / They* **admire** *the actor / him.*
Passive   *The actor / He* **is admired** *by the students / them.*

+	I am ('m) admired. You/we/they are ('re) admired. He/she/it is ('s) admired.
–	I am ('m) not admired. You/we/they are not (aren't) admired. He/she/it is not (isn't) admired.
?	Am I admired? Are you/we/they admired? Is he/she/it admired?

Unit 12

Past continuous

was/were + *-ing*

+	I/he/she/it was swimming. You/we/they were swimming.
–	I/he/she/it was not (wasn't) swimming. You /we/they were not (weren't) swimming.
?	Was I/he/she/it swimming? Were/you/we/they swimming?

Past continuous and past continuous

Two past activities at the same time (often with *while*):
We **were eating** *chocolate* **while** *the teacher* **was talking**.

Past continuous and past simple

Past activity beginning before an event and continuing until or after it. The event is usually *when* + **past simple**:
We **were eating** *chocolate* **when** *the teacher* **arrived**.

Unit 13

Modal verbs (possibility and probability)

Certainty (I'm sure it is true) – *it/they* **must be**
Possibility (perhaps it's true) – *it/they* **might be**, *it* **could be**
Impossibility (I'm sure it isn't true) – *it/they* **can't be**
These verbs have only one form.

That **must be** *John's brother.* [He looks exactly like John, so I feel certain.]
That **might/could be** *John's brother.* [He looks a bit like John, so I think it's possible they are brothers.]
They **can't be** *John's brothers.* [They look completely different from John, so I don't believe it's possible that they are his brothers.]

Unit 14

used to

+	I/he/she/it/you/we/they used to eat chocolate.
–	I/he/she/it/you/we/they did not (didn't) use to eat chocolate.
?	Did I/he/she/it/you/we/they use to eat chocolate?

Used to shows something was true in the past but is not true now:
I **used to watch** *westerns.* [I don't watch them now.]
We **used to see** *horses in the field.* [We don't see them now.]
There **didn't use to be** *a sports centre in the city.* [There is now.]
Did *there* **use to be** *less traffic?* [I know there's a lot of traffic now, I want to know if it has increased.]

Adjective order

1 opinion   **2** size   **3** description   **4** colour   **5** material
an amazing long stripey green wool scarf
a useful little old red plastic bag

too + adjective and not + adjective + enough

too + adjective (+ *for* x)
This skirt is **too big** *for me.* [I need a smaller one.]
The room is **too warm**. [We feel uncomfortably hot.]

not + adjective + *enough* (+ for x)
This hat isn't **big enough** *for me.* [I need a bigger one.]
The room isn't **warm enough**. [We feel uncomfortably cold.]

Unit 15

Modal verbs (permission and obligation)

can
Can never changes.

+	I/you/he/she/it/we/they can dance.
–	I/you/he/she/it/we/they can't dance.
?	Can I/you/he/she/it/we/they dance?

have to
We use the tenses of **have**.
Present

+	I/you/we/they have to dance. He/she/it has to dance.
–	I/you/we/they don't have to dance. He/she/it doesn't have to dance.
?	Do I/you/we/they have to dance? Does he/she/it have to dance?

Past

+	I/you/he/she/it/we/they **had to dance**.
-	I/you/he/she/it/we/they **didn't have to dance**.
?	**Did** I/you/he/she/it/we/they **have to dance**?

Permission

can, can't + verb
*You **can** sit here.* [This chair is free, you are allowed to sit here.]
*You **can't** sit here.* [This chair isn't free, you aren't allowed to sit here.]

Obligation

(don't) have to + verb
*You **have to** sit here.* [You aren't allowed to sit in any other chair.]
*You **don't have to** sit here.* [You are allowed to choose your chair.]

Adverbs

Regular adverbs

- Most adjectives add *ly*:
  quiet → *quietly, strange* → *strangely,
  beautiful* → *beautifully*
- Adjectives ending in *le*:
  drop *e* and add *y* (e.g. *sensible* → *sensibly*)
- Adjectives ending in *y*:
  change *y* to *i* + *ly* (e.g. *lazy* → *lazily*)

Irregular adverbs

Some adverbs are the same as their adjectives:
fast, hard, late, early
*She's a **fast** runner. She runs **fast**.*
*I had an **early** phone call. He phoned me **early**.*
***Well** is the adverb from **good**.*
*They're **good** dancers. They dance **well**.*

Unit 16

going to future

+	I am ('m) **going to** eat this chocolate. You/we/they **are** ('re) **going to** eat this chocolate. He/she/it **is** ('s) **going to** eat this chocolate.
-	I am ('m) **not going to** eat this chocolate. You/we/they **are not (aren't) going to** eat this chocolate. He/she/it **is not (isn't) going to** eat this chocolate.
?	**Am** I **going to** eat this chocolate? **Are** you/we/they **going to** eat this chocolate? **Is** he/she/it **going to** eat this chocolate?

Going to is used

- to talk about what we plan to do:
  *We're **going to** watch a football match this evening.*
  *I'm **not going to** play tennis next weekend.*
- to describe a future event which we feel sure about:
  *Jane has made some coffee. She's **going to** drink it.*
  *You're carrying a heavy bag. You're **going to** drop it.*

Present tense following *when, until, after* in future time

*After I **leave** school I'm going to get a job.*
*He isn't going to get up **until** we **phone** him.*
*Are you going to travel by bus **when** you **visit** Australia?*

The time

It's At	five, ten, twenty-five, etc. (a) quarter three, nine, sixteen, etc. minutes	to past	one, two … twelve, etc. midday. midnight.
	half	past	
	midday/midnight.		
	one, two … twelve, etc. o'clock.		

Unit 17

will future

+	I/you/he/she/it/we/they **will ('ll) be** successful.
-	I/you/he/she/it/we/they **will not (won't) be** successful.
?	**Will** I/you/he/she/it/we/they **be** successful?

will and going to

Both talk about the future. (See also Unit 16.)
***Will** is used to say what we *believe*, but are not *certain* about the future:
*I'm going to join a tennis club because I'**ll meet** some good players there.* [I believe they have some good players.]
*Why are you going to watch that DVD? You **won't enjoy** it.*
[I don't think it's your kind of film.]
*They're going to arrive late. **Will** they **be** hungry?*
[I want to know your opinion.]

everyone, no one, someone, (not) anyone everybody, nobody, somebody, (not) anybody

+	**Someone/Somebody** has opened the window. [I don't know who.] **Everyone/Everybody** has left the house. [all the people]
-	There isn't **anyone/anybody** with me. There is **no one/nobody** with me. **No one/Nobody** came here with me. **not anyone, not anybody** = **no one, nobody** (**anyone/anybody** is not the same as **no one/nobody**)
?	Is there **anyone/anybody** in the house?

All these words are followed by a singular verb.

Unit 18

Past perfect

Past simple of *have* + past participle

+	I/he/she/it/you/we/they **had eaten** the chocolate.
-	I/he/she/it/you/we/they **had not (hadn't) eaten** the chocolate.
?	**Had** I/he/she/it/you/we/they **eaten** the chocolate?

Past perfect and past simple with *when / by the time*

She **had eaten** the chocolate **when / by the time** we **came** home.
OR **When / By the time** we **came** home, she **had eaten** the chocolate. [She ate it *before* we arrived.]

Past simple and past simple with *when*

She **ate** the chocolate **when** we **came** home.
OR **When** we **came** home, she **ate** the chocolate.
[She didn't eat it *until* we arrived home.]

Unit 19

Verbs and expressions + *to* and *-ing*

+ *to*

agree   allow   arrange   begin*   continue*
decide   expect   hope   learn   like   need
offer   plan   promise   refuse   seem   start*
stop**   try**   want   would like

+ *-ing*

be afraid of   begin*   be fed up with   be good at
be interested in   continue*   don't mind   enjoy
like   look forward to   love   prefer   start*
stop**   try**

*These verbs can be followed by *to* or *-ing* **without** changing the meaning.
** These verbs can be followed by *to* or *-ing* **with** a change in the meaning.

He **stopped eating** chocolate. [He didn't eat chocolate after that time.]
He **stopped to eat** chocolate. [He stopped working/walking *etc.* because he wanted to eat some chocolate.]
He **tried joining** a sports club. [He joined a sports club to find out if it was useful.]
He **tried to join** a sports club. [He wanted to join a sports club but he couldn't.]

make and *let*

These verbs are followed by another verb without *to* or *-ing*:
The teacher **let** the students **go** home early.
[The teacher *allowed* the students to go home early.]
The teacher **made** the students **go** home early.
[The teacher *forced* the students to go home early.]

Unit 20

Comparison of adverbs

Regular adverbs
adverbs ending -**ly**:
carefully, more carefully, most carefully
Alan worked **more carefully** than Judy.
Hazel worked **the most carefully**.

Irregular adverbs
adverbs which are the same as adjectives:
fast, faster, (the) fastest
hard, harder, (the) hardest
late, later, (the) latest
early, earlier, (the) earliest
She runs **faster** than him.
I run **(the) fastest**.
They get up **earlier** than us.
He gets up **(the) earliest**.

well, badly
well, better, (the) best
badly, worse, (the) worst
David played **better** than Michael.
John played **(the) best**.
Donna played **worse** than Mandy.
Jill played **(the) worst**.

Comparative sentences

more … than
less … than
not as/so … as
Alan worked **more carefully than** Judy.
= Judy worked **less carefully than** Alan.
= Judy didn't work **as carefully as** Alan.

so and *such*

so + adjective or adverb (*that*)
so + adjective:
The work was **so easy** (that) we finished in ten minutes.
so + adverb:
He worked **so slowly** (that) he didn't finish until midnight.

such a + (adjective) noun (*that*)
* *such a* + countable noun:
  He drove at **such a speed** (that) I felt frightened.
* *such* + uncountable noun:
  He talked **such** nonsense (that) they laughed.
* *such a* + adjective + countable noun:
  It was **such an easy exercise** (that) we finished in ten minutes.
* *such* + adjective + plural noun:
  They were **such slow workers** (that) they didn't finish until midnight.
* *such* + adjective + uncountable noun:
  It was **such easy work** (that) we finished in ten minutes.

Connectives

so, because/as, but, although, either … or
* the result of an event or action:
  I was hungry **so** I ate the chocolate.
* the reason for an event or action:
  I ate the chocolate **because/as** I was hungry.
* contrasting or comparing:
  The chocolate was expensive **but** it wasn't good.
  Although the chocolate was expensive, it wasn't good.
* giving two alternatives:
  She can **either** eat the chocolate **or** give it to her mother.

Unit 21

have something done

I/you/he/she/it/we/they + tense of *have* + noun + **past participle**:

*I'm **having** my hair **coloured** tomorrow.*
*He **doesn't have** his hair **coloured**.*
***Did** you **have** your hair **coloured**?*

Reported speech

Reported requests

Ask someone (not) to do something

Direct speech	Reported speech
Please shut the door.	*He **asked** her **to** shut the door.*
Please don't open the door.	*He **asked** her **not to** open the door.*

Reported commands

Tell someone (not) to do something

Direct speech	Reported speech
Shut the door!	*He **told** her **to** shut the door.*
Don't open the door!	*He **told** her **not to** open the door.*

Possessive pronouns and adjectives

Name /noun	Pronouns							
John /the boy	**subject**	I	you	he	she	it	we	they
John /the boy	**object**	me	you	him	her	it	us	them
Possessive forms								
John's /the boy's	**adjective**	my	your	his	her	its	our	their
John's /the boy's	**pronoun**	mine	yours	his	hers	its	ours	theirs

John's friend	a friend **of John's**
the boy's friend	a friend **of the boy's**
his friend	a friend **of his**
my friend	a friend **of mine**
your friend	a friend **of yours**

Unit 22

Reported speech

Reported speech → Direct speech

- Past simple → Present simple:
  *She said she **wanted** coffee.*
  → '*I **want** coffee.*'
  *He said he **didn't want** tea **then**.*
  → '*I **don't want** tea **now**.*'

- Past continuous → Present continuous:
  *She said she **was making** coffee.*
  → '*I'm **making** coffee.*'
  *She said she **wasn't making** tea.*
  → '*I'm **not making** tea.*'

- *would* + verb → *will* future:
  *He said he**'d (would) have** coffee.*
  → '*I'll **have** coffee.*'
  *He said he **wouldn't have** tea **there**.*
  → '*I **won't have** tea **here**.*'

- Past perfect → Present perfect:
  *She said she**'d (had)** already **made** coffee.*
  → '*I've already **made** coffee.*'
  *She said she **hadn't made** tea.*
  → '*I **haven't made** tea.*'

- Past perfect → Past simple:
  *She said she**'d (had) bought** it **the day before / the previous day**.*
  → '*I **bought** it **yesterday**.*'
  *She said she **hadn't bought** tea **that day**.*
  → '*I **didn't buy** tea **today**.*'

Unit 23

Relative clauses

- Subject of relative clause: person/people
  I saw a **student**. **He** was in my class.
  → *I saw a **student who/that** was in my class.*

- Subject of relative clause: thing
  I saw a **jacket**. **It** was very expensive.
  → *I saw a **jacket which/that** was very expensive.*

- Object of relative clause: person/people
  I phoned **the hairdresser**. My friend recommended **him**.
  → *I phoned **the hairdresser who/that** my friend recommended.*
  OR *I phoned **the hairdresser** my friend recommended.*

- Object of relative clause: thing
  I made a **cake**. Everyone liked **it**.
  → *I made a **cake which/that** everyone liked.*
  OR *I made a **cake** everyone liked.*

- Relative clause: *where* (place)
  I know a **club**. The music is great **there**.
  → *I know a **club where** the music is great.*

- Relative clause: *whose* (person/people)
  I phoned **the woman**. You gave me **her** name.
  → *I phoned **the woman whose** name you gave me.*

Adjective + preposition + noun/pronoun/ -ing

afraid of   angry about something / with someone
bad/good at   different from   excited about
fed up with   full of   interested in   keen on
kind of   nervous of   worried about   tired of

Unit 24

Past passive

Past simple of *to be* + past participle
(For past participles see Unit 8 and irregular verb list on page 216.)

Active   *The students **admired** the actor / him.*
            *The students **admired** the singers / them.*
Passive   *The actor / He **was admired** by the students.*
            *The singers / They **were admired** by the students.*

+	I/he/she/it **was admired.** You/we/they **were admired.**
–	I/he/she/it **was not (wasn't) admired.** You/we/they **were not (weren't) admired.**
?	**Was** I/he/she/it **admired?** **Were** you/we/they **admired?**

Future passive

will be + past participle
(For past participles see Unit 8 and irregular verb list on page 216.)

Active   *The students **will admire** the actor/him.*
            *The students **will admire** the singers/them.*
Passive   *The actor/He **will be admired** by the students.*
            *The singers/they **will be admired** by the students.*

+	I/he/she/it/you/we/they **will be admired.**
–	I/he/she/it/you/we/they **will not (won't) be admired.**
?	**Will** I/he/she/it/you/we/they **be admired?**

Unit 25

Reported questions

Wh- questions

*I asked **what** the problem **was**.*
→ ***What is** the problem?*
*She asked **which** book **I wanted**.*
→ ***Which** book **do you want?***
*He asked **how much I had ('d) paid** for it.*
→ ***How much did you pay** for it?*
*They asked her **where she had hidden** the chocolate.*
→ ***Where have you hidden** the chocolate?*
*We asked her **when she would explain**.*
→ ***When will you explain?***

Yes/no questions + if or whether

*I asked them **whether they liked** chocolate.*
→ ***Do you like** chocolate?*
*He asked me **if I was going to sing**.*
→ ***Are you going to sing?***
*She asked me **if I would make** coffee.*
→ ***Will you make** coffee?*
*I asked them **if they'd seen** my mobile.*
→ ***Have you seen** my mobile?*

too much, too many, not enough

- *too much* + uncountable noun:
  *We've got **too much homework**.*

- *too many* + plural countable noun:
  *You ask **too many questions**.*

- *not enough* + plural countable/uncountable noun:
  *There are**n't enough chocolates** for everyone.*
  *I haven**'t had enough time** to learn these rules.*

Verbs with two objects

give + person + object → *give* + object + *to* person
*The teacher gave **the boy** extra homework.*
→ *The teacher gave extra homework **to the boy**.*
*Annie sent **me** an email.*
→ *Annie sent an email **to me**.*

Unit 26

First conditional

Used for possible conditions.
Condition: ***if/unless*** + **present tense**
Result: **future tense**
Either the condition or the result can be first in the sentence.
If the condition clause is first, there is a comma after it.
There is no comma if the result clause is first.
*If you **leave** the party early, you**'ll miss** the fireworks.*
= *You**'ll miss** the fireworks **if** you **leave** early.*
= *You**'ll see** the fireworks **if** you **stay** until midnight.*
= *You**'ll miss** the fireworks **unless** you **stay** till midnight.*
= *If you **don't stay** till midnight, you**'ll miss** the fireworks.*

if and when

When means the speaker is **certain** that something will happen:
*I'll be very nervous **when** I take the exam.* [I'm certain that I'm going to take the exam.]
If means the speaker is **not certain** that something will happen:
*I'll be very happy **if** I pass the exam.* [Perhaps I'll pass the exam.]
*I'll be very sad **if** I fail the exam.* [Perhaps I'll fail the exam.]

Unit 27

Verb/preposition + reflexive pronouns

myself, yourself, himself, herself, itself, ourselves, yourselves, themselves
The **subject** of the verb/preposition is the same as its **object**:
*A **boy** of fifteen should know how to look after **himself**.*
*Remember to give **yourself** plenty of time to reach the airport.*
***They** never care about other people, only about **themselves**.*

each, every, all + noun

each/every + singular countable noun
each of + a plural countable noun
all + plural countable/uncountable noun
***Every** student had some chocolate.*
***Each** student had some chocolate.*
***Each of** my friends had a different sweet.*
***All** the students had some chocolate.*
***All** the chocolate was eaten.*

every/all + morning/night/week/month etc.

Every morning = more than one morning
All morning = the whole of one morning
*He visits his grandmother **every week**, usually on Sundays.*
*I've been ill **all week** and couldn't go to work.*
*We live in Poland but we spend the summer in Spain **every year**.*
*The storm continued **all night** and no one could sleep.*

Unit 28

Second conditional

Used for nearly or completely impossible conditions (compare Unit 26).

Condition:	**if /unless** + past tense
Result:	**would** verb

Either the condition or the result can be first in the sentence.
If the condition clause is first, there is a comma after it.
There is no comma if the result clause is first.

Nearly impossible:
*If you **left** the party early, you**'d miss** the fireworks.* [But I don't believe you will leave early.]
= *You**'d miss** the fireworks if you **left** early.*
= *You**'d see** the fireworks if you **stayed** until midnight.*
= *You**'d miss** the fireworks **unless** you **stayed** till midnight.*
= *If you **didn't stay** till midnight, you**'d miss** the fireworks.*

Completely imposssible:
*If I **was** a film star, I **would** ('d) **live** in Los Angeles.* [I'm not a film star, so I don't live there.]
= *I **would** ('d) **live** in Los Angeles if I **was** a film star.*
= *I **wouldn't live** here if I **was** a film star.*
*I **wouldn't act** in a film **unless** I **liked** the director.*
= *If I **didn't like** the director, I **would** ('d) **refuse** to act in a film.*

Unit 29

so + verb or neither/nor + verb

We use *so* + verb and *neither/nor* + verb to agree with another speaker.
The verb must match the tense in the other speaker's sentence.
So is used to reply to a positive sentence.
Neither/Nor are used to reply to a negative sentence.
(Compare short answers in Unit 9.)

I'm fifteen.	*So **am** I.*
	*So **are** we/they.*
	*So **is** he/she.*
*We're **not** allowed to drive.*	*Nor/Neither **am** I.*
	*Nor/Neither **are** we/they.*
	*Nor/Neither **is** he/she.*
*He often **catches** this bus.*	*So **do** I/we/they.*
	*So **does** he/she.*
*He **doesn't like** cycling.*	*Nor/Neither **do** I/we/they.*
	*Nor/Neither **does** he/she.*
*We**'ve bought** return tickets.*	*So **have** I/we/they.*
	*So **has** he/she.*
*They **haven't bought** tickets yet.*	*Nor/Neither **have** I/we/they.*
	*Nor/Neither **has** he/she.*
*I **caught** the train yesterday.*	*So **did** I/he/she/we/they.*
*She **didn't come** to school.*	*Nor/Neither **did** I/he/she/ we/they.*
*I'll **phone** her later.*	*So **will** I/he/she/we/they.*
*I **won't** forget.*	*Nor/Neither **will** I/ he/she/ we/they.*
*They're **going to** get off the bus.*	*So **am** I.*
	*So **are** we/they.*
	*So **is** he/she.*
*I **must** hurry.*	*So **must** I/he/she/we/they.*
*We **hadn't noticed** the time.*	*Nor/Neither **had** I/he/she/ we/they.*

Polite questions

Can you tell me ... ? Can you remember ... ? Do you know ... ? I'd like to know .... Can you find out ... ? etc.	+ reported question.

For reported questions see Unit 25.

Unit 30

hardly

Hardly means *almost not*. We don't use *not* with *hardly*.

hardly any (of) / anyone, anybody etc. + noun
*I have **hardly any homework**.* [almost none]
***Hardly anyone** enjoys homework.* [almost no one]
***Hardly any of my friends** are older than me.* [almost none of them]

hardly (ever) + verb
*We **hardly ever have** a free evening.* [almost never]
*She **hardly understood any of** our jokes.* [almost none]
*They **hardly ate** anything.* [almost nothing]

before and after + -ing

The subject of the *-ing* verb must be the same as the subject of the other verb:
*I wrote an email to my parents **before going** to bed.*
[before I went to bed] [**not** before they went to bed]
*They'll certainly phone us **after arriving** home.*
[after they arrive] [**not** after we arrive]
***Before leaving** the train, check that you have all your luggage.*
[before you leave]
***After using** these books, please return them to the correct shelf.*
[after you use]

Key to phonetic symbols

Vowels

Sound	Example
/ɑː/	cart
/æ/	cat
/aɪ/	like
/aʊ/	now
/e/	tell
/eɪ/	say
/eə/	there
/ɪ/	big
/iː/	steep
/ɪə/	here
/ɒ/	pop
/əʊ/	phone
/ɔː/	four
/ɔɪ/	boy
/ʊ/	took
/uː/	pool
/ʊə/	tour
/ɜː/	third
/ʌ/	fun
/ə/	again

Consonants

Sound	Example
/b/	be
/d/	do
/f/	find
/g/	good
/h/	have
/j/	you
/k/	cat
/l/	like
/m/	me
/n/	no
/p/	put
/r/	run
/s/	say
/t/	tell
/v/	very
/w/	well
/z/	zoo
/ʃ/	shoe
/ʒ/	television
/ŋ/	sing
/tʃ/	cheap
/θ/	thin
/ð/	this
/dʒ/	joke

Irregular verb list

Verb	Past simple	Past participle	Verb	Past simple	Past participle
be	was were	been	lend	lent	lent
beat	beat	beaten	let	let	let
become	became	become	lie	lay	lain
begin	began	begun	light	lit	lit
bend	bent	bent	lose	lost	lost
bite	bit	bitten	make	made	made
bleed	bled	bled	mean	meant	meant
blow	blew	blown	meet	met	met
break	broke	broken	pay	paid	paid
bring	brought	brought	put	put	put
build	built	built	read	read	read
burn	burnt/burned	burnt/burned	ride	rode	ridden
buy	bought	bought	ring	rang	rung
catch	caught	caught	rise	rose	risen
choose	chose	chosen	run	ran	run
come	came	come	say	said	said
cost	cost	cost	see	saw	seen
cut	cut	cut	sell	sold	sold
dig	dug	dug	send	sent	sent
do	did	done	set	set	set
draw	drew	drawn	shake	shook	shaken
dream	dreamt/dreamed	dreamt/dreamed	shine	shone	shone
drink	drank	drunk	shoot	shot	shot
drive	drove	driven	show	showed	shown
eat	ate	eaten	shut	shut	shut
fall	fell	fallen	sing	sang	sung
feed	fed	fed	sink	sank	sunk
feel	felt	felt	sit	sat	sat
fight	fought	fought	sleep	slept	slept
find	found	found	slide	slid	slid
fly	flew	flown	smell	smelt/smelled	smelt/smelled
forget	forgot	forgotten	speak	spoke	spoken
forgive	forgave	forgiven	spell	spelt/spelled	spelt/spelled
freeze	froze	frozen	spend	spent	spent
get	got	got	spill	spilt	spilt
give	gave	given	spoil	spoilt	spoilt
go	went	been/gone	stand	stood	stood
grow	grew	grown	steal	stole	stolen
hang	hung	hung	stick	stuck	stuck
have	had	had	sweep	swept	swept
hear	heard	heard	swell	swelled	swollen
hide	hid	hidden	swim	swam	swum
hit	hit	hit	take	took	taken
hold	held	held	teach	taught	taught
hurt	hurt	hurt	tear	tore	torn
keep	kept	kept	tell	told	told
kneel	knelt	knelt	think	thought	thought
know	knew	known	throw	threw	thrown
lay	laid	laid	understand	understood	understood
lead	led	led	wake	woke	woken
learn	learnt/learned	learnt/learned	wear	wore	worn
leave	left	left	win	won	won
			write	wrote	written

Answers and recording scripts

Unit 1
page 10
Introduction

1

a cycling **b** horse riding **c** skiing **d** basketball
e sailing **f** table tennis **g** volleyball **h** tennis
i gymnastics **j** surfing **k** windsurfing **l** hockey
m football **n** rugby **o** athletics

Corpus spot

play	do	go
football	athletics	swimming
basketball	gymnastics	cycling
hockey		horse riding
rugby		sailing
table tennis		skiing
tennis		surfing
volleyball		windsurfing

a play **b** go **c** play **d** go **e** do

page 11

3

Suggested answers

bike – cycling
boat – sailing
net – football (part of goal), hockey, table tennis, tennis, volleyball
sail – sailing, windsurfing
stick – hockey (**not** skiing – skiers use *poles*)

bat – table tennis
board – surfing, windsurfing
helmet – cycling (**not** horse riding – riders wear a *hard hat*, **not** a *helmet*)
racket – tennis
skis – skiing

Listening

1

a snowfering **b** bossaball **c** karting **d** curling

2

a speaker 2 **b** speaker 1 **c** speaker 4 **d** speaker 3

Recording script 1 02

Speaker 1: We always wear <u>shorts</u>. We sometimes wear shoes, but I usually have <u>bare feet</u>.

Speaker 2: <u>We have a board like the board we use for snowboarding and we use a kind of sail.</u>

Speaker 3: We use special <u>stones</u> and <u>brushes</u> and we play on ice.

Speaker 4: You can go up to 45 kph, so you wear a <u>helmet</u>, but it's not very dangerous – really!

3

b (in the) summer
c special stones and brushes
d it's a kind of chess (on ice)
e (up to) 45 kph
f a kind of small racing car
g on the snow (on the lakes and fields)
h a board (like the board they use for snowboarding) and a kind of sail

Recording script 1 03

We always wear shorts. We sometimes wear shoes, but I usually have bare feet. It's called bossaball. It's a new sport. It's like a kind of volleyball with trampolines. It's fun in the sun and we usually play <u>in the summer</u>.

We use <u>special stones and brushes</u> and we play on ice. It's called curling. It's a very old sport. People sometimes say <u>it's a kind of chess on ice</u>. It's exciting and it's quite skilful. We sometimes wear special shoes.

<u>You can go up to 45 kph indoors</u> so you wear a helmet, but it's not very dangerous – really! It's called karting. We use <u>a kind of small racing car</u>. It's got a real engine. Champion racing drivers often begin in them.

The weather's very cold and windy in Canada in winter and there's always ice and snow <u>on the lakes and fields</u>. It's called snowfering. <u>We have a board like the board we use for snowboarding and we use a kind of sail.</u> It's a kind of windsurfing <u>on the snow</u>. It's wonderful.

4

1 It's fun (in the sun).
2 It's exciting (and it's quite skilful).
3 It's not very dangerous.
4 It's wonderful.

page 12

Language focus

a kind of

b It's a kind of bat.
c It's a kind of surfing on water.
d It's a kind of tennis.
e It's a kind of team game.
f It's a kind of car.
g It's a kind of windsurfing on the snow.

Present simple + frequency adverbs

Grammar spot

Frequency adverbs go <u>before</u> a main verb but <u>after</u> an auxiliary verb and *to be*.

1

Suggested answers

b Cyclists sometimes go very fast.
c Footballers are often very rich.
d Surfers always get wet.
e Gymnasts never wear helmets.
f There are usually two people in a tennis match.
g Good athletes never smoke.

Corpus spot

a She <u>often comes</u> to my house.
b I <u>sometimes meet</u> them in my free time.
c At weddings people <u>are usually</u> happy and have fun together.
d I don't <u>often go</u> to the countryside.
e He <u>doesn't usually</u> make jokes.
f We have a basketball team and we <u>often play</u> against other teams.

page 13

«Pronunciation»

2

/aɪ/	/iː/	/ɪ/
quite	*steep*	*hill*
like	field	little
kind	knee	stick
ice	people	big
line	street	rich
ride	wheel	
bike	team	

4

ee	ie	eo	ea

page 14

Exam folder 1

Reading Part 1

2

1 email (the typeface and layout suggest an email)
2 notice (the style shows that this is a notice and the words suggest it is for anyone to read)
3 text message (the typeface and layout suggest a text message)
4 telephone message (the word *phone*)
5 Post-it note (*Here's* means the note is stuck to something, e.g. a leaflet)

4

2 B	3 A	4 C	5 A

Unit 2

page 16

Introduction

2

a Stefan b Mike c Mandana d Julia
e Kurt (not heard) f Anastasia (not heard)

Recording script 1 05

Stefan: Hello, <u>Mandana</u>?

Mandana: Yes. Is that <u>Stefan</u>?

Stefan: Yes, I'm meeting you this afternoon. What do you look like?

Mandana: Oh, well, <u>I've got short dark hair and dark eyes</u>. I'm average height. What about you?

Stefan: Right, er, I'm not very tall, but I'm broad-shouldered and <u>I've got blue eyes. My hair is fair and it's quite short and curly.</u>

Julia: Hi <u>Mike</u>, this is <u>Julia</u>. I'm meeting you at the coach station tomorrow.

Mike: Oh, right. What do you look like?

Julia: Well, <u>I'm slim, and I've got fair hair. It's wavy and shoulder-length. I've got green eyes.</u> And you?

Mike: Er, I'm tall, <u>with short dark hair and I've got a moustache.</u>

Julia: OK. See you tomorrow.

Corpus spot

a She is *tall* and slim. b He's got short fair *hair*.

page 17

Reading

1

2 Travel 3 Accommodation 4 Contacts 5 Travel
6 Accommodation

2

	Elena	Adrian	Carola	Henry	Sandra	Maggie
a	✓				✓	
b	✓					
c	✓		✓			
d		✓				
e			✓			
f		✓		✓		
g						✓

page 18

Language focus

want, like, would like and *have got*

Grammar spot
a going   b going   c to go   d to go

1
b Would   like   likes
c have   got   haven't got
d Does   like   's/has got
e do   like   like
f Would   like   don't like
g 'd/would like   likes
h 'd/would like   have   got   haven't got

page 19

«Pronunciation»

1
No, they don't.

2

/juː/	/ʌ/	/ɒ/
university	*fun*	*pop*
music	become	long
Tuesday	some	doctor
you	other	want
future	club	cost
	above	
	discuss	

3

Recording script 1 06

university fun pop music become some Tuesday other club long you above doctor discuss want cost future

4
/juː/ is heard in *university, students, music*
/ʌ/ is heard in *become, some, fun, run, club, above, other, brother*
/ɒ/ is heard in *want, doctor, lot, shop, got, long*

page 20

Exam folder 2
Listening Part 3

2
b I have a huge breakfast at about <u>half past eight</u>.
c <u>I'm studying</u> geography.
d I usually study in my room <u>in the afternoon</u>.
e I <u>enjoy</u> spending time with my friends.
f I <u>would like</u> to travel round the world.

Recording script 1 08

Dan: My name is Dan Jones and I'm a third year student at Southgate University. My days are really busy because my hobby is tennis and I play in national matches, so I have to practise a lot.
My day begins at 6 am. I get up and go straight to the gym before breakfast. <u>I always go there by bicycle</u> because the fresh air wakes me up. After an hour or so I come back to the university and then <u>I have a huge breakfast at about eight thirty</u>. Oh, I always have a shower of course before breakfast or nobody would sit next to me! From 9.30 until 1.00, I go to lectures. <u>My subject is geography</u>. Then all the students have lunch together in the canteen at 1 o'clock. <u>I usually study in my room after lunch</u> – that is, except for one afternoon a week when we play matches, sometimes against another university. They're always on Wednesday afternoons. In the evenings <u>I like spending time with my friends</u> – we sometimes go to the cinema or to a disco. When I leave university next year, <u>I want to travel round the world</u>.

4
b eight thirty   c My subject is   d after lunch
e like   f want

6
1 gym   2 8.15 / (a) quarter past eight   3 biology
4 library   5 Friday   6 watching TV   7 nurse

Recording script 1 09

Katy: My name is Katy Williamson and I'm a student at Southgate University. I'm the captain of the university women's football team. Women's football is becoming more and more popular and the team is really busy playing matches all over the country.
I get up at 6 am and at 6.30 I go to the <u>gym</u>. I always walk. I usually spend about an hour there and I walk back to the university and have a huge breakfast in the student canteen at <u>about a quarter past eight</u>. I meet all my friends there, so breakfast sometimes takes a long time. Lectures are from 10 o'clock until about 1. I'm studying <u>biology</u> so I spend quite a lot of time in the laboratories. I usually have lunch in the canteen but I sometimes go to a café over the road. After lunch I usually study in the <u>library</u>. There's sometimes football practice between 5 and 6, so I have to work hard to finish all my work before then. We play matches against other university women's teams on <u>Friday</u> afternoons, so I have to make sure I'm always free then. Then I have my evening meal – usually in the canteen because it's cheaper there. In the evenings I like <u>watching TV</u> – I'm usually too tired to do anything else. And I go to bed really early, about 10.
When I leave university next year, I want to be a <u>nurse</u>, but I'll continue playing football as a hobby because I love it.

page 21

Writing folder
Writing Parts 1, 2 and 3

1

a There are ten. We use them at the beginning of sentences, for someone's name and for the pronoun '*I*'. They are also used for place names, days of the week and months.

b To show the beginning and end of each piece of spoken language. These could also be double (" ").

c There are four. Three replace missing letters. (In speech and informal written English, these forms are correct. PET students can use them throughout the exam.) One is used to show possession; there is no letter missing.

d With a full stop.

e At the end of a question.

f Between the two halves of a sentence, especially before words like *but* and *so*, but not usually before *and* or *that*; between items in lists, until the last item, which is preceded by *and*; in addresses, and at the beginning and end of letters (although in the PET exam you would not lose marks for omitting these).

g The only other punctuation mark PET students may want to use is the exclamation mark. Remember that in English it is always at the end of a sentence. We normally use it to express surprise, humour or excitement. Be careful not to use it too much.

PET students may meet colons, semicolons and dashes in printed texts, dialogues, lists, etc. but do not need to use them.

2

the student's books = the books of one student
the students' books = the books of two or more students

3

a My brother and I usually watch football matches at my grandparents' flat because their television's very big.

b On Thursday I'm going to the match between Italy and Scotland with Dad and Uncle Ian.

c We're travelling in my uncle's car to Edinburgh and after the match, we're staying at the Norton Hotel.

d Then on Friday morning my uncle and I are visiting Edinburgh Castle and my father's going to the National Gallery and a museum.

4

Dear Pia,
How are you? I must tell you about a new club in my town./!
It's in Oxford Road and I think you'd love it. We can play tennis and go swimming and there's a small gym.
I made a new friend there last Sunday. Her name's Jessica. She's from Canada and she's got blonde hair and she makes me laugh. She's a good dancer too. I hope you can come here soon and meet her.
With love,
Andy

Corpus spot

a In my country, all the women wear new clothes at weddings.
b I like the London streets with their red telephone boxes.
c There are a lot of friendly people at the club.
d I look after the children when their parents are working.
e During the break we talk about our lives and our friends.

Unit 3
page 22

Introduction

1

a Speaker 3 b Speaker 1 c Speaker 6 d Speaker 5
e Speaker 7 f Speaker 4 g Speaker 2

Recording script 1 10

1 I look after the passengers on an aeroplane.
2 I design roads and bridges.
3 I help people in a fashion shop.
4 I cut people's hair.
5 I mend engines and change tyres.
6 I sell cars and vans.
7 I design websites.

2

a shop assistant b flight attendant c (car) salesman
d mechanic e website designer f hairdresser g engineer

3

Suggested answers

a The shop assistant's tidying some clothes.
b The flight attendant's bringing the pilots some food.
c The salesman's working at his computer.
d The mechanic's having a break.
e The website designer's plugging in her computer.
f The hairdresser's holding a mirror.
g The engineer's looking at a plan.

page 23

Listening

2

He is a security officer in a shopping mall.
He's talking to a police officer.

Recording script 1 11

Security officer: Grand City Mall. Security.

Police officer: Hello, Security? This the police. We have a report that there's a thief in the shopping mall.

Security officer: Oh, yeah? What kind of a thief?

PO: A shoplifter. Someone who steals clothes and things from shops. Can you see anyone? Does anyone look like a thief?

SO: I can see ... oh, about six people on the security cameras. And you.

PO: Oh. Well, one of the others is a criminal. Does one of them look like a criminal? Is one of them carrying a big bag?

SO: Er, no. I can tell you what they're doing.

PO: OK. Go ahead.

SO: Well, first, there's a woman. She's painting a picture of a child. She's got a box.

PO: A big box?

SO: No, no. A box of paints. She's an <u>artist</u>. She paints pictures of the children and sells them to their parents. I know her. Then, there's a young woman. She's standing near the fountain. A man is taking a photograph of her. He's got a casc.

PO: Is it a big case?

SO: Yeah, but the case has got different cameras in it. He's a fashion <u>photographer</u> and she's a <u>model</u>. He takes photos all the time and sells them to magazines.

PO: OK. So – anyone else?

SO: There's another man. He's standing outside a shop. He's holding a notebook. He's looking up and down the mall and he's writing something in his notebook.

PO: Does he look like a thief?

SO: No, he's not a thief. He's a <u>journalist</u>. He often walks round to see what news he can find. He always writes everything in his notebook.

PO: Is that all you can see?

SO: There's the <u>bank guard</u>. He's standing near the door of the bank.

PO: He's not a thief!

SO: Probably not. I know him. He's too lazy. He never does anything.

PO: Isn't there anyone else?

SO: The only other person I can see now is a woman with short grey hair. I don't know her but she doesn't look like a thief.

PO: Short grey hair? Aha! What's she doing?

SO: She's walking through the mall.

PO: Is she carrying a big bag?

SO: No, she isn't *carrying* a big bag.

PO: Oh.

SO: But she's pulling a shopping bag on wheels. It's quite big.

PO: That's her! She looks like a housewife. She steals things and puts them in the bag. Everyone thinks she's got shopping in it. OK, watch her carefully. I'm coming to arrest her.

3

> **1** artist   **2** photographer   **3** model
> **4** journalist   **5** bank guard

Language focus

Present simple and present continuous

1

> **b** is standing   **c** sells   **d** is pulling   **e** steals
> **f** isn't looking   **g** does   **h** is taking   **i** sells
> **j** isn't stealing   **k** is writing

> **Grammar spot**
> We use the *present simple* to talk about what we usually do. We use the *present continuous* to talk about what we're doing now.

page 24

2

usually	this week only
She does lessons all day.	She isn't doing any homework.
She studies at home in the evening.	She's working in a hotel.
She plays volleyball after school.	She's having meals with her colleagues.
She doesn't wear her best skirt every day.	She's speaking French with hotel guests.

3

> **b** 'm doing   **c** 'm working   **d** aren't / 're not working
> **e** 'm helping   **f** like   **g** prefer   **h** are staying   **i** understand
> **j** get up   **k** 'm starting   **l** 'm looking forward to

Recording script 1 12

Sonia: Hi, Granny. How are you?

Granny: Oh, not bad. How's school?

Sonia: <u>I'm not going</u> to school this week.

Granny: Why not? Are you ill?

Sonia: No, <u>I'm doing</u> work experience. <u>I'm working</u> in a hotel.

Granny: I hope you<u>'re not working</u> in the kitchen. You're not good at cooking!

Sonia: No, I'm not in the kitchen. <u>I'm helping</u> the receptionist and the manager.

Granny: Is that nice?

Sonia: Yes. Well, I <u>like</u> working with the manager, she's really friendly. But I <u>prefer</u> helping the receptionist because I can talk to the guests. I can practise my French because some French people <u>are staying</u> in the hotel. I <u>understand</u> almost everything they say. Isn't that great?

Granny: Yes, that's very good.

Sonia: Yes. But I am tired. When I go to school, I <u>get up</u> at half past seven, but this week I<u>'m starting</u> work at seven o'clock.

Granny: Oh, well, you can have a good rest at the weekend.

Sonia: Oh, yes. I<u>'m looking forward to</u> it.

> **Grammar spot**
> **b** Are those jeans new? <u>I like</u> them very much.
> **c** <u>We think</u> this CD is very expensive.
> **d** <u>Do you want</u> some coffee?
> **e** I can't phone you because <u>I don't know</u> your number.
> **f** The teacher is speaking quickly and <u>I don't understand</u> what she's saying.
> **g** My friends are watching a pop programme on TV but <u>I don't like</u> it, so I'm listening to my MP3 player.

page 25

Short answers

1

> **b** 1 **c** 5 **d** 7 **e** 2 **f** 8 **g** 6 **h** 4

«Pronunciation»

1

> **a** cat 3 cart 2 cut 1
> **b** bag 1 bug 2
> **c** carry 2 curry 1
> **d** match 1 March 3 much 2

Recording script 1 13

a I've got a <u>cut</u> on my knee.
  Can you move the <u>cart</u>?
  Where is the <u>cat</u> exactly?
b There's a <u>bag</u> on the table.
  I can see a <u>bug</u> under your chair.
c Would you like some <u>curry</u>?
  Please <u>carry</u> that for her.
d We can meet at the <u>match</u>.
  There isn't <u>much</u> here.
  They often stay here in <u>March</u>.

3

> Same sound as cat /æ/: can
> Same sound as cart /ɑː/: can't are aren't
> Same sound as cut /ʌ/: does doesn't must mustn't

«Activity» Spot the difference

> **Suggested answers**
> The model isn't standing by the fountain, she's talking to the journalist.
> The artist isn't painting a picture, she's showing a child the picture.
> The journalist isn't writing in his notebook, he's talking to the model.
> The bank guard isn't standing near the door of the bank, he's having a cup of coffee.
> The photographer isn't taking a photo of the model, he's taking a photo of the thief.
> The police officer isn't sitting in his car, he is running after the woman with the bag.

page 26

Exam folder 3
Speaking Part 3

1

> **a** 6 **b** 7 **c** 5 **d** 3 **e** 1 **f** 4 **g** 2

2

> **Suggested answers**
> **a** She's in an office.
> **b** She's slim and she's got long, wavy hair.
> **c** She's wearing a green dress.
> **d** She's hard-working/untidy.
> **e** She's reading an email and eating a sandwich.
> **f** I wouldn't like to do this.
> **g** Because I don't like office work. It's boring.

page 27

Reading Part 5

1

> 2 C   3 B

2

> 1 B   2 A   3 D

Unit 4
page 28

Introduction

1

> **b** ballet   **c** magic show   **d** music festival
> **e** musical   **f** film

2

> **Suggested answers**
> **a** 1   **b** 4   **c** 6   **d** 3   **e** 5   **f** 2

page 29

Reading

1

> **B** Children **C** Music **D** Clubbing **E** Dance shows
> **F** Music

2

> **b** B* and F   **c** A   **d** C and E   **e** A   **f** B and F
>
> *The expression Big Top is mainly used for the big tent used by circuses, although it is sometimes borrowed for other entertainments taking place in an outsize tent. So the circus is outdoors but inside a tent.

> **Vocabulary spot**
> 1 a   2 b   3 c

> **Corpus spot**
> If something or someone is *funny*, it/he/she makes you laugh. If something is *fun*, you enjoy doing it.
> **a** fun   **b** funny   **c** fun

page 30

Language focus

Prepositions of time

1

> **1** the circus   **2** the cinema   **3** the nightclub

Recording script ●1 16

Conversation 1

Sara: I know. It sounds good. I'd like to go.

Ed: I'm taking my little brother. Would you like to come too?

Sara: That would be great. I love the noise, the music and all the excitement. The last time I went was in 2005 when I was ten.

Ed: Oh, really? Well, I like the clowns best. Are you free today or tomorrow? The afternoon show is best for my brother.

Sara: Sorry, I'm busy then. I'm going to the cinema this afternoon – I've got the tickets so I can't change it – and I'm playing tennis tomorrow afternoon.

Ed: Oh, well … can you go at the weekend? It finishes on 29 August. That's Saturday.

Sara: I'm free on Saturday afternoon.

Ed: Good. I'm free then, too. It only comes once a year, so we mustn't miss it.

Conversation 2

Sam: Hi, Juliet, it's Sam here. Have you got the tickets yet?

Juliet: Yeah, for tonight.

Sam: What time does it start?

Juliet: Just a minute. I'll look. Er, it starts at a quarter to eight.

Sam: Oh, you know I work in a shop on Wednesdays? In the city centre. Well, there's a sale this week so I'm working late. I have to tidy the shop at the end of the day, so I'm working till seven thirty this evening. I usually finish at seven o'clock, which is better.

Juliet: Don't worry. There are lots of adverts before the film actually starts.

Sam: OK. See you later then. Outside?

Juliet: See you there. Bye.

Conversation 3

Max: It's so boring here in August, Rachel. There's nothing to do.

Rachel: There are lots of good things on at the moment. What are you doing next weekend? My mum's going to see a dance show on Sunday afternoon. We can go with her.

Max: Oh, boring. And I don't like going to things like that in the afternoon.

Rachel: Well, there's the rock festival in the park. That looks good. I like listening to music outside in the summer. But it's very expensive.

Max: Mm. I've only got £10.

Rachel: Well, would you like to go to the new nightclub? I went there last week on my birthday. It's only £8 before eleven. We can go on Saturday.

Max: I'd really like to go to the rock festival, but OK then. Shall we meet at your house?

Rachel: Yeah. About nine?

Max: See you then.

2

> **b** today   **c** this afternoon   **d** tomorrow afternoon
> **e** at the weekend   **f** on 29 August   **g** on Saturday afternoon
> **h** at a quarter to eight   **i** on Wednesdays   **j** this week
> **k** at the end of the day   **l** at 7 o'clock   **m** in August
> **n** at the moment   **o** next weekend   **p** on Sunday afternoon
> **q** in the afternoon   **r** in the summer   **s** on my birthday
> **t** on Saturday

3

on	at
29 August	the weekend
Saturday afternoon	a quarter to eight
Wednesdays	the end of the day
Sunday afternoon	7 o'clock
my birthday	the moment
Saturday	

in	no preposition
2005	today
August	this afternoon
the afternoon	tomorrow afternoon
the summer	this week
	next weekend

Grammar spot

We use *on* before days of the week and dates.
We use *at* before times, *the weekend*, *the end of the day*, *the moment*.
We use *in* before months, seasons and years.
We use *no preposition* before *today*, *tomorrow (morning)*, *this/next (afternoon, week)*.

page 31

4

> **b** on   **c** –   **d** on   **e** at   **f** in   **g** in
> **h** on   **i** in   **j** at   **k** –   **l** at

≪Pronunciation≫

1

> Monday   2 syllables
> Tuesday   2 syllables
> Wednesday   2 syllables
> Thursday   2 syllables
> Friday   2 syllables
> Saturday   3 syllables

2

Recording script 🔵 17

Sunday   Monday   Tuesday   Wednesday
Thursday   Friday   Saturday

3, 4

Recording script and answers 🔵 18

■ January   ■ February   ■ March   ■ April   ■ May   ■ June   ■ July
■ August   ■ September   ■ October   ■ November   ■ December

5, 6

Recording script 🔵 19

the twenty-eighth of April   the fifteenth of August
the third of February

7

> We *write* 15th January or 15 January but we *say* the fifteenth of January or January the fifteenth.

Present continuous for future plans

Grammar spot

We use the *present simple* to talk about what we usually do. We use the *present continuous* to talk about future plans.

Possible answers

b He's/is going (horse) riding next Monday.
c He's/is having lunch with a friend on Thursday.
d He's/is playing basketball tomorrow afternoon.
e He's/is going camping on 15th January.
f He's/is going to a party at the weekend.

《Activity》 **Diary**

> You are both free on Saturday evening.

page 32

Exam folder 4
Listening Part 1

2

a No. Sophia is not very good at tennis.
b No. They can't play hockey with two people.
c Yes. Greg says *We could go out on our bikes. Let's cycle …*
d Yes. *Great idea* tells you that they agree.

Recording script 🔵 20

1   What do they decide to do tomorrow?
Greg: This weekend is so boring. Let's go out and do something tomorrow. I'd like to do some sport. Would you like to play tennis with me?

Sophia: I'm not very good at tennis. My best sport is hockey. I'd like to have a game tomorrow.
Greg: Don't be silly. We can't play hockey with just two people. We could go out on our bikes. Let's cycle to the lake and take a picnic.
Sophia: Great idea.

4

| 2 B | 3 C | 4 A | 5 A |

Recording script 🔵 21

2   Which shop are they going to first?
Woman: I want some shampoo to take on holiday. The chemist is at the other end of the shopping centre. So let's go and look for your swimming costume first.
Girl: Oh, yes. There's a really nice one in the sports shop over there.
Woman: OK. And remind me to buy something to read on the plane. The bookshop is next to the chemist's.

3   When is Tim meeting his father?
Man: Have a good time, Tim. Don't forget we're meeting tomorrow morning outside the railway station at eleven.
Tim: Dad, that's much too early. I'm going out with Simon tonight. We're spending the evening at a nightclub. We're staying there till midnight. I can't meet you until the afternoon. Two o'clock is better.
Man: OK. But don't be late. And have a good evening.

4   Where are they going on Saturday evening?
Boy: I've got an invitation to a concert on Saturday evening. Euan is playing the violin and he says I can have two free tickets. Do you want to come?
Girl: Well, I've got two tickets for the rock band at the Town Hall on Saturday evening. It starts at eight o'clock, but I can go with someone else.
Boy: Oh, I'm coming with you to that. Please?
Girl: OK. And don't forget we're taking your little brother to the cinema on Saturday afternoon.

5   When is Paula's birthday party?
Woman: You know Paula's sixteen soon?
Man: Surely not! Time passes so quickly. Now, let me see, when is her birthday? It's the fifteenth of May, isn't it?
Woman: That's right. It's on a Monday. So the party's two days before, on the thirteenth. That's a Saturday.

page 33

Writing folder
Writing Part 2

2

Only email **b** covers all three points in the question.
Email **a** says what she would like to do but omits two
elements of the question – time of arrival and where to
meet. This answer would not get a good mark even though
the English is good.
Email **c** omits to arrange a meeting place.

3

No, because it is not long enough.

Unit 5
page 34
Introduction

1

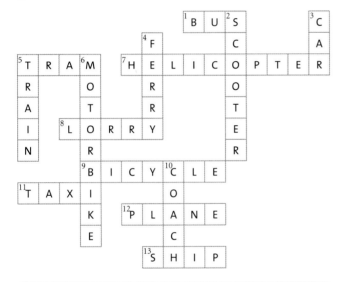

Corpus spot

a by car
b on foot
We go *by* car, train, bicycle, plane, boat but we go *on* foot.

4

AIR	LAND		WATER
helicopter	coach	car	ferry
plane	lorry	bicycle	ship
	motorbike	scooter	
	bus	taxi	
	tram	train	

Vocabulary spot

truck = lorry   *cab* = taxi   *freeway* = motorway

page 35
Listening

1

In an airport.

2

1 c   **2** d   **3** a   **4** g   **5** b   **6** h

Recording script 1 22 **and answers to Grammar spot below**

1

Man: Hello, can you help me? <u>I need a hotel room for tonight</u>. Near the airport.
Woman: Certainly, sir. I can book you a room.
Man: And can you call a taxi to take me there?
Woman: Oh, <u>you don't need a taxi</u>. There's a free bus.

2

Man: Passport, please. How long are you staying in the United Kingdom?
Woman: Only two weeks. Why? <u>Do I need a visa?</u>
Man: No, you don't. Enjoy your stay.

3

Woman: Good morning, sir. How many cases have you got?
Man: Just this one.
Woman: Right. Here's your boarding pass.
Man: <u>Do I need to go to the departure lounge now?</u>
Woman: Yes please, sir.
Man: OK. Thank you.

4

Woman 1: <u>Do we need to buy anything else before we leave?</u>
Woman 2: I don't think so. Well, we haven't got any shampoo.
Woman 1: Oh, <u>we don't need to buy that. The hotel has got everything we need.</u>
Woman 2: Oh, fine.

5

Woman: I've got this camera and this watch. The camera was a thousand dollars and the watch was a hundred. <u>Do I need to pay any tax?</u>
Man: Well, <u>you needn't pay any tax on the watch. But you need to pay tax on the camera.</u>
Woman: Oh, OK.

6

Man: Good afternoon. I want to fly to Madrid as soon as possible. In business class, please.
Woman: I can put you on the five o'clock flight. Is that all right?

Man: Yes, that's great. <u>I need to come back on Saturday evening.</u>

Woman: No problem.

Man: <u>Do I need to reconfirm my return flight?</u>

Woman: <u>No, you needn't do that.</u> It's all arranged.

Man: Thank you very much.

Language focus

Need

1

a a hotel room
b a taxi
c a visa
d go to the departure lounge
e nothing
f yes – on the camera but not on the watch
g on Saturday evening
h no

Grammar spot

Need + noun

+	I **need** a taxi. He needs a taxi.	-	I **don't need** a visa. He doesn't need a visa.	?	Do I need a boarding pass? Does he need a boarding pass?

Need + verb

+	I **need to** buy some shampoo. He needs to buy some shampoo.	-	I don't need to pay / I needn't pay any tax. He **doesn't need to** pay / He **needn't** pay any tax.	?	**Do I need to** reconfirm my flight? Does he need to reconfirm his flight?

Needn't is only used before a **verb**, not a **noun**. *Needn't* isn't used in a question.

page 36

2

b Do you need   **c** Do we need to   **d** don't need to / needn't
e need to   **f** I need to   **g** doesn't need
h don't need to / needn't

Countable and uncountable nouns

1, 2

Countable (singular)	Countable (plural)	Uncountable
a camera a coat an address book a passport a mobile phone a sleeping bag a toothbrush a backpack	*some magazines* some photos	*some shampoo* some money some chocolate some tea some sunscreen

Grammar spot

Countable nouns can be singular or plural. **Uncountable** nouns cannot be plural. We use *a* or *an* before **countable** nouns. We use *some* before **uncountable** nouns and plural **countable** nouns.

a glass or a bottle of water
a packet of tea
a bar of chocolate
a loaf of bread

3

Suggested answers

Things Joe needs to take	Things Joe doesn't need to take
a passport a camera some money an address book (so he can send postcards) some magazines (to read on the journey) a mobile phone	a coat (it's hot in Brazil) any shampoo any chocolate any photos of his family a sleeping bag (he's staying with a family) any tea any sunscreen a toothbrush (he can buy a toothbrush, sunscreen and shampoo when he gets there)

Corpus spot

a I have a lot of <u>work</u> to do at home tonight.
b We can eat <u>fish</u> and big plates of salad.
c We came to a set of traffic <u>lights</u>.
d Listening to English <u>music</u> is good.
e I have a lot of <u>furniture</u> in my room.
f My friend Noelia always gives me good <u>advice</u>.
g They travel to other <u>countries</u> every year.

page 37

Expressions of quantity

Grammar spot

left-hand column: *countable nouns*
right-hand column *uncountable nouns*

b much   **c** lots of   **d** several   **e** a few   **f** a lot of
g a couple of   **h** much   **i** a little

≪Pronunciation≫

1

b a of   **c** to   **d** a of   **e** to   **f** some

2

The words you filled in all have a schwa sound: /ə/.

3, 4

Answers and recording script 🔟24

a I need⟨a⟩hotel room.
b You need⟨to⟩pay tax.
c I want⟨some⟩shampoo.
d I'd like⟨to⟩go swimming.
e He's got⟨a⟩few magazines.
f I've got⟨a⟩new pair⟨of⟩shoes.

page 38

Exam folder 5
Reading Part 2

2

> **1** d **2** a **3** e **4** b **5** f
>
> Suitcase **c** does not belong to anyone.
> **1** Karen likes <u>pop music</u> and dancing in discos and she would like to find a hotel where she can <u>swim</u> every day. She also enjoys using a gym.
> **2** Tom needs to find a quiet hotel in the country which has a good restaurant. He is taking some <u>work</u> on holiday with him and needs to hire a room for a business meeting in the hotel.
> **3** Maggie would like to relax in her hotel, <u>sunbathing</u>, swimming and <u>reading</u>. She wants to stay somewhere quiet with a good restaurant.
> **4** John wants to stay in the mountains. He likes <u>walking</u> and is interested in flowers and <u>birds</u>. He wants to stay in a family hotel.
> **5** Mike wants to spend his holiday <u>sightseeing</u> in the city. He likes taking <u>photographs</u> of the places he visits and wants a hotel which can organise trips. He would like a hotel with a swimming pool.

page 39

5–8

Karen: **E**

Hotels	A	B	C	D	E	F	G	H
disco?			✓		✓			
swimming?					✓			
gym?					✓			

Tom: **F**

Hotels	A	B	C	D	E	F	G	H
in the country?				✓		✓		✓
good restaurant?						✓		
room for meeting?						✓		

Maggie: **B**

Hotels	A	B	C	D	E	F	G	H
quiet?		✓		✓		✓		✓
swimming?		✓						
restaurant?		✓						

John: **H**

Hotels	A	B	C	D	E	F	G	H
family hotel?	✓				✓			✓
walking in the mountains?								✓
flowers and birds?								✓

Mike: **A**

Hotels	A	B	C	D	E	F	G	H
city?	✓		✓		✓		✓	
swimming pool?	✓				✓			
organises trips?	✓							

Unit 6
page 40

> **Vocabulary spot**
> **Answer**
> *I had a good education* means *I went to a good school.*

page 41

Reading

1

> **A** Mavis Carver (girls being addressed by their surnames is very old-fashioned)
> **B** Neil Johnson (it was an 'all boys' school)
> **C** Anita Green (computer rooms have only existed in the past twenty years)

2

> **Suggested answers**
> **A** (about) 1935 / in the 1930s **B** 1965 / in the 1960s
> **C** 2005 / this century

Language focus

Adjectives describing feelings and opinions

2

> **Good feelings** important, interested, fun, friendly, happy, confident
> **Bad feelings** frightened, angry, miserable, terrible, difficult, tired

page 42

-ing and *-ed* adjectives

1

> **b** frightened **c** tired **d** amused **e** interested **f** worried

2

> **b** amusing **c** worrying **d** interesting **e** tiring **f** boring

Grammar spot

We use *-ing* adjectives to describe the thing (or person) that *causes* the feeling.
We use *-ed* adjectives to describe the person who *has* the feeling.

Corpus spot

a bored   b interesting   c interested   d relaxed
e surprised   f boring   g embarrassing   h excited
i surprising   j amazed

Past simple

1

List A   arrived, asked, helped, looked, realised, showed,
          started, stopped, studied, used, walked, wanted
List B   was/were, became, began, could, felt, found, got, gave,
          went, made, met, took, told

2

List A verbs are regular verbs. List B are irregular verbs.

page 43

Grammar spot

a You use *was* and *were* in the same way as *is* and *are* in the present.
b *did*

3

b Were there any boys in the hall?
c Did she walk to school alone?
d Did the teacher give the girls any books?
e Was Mavis's first lesson in the classroom?

4

2 e   3 b   4 c   5 d

7

b were   c worked   d didn't learn   e Did   go
f made   g became   h taught   i Did   attend
j believed   k didn't/did not need   l had   m stayed

«Pronunciation»

2

Recording script ①25

checked   enjoyed   kissed   looked   mended
needed   prepared   realised   showed   stopped
studied   used   walked   wanted   wished

3

/d/   enjoyed   prepared   realised   showed   studied   used
/t/   checked   kissed   looked   stopped   walked   wished
/ɪd/   mended   needed   wanted

Exam folder 6
Listening Part 2

2

In the recording, the taxi driver is male and the passenger is female; the passenger is worried; the bags are in the boot.

Recording script ①26

Man: On my first day as a taxi driver, my first passenger was a woman who wanted to go to the airport. She was in a hurry because she needed to be at the airport at 10.30 to check in. She had lots of bags with her. Anyway, she got in the car and put the bags in the boot and we set off. I drove fast and we were lucky because there were no traffic jams. <u>We got to the airport at exactly 10.15.</u> Her flight was to New York where her sister lived and it left at 12.20. She got out of the car and started to look for her purse. Then she looked across at the airport. She suddenly looked very annoyed. She took her ticket out of her bag and showed it to me. I realised the mistake. <u>She didn't tell me which airport to go to, so this was the International Airport. Her flight went from the City Airport</u> – about an hour away. She refused to pay me anything so it wasn't a very good start for me.

3

a to check in   b they arrived at the airport   c 12.20
d no   e no

4

1 A   2 C

5

See underlining in recording script above.

7

1 A   2 C   3 B

Recording script ①27

Woman: When I was about 18, I started a new job in the kitchen of a restaurant. I liked cooking and I wanted to be a chef so I was really pleased to have this job. In fact on the first morning I woke up very early and I went to the restaurant at about 7.30. <u>I just didn't want to wait any longer. I wanted to be in that kitchen!</u> Luckily, the restaurant was open. The chef met me and showed me what to do. But at about nine o'clock the chef felt ill and went home. <u>It was a terrible day. I was the only one in the kitchen</u> and the restaurant was very busy. The waiters came to the kitchen and ordered the food for the customers and I made it. The waiters helped me to find things. Twice I made a mistake and the customers got the wrong food. <u>But it wasn't a problem – in fact both of the customers ate the food and then came to the kitchen to say the food was really delicious.</u> And the waiters got a big tip.

page 45

Writing folder
Writing Part 3
2

> **C** answers the question. It says something about the school and says what the writer likes. **A** doesn't understand the question and writes from the person who is coming to the school rather than the person who is already there. **B** gives only negative information about the school and spends too much time writing about the city.

3

> computers, sports, friends, size, timetable, laboratories, swimming pool, teachers

Units 1–6 Revision
page 46

Vocabulary
2

> **b** engineer   **c** slim   **d** ferry   **e** guest
> **f** century   **g** joke   **h** factory   **i** performance

Reading
3

> **b** No, he didn't.   **c** Yes, he does.   **d** Yes, they do.
> **e** No, there weren't.   **f** Yes, he did.   **g** Yes, there were.
> **h** No, he doesn't.   **i** No, he didn't.   **j** No, he wasn't.
> **k** No, they didn't.   **l** Yes, they are.   **m** Yes, he is.

page 47

Vocabulary
4

> **b** became   **c** finished   **d** summer   **e** job   **f** excited
> **g** hard-working   **h** tired   **i** boring   **j** exciting
> **k** take   **l** describe   **m** share   **n** helped   **o** design

Grammar
5

> **2** B   **3** A   **4** C   **5** A   **6** A

6

> **2** C   **3** C   **4** B   **5** A   **6** A

7

> **b** I couldn't   **c** Did you go   **d** I went   **e** Was it   **f** it was
> **g** We saw   **h** I don't usually like   **i** I enjoyed
> **j** the concert began   **k** it ended   **l** we met   **m** you had
> **n** I didn't do   **o** Are you going   **p** My cousin's giving
> **q** Do you want   **r** He always has   **s** he knows
> **t** I didn't realise

Unit 7
page 48

Introduction
1

> **2** car park (J)   **3** nightclub (A)   **4** museum (G)   **5** library (H)
> **6** theatre (F)   **7** bus station (B)   **8** newspaper kiosk (C)
> **9** swimming pool (D)   **10** petrol station (E)

page 49

> ### Grammar spot
> **a** opposite
> **b** in front of; behind; next to / beside
> **c** between

Listening
1

> **1** petrol station   **2** shopping centre   **3** skateboard park

Recording script ●1 **28**

Conversation 1

Woman: OK. Turn right at the next roundabout and then take the second turning on the left. It's on your left on the corner opposite a supermarket.

Man: I'm sorry. Could you say that again, please?

Woman: Go down here. When you reach the roundabout, turn right. It's a one-way street. OK?

Man: Yes.

Woman: So, after the roundabout you don't take the first turning on the left, you take the second. You'll see it then. There's a supermarket on the other side of the road. All right?

Man: Yes. I see. Thank you very much for your help.

Woman: You're welcome.

Conversation 2

Man: It's near the market square, which is a pedestrian area. It's not far to walk from here.

Woman: Where can I leave my car?

Man: OK, well, at the next crossroads turn right, then turn right again. You'll see the entrance to the car park just on the right. Park your car there, then you can walk across the road and you're there. There's a pedestrian crossing.

Woman: Thank you.

Conversation 3

Girl: Yes, of course. Are you on foot?

Boy: I'm sorry, I don't understand.

Girl: Are you walking?

Boy: Yes.

Girl: Good. That's easy then. Go straight down this road past the town hall. Then turn left at the traffic lights into Queen Street. Walk down there to the market square and walk across the square. Go straight on and it's at the next crossroads on the corner.

2

> **a** Could you … need to find
> **b** could you tell me the way to
> **c** can you tell me the way to
> *Could* is more polite than *can*. We also use *please* a lot in English.
> **d** I'm sorry. Could you say that
> **e** sorry
> British people often say nothing in reply to *Thank you*, but *You're welcome* is a possible answer.

Recording script ⑴29

Conversation 1

Man: <u>Could you help me, please? I need to find a petrol station.</u>

Woman: OK. Turn right at the next roundabout and then take the second turning on the left. It's on your left on the corner opposite a supermarket.

Man: <u>I'm sorry. Could you say that again, please?</u>

Woman: Go down here. When you reach the roundabout, turn right. It's a one-way street. OK?

Man: Yes.

Woman: So, after the roundabout you don't take the first turning on the left, you take the second. You'll see it then. There's a supermarket on the other side of the road. All right?

Man: Yes. I see. Thank you very much for your help.

Woman: You're welcome.

Conversation 2

Woman: <u>Excuse me, could you tell me the way to the shopping centre, please?</u>

Man: It's near the market square, which is a pedestrian area. It's not far to walk from here.

Woman: Where can I leave my car?

Man: OK, well, at the next crossroads turn right, then turn right again. You'll see the entrance to the car park just on the right. Park your car there then you can walk across the road and you're there. There's a pedestrian crossing.

Woman: Thank you.

Conversation 3

Boy: <u>Excuse me, can you tell me the way to the skateboard park, please?</u>

Girl: Yes, of course. Are you on foot?

Boy: <u>I'm sorry. I don't understand.</u>

Girl: Are you walking?

Boy: Yes.

Girl: Good. That's easy then. Go straight down this road past the town hall. Then turn left at the traffic lights into Queen Street. Walk down there to the market square and walk across the square. Go straight on and it's at the next crossroads on the corner.

Language focus

Directions

> **b** second turning on   **c** straight on / straight down this road
> **d** Turn left   crossroads   **e** Turn   into
> **f** Turn right   roundabout   **g** corner

≪Pronunciation≫

1, 2

/aʊ/	/ɔː/
out	or
round	sports
town	course
about	corner
down	hall
how	board
	walk

3

> /aʊ/ down roundabout town outside
> /ɔː/ corner walk course hall skateboard sports

page 50

Prepositions of movement

> **Suggested answers**
> **b** along   **c** up   **d** through   **e** around   **f** across
> **g** off   **h** over

Comparative adjectives

1

> **b** cheaper   **c** safer   **d** bigger   **e** more exciting
> **f** more fashionable   **g** noisier   **h** more popular
> **i** more common   **j** better

> **Grammar spot**
> Most one-syllable adjectives (e.g. *light*) add *er*.
> One-syllable adjectives ending in e (e.g. *safe*) add *r*.
> Most adjectives ending in a *vowel* and a consonant (e.g. *big*) double the consonant and add *er*.
> Most adjectives with more than one *syllable* (e.g. *popular*) use *more* (e.g. *more popular*).
> Adjectives ending in y (e.g. *noisy*) usually change y to *i* and add *er*.
> *Good* and *bad* are irregular and become *better* and *worse*.

3

Add *er*	steeper stronger older richer
Add *r*	nicer wider
Double the last letter and add *er*	thinner wetter
Use *more*	more famous more popular more difficult more miserable
Change *y* to *i* and add *er*	friendlier lazier busier tidier
Irregular	worse better

page 51

4

Possible answers

c Skateboarding is not as/so safe as cycling.
d A skateboard is not as/so big as a mountain bike.
e Cycling is less exciting than skateboarding.
f Skateboards are less fashionable than mountain bikes.
g Mountain bikes are not as/so noisy as skateboards.
h Mountain bikes are less popular than skateboards.
i Mountain bikes are not as/so common as skateboards.
j Skateboards are not as/so good as mountain bikes for long journeys.

Grammar spot

Mountain bikes are more fashionable *than* skateboards.
= Skateboards are not as/<u>so</u> fashionable *as* mountain bikes.
= Skateboards are *less* fashionable *than* mountain bikes.

Corpus spot

b I would like to buy a new TV that is <u>bigger</u> than my old one.
c Hotels are <u>cheaper</u> here than in the city.
d My parents are not <u>as/so</u> excited as I am about the holiday.
e Modern furniture is <u>easier</u> to clean than old furniture.
f This supermarket is <u>better</u> than the other one.
g I think he is <u>taller</u> than I told you.
h I'm not as good at tennis <u>as</u> you are.

5

b Steve is hotter than John. / John isn't as/so hot as Steve.
c Sue's homework is worse than Jack's (homework). / Jack's homework isn't as/so bad as Sue's (homework).
d The taxi is less slow than the school bus. / The taxi isn't as/so slow as the school bus.
e The Amazon is wider than the Thames. / The Thames isn't as/so wide as the Amazon.
f Jill is sadder than Liz. / Liz isn't as/so sad as Jill.
g The ring is less expensive than the watch. / The ring isn't as/so expensive as the watch.
h The shorts are dirtier than the T-shirt. / The T-shirt isn't as/so dirty as the shorts.

page 52

Exam folder 7
Reading Part 3

3

The city of Lincoln is 2,000 years old and there are a lot of interesting buildings to see. <u>The cathedral is in the north of the city just outside the main city centre. You can walk to many of Lincoln's other attractions from the cathedral. It's not far from the castle.</u> There is a wonderful view of the city from there. <u>Behind the castle is The Lawn, an old hospital, which is now a museum with shops and a café. You can sit in the beautiful gardens to have lunch or a coffee.</u> There is a car park a few metres from the café.

During the summer, walking tours leave from <u>the Tourist Information Centre, which is next to the castle.</u> They are not expensive, last about an hour and visit all the main attractions. There are some very interesting museums. The Toy Museum is near the Tourist Information Centre and has children's toys and games from the last century.

There are shops and a market in the old city centre. There are two shopping centres – one is the <u>Waterside Centre opposite the market</u> and the other is <u>St Mark's Shopping Centre. St Mark's is newer than the Waterside Centre</u> and is just south of the main city centre. Go straight down the High Street from the city centre and it is on the right.

<u>In the middle of the city centre, there are some beautiful spots away from the crowds.</u> For example, <u>you can walk by the river or take a boat trip. Trips leave from Bayford Pool.</u>

You can travel to Lincoln by train, bus or car. It is 216 km from London. The bus station is beside the river and <u>the railway station is a few minutes' walk away from the bus station on the other side of St Mary's Street.</u>

4

1 A

5

2 B **3** B **4** A **5** A **6** A

page 53

Corpus spot

These sentences from the text will help you correct the mistakes.

... just outside the main city centre (**a**)
It's not far from (**b**) the castle.
There is a wonderful view of the city from there. (**c**)
Behind the castle ... (**d**)
There is a car park a few metres from the café. (**e**)
... the Tourist Information Centre, which is next to the castle. (**f**)
The Toy Museum is near the Tourist Information Centre (**g**)
The bus station is beside the river (**h**)
... the railway station is a few minutes' walk away from the bus station (**i**)

Answers

a We will meet 15 minutes before the film starts <u>outside</u> the cinema.
b My flat isn't too far away <u>from</u> the town centre.
c There is a lovely view of the sea <u>from</u> the window.
d We saw a big tree and <u>behind it</u> was a lake.
e The cinema is a few metres <u>from</u> the Underground station.
f In my room there is a radio next <u>to</u> the TV.
g I live in the south of France <u>near</u> Toulouse.
h I am staying in a small town <u>beside</u> a large forest.
i He works only one block away <u>from</u> where I am working.

Unit 8
page 54

Introduction
4, 5

Answers and recording script **1** **32**

a Congratulations! (They're getting married.)
b Good luck! (They're taking an exam.)
c Happy birthday! (It's the boy's birthday. Also possible: *Many happy returns*, or *Congratulations* for a special birthday, e.g. 18 or 60.)
d Have a good journey! (They're starting a journey. Also possible: *Enjoy your trip*.)
e Enjoy your meal! (They're having a meal.*)
f Well done! (He's won a race. Also possible: *Congratulations*.)
g Happy anniversary! (It's their wedding anniversary. Also possible: *Congratulations*.)
h Have a nice weekend! (They're leaving work. Also possible: *See you on Monday*.)
* There is no set expression used by English speakers at the beginning of a meal. *Enjoy your meal* is normally said by the waiter, not a fellow diner.

page 55

Reading
1

Photo **a** shows a traditional church wedding. With lots of guests, this will cost thousands of pounds and is traditionally paid for by the bride's father, though costs are often shared now.

Photo **b** shows a beach in an exotic location, where a wedding can take place. The bride and groom fly out, get married and stay there for their honeymoon. This is an increasingly popular trend with couples who want a 'romantic' wedding and honeymoon, but cannot afford or do not wish to spend so much on the wedding.

Photo **c** shows a registry office wedding (the most usual way to get married in the UK nowadays).

Photo **d** shows a wedding in a licensed wedding venue.

2

a Nigel and Fiona b Anna and Jay c Dawn and Gary
d Lorne and Esmerelda

3

b A new bikini and some sunscreen.
c Their family and friends.
d When they come back.
e Because they're both very famous.
f The rings.
g Because no one can disturb them there on their honeymoon.
h All their friends and their parents and all their relations.
i Fiona's parents.
j (They've booked) a band.
k Because they're keeping that a secret until their wedding day.
l Because she doesn't know who's accepted and who's refused (their secretaries have organised everything).
m To a good restaurant. Back to work.
n Because they're too busy to go away (this year).

page 56
4

b 9 keep a secret
c 2 book a band
d 3 organise a barbecue
e 7 refuse an invitation
f 1/8 make an appointment/mistake
g 6 rent a cottage
h 5 hire a car
i 8/1 make a mistake/appointment

Corpus spot

a I often go there and <u>have</u> a barbecue with my friends.
b I had a rest and I <u>made</u> a plan for my holiday.
c My friend is leaving next week so we'd like to <u>have</u> a party.
d I will <u>make</u> some reservations because this is a busy time of year.
e I hope you don't <u>make</u> the same mistake as me.
f His name is John and we <u>are</u> the same age.

Language focus

Present perfect; *just*, *already* and *yet*

1

b 've/have told c 've/have rented d haven't planned
e haven't told f 've/have booked g 've/have sent
h has accepted; has refused i 's/has made

Grammar spot
Formation

verb	past simple	past participle
open	opened	*opened*
plan	*planned*	planned
organise	organised	*organised*
send	*sent*	sent
tell	told	*told*
make	*made*	made
take	*took*	taken
eat	ate	*eaten*
be	was/were	*been*
go	*went*	gone

Meaning
a past simple
b present perfect

2

Suggested answers

b He's broken the chair.
c He's dropped his glass.
d They've lost the key.
e They've eaten all the food.
f She's spilt some juice.
g They've drunk all the fizzy drinks.
h They've made a terrible mess.

3

b Have you washed the glasses yet?
Yes, I've just washed them.
c Have you tidied the living room yet?
Yes, I've just tidied it.
d Have you found the key yet?
Yes, I've just found it.
e Have you thrown away the rubbish yet?
Yes, I've just thrown it away.
f Have you bought any/the food yet?
Yes, I've just bought some/it.
g Have you mended the chair yet?
Yes, I've just mended it.

Grammar spot

a just **b** already **c** yet **d** already **e** yet **f** yet

4

b already **c** yet **d** yet **e** already **f** already

《Pronunciation》

1, 2

Answers and recording script 1️⃣ 33

the third of July
the first of January
the twenty-fifth of March
the twenty-fourth of October
the second of February

3

Answers and recording script 1️⃣ 34

(the) 11(th of) November   (the) 12(th of) June
(the) 14(th of) December   (the) 20(th of) April
(the) 21(st of) August   (the) 22(nd of) September

page 58

Exam folder 8
Speaking Part 3
1

1 **d** At Christmas time many people decorate real or plastic trees.

2 **c** On St Valentine's Day people traditionally send an anonymous card or present to the person they love or admire.
3 **b** Eggs have pre-Christian associations with spring, but chocolate eggs are part of the Easter celebrations enjoyed by most UK children, whether their families are churchgoers or not.
4 **a** Notting Hill is a very large public carnival which takes place in London. There are thousands of bands and dancers of many kinds, but especially from the Afro-Caribbean communities.

2

It does not matter if you do not know what festival your photograph shows.
Photograph a shows the Holi festival in India.
Photograph b shows the ice festival at Lake Shikotsu in Japan.

page 59

Writing folder 8
Writing Part 2
2

a Matthew   **b** Ben   **c** Catherine

3

Dear *Matthew*,
I'm having a birthday party next Friday. <u>Would you like to come</u> (*these words invite Matthew to the party*)? <u>All our friends from school are coming and some of my family</u> (*these words tell him who is coming*). I live in the city centre. <u>Take a bus to the bus station, then you can walk from there</u> (*these words suggest how to get there*).

4

Card b
Dear *Ben*,
<u>Thank you very much for the book you sent me for my birthday</u> (*these words thank him for the present*). <u>I spent the day with my family and I went to a nightclub in the evening with my friends</u> (*these words describe what you did on your birthday*). <u>Can you tell me when your birthday is</u> (*these words ask him when his birthday is*)?

Card c
Dear *Catherine*,
<u>Thank you for inviting me to your birthday party next week</u> (*these words thank her*). <u>I'm sorry but I can't come</u> (*these words apologise*) <u>because my brother and his wife are visiting us with their new baby</u> (*these words explain why you can't go*). I hope you enjoy the party.

5

Sample answers

Dear Emily,
Thank you for inviting me to the concert with you next Saturday. I'm sorry but I can't come with you because I'm going to the seaside for the weekend with my family. I hope

you enjoy it.
Best wishes,
Hans

Dear Tim,
I went to the city centre last Saturday. A friend gave me a lift on his motorbike. We went to the cinema and then to a café. Would you like to come with us next weekend?
All the best,
Jakub

Corpus spot

a go   b come

Unit 9
page 60

Introduction

1

They are lifting weights, exercising on a rowing machine, and exercising on an exercise bike.
The weightlifter is exercising his arms, but also muscles all over his body – chest, shoulders, neck, back, legs, stomach.
The rower is exercising her arms and legs and also other muscles, such as her stomach muscles.
The cyclist is mainly exercising her legs.

2

a finger	h forehead	o neck
b thumb	i lip	p chin
c shoulder	j cheek	q knee
d wrist	k brain	r ankle
e elbow	l lung	s toe
f chest	m heart	
g eyebrow	n stomach	

page 61

3

The woman on the cycling machine would use about 450 calories in 30 minutes, the woman on the rowing machine about 300 and the man lifting weights about 110.

4

washing the dishes – about 85 calories
playing the drums – about 150 calories
watching TV – about 35 calories
playing tennis – about 250 calories
running upstairs – about 550 calories
sweeping the floor – about 130 calories
playing the guitar – about 75 calories
swimming – about 330 calories

Listening

1

a His son has hurt his wrist.
b She has a cough and a sore throat.
c Her husband has a pain in his chest and he feels sick.

d The child has a stomach ache.
e The boy has sore eyes.
f The child has earache and a temperature.

Recording script ①35

a

Nurse: Hello. Healthlink Phone Line. Can I help you?
Man: Oh, yes, thank you. My son fell over at school today. He was playing football. His arm hurts, well, his wrist really.
Nurse: Did he hit his head?
Man: No, he didn't.
Nurse: Can he move his fingers?
Man: No, he can't. He can't move them at all.

b

Nurse: Hello. Healthlink Phone Line. Can I help you?
Girl: Hello. I've got a cough and a sore throat. I cough all the time, especially at night. I can't stop and I can't sleep.
Nurse: Have you got a cold at the moment?
Girl: No, I haven't. I had one last week but it's gone. Now I've got this cough.

c

Nurse: Hello. Healthlink Phone Line. Can I help you?
Woman: Oh, yes. My husband isn't feeling well. He's got a pain in his chest. He's usually very healthy. I don't understand it.
Nurse: Does he feel sick?
Woman: Yes, he does.

d

Nurse: Hello. Healthlink Phone Line. Can I help you?
Man: Oh, hello. I'm sorry to bother you, but I'm looking after a friend's daughter and she has a terrible stomach ache.
Nurse: Does she have a headache?
Man: Yes, she does.
Nurse: Has she eaten a lot today?
Man: No, she hasn't. Well, let me see. She had a big breakfast. Then we went to the cinema and she had a burger and chips at lunchtime, oh, and some popcorn. Since then she's only had a bar of chocolate and a drink. Should I take her to the doctor's?

e

Nurse: Hello. Healthlink Phone Line. Can I help you?
Boy: Yes. Hello. I've got sore eyes. I can't open them very well.
Nurse: Have you spent a lot of time working at a computer this week? Are you very tired?
Boy: No, I'm not. I'm not working this week. I'm relaxing at home.
Nurse: Do you wear glasses or contact lenses?
Boy: No, I don't.

f

Nurse: Hello. Healthlink Phone Line. Can I help you?

Woman: Hello. My son's got earache. He cried all night. He's just stopped at last so I decided to phone. I don't want to ring the doctor at the weekend.

Nurse: Is he hot?

Woman: Yes, he is. He's got a temperature.

Nurse: Has he taken any aspirin or paracetamol?

Woman: Yes, he has. Just now.

4

> **a** go to the hospital   **b and d** stay at home
> **c** call an ambulance   **e and f** go to the doctor's

Recording script ① 36

a

Nurse: You should take him to the hospital. It's probably broken.

Man: OK. Thanks. We'll go now.

b

Nurse: People often have a cough for a few days after a cold. Why don't you take some cough mixture before you go to bed? Why don't you take a warm drink to bed with you too, and you should sleep with at least two pillows. Your cough will soon be better.

Girl: I hope so. Thank you.

c

Nurse: You should call an ambulance to take him to hospital. You'd better dial 999 at once. Can you do that now?

Woman: Yes, of course.

d

Nurse: You don't need to see a doctor. She shouldn't eat any more food today. But she should drink lots of water.

Man: OK. Thank you.

e

Nurse: Why don't you wash your eyes in warm water? And get an appointment with your doctor because you probably need some antibiotics.

Boy: Thanks for your help.

f

Nurse: Well, why don't you give him some more paracetamol after four hours? And you'd better phone the doctor. You can get an emergency appointment.

Woman: Thanks very much.

page 62

Language focus

Illnesses and advice

1

> **b** I've got earache.   **c** I've got a cough.   **d** I've got a cold.
> **e** I've got a sore eye.   **f** I've got a pain in my chest.
> **g** My arm hurts / is broken.   **h** I feel sick.

2

> **b** don't you take   **c** should call   **d** shouldn't eat
> **e** don't you wash   **f** better phone

Recording script ① 37

a You should take him to the hospital.

b Why don't you take some cough mixture?

c You should call an ambulance.

d She shouldn't eat any more food today.

e Why don't you wash your eyes in warm water?

f You'd better phone the doctor.

Expressions with *at*

> **b** all   **c** night   **d** the moment   **e** lunchtime   **f** home
> **g** last   **h** the weekend   **i** least   **j** once

> **Corpus spot**
> **a** The weather is cold <u>at</u> night.
> **b** I get bored staying <u>at</u> home doing nothing.
> **c** ✓
> **d** That's all I have to tell you <u>at</u> the moment.
> **e** We usually go to the beach <u>at</u> the weekend.
> **f** ✓

page 63

Short answers

1

> **b** 9   **c** 8   **d** 2   **e** 7   **f** 3   **g** 6   **h** 5   **i** 1

> **Grammar spot**
>
> | Question | Short answer |
> |---|---|
> | Present simple | *does, do or doesn't, don't* |
> | Past simple | *did or didn't* |
> | Present perfect | *has, have or hasn't, haven't* |

2

> **b** Yes, I do.   **c** Yes, he/she is.   **d** Yes, they are. / No, they aren't.
> **e** Yes, I am.   **f** Yes, it is. / No, it isn't.   **g** No, I haven't.
> **h** No, he/she hasn't.   **i** Yes, I/we do. / No, I/we don't.

###《Pronunciation》

1

> **b** h<u>e</u>lp   **c** fr<u>ie</u>nd t<u>a</u>kes tr<u>ai</u>n
> **d** h<u>ea</u>lthy br<u>ea</u>kfast d<u>ay</u>   **e** h<u>ea</u>d p<u>ai</u>n
> **f** br<u>ea</u>k   **g** gr<u>ea</u>t pl<u>ay</u> tod<u>ay</u>

3

Recording script ① 38

a My son fell over.

b Can I help you?

c My friend takes the train to college.

d I eat a healthy breakfast every day.

e I hit my head and now I've got a pain.
f Don't break that glass.
g I saw a great play today.

4

> /eɪ/ takes train day pain break great play today
> /e/ fell help friend healthy breakfast head
> Spellings of /eɪ/: *a, ai, ay, ea*
> Spellings of /e/: *e, ea, ie*

page 64

Exam folder 9
Reading Part 4

1

> **A** Text 2 is advising: *You should try it. You really shouldn't work hard all the time. Why don't you join the health club?*
> **B** Text 4 is apologising: *It was very rude of me. I'm really sorry.*
> **C** Text 3 is advertising: *special discount; Don't miss the chance to join.*
> **D** Text 1 is complaining: *I am not happy about this because it is very dangerous.*

2

> **A** The writer of text 4 has this opinion: *The equipment in the gym is old and is sometimes difficult to use.*
> **B** The writer of text 3 has this opinion: *There is no other club in town which is as good as this one.*
> **C** The writer of text 2 has this opinion: *I use the pool there because it's brilliant. The gym is OK.*
> **D** The writer of text 1 has this opinion: *There were no instructors.*

3

> **A** Text 3 states this: *phone me, Mick Smith, the manager*
> **B** Text 1 states this: *I joined your health club last week. / I came in for the first time on Thursday.*
> **C** Text 4 states this: *I go to the club every Sunday afternoon*
> **D** Text 2 states this: *I go ... at least twice a week*

Unit 10
page 66

Introduction

1

> 1 notice in window
> 2 birthday card
> 3 anniversary card
> 4 Post-it note
> 5 business letter
> 6 someone sending a text message
> 7 postcard
> 8 someone writing an email

2

> **a** birthday card (2)
> **b** Post-it note (4)
> **c** text message (6)
> **d** anniversary card (3)
> **e** business letter (5)
> **f** email (8)
> **g** postcard (7)
> **h** notice in window (1)

Vocabulary spot

> We begin letters and emails: *Dear (Name)*. Emails are also often started with *Hi (Name)*.
> Note that it is not normal to write *Dear Friend* in English.
> We end a letter or email to a friend: *All the best, / (With) Best wishes, / (With) Love (from)*
> 'Love' is more commonly used by women and children, but men may use it to close female friends and relatives.
> We end a letter or email to a stranger: *Yours sincerely,*

4

> | :) | I'm happy. / This is a joke. |
> | :(| I'm sad. |
> | :{ | I have a moustache. |
> | :o | I'm surprised. |
> | CU | See you. |
> | 4U | For you. |
> | 2U | To you. |
> | CUL8R | See you later. |
> | RUOK? | Are you OK? |
> | YRUX? | Why are you cross? |
> | 2b/nt2b=? | To be or not to be, that is the question. (First line of a famous speech in Shakespeare's play *Hamlet*) |

page 67

Reading

1

> Mike's letters/emails: **a, c, f, h**
> Maria's letters/emails: **b, d, e, g**

2

> Mike 2 – **f**   Mike 3 – **h**   Mike 4 – **c**
> Maria 2 – **d**   Maria 3 – **g**   Maria 4 – **e**

3

> **b** (Because) they've moved to another town.
> **c** (Because) he hasn't studied English since secondary school.
> **d** Yes, he has.
> **e** She's reserved a room in the hostel for him.
>
> **g** Last year.
> **h** Three years ago.
> **i** The Gibsons.
> **j** When he was a child / Ten years ago.

page 68

Language focus

Present perfect and past simple; *ago, for, since, in*

Grammar spot

◄──── I've worked here **since** 2007. ────►
◄──── I've worked here **for** (three) years. ────►

I started this job **in** 2007.
I started this job (**three**) years **ago**.

a present perfect   **b** present perfect
c past simple   **d** past simple

1

b Did you have   **c** was   **d** met   **e** Have you been
f I've been   **g** I've learnt   **h** Have you been   **i** I have
j was   **k** I visited   **l** I didn't come   **m** I've found   **n** I arrived

2

b 've/have already earned   **c** began   **d** gave   **e** told
f didn't want   **g** got   **h** 've/have sold   **i** bought
j 've/have spent

3

b ago   **c** since   **d** for   **e** since   **f** ago

Corpus spot

a since (since college = since we were at college)
b ago   **c** since   **d** ago   **e** for

page 69

Corpus spot

a been   **b** gone   **c** gone   **d** been   **e** been
f gone   **g** been

Have you ever ...?

b Have you ever bought something online?
c Have you ever been to Bangkok?
d Have you ever been to a pop concert?
e Have you ever ridden a bike?
f Have you ever been to a wedding?

«Pronunciation»

1

/ɪz/
glasses
bridges
hairbrushes
matches

Recording script **1** 39

a He needs new <u>glasses</u>.
b There are ten <u>bridges</u> in the city.
c I bought two new <u>hairbrushes</u>.
d There are three football <u>matches</u> tomorrow.

2

/s/	/z/
books	*schools*
shops	*legs*
chips	*shoes*
cakes	*lessons*
boots	

3

Recording script **1** 41 and answers

a My father play<u>s</u> tenni<u>s</u> very well. /z/ /s/
b My back ache<u>s</u>. /s/
c He never catche<u>s</u> the ball. /ɪz/
d She swim<u>s</u> every day. /z/
e He like<u>s</u> travelling. /s/
f She stay<u>s</u> at home on Sunday<u>s</u>. /z/, /z/
g He never finishe<u>s</u> work early. /ɪz/
h He eat<u>s</u> salad every day. /s/
i She always watche<u>s</u> him when he play<u>s</u> football. /z/, /ɪz/, /z/
j He hope<u>s</u> to be a scientist. /s/
k The hotel arrange<u>s</u> everything. /ɪz/

page 70

Exam folder 10

Listening Part 1

1

The question is about how the woman travelled: by car/
driving, by bus or by train.

2

Suggested answers

2 hotel, campsite, beach (tall, floor)
3 beard, short hair, glasses
4 journalist, photographer, actress
5 CD, calendar, picture

3

1 A   **2** C   **3** A   **4** B   **5** B

Recording script **1** 42

For each question, there are three pictures and a short
recording.
Choose the correct picture and put a tick (✔) in the box
below it.
1 How did the woman travel?
Woman: Hi, I got here safely. <u>I drove in the end</u> because I
was late last time when I took the train. It was raining, so
I didn't want to wait for the bus.

2 Where did the man stay?

Man: We were on the top floor of the hotel and we expected to have a lovely view. But <u>our hotel only had four floors</u> and there was a much taller hotel between us and the sea so we couldn't see much. There was a nice campsite next to the beach so next time we're going there.

3 Which is the girl's brother?

Boy: I was walking through town yesterday and your brother stopped to say hi. I didn't recognise him – he looks so different.

Girl: I suppose so. <u>He's grown a beard and he wears glasses</u> now.

Boy: And his hair's really short, too.

4 Which job is Alice doing now?

Man: Is Alice working as an actress now? She was still training last time I saw her.

Woman: Oh, she didn't finish that course. It's difficult to get a job, you know. She's working on the local newspaper now <u>as a photographer</u>.

Man: Really? I always expected her to be a journalist – she was so good at writing when she was at school.

5 What has the boy bought his mother?

Girl: Toby, have you bought a birthday present for mum yet?

Boy: Of course I have. <u>I've got her a calendar</u>, a film one, with pictures of her favourite actors and singers.

Girl: Oh, that was a good idea. I've got her a CD.

Boy: I nearly got her a CD but I couldn't decide which one.

page 71

Writing folder
Writing Part 3

2

Mirza's letter answers the questions, but it is not a good answer because it is too short and simple.

3

Suggested answer

<u>Thanks for your letter.</u> I don't go to a fitness centre. <u>There's one near our house and my brother joined it last year. He says it's good.</u> I prefer to do sport outdoors. There's a sports ground near our house. <u>I go there on Saturdays and play football with my friends. On Sundays we have matches against other teams.</u> I go swimming quite often. <u>I usually go to the big pool</u> in the city centre, but sometimes we go surfing in the sea. I really like that and I think it's a great way to keep fit.
All the best,
Mirza

The other sentences don't answer the question.

Grammar spot

I look forward to hearing from you.

Unit 11
page 72

Introduction

1

b 1 (Chile) **c** 6 (Portugal) **d** 5 (Italy)
e 2 (the USA) **f** 7 (Australia) **g** 4 (Kenya) **h** 3 (Mexico)

2

b Italy **c** The USA Mexico **d** Kenya **e** Japan Australia
f Chile **g** Portugal

page 73

Listening

2

Rory's answers
1 C 2 B 3 B 4 C 5 A 6 C 7 A 8 C 9 B 10 A

Recording script 2 02 (underlining refers to answers for Exercise 5)

Question master: And now, Rory – are you ready? You have ten questions. Number 1 – which is the smallest ocean in the world? Is it (a) the Atlantic Ocean, (b) the Indian Ocean, or (c) the Arctic Ocean?

Rory: The Arctic Ocean.

Question master: Number 2 – which is the longest border in the world? Is it (a) between the USA and Canada, (b) between the USA and Mexico, or (c) between Argentina and Chile?

Rory: <u>Oh, just a moment.</u> I think it's between the USA and Mexico.

Question master: Number 3 – where is the wettest place in the world? Is it (a) in India, (b) in Colombia, or (c) in Nigeria?

Rory: <u>Er, I'm sorry, could you repeat that, please?</u>

Question master: Of course. Where is the wettest place in the world? Is it (a) in India, (b) in Colombia, or (c) in Nigeria?

Rory: I think it's in Colombia.

Question master: Number 4 – which planet is the largest? Is it (a) Earth, (b) Venus, or (c) Jupiter?

Rory: Jupiter.

Question master: Number 5 – in which country is the busiest airport in the world? Is it (a) in the USA, (b) in Japan, or (c) in Greece?

Rory: <u>Er, I'm not sure.</u> The USA.

Question master: Number 6 – which island is the biggest? Is it (a) Great Britain, (b) Greenland, or (c) Cuba?

Rory: I think it's Great Britain. No, <u>let me try again.</u> Cuba – that's my answer.

Question master: Number 7 – which continent has the most people? Is it (a) Asia, (b) Australasia, or (c) Africa?

Rory: <u>Let me think</u> – it's not Australasia. I think it's Asia.

Question master: Number 8 – which city is the most expensive to live in? Is it (a) Geneva, in Switzerland, (b) Paris, in France, or (c) Tokyo, in Japan?

Rory: Tokyo.

Question master: Number 9 – where is the deepest valley in the world? Is it (a) in the USA, (b) in China, or (c) in Kenya?

Rory: <u>I'm sorry, I don't know.</u>

Question master: Have a guess.

Rory: China.

Question master: And the last question. Number 10 – which country is the farthest from the equator? Is it (a) Portugal, (b) Australia, or (c) Peru?

Rory: <u>Just a moment.</u> Portugal.

Question master: Thank you, Rory. You got seven correct answers and three wrong answers.

4

Rory got 2, 6 and 9 wrong.

Recording script 2 ▪03

Question master: And here are the answers.

Number 1. Rory, you were correct. The Arctic Ocean is the smallest ocean. It is 14,351,000 square kilometres.

Number 2. Rory, you were wrong. The longest border in the world is between the USA and Canada and it's 6,416 kilometres long.

Number 3. Rory, you were correct. The wettest place in the world is Tutunendo in Colombia and it has 11,770 millimetres of rain every year.

Number 4. Rory, you were correct. The largest planet is Jupiter and it is 142,800 kilometres wide.

Number 5. Rory, you were correct. The busiest airport is in Atlanta in the USA. About seventy-five million passengers use it every year.

Number 6. Rory, you were wrong. Greenland is the biggest island. It has an area of 2,175, 000 square kilometres.

Number 7. Rory, you were correct. Asia is the continent with the most people. More than three billion people live there.

Number 8. Rory, you were correct. Tokyo is the most expensive city in the world to live in.

Number 9. Rory, you were wrong. The deepest valley in the world is in Kenya. The Great Rift Valley is 1,250 metres deep.

And number 10. Rory, you were correct. Portugal is 4,200 kilometres from the equator, so is the farthest.

Well, congratulations, Rory. You have won our fourth prize ...

5

Oh, just a moment
Er, I'm sorry, could you repeat that, please?
Er, I'm not sure.
Let me try again.
Let me think.
I'm sorry, I don't know.

Language focus

Superlative adjectives

1

Adjective	Comparative	Superlative
small	smaller	the smallest
long	longer	the longest
wet	wetter	the wettest
large	larger	the largest
busy	busier	the busiest
big	bigger	the biggest
expensive	more expensive	the most expensive
deep	deeper	the deepest
far	farther/further	the farthest/furthest
good	better	the best
bad	worse	the worst

Grammar spot

Most one-syllable adjectives (e.g. *small*) add **est**.

One-syllable adjectives ending in *e* (e.g. *large*) add **st** .

Most adjectives ending in a **vowel** and a consonant (e.g. *wet*) double the consonant and add **est**.

Most adjectives with more than one **syllable** (e.g. *expensive*) use *the* **most**.

Adjectives ending in *y* (e.g. *busy*) usually change *y* to *i* and add **est**.

Far, **good** and **bad** are irregular and become *the farthest/ furthest*, **the best** and **the worst**.

page 74

2

Possible answers

William is the happiest, the friendliest and the most confident.
Charlie is the most serious, the shyest and the kindest.
Michael is the angriest, the most hard-working and the most interesting.

Corpus spot

a Vilnius is the <u>biggest</u> town in my country.
b That's the <u>worst</u> joke I've ever heard.
c The <u>cheapest</u> hotels are near the railway station.
d Those four days were the <u>happiest</u> in my life.

Numbers and measurements

1

mm millimetre(s)   **cm** centimetre(s)   **m** metre(s)
km kilometre(s)   **km²** square kilometre(s)

3

b 6,416 km **c** 11,770 mm **d** 142,800 km **e** 75,000,000
f 2,175,000 km²
For recording script, see Listening, Exercise 4.

Countries, nationalities, languages

1

Language	Nationality	Country
a Greek	Greek	Greece
b Polish	Polish	Poland
c Japanese	Japanese	Japan
d Russian	Russian	Russia
e German	German	Germany
f Italian	Italian	Italy

2

Language	Nationality	Country
Spanish	Spanish	Spain
Spanish	Mexican	Mexico
French	French	France
Portugese	Brazilian	Brazil
English	Australian	Australia

3

At the time of writing there are 6,912 living languages in the world (according to www.ethnologue.com).

page 75

Present passive

2

invented	carried
led	kept
made	lit
	played

3

b is lit **c** is carried **d** is kept **e** is invented
f aren't/are not made **g** are always led
h aren't/are not played

4

Questions
Are cars driven on the left in Australia or Italy?
Is baseball played in the United States or Russia?
Are kilometres used in Canada or Mexico?
Is rice produced in China or Switzerland?

Answers
Cars are driven on the left in Australia. They aren't driven on the left in Italy.
Baseball is played in the United States. It isn't played in Russia.
Kilometres are used in Mexico. They aren't used in Canada.
Rice is produced in China. It isn't produced in Switzerland.

1

cheese /tʃ/ shampoo /ʃ/

2, 3

Answers and recording script
The words in **bold** are in the wrong column.

cheese	shampoo
Chinese	shy
teacher	special
much	information
cheap	ocean
brush	**lunch**
question	**picture**
temperature	machine

Exam folder 11

page 76

Reading Part 5

1

1 D **2** A **3** B **4** C

2

1 C **2** D **3** B **4** A

3

1 D **2** A **3** C **4** B

4

1 B **2** A **3** C **4** D

6

a to the North Pole **b** they walked **c** in a freezer; to prepare for the trip **d** by plane **e** a cake

page 77

7

1 B **2** C **3** A **4** C **5** D
6 D **7** B **8** C **9** A **10** B

Unit 12

page 78

Introduction

2

The obvious answer is book **d**, but some of the others are also possible.

3

2 c   3 a   4 e   5 d   6 b

4

The biography (book **a**) is non-fiction. The others are fiction.

page 79

Reading

2

a Somebody was screaming very loudly.
b She got out of bed. She put on a T-shirt and some jeans and went out of her room.
c (She talked to) Adriana and Martin Audley.
d (They saw) a police car, some people and something else / Frank Shepherd's body.
e Because she was frightened/upset. / Because Frank was dead.

Language focus

Past continuous and past simple

1

a 3   **b** 2   **c** 1

Grammar spot

Sentences **a, b, c** tell us about events that happened.
Sentences **1, 2, 3** tell us what was happening around the time of those events.

page 80

2

b were waiting   **c** was walking   **d** was standing
e was carrying   **f** was helping   **g** were getting
h was reading   **i** wasn't lying   **j** was sitting   **k** was laughing

3

Suggested answers

a the girl / the doctor / the writer / all three   **b** nothing
c a secret message   **d** because her plan was successful

Grammar spot

While + **past continuous** + **past continuous** describes two activities that were happening at the same time.

When + **past simple** + **past continuous** describes an event that happened during a longer activity, or interrupted it.

4

b While Georg was cooking breakfast, Kurt was having a shower.
c While Georg was playing basketball, Kurt was sleeping.
d While Georg was having lunch, Kurt was still sleeping.
e While Georg was working in the library, Kurt was buying some new CDs.

f While Georg was walking home, Kurt was listening to music.
g While Georg was watching television, Kurt was still listening to music.
h While Georg was going to bed, Kurt was driving to work.

5

Suggested answers

b were playing tennis.   **c** was cooking.   **d** were going home on their motorbike.   **e** was putting petrol in his car.

6

Suggested answers

b Were Georg and Kurt watching football on television when the phone rang?
No, they weren't watching football on television, they were playing tennis.
c Was Kurt having a shower when the phone rang?
No, he wasn't having a shower, he was cooking.
d Were Georg and Kurt sitting in a café when the phone rang?
No, they weren't sitting in a café, they were going home on their motorbike.
e Was Kurt writing an email when the phone rang?
No, he wasn't writing an email, he was putting petrol in his car.

page 81

7

b shut   **c** pulled   **d** switched   **e** took   **f** was reading
g heard   **h** switched   **i** listened   **j** was happening
k was looking   **l** was walking   **m** was standing   **n** came

8

b tried   **c** hit   **d** fell   **e** was trying   **f** heard   **g** ran
h jumped   **i** drove   **j** was still lying   **k** arrived

«Pronunciation»

1

Don't sh**oo**t! /uː/   P**u**t the gun down! /ʊ/

2, 3

/uː/   *pool, too*, you, too, school, rules, blue, cool, suit, true, you
/ʊ/   *full*, would, book, look, good, cook, put, pull, stood, foot

«Activity» What can you say about a book?

Suggested answers*

Sentences which mean *I love this book*:   a, c, i, j, p
Sentences which mean *Other people like this book*:   b, e, g, m, r
Sentences which mean *I don't like this book*:   f, h, l, n
Sentences which tell you a fact about the book: d, k, o, q, s
*Some sentences may appear in more than one list (e.g. **b** and **m** might also be facts).

«Activity» Write a review

Sample review
The book is called The Double Bass Mystery *and it's by Jeremy Harmer.*
It's fiction. It's a crime story about a murder and it takes place in Barcelona. The heroine is Penny, an English musician. It's an exciting story and I think it's a great book for a boring journey.

Exam folder 12

page 82

Speaking Part 1

2

b what's your surname
c How do you spell it?
d where do you come from?
e do you work or are you a student
f What do you study?
g where do you live?
h And what do you do?
i Could you speak more slowly, please?
j do you enjoy studying English?
k Could you repeat that, please?

Writing folder

page 83

Writing Part 3

2

a 3 b 4 c 6 d 2 e 5 f 1

3

Sample answers

a
It was a key with the name of a bank on it. I took it to the bank. A man was talking to the manager. 'I must have my money!' he shouted.
'We need the key,' said the manager.
'Is this the key?' I asked.
They were very surprised. I explained where I found it.

b
I explored the shops and then walked home. I was happy until I reached Oxford Road. Suddenly I felt worried. I couldn't remember the number of our house. All the houses were new. Which was our house? I didn't know.
I got out my mobile.

c
We ran down the hill to the road. We wanted to catch a bus, but it didn't arrive.
It was very cold and almost dark. We walked to the village. We wanted a lift to the city, but we couldn't find one. We walked for a long time.

d
Suddenly, the phone rang.
'Hi, John. Can you meet me at the club?' said Lee.
John walked sadly to the club. 'Lee doesn't remember it's my birthday,' he thought. When he went in, all his friends were waiting for him.
'Happy birthday, John!' they shouted.
Everything was ready for a party. John was very surprised. At the end, he thanked his friends.

e
'It's a secret,' he answered. 'But I can tell you that it's dangerous. A journalist went to meet this man last year. We haven't seen him since he got into the man's car. I'm meeting him in a park. My friends are already hiding behind the trees. I must go now.'

f
One night last week she caught a mouse. When I opened the back door she was sitting on the step with the mouse in her mouth. She dropped it at my feet. I didn't know what to do. I didn't want to touch it.
Sheba went into the house and fell asleep on my chair. I put on some gloves and picked up the mouse.

Corpus spot
a looking for   b searched   c looking for
d looked for   e searched

Units 7–12 Revision

page 84

Grammar

2

b ever   c never   d in   e since
f already   g yet   h while   i for   j on

Reading

3

1 B 2 D 3 C 4 A 5 B 6 A 7 D 8 A 9 B 10 C

page 85

Grammar

4

b This is the <u>funniest</u> book I've ever read.
c Portuguese is <u>spoken</u> in Brazil.
d This cinema is less modern <u>than</u> the one in my town.
e The café is in <u>a/the</u> corner of the park.
f Why <u>don't you</u> phone the doctor?
g The weather here is <u>hottest</u> in July.
h This is the <u>worst</u> painting I've ever done.
i Could you <u>speak</u> more slowly, please?
j My racket wasn't as expensive <u>as</u> my teacher's.
k Natalya is from <u>Russia</u>. / Natalya is <u>Russian</u>.

Vocabulary

5

> **b** straight **c** crossroads **d** down/along/up
> **e** roundabout **f** over **g** on **h** pedestrian **i** across
> **j** past **k** right **l** one-way **m** left **n** on **o** opposite

6

> *roundabout* corner entrance fountain stadium
> turning
> *wedding* anniversary birthday carnival festival
> honeymoon
> *cough* ankle neck thermometer throat tongue
> *border* continent desert island ocean valley

Unit 13

page 86

Introduction

1

> **a** mirror **b** chest of drawers **c** telephone **d** cupboard
> **e** dishwasher **f** (desk) lamp **g** sofa **h** chair

2

> **1** h **2** b **3** a **4** e **5** d **6** g **7** f **8** c

> **Vocabulary spot**
> **a** cost **b** afford **c** is **d** worth

page 87

Listening

1

> **a** 4 (Neil) **b** 2 (Patricia) **c** 1 (Ian) **d** 3 (Adam)

Recording script 2 09

1

I'm Ian. I'm a student, so I'm not rich but I've found a good way to save money. I don't pay rent. My home has a very small kitchen and a living room downstairs. There are curtains and carpets – it's very comfortable. I've got central heating, and on the first floor there's a little bathroom and my bedroom. I can't give you my address because I often move. You see, when I get bored of the view, I can drive my home away and park somewhere new!

2

I'm Patricia. My husband and I were looking for a traditional house when we found our unusual home. It's in two old railway carriages. They've been here since 1902. The carriages stand side by side, the sitting room and dining room are between them and there's a normal roof over the whole building. We enjoy living here and our guests enjoy visiting us.

3

My name's Adam. I'm fifteen. My home is twelve metres above the ground. I made it myself. I didn't use any nails, only ropes, so I haven't damaged any branches. I use solar power to heat it and I have a proper kitchen, and a shower and so on. I've got my hi-fi up here and there's plenty of space for guests. Sometimes the tree moves when the wind blows, but my house hasn't fallen down yet, so I'm not really worried.

4

I'm Neil and I rent this amazing place between London and Brighton. It's two towers. The windows have a view of the railway line and it could be noisy for some people, because you hear the trains passing through the tunnel under it every hour, but I don't mind the noise because I'm a party animal. I enjoy giving enormous parties with really loud music because there aren't any neighbours to complain. It's perfect for me.

2

	Ian	Patricia	Adam	Neil
dining room		✓		
bathroom	✓			
shower			✓	
roof		✓		
towers				✓
windows				✓
curtains	✓			
carpets	✓			
hi-fi			✓	
central heating	✓			
solar power			✓	

3

> **b** He drives his home away and parks somewhere new.
> **c** They were looking for a traditional house.
> **d** (It's) between the two railway carriages.
> **e** He used ropes.
> **f** Because it hasn't fallen down yet.
> **g** Because he's a party animal.
> **h** Because (he enjoys giving enormous parties with loud music but) there aren't any neighbours to complain.

page 88

Language focus

could/might/must/can't + be

> **Grammar spot**
> **1** must be **2** can't be **3/4** might be / could be

1

a a double bass **b** a football boot

2

2 must **3** can't **4** might **5** could

Prepositions of place

Corrections are suggested for the false sentences.
b The toilet is near/beside a cupboard.
c There's a mirror above the basin.
d true
e There's a window behind the toilet.
f true
g There's a tall cupboard in the corner.
h true
i We can see towels inside some of the drawers.
j true

page 89

Rooms and furniture

1

Rooms	Furniture
kitchen	cupboards, fridge, table, chairs
bedroom	bed, wardrobe
bathroom	shower, toilet
living room	chairs, coffee table
study	table, chair, bookshelves
hall	

2

Suggested answers

bathroom	basin, bath, mirror
living room	sofa, clock, television
bedroom	clock, chest of drawers, wastepaper basket, bedside table, poster, mirror, desk, pillows
kitchen	cooker, sink, dishwasher, washing machine
study	desk, wastepaper basket, poster, clock
all/most rooms	central heating, curtains, carpet, air conditioning

≪Pronunciation≫

1

/ʒ/ televi**s**ion   /dʒ/ **j**oke

2, 3

/ʒ/ *measure*, revision, pleasure, usually, leisure, decision, unusual
/dʒ/ *jeans*, fridge, lounge, college, jogging, generous, wages, Bridge, just, giraffe

Exam folder 13

page 90

Reading Part 2

1

1
Alma <u>doesn't like cities</u> and wants to live <u>somewhere quiet with an English family</u>. She wants to do a <u>full-time course</u>.

2
Kostas enjoys <u>city life</u>. He wants to do a <u>part-time course</u> and have a part-time job as well. <u>He is not interested in going on trips or doing activities with the college after his classes</u>. He wants to <u>rent his own flat</u>.

3
Margarita would like to live in a <u>hostel with other students</u>. She wants to do a <u>full-time course</u>. She likes to play <u>sport</u> in her free time.

4
Tomek is looking for a <u>full-time four-week course</u> at a college which organises <u>social activities for students</u>. He <u>doesn't mind living in the city or the country</u> but he wants to <u>stay with a family</u>.

5
Hiroki wants to do a <u>part-time course</u> at a <u>college which can arrange his accommodation</u>. He loves <u>walking</u>, so he wants to be <u>near the countryside</u>. He <u>doesn't enjoy organised trips and activities</u>.

2

a A C H   **b** A H   **c** H   **d** H

page 91

3

2 B **3** E **4** G **5** C
A, D and F are not used.

Corpus spot

1 a I want to *do/take* a course here in England.
 b We're going to *do/take* the same course.
 c Last year I *did/took* an English course in Bristol.

2 a did/took **b** is doing/taking **c** Have (you) done/taken

Unit 14

page 92

Introduction

2

1 A	**2** C	**3** B	**4** B	**5** D	**6** D
7 C	**8** B	**9** D	**10** A	**11** C	**12** A

Recording script 2 11

1 Those heels are too high for her.
2 That jacket is very fashionable.
3 Those leather trousers are extremely tight.

4 That's a lovely striped scarf.

5 The shorts are enormous – they're very big and loose.

6 Those trainers look comfortable.

7 I love the material that the grey suit is made of but the colour's very dull.

8 The dark blue hat is very nice.

9 He should take that awful baseball cap off.

10 The sleeveless dress looks fairly cool because of the thin material.

11 What a horrible pattern on that silk tie. I prefer plain ties.

12 The colours are too bright and the orange belt doesn't match.

3

high heels	fashionable jacket
leather trousers	striped scarf
enormous shorts	comfortable trainers
grey suit	dark blue hat
awful baseball cap	sleeveless dress
silk tie	orange belt

page 93

Reading

1

top left paragraph – photo c
top right paragraph – photos a
bottom left paragraph – photos b
bottom right paragraph – photo d

top left paragraph – 1960s
top right paragraph – 1920s
bottom left paragraph – 1950s
bottom right paragraph – 1990s

page 94

Language focus

Used to

1

Suggested answers
In the 1920s men used to wear flat caps.
In the 1920s women used to wear beads.
In the 1950s women didn't use to wear very short skirts.
In the 1950s men used to wear narrow trousers.
In the 1950s men didn't use to wear big ties.
In the 1950s women used to wear gloves.
In the 1960s men used to wear big ties.
In the 1960s men didn't use to wear baseball caps.
In the 1990s women didn't use to wear shiny black boots.
In the 1990s teenagers didn't use to wear white socks.

Grammar spot

+ In the 1920s, women *used to* wear hats.
− In the 1950s, women *didn't use to* have short skirts.
? In the 1970s, did men *use to* wear ties?

2

b What time did you use to get up?
c What time did you use to go to bed?
d What did you use to do at weekends?
e What did you use to enjoy doing?

«Activity» *Used to*

Suggested answers
The statue used to be near the building on the left.
The building at the back used to be narrower.
The building on the right used to be a shop.
People used to meet there.
There used to be a kind of seat.
There didn't use to be a tree / any cars / traffic lights / street lights / street signs / railings / marks on the road.

«Pronunciation»

1

a The odd word out is *cough* – all the words contain the letters *gh* but they are pronounced silently in all the words except *cough*, which has an /f/ sound.
b The odd word out is *enough* – all the words have a /f/ sound but it is spelt *gh* in *enough* and *ph* in the other words.
c The odd word out is *fashion* – all the words have a /f/ sound but it is spelt *f* in *fashion* and *ph* in the other words.

3

f – this is the most common spelling of the sound /f/
ph – a few words spell the sound /f/ as *ph*

gh – there are some common words in which **gh** is pronounced /f/, e.g. *laugh, cough, enough* and *rough*. But also, **gh** is often silent, e.g. *right, might, sight, thought, bought*.

page 95

Too and *enough*

1

b are too big
c aren't long enough
d is too bright
e are too dark

Grammar spot

We use *not* with *enough*.
Too goes before an adjective.
Enough goes after an adjective.

2

short–long   thin–thick   loose–tight   large–small
low–high   narrow–wide   plain–patterned

3

b wide enough   **c** high enough   **d** is too   **e** is too

Adjective order

1

Opinion	Size	Description	Colour	Material	Noun
–	long	shiny	black	plastic	boots
wonderful	–	patterned	–	–	shirts
–	short	–	white	cotton	socks

2

Yes, they are.

3

b a warm brown coat c a beautiful old wooden desk
d an amazing short silk dress e a brilliant new film
f some fashionable black cotton shorts g a shiny glass table

page 96

Exam folder 14
Listening Part 4

1

Sandy is a boy; Megan is a girl; their conversation is about jobs.

2

1 Megan's new job 2 photography/models 3 bookshops
4 Sandy's job 5 photography 6 a magazine
Their jobs could be photographer, working in a bookshop or working for a magazine.

3

1 B 2 B 3 A 4 A 5 B

4

like: interesting, great, brilliant, exciting
dislike: awful, not interesting enough, miserable, depressing, boring

5

agree: Of course, Exactly
disagree: You're wrong there, I don't think so, That's not a good idea.

6

1 A 2 B 3 B 4 B 5 A 6 B

Recording script 2 13

You will hear a conversation between a boy, Sandy, and a girl, Megan, about their jobs. Decide if each sentence is correct or incorrect. If it is correct, put a tick (✓) in the box under A for YES. If it is not correct, put a tick (✓) in the box under B for NO.

Megan: Hi, Sandy. How are you? I haven't seen you for ages.

Sandy: OK, I suppose. Are you OK?

Megan: Oh, yes. I've got this <u>great job</u>, you see. I work on a fashion magazine. <u>It's what I've always wanted to do. It's brilliant.</u> And it's in the centre of town, near where I live.

Sandy: So what do you do exactly?

Megan: Well, at the moment I go along with the photographer when he takes the photos of the models for the magazine. They have lots of pages of the latest fashions.

Sandy: So you're a photographer now?

Megan: Well, not yet … I'm doing a course. <u>I help him to carry the equipment.</u> What about you? I haven't seen you since we left art college. Are you working?

Sandy: Well, I am, but I want to be a photographer too, you know. And I've got a really awful job at the moment in a bookshop.

Megan: What's wrong with that? Why are you miserable about it? Bookshops are very interesting places.

Sandy: Not this one. It's an extremely depressing bookshop – like all bookshops, in fact.

Megan: Well, <u>you're wrong there.</u> Why don't you try to get a job in that new bookshop, you know, in Spring Street? It opened last week. It looks interesting.

Sandy: Not interesting enough for me. <u>I want to do something more exciting</u> – that's why I want to become a photographer.

Megan: But photography is a very tiring job – busy all day. And no time to relax.

Sandy: Exactly, so it's not boring. And <u>I've already done a photography course.</u> I'm always out taking photographs.

Megan: Are you?

Sandy: Yes, so could you ask if I can have a job on your magazine?

Megan: <u>I don't think so. That's not a good idea.</u> You see, the photographer only needs one assistant and that's my job.

Sandy: Oh. But could I come and watch one day?

Megan: Of course. People often come and watch. But don't talk to anyone – they're all too busy.

page 97

Writing folder
Writing Parts 2 and 3

2

Five: lamp, cushions, mirror, (bed) cover, (three) posters

3

Suggested answers

There are lots of possible answers.
I went shopping this morning and I bought some things for my *new* flat. I got a *lovely/amazing, large/big/tiny/small, new/modern/shiny, any colour, plastic* lamp in that new shop near the station. Then I found some *lovely/amazing, large/big/tiny/small, new/modern/soft, any colour/colourful, cotton* cushions to match my *comfortable, new, leather* sofa. They look nice. Then I bought a *lovely/amazing, large/big/tiny/small, new/modern/shiny, any colour, plastic* mirror which I've put on my *large/big/tiny/small, new/modern/wooden* chest of drawers. It was cheap. I'd like to buy a *large, new/modern, wooden* bed but I can't afford it, so I bought a *lovely/amazing, new, any colour/colourful, cotton* cover instead. The bed I've got is old. When I was coming home I walked through the market and I saw some *amazing/crazy/lovely, colourful* posters, so I bought three.

5

Suggested answer

Dear Sarah,
We had a very *long/difficult/bad* journey here because the weather was *wet/windy/bad*, so the ferry was late. We are staying in a(n) *interesting/pretty/small* town. We have a *nice/big/pretty* room with a *beautiful/wonderful/lovely* view. I like the sea best. The water is *clean/warm*.
Love,
Rosie

6

Sample plan

What kind of?
modern   fashionable   comfortable   unusual
names of clothes/shops

Bought recently
one or two things   where   expensive/cheap
colour   how I feel

Sample answer for Writing folder Unit 14
Dear Jenny,
I go shopping on Saturdays with my friends. There's one shop which is our favourite because it has fashionable clothes, but they aren't too expensive. I like buying T-shirts in bright colours. Last week I bought a red one and a yellow one. I usually wear jeans and trainers. I have three pairs of trainers and I'm saving my money to buy another pair. When I go out I sometimes wear a skirt and shoes with high heels. I don't usually wear a coat. I have a short blue jacket which I put on when it's very cold. Write to me soon.
Love,
Rose

Unit 15
page 98
Introduction

1

Answers for the UK	
When you are 16:	**In the UK**
you can buy a pet.	12
you can vote in elections.	18
you can get a tattoo.	18
you can work full-time.	16
you can buy fireworks.	16
you can buy lottery tickets.	16
you can get a pilot's licence.	17
you can ride a scooter.	16
you can learn to drive a car.	17
you can give blood.	17
you can get married (if your parents agree).	16

Listening

b false   **c** false   **d** true   **e** true

Recording script 2 14

Ryan: You know, Martha, I want to do something really exciting this summer. I went sky-diving last year and it was great. I'd really like to know more about the marathon you did in Morocco. How did you get on?

Martha: Well, I enjoyed it. It's not really dangerous if you behave sensibly, but it certainly tests your strength and personality. When I set off, I didn't know if I was strong enough to do it. You have to pass a medical examination before you go but apart from that anybody can do it. In fact the oldest competitor to finish was 76.

Ryan: I'm a bit younger than that so maybe I have a chance. So, what do you have to do? Why is it so hard?

Martha: Well, it's a 230-kilometre marathon across the desert and you have to finish the run in seven days.

Ryan: And I suppose it's hard running on sand.

Martha: Yes, it is, but the worst thing is that you have to carry your own food for the seven days.

Ryan: And I'm sure you need a lot of water as well.

Martha: You don't have to carry water for seven days because you're given water each day. You have to take a good water bottle with you. It's very important to drink enough. You can take other drinks to mix with the water if you like.

Ryan: And where do you sleep?

Martha: In tents. You don't have to carry those. The organisers do that, but you have to bring your own sleeping bag. You fall asleep very quickly in the evening because you're so tired but you can't stay in your tent after sunrise in the morning. You have to get up quickly when the organisers call everyone. They do it very noisily because some people are amazingly heavy sleepers.

Ryan: <u>So, do you have your own tent?</u>

Martha: <u>No,</u> and you need to get on with the other people in your tent because you spend a lot of time with them.

Ryan: And what about the organisers?

Martha: They don't run with you, of course. And they live separately. The competitors can't go into their camps. They have much nicer food and are more comfortable.

Ryan: So, does it get boring running for hours at a time?

Martha: Not really, but you can take an MP3 player if you want. Just remember everything goes in your backpack and you carry it in the heat. <u>It's normally about 40 degrees in the daytime</u> and it sometimes gets hotter than that, but it's cold at night. When you first arrive, when you get off the plane, you can't believe how hot it is! Anyway, I have some work that I need to get on with. Why don't you look at the website – then you can decide. And I'll find my photographs to show you.

Ryan: Oh, thanks.

page 99

Language focus

Can, can't; have to, don't have to

1

> You have to: **a, b, f** You can't: **g, h**
> You can: **d, i** You don't have to: **c, e**

> **Grammar spot**
> It is a rule: *have to* *can't*
> If you want: *can* *don't have to*

2

> **b** do we have to **c** don't have to **d** can **e** can't
> **f** have to **g** do students have to **h** don't have to

Phrasal verbs with *get*

> **b** up **c** on with **d** off **e** on with

page 100

Had to, didn't have to

1

> I had to arrive several hours before the jump.
> I didn't have to take any special clothes with me.

4

> **b** didn't have to **c** Did you have to **d** didn't have to
> **e** had to **f** didn't have to **g** Did they have to
> **h** had to

3

/ə/ nervous	/ʌ/ young	/ɔː/ bought	/aʊ/ house
dangerous flavour	enough touch	thought ought	shout out

page 101

Adverbs

1

> **b** comfortable **c** noisy

> **Grammar spot**
> Add **ly** (*perfect* → *perfectly*)
> Change *y* to *i* and add **ly** (*noisy* → *noisily*)
> For adjectives ending in *le*, take off *e* and add *y* (*comfortable* → *comfortably*)

2

> cheerfully heavily perfectly confidently
> loudly quickly gently

3

> **b** cheerfully **c** loudly **d** confidently **e** quickly
> **f** gently **g** heavily **h** perfectly

> **Corpus spot**
> **a** easily
> **b** Luckily
> **c** completely

≪Activity≫ Adverbs

1

> angrily quickly quietly nervously miserably lazily
> happily secretly seriously slowly loudly sleepily
> excitedly

page 102

Exam folder 15
Reading Part 1

1

> **a** in a fair or theme park **b** children less than five years old
> **c** children five years old or older

2

> **A** is correct (*less than five years old* = under five; *cannot go alone* = must have an adult with them)
> **B** is wrong because the sign says nothing about groups
> **C** is wrong because adults can go on the ride with children

3

a This entrance *is* closed until 11 am today. Use *the* other entrance beside *the* café.

b by an entrance **c** one **d** two

4

a yes
b no (*after today* means *forever*)
c B
d A is wrong because *after today* doesn't mean the same as *until 11 am today*.
C is wrong because the park is open before 11 am.

page 103

5

Please remain in *your* seats until *the* ride stops completely.

6

B is correct.
A is wrong because the notice is about when the ride stops, not when it starts.
C is wrong because the notice does not tell people to wait after the ride stops.

7

A

8

B

Unit 16

page 104

Corpus spot
a did   **b** do

page 105

Reading

1

It is about students' plans when they finish their exams.

2

2 a **3** g **4** c **5** b **6** e **7** h **8** f

page 106

Language focus

Going to

1

Suggested answers
b She's going to take a photo.
c He's going to dive into the water.
d They're going to borrow some books.
e He's going to ride his motorbike.

4, 5

2 h **3** a **4** c **5** b **6** f **7** e **8** g

Recording script 2 ▪17

Liz: Hi, Sam. What are you doing?

Sam: I'm making a poster. Do you want to help me?

Liz: I'm afraid I can't. I'm going to watch the football on television. Aren't you going to watch it?

Sam: No, not this time. I'm going to join a demonstration in the city centre.

Liz: Why?

Sam: Because the council is going to build a new car park.

Liz: So what's wrong with that?

Sam: Because they're going to put it by the market, you know, where Space Party is? The club we went to last week. That's where they're going to build it. Would you like to come on the demonstration?

Liz: Another time perhaps. Anyway, I think the car park's a good idea. There isn't enough parking in the town.

Sam: But it's a really bad idea. It isn't going to make things better for teenagers.

Liz: Why not?

Sam: Because they're going to knock down Space Party. So what are we going to do at weekends? Space Party's the only place to go to in this town.

Liz: OK, but what are you and your friends going to do to stop it?

Sam: We're going to stand in the shopping centre and we're going to tell people what's happening.

Liz: Well, good luck. Now I'm going to watch the match.

Sam: OK. You can tell me about it when I get home.

page 107

Present tense following *when, until, after*

Grammar spot

When we talk about *future* time, a *present* tense follows the adverbs *when, until* and *after*.

Suggested answers
b comes **c** gets **d** pay **e** finish **f** gets **g** get

The time

1, 2

b 3.25 **c** 4.45 **d** 7.30 **e** 8.35 **f** 11.57

Recording script 2 18

a
Man: Excuse me, what's the time, please?
Woman: It's ten to one.
b
Woman: Can you tell me the time, please?
Man: It's twenty-five past three.
c
Man: What time does the bus leave?
Woman: At quarter to five.
d
Woman: What time is it now?
Man: It's half past seven.
e
Man: What's the time of the next performance?
Woman: It starts at twenty-five to nine.
f
Woman: Excuse me, can you tell me the time, please?
Man: Of course. It's exactly three minutes to twelve.

3

b twenty-five past three *or* three twenty-five
c quarter to five *or* four forty-five
d half past seven *or* seven thirty
e twenty-five to nine *or* eight thirty-five
f three minutes to twelve *or* eleven fifty-seven

Note: In Britain, the first alternatives are more common in speech and the second alternatives are more formal, used on the radio, etc. The twenty-four-hour clock is commonly used in timetables etc., but rarely in speech.

Vocabulary spot

a what's **b** tell **c** know **d** it

⟪Activity⟫ Making plans

1

Sunday morning: skateboarding at 10.45
Sunday afternoon: cinema at 2.30

Recording script 2 19

1

George: Marco, would you like to see an English film on Sunday afternoon?
Marco: Oh, yes. I'd really like that. What time?
George: It starts at twenty-five to three.
Marco: Fine. I can be at the cinema at half past two.
George: Good. See you on Sunday.
Marco: Yeah. Bye.

2

Oscar: Hi, Marco. Oscar here. You know we have an exam on Monday?
Marco: How can I forget?
Oscar: Well, Philippe and I are spending Sunday afternoon together. We're going to study some English grammar. Would you like to join us?
Marco: I'm afraid I can't. Another time perhaps.
Oscar: Oh, OK.
Marco: Thanks for asking me, anyway.

3

Peter: Marco? Do you want to come skateboarding this weekend? Sunday afternoon?
Marco: I'm sorry, I'm going to be busy then. What about Sunday morning?
Peter: Yes, but not too early!
Marco: OK. Let's meet at quarter to eleven.
Peter: All right. See you then.

page 108

Exam folder 16

Listening Part 2

1

a a radio interview
b two (one woman and an interviewer)
c It's about a trip she's going to make.

2

She won a prize.

3

2 e **3** f **4** d **5** b **6** a

4, 5

1 A **2** A **3** B **4** B **5** C **6** A

Recording script 2 20

You will hear a radio interview with a woman called Philippa about a trip she is going to make.

For each question, put a tick (✓) in the correct box.

Jim: Welcome to Travellers' Talk, our weekly programme about travel and holidays. I'm Jim Baker and my first guest this morning is Philippa Berry, who won first prize in last month's competition. Philippa, remind listeners how you won the competition.

Philippa: <u>I wrote a poem called *The Traveller*</u>. It tells the life story of a very old man.

Jim: And Philippa has won a thousand pounds to spend on a holiday. Philippa, congratulations.

Philippa: Thank you.

Jim: Now tell us about the journey you've planned.

Philippa: Well, first of all, I decided that I didn't want to go alone because I haven't been abroad alone before. I asked my family and one or two friends to come with me. But I'm going to be away for six weeks and that's too long for most of them. My brother loves travelling, but he's got exams and my best friend says it's too expensive. So <u>I'm joining a tour organised by a travel agent</u>. We travel together but we don't have to stay together all the time, so that'll be just right for me.

Jim: And when are you leaving?

Philippa: Well, I have to use my ticket before the end of this year and these tours only go once a year so I had to decide immediately. In fact <u>we set off two weeks from today</u>.

Jim: And where are you going first?

Philippa: Well, we start by flying from London to Amsterdam, where we catch a plane for the United States. <u>We spend three days in New York</u> and then we travel by bus across the States to California.

Jim: I expect you're really excited about it.

Philippa: Yes, I am. <u>But the part of the holiday I'm looking forward to most is the bus journey from one side of the States to the other</u>. We're going to see all kinds of wonderful scenery and I'm hoping to take some good photographs of mountains and that kind of thing. It's my hobby. Of course, I'll be pleased to visit the big cities too.

Jim: And when your trip is over, what then?

Philippa: <u>After I get home, I'm planning to have a show of the photographs I take</u>. It's going to be in the city library, where I had a holiday job. They have space in the library for things like that and the librarian has very kindly said that I can use it for one week.

Jim: Well, that's great. Thank you, Philippa, for telling us about your plans. Now, we need to talk about this week's competition …

page 109
Writing folder
Writing Part 1

1

> A and B are grammatically incorrect. C is correct.

2

> A is correct.
> B is grammatically incorrect. You cannot say *The new pool has been open since two days*.
> C doesn't make sense.

3

> **3** bigger/larger than   **4** open   **5** not go
> **6** 've/have never been   **7** to go   **8** small   **9** lent me
> **10** spent

Unit 17
page 110

Introduction

1

> **Suggested answers**
> **1** News   **2** Police drama   **3** Children's programme
> **4** Costume drama

2

> **2** Children's programmes   **3** Documentary
> **4** Game shows   **5** Costume drama   **6** Police drama
> **7** Soaps   **8** Sport

3

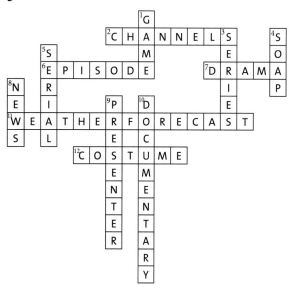

page 111

Listening

3

> **b** a job, some money **c** to ask about the chef's job

Recording script ②22

Nathalie: Hello, Mario, how are you?

Mario: Fine, Nathalie, but busy. My chef left last week. I have to do all the cooking myself and I'm so tired.

Nathalie: Perhaps I can help. I'm looking for a job. I need to earn some money.

Mario: But can you cook?

Nathalie: Cook? Oh, well, you know, yeah. I'm sure I'm exactly the person you're looking for.

Mario: Well, actually, I saw a woman yesterday, but she wasn't sure. Can you start tomorrow?

Nathalie: Sure. The sooner the better.

Mario: Because this woman lives a long way away. She's phoning me this morning. Come and see me later. If she doesn't want the job, you can have it.

Nathalie: Oh, thank you, Mario. Bye.

4

> **b** a picture of a car **c** a red car like the one in the picture

Recording script ②23

Adam: Morning, Karim. Are you going to work already?

Karim: Hi, Adam. Yes, Mario hasn't got a chef and I'm going to help him. Anyway, I want to talk to Claudia. You know I'm going to buy her car?

Adam: Yeah? That'll be really useful.

Karim: And it's good value. It's almost new. Like this one in this magazine, see?

Adam: Oh, right. I saw one like that near Claudia's place yesterday, it was a different colour. There was a fair-haired girl in it, but it had –

Karim: Claudia's car is red.

Adam: Really?

Karim: Anyway, I must go. See you.

Adam: But Karim, that car I saw, that was red –

Karim: Bye, Adam.

Adam: – but its headlights were smashed. Oh, well. Perhaps it wasn't Claudia's car.

5

> **b** true **c** false **d** false **e** false **f** true

Recording script ②24

Karim: Hi, Claudia.

Claudia: Hi, Karim. Do you still want to buy my car?

Karim: Sure. I can give you the money tomorrow.

Claudia: Oh, Karim, that's great. I need the money this week. I have to pay my college fees for next year.

Karim: No problem. I know it's a good car. It's never been in an accident, has it?

Claudia: Oh, no. I've looked after it very carefully.

Nathalie: Hi, Claudia.

Claudia: Hey, Nathalie, what are you doing here? Oh, I forgot to ask you. Did you put some petrol in my car on Sunday? When you borrowed it?

Nathalie: Oh, er, yeah. Actually, I want to see Mario. I need to ask him something.

Claudia: Are you going to come and work as a waitress here with me, Nathalie? That'll be a good laugh. But I don't think we need another waitress. He wants a new chef. Go through to the kitchen.

Nathalie: Thanks, Claudia.

Karim: Perhaps Nathalie'll be the new chef.

Claudia: I don't think so. She can't boil an egg! Look, Karim, before we get busy in here, I'm going to go and buy a magazine, OK?

Karim: Sure.

Claudia: I'll be back in a minute.

Nathalie: Hey, Karim. Oh, where's Claudia? I want to tell her some news.

Karim: Yeah?

Nathalie: Yes. I'm going to be the new chef. She'll be really surprised when I tell her.

Karim: But Nathalie, you can't cook.

Nathalie: Why do you think that?

Karim: Claudia told me.

Nathalie: Well, Mario doesn't know. And Claudia won't tell him. She's my friend. I'm sure I can keep the job until Mario pays me at the end of the week. I need some money very quickly.

Karim: But the café will lose all its customers!

Nathalie: Oh, come on, Karim. Anyway, I must go now. Please don't tell Mario.

Adam: After you.

Nathalie: Thank you. Bye.

Adam: Hi, Karim. Who was that?

Karim: Oh, hello, Adam. That was Nathalie. She shares a flat with Claudia.

Adam: But that's the girl –

Mario: Hey, Karim, where's Claudia? I've got some good news. I've found a chef!

Claudia: Hey, I'm back.

Adam: Claudia …

Karim: Mario …

Mario: Good. We've got customers. We'll talk later.

Announcer: What will happen next? Will Mario find out about Nathalie's cooking? Will Claudia find out about her car?

page 112

Language focus

Will future

2

> **Suggested answers**
> **a** To mend Claudia's car.
> **b** Yes, he will probably find out.
> **c** Yes, Adam will probably tell Karim, and he will tell Claudia.
> **d** There will be problems in the kitchen! / Mario won't be happy. He won't pay Nathalie.

3

> **Possible answers**
> **b** will go to university.   **c** will be hotter.
> **d** will give us less homework.   **e** will have a good job.

4

> **Possible answers**
> **b** I won't see them very often.
> **c** we won't use any central heating.
> **d** we won't be tired.   **e** I won't go to school.

Talking about the future

> **Grammar spot**
> Nathalie uses *going to* for a definite plan, *will* for a prediction and *the present tense* after *when*.

1

> **b** is/'s going to leave   will/'ll get   hears
> **c** am/'m not going to join   will/'ll be   tell
> **d** is/'s going to give   will not/won't enjoy   gives will/'ll help

Everyone/everybody, no one/nobody, someone/ somebody or anyone/anybody

1

> **a** Everyone/Everybody
> **b** No one/Nobody
> **c** Mario is.

> **Grammar spot**
> **a** No one **b** anyone **c** someone **d** anyone **e** anyone
> We use a *singular* verb with these words.

page 113

> **Corpus spot**
> **a** There isn't <u>anybody</u> on the beach.
> **b** We looked for my ring but <u>no one</u> found it.
> **c** I saw that everybody <u>was</u> dancing.

«Activity» Everyone has something

1

> **The things are:** a laptop, a mirror, a sculpture, a plant, a blind, a lipstick, a desk, a hairdryer, an exercise bike and football boots

«Pronunciation»

1

> **a** /ɑː/   large car   **b** /ɔː/   all sore   **c** /ɜː/   third turning

2

/ɑː/	/ɔː/	/ɜː/
can't	talk	hurts
dark	saw	shirt
aren't	morning	earn
harder	more	dirty
half	doors	learn
	story	work
		heard

page 114

Exam folder 17
Reading Part 4

1

> The text is a letter, and it is from a class of students.

2

> **2** The reason(s) why the students think Parson's Place is important.
> **3** Something will cause traffic jams.
> **4** What the ordinary people will do, or what will happen to them.
> **5** The students have made a poster.

4

> **a** Few people know ... our town (lines 2–3)
> **b** It is a beautiful natural area ... roads nearby (lines 4–6)
> **c** the second paragraph
> **d** the average family
> **1** D   **2** C   **3** A   **4** D   **5** B

Unit 18
page 116

Introduction

1

> **a** comedy *Mr Bean* **b** musical   *Mamma Mia!*
> **c** science fiction film   *Star Wars* **d** horror film   *The Mummy*
> **e** animation/cartoon   *Ice Age*
> **f** action film   *The Dark Knight*
> **g** love story   *Titanic*
> **h** historical film   *The Other Boleyn Girl*

page 117

Reading

2

> ten minutes

3

The actors ...	The film crew ...
went to the make-up room ✓	set up the lights ✓
went to the dressing room ✓	moved the cameras ✓
read the scripts ✗	checked the microphones ✓

4

> **b** false **c** true **d** false **e** false

page 118

Language focus

Past perfect

1

> **b** had visited the make-up artist.
> **c** had set up the lights.
> **d** had cleared the rubbish.
> **e** had told everyone what to do.
> **f** hadn't checked the microphones.
> **g** had shot ten minutes of the film.
> **h** had been there for ten hours.

Past perfect and past simple

1

> Two things happened almost at the same time in Sentence B.
> One thing happened before another in Sentence A.

> **Grammar spot**
> When two things happen almost at the same time, we use the *past simple* tense in both sentences.
> When one event happens before another, we use the *past perfect* tense for the event that happened first and the *past simple* tense for the second event.

2

> **b** had **c** hadn't finished **d** welcomed **e** had been
> **f** was **g** had changed **h** didn't recognise

page 119

3

> **b** had lived **c** met **d** hadn't seen **e** reminded
> **f** had dug **g** had put **h** had written **i** had covered
> **j** decided **k** found **l** started **m** was **n** took
> **o** read **p** had written **q** were **r** didn't know

1

> *holiday* and *telephone* have a different sound in the last syllable

3

ending in er(s)	ending in or(s)	ending in tion	ending in ant or ent
teenager	*actors*	fiction	different
letters	visitor	action	assistant
teacher	director	question	instrument

4

Recording script 2 28

actors fiction different visitor teenager letters action assistant question director instrument teacher

page 120

Exam folder 18

Listening Part 3

1

> **a** a programme **b** Box office **c** performances
> **d** screens **e** Discounts

2

> **a** a time
> **b** a day of the week or a date
> **c** a place, e.g. a bank or a supermarket
> **d** director, photography, actor, etc.
> **e** a foreign language
> **f** a type of person, e.g. children, adults
> **g** a price
> **h** a phone number

3

> **1** a day of the week or a date **2** a person
> **3** something that is connected with the film (see 2d)
> **4** a language **5** a person **6** a time

4, 5

> **1** Monday **2** director **3** photography **4** Spanish
> **5** Princess **6** 9.30

Recording script 2 29

You will hear a recorded message giving you information about films.
For each question, fill in the missing information in the numbered space.

Message: Welcome to the Victoria Cinema Information Line.

Here is a list of films for the week starting July 7th. There are three performances each day of *One Summer Night* at 5 pm, 7.30 pm and 10 pm, except <u>Monday</u>, when there is only one chance to see it at 7.30 and Sunday, when there is no performance.

Every afternoon there is a showing of *The Violinist* at 2.30 pm and after the performance on Wednesday, the <u>director</u>, Mark Hawkins, will give a lecture about the film. This is included in the ticket price.

Our late-night film is *Dead Men's Shoes*, which is coming to the cinema for the second time. It is set in the Canadian mountains and stars the well-known actor Jim Harrison. It recently won a prize for its <u>photography</u>.

Our foreign-language film this week is called *A Dangerous Game* and is showing on Saturday afternoon at 5 pm. Although the director is actually Swedish, the film is in <u>Spanish</u> with subtitles in English.

There are two films showing in our Saturday morning Film Club for children. The film at 10 am is suitable for children aged between 5 and 10 and is called *The Young Princess*. It is about the adventures of a young girl whose father becomes king of his country by mistake. At 11.30 we are showing *The Mad Professor*, which is a comedy. All tickets are £4.50 except for children and senior citizens who pay £3.50.

The box office is open from 2 pm until 8.30 pm but our telephone booking line is open in the morning from 10.30 am and you can book tickets with a credit card until <u>9.30</u> pm if you ring 0987 34872. There is a charge of 50p for tickets bought by telephone.

Thank you for calling the Victoria Cinema Information Line.

page 121

Writing folder
Writing Part 2
1

> **a** tomorrow afternoon **b** this weekend **c** last night

2

> **Suggested answers** (useful language is in brackets)
> **1**
> • say what the house is like: *present simple* (It's a traditional farmhouse.)
> • say what you have done this morning: *present perfect* (I've helped with the animals.)
> • tell him/her your plans for the rest of the weekend: *present continuous / going to* (We're going (to go) for a walk in the woods tomorrow.)

2
> • say how you plan to get there: *present continuous / going to* (I'm coming / I'm going to come by train.)
> • ask about what you will all do: *future / going to* (What will we do? / What are we going to do?)
> • tell them what time you will arrive: *present continuous / future / going to* (I'm arriving at 10.30 / I'll be at the station at 10.30 / I'm going to arrive at 10.30.)

3
> • say what you enjoyed most: *past simple* (I really enjoyed helping with the animals.)
> • tell him/her about your journey home: *past simple* (I had an easy journey home.)
> • tell him/her your plans for next weekend: *present continuous / going to* (Next weekend I'm having a party / I'm going to have a party.)

Units 13–18 Revision
page 122
Vocabulary
2

> **b** tower **c** coast **d** rope **e** tunnel **f** on
> **g** square **h** in **i** from **j** entrance **k** instructions

3

> Dear Hanna
> How are you? I *hope* you're well.
> I'm fine. I went *shopping* yesterday with my *friend* Emilia *because* it was my birthday and I *received/had received* some money.
> I saw a *beautiful* jacket in my *favourite clothes* shop. I tried it on *and* it was *comfortable*. But I *thought* it was *too* expensive. Then Emilia showed me the ticket – it was half *price*! I bought it, *then* we decided to go to a *restaurant* which is near *there*. We had a very good day.

4

> **b** sofa **c** curtain **d** amazing **e** gloves
> **f** sensible **g** cooker **h** save

page 123
Grammar
5

> **2** A **3** C **4** B **5** B **6** C

6

> **2** B **3** C **4** A **5** A **6** B

7

> **b** could/might **c** mustn't/can't **d** can't
> **e** don't have to **f** used to **g** has to **h** don't have to
> **i** have to **j** could/might **k** need

Unit 19

page 124

Introduction

1

> **b** daughter **c** uncle **d** husband **e** sister
> **f** stepmother **g** half-sister **h** nephew **i** niece
> **j** brother-in-law **k** cousin **l** ex-wife

page 125

Listening

1

> Rebecca (oldest): Your parents worry about you.
> George (youngest): You're always the baby. / They never let you grow up.
> Charlotte (middle): You don't have a special place in the family.
> Peter (only): It's difficult to make friends.

Recording script 2 30

a: My name's Rebecca. My brother's five years younger than me. My parents didn't make me look after him but I enjoyed it. I used to <u>look forward to</u> <u>playing</u> with him when I came home from school but I sometimes got <u>fed up with reading</u> the same stories hundreds of times. But all those afternoons with my brother were good practice because now I have my own son and <u>I'd like to have</u> more children. My son is like me in lots of ways except he's really untidy and I'm the opposite. The worst thing about being the oldest is that your parents <u>begin to worry</u> about you from the moment you're born and they <u>continue to worry</u> because you're always the first to do everything.

b: I'm George and I have three older sisters so I was really spoilt when I was a child but I didn't mind that. I never worried about anything – I was always laughing and I think I <u>started to tell</u> jokes when I was about two years old. But when I was about 14 I <u>stopped doing</u> what everyone told me and then I had two parents and three sisters getting angry with me. That's the problem really with being the youngest – everyone <u>continues seeing</u> you as the baby even when you're an adult. They never let you grow up.

c: I'm Charlotte and I have an older sister who is clever, pretty and has a lovely singing voice, in fact she's good at everything, and a younger brother who is good-looking, clever, oh what else, he's really good at playing football. Then there's me. I <u>try to be</u> nice to them both but I'm really jealous because they always <u>seem to do</u> everything right and I do everything wrong. So I always <u>arrange to spend</u> a lot of time with my mates. I think it's hard for middle children because they don't have a special place in the family.

d: My name is Peter. I was never jealous of my friends who had brothers and sisters because my parents loved taking me with them when they went out so I spent a lot of time with adults. I enjoyed that. I have quite a few cousins and I used to see them sometimes but I didn't <u>want to share</u> my parents with anyone. I don't think I ever <u>learnt to play</u> with other children – I <u>preferred reading</u> and I spent a lot of time doing homework. I think only children sometimes find it difficult to make friends so that's a disadvantage. I only really <u>began making</u> friends when I went to university and <u>started spending</u> a lot of time with people of my own age.

2, 3

> Oldest children *Rebecca*
> • <u>expect</u> to do well
> • are <u>good at</u> looking after other people ✓
> • <u>need</u> to keep everything tidy ✓
> • <u>like</u> keeping rules
>
> Youngest children *George*
> • <u>love</u> taking risks
> • have a good sense of humour ✓
> • often <u>refuse</u> to do what other people tell them ✓
> • are <u>interested in</u> studying artistic subjects
>
> Middle children *Charlotte*
> • are <u>good at</u> solving arguments
> • enjoy being with other people ✓
> • are good managers and leaders
> • <u>don't mind</u> changing their plans
>
> Only children *Peter*
> • <u>prefer</u> being with adults ✓
> • are quite serious ✓
> • are <u>afraid of</u> failing
> • are hard-working ✓

> **Corpus spot**
>
> **a** <u>I agree</u> with you about the new restaurant.
> **b** <u>Do</u> you agree about that?
> **c** I hope she <u>will agree</u> to come with us tomorrow.
> **d** My friend <u>agreed</u> to meet me at 7.30.

page 126

Language focus

Words followed by *to* or *-ing*

1

Verbs and expressions followed by *to*	Verbs and expressions followed by *-ing*
expect	*be good at*
need	like
refuse	enjoy
	don't mind
	love
	be interested in
	be afraid of

2

Verbs and expressions followed by *to*	Verbs and expressions followed by *-ing*
would like	look forward to
begin	be fed up with
continue	stop
start	continue
try	prefer
seem	begin
arrange	start
want	
learn	

begin, *continue* and *start* are in both columns

3

hope, *agree*, *promise*, *plan*, *decide* and *offer* are all followed by *to*

4

Make and *let* are followed by the infinitive without *to*.
Possible answers

When I was five years old ...
... my parents let me buy sweets on Saturdays.
... my parents made me go to bed at 7.30.

When I was ten years old ...
... my parents let me go to the shops with a friend.
... my parents made me do my homework before dinner.

Corpus spot
a Don't forget <u>to write</u> to me.
b I am enjoying <u>being</u> here on holiday.
c I am looking forward to <u>hearing</u> from you soon.
d We decided <u>to catch</u> the train back.
e My parents didn't <u>let me stay</u> in the hotel alone.
f When we finished <u>eating</u>, I went to my house.
g I would like to <u>meet</u> you and your family.
h I am <u>interested in joining</u> this club.

5

b to be c to go d to sit e being f being

g doing h to live/living i seeing j to meet k to do
l seeing m saying

page 127
Giving advice

2

You should	Why don't you	You ought to
You shouldn't	You'd better	

«Pronunciation»
1

Think and *thing* are the odd ones out because *th* is pronounced /θ/.

2

/ð/	/θ/
their	*thirsty*
that	thank
they	both
although	birthday
weather	thirty
	bath
	teeth
	Thursday
	mouth
	thousand

page 128

Exam folder 19
Reading Part 5

Check!
a Read through the whole text.
b (o)
c Read the words around the space and check the grammar and meaning.
d Guess.
e On the separate answer sheet.

1

1 A	2 C	3 B	4 B	5 D	6 C	7 D	8 B	9 B	10 D

page 129
3

1 A	2 A	3 B	4 A	5 B	6 D	7 B	8 A	9 C	10 D

Unit 20
page 130

Introduction
1

a drum b flute c electric guitar
d keyboard / electronic piano e trumpet f violin

4

in a classical concert:	violin, flute, piano, trumpet, cello, double bass, oboe, drums, clarinet, horn
in a jazz concert:	drums, trumpet, piano, saxophone, clarinet, double bass, trombone
in a rock concert:	drums, electric piano/keyboard, electric guitar

5

Possible answers
hip-hop, pop, heavy metal, dance, blues, country, traditional

6

-er	-or	-r	-ist
trumpeter	actor	dancer	*guitarist*
drummer	director	manager	pianist
employer		diver	violinist
photographer			artist
farmer			journalist
reporter			novelist
teacher			

Reading

1

a Eastside b Texas Team c The Storm d Third Avenue

page 131

Language focus

Comparison of adverbs

1

b Third Avenue c Texas Team d The Storm e Eastside
f Third Avenue g The Storm

2

a Mara, the singer, sang more confidently than the other singers.
b They danced less professionally than the other bands.
c The violinist didn't play as loudly as the other musicians.

Grammar spot
They have the same meaning.

3

a Texas Team danced less professionally than the other bands.
   Texas Team didn't dance as professionally as the other bands.
   The other bands danced more professionally than Texas Team.
b The violinist in Texas Team didn't play as loudly as the other musicians.
   The violinist in Texas Team played less loudly / more quietly than the other musicians.
   The other musicians played more loudly / less quietly than the violinist in Texas Team.

4

a The Storm's drummer didn't play as loudly as the other drummers.
   The Storm's drummer played more quietly / less loudly than the other drummers.
   The other drummers played less quietly / more loudly than The Storm's drummer.
b Jason played much better than the other guitarists.
   The other guitarists didn't play as well as Jason.
   The other guitarists played less well than Jason.
c The Eastside singers didn't sing as well as the other singers.
   The Eastside singers sang less well than the other singers.
   The other singers sang better than the Eastside singers.

page 132

So and such

1

First: The Storm   Second: Third Avenue
Third: Eastside   Fourth: Texas Team

Recording script

Judge: Thank you to all the competitors. I won't say much because I know you're all anxious to hear the results – it was a very difficult decision and I'll start with the band which came fourth. That's Texas Team, who are the youngest group here today. Unfortunately, the violinist played so quietly that we couldn't hear him. So <u>bad luck</u> to Texas Team. Third was Eastside. They are such good dancers they should enter for a dance competition. And with a bit more practice on the music they'll do very well. In second place is Third Avenue. They did well, especially their young guitarist, but the singer looked so unhappy we thought maybe he didn't want to win! <u>Never mind</u> – you nearly won, so <u>better luck next time</u>. <u>Congratulations</u> to The Storm who are our winners today. The singer had such a great voice that we had to give them first place. <u>Well done</u>.

2

b such good dancers c so unhappy d such a great voice

Grammar spot
So is used before *an adjective* or *an adverb*.
Such is used before *an adjective + noun* or a noun.

Such + (adjective) + plural or uncountable noun	Such a + (adjective) + singular noun
good dancers	great voice
loud drums	difficult decision
nice food	

Corpus spot
a She is <u>such a</u> kind woman.
b My grandparents are always <u>so</u> happy together.
c She has <u>such a</u> pretty face.

3

b They danced so well (that) I wanted to watch them for ever.
c The concert was in such a small room (that) there wasn't space for everyone.
d The seats were so expensive (that) we couldn't afford to go.
e The fans made such a terrible noise (that) we couldn't hear the band.
f We had such good seats (that) we could see very well.

Congratulating and choosing

1

> Expressions to use when someone has won:
> *Congratulations, Well done*
>
> Expressions to use when someone has lost:
> *Bad luck, Never mind, Better luck next time*

«Pronunciation»

1

> **Answers and recording script** 2 37
> see/sea sun/son there/their where/wear
> wood/would hour/our hear/here won/one

2

> **b** Where wear **c** here hear
> **d** their there **e** sea see **f** would wood
> **g** son sun **h** Our hour

page 133

Connectives

1

> **b** but **c** Although **d** so **e** because/as **f** as/because
> **g** as soon as **h** either **i** or

2

> **Michelle:** I try to go to the gym three times a week because I like to keep fit.
> **Anika:** I go shopping or I go swimming.
> **Mark:** I go racing on my motorbike, although I'm not very good at it.
> **Tanya:** I'm busy writing songs for the band, so I don't have much spare time at the moment.

Grammar spot

> **a** We use *because* or *as* when we give a reason for something.
> *I didn't go swimming **because/as** I had a cold.*
> **b** We use *so* to give the result of something.
> *The bus didn't come **so** I walked to the city centre.*
> **c** We use *either* and *or* in the same sentence to give two different choices.
> *We can **either** stay at home **or** go for a walk.*
> **d** We use *although* or *but* to contrast or compare two ideas.
> *The film was funny **but** it was too long.*
> ***Although** the film was funny, it was too long.*

page 134

Exam folder 20
Listening Part 1

> **Check!**
> **a** the pictures and the questions **b** what the people will talk about / vocabulary **c** listen carefully the second time **d** guess **e** twice

> 1 C 2 C 3 B 4 C 5 A

Recording script 2 38

For each question, there are three pictures and a short recording.

Choose the correct picture and put a tick (✓) in the box below it.

1 Where will they meet?

Woman: Are you going to the city centre?

Man: Yes, do you want a lift?

Woman: Yes, please. Can you take me to the library? Then I need to go to the supermarket.

Man: OK. I'm going to the bank so <u>I'll see you in the supermarket car park</u> at four. Oh, and can you take back these library books for me?

2 What time will the boy catch the bus?

Girl: Hi, Alex, this is Mandy. You know we agreed to meet at a quarter past six? Well, we'll have to meet an hour later at a quarter past seven because I have to look after my sister while my mum is out.

Boy: Mm … my bus only leaves once an hour so I can get the one <u>at a quarter to six or at a quarter to seven</u>.

Girl: Well, <u>get the later one</u>. That'll give me more time too.

Boy: OK. See you tonight then.

3 Which band does Robert play in?

Girl: Robert's just joined a band, you know.

Boy: Is he playing guitar in it?

Girl: <u>They've already got a guitarist, so he's the singer. There's a keyboard player too.</u> They used to have a drummer but he left.

Boy: We must go and see them play.

4 Which is Lisa's new T-shirt?

Girl 1: Have you seen Lisa's new T-shirt? It's amazing.

Girl 2: What's it like?

Girl 1: <u>It's sleeveless with a high neck and it's got red and green stripes.</u>

Girl 2: Ugh.

5 What will the weather be like tomorrow?

Man: And here is the weather forecast for today and tomorrow. The fine weather will continue today, so enjoy it while it lasts because <u>tomorrow we'll have cloudy skies</u> again. There won't be any rain but it won't be very warm, I'm afraid.

page 135

Writing folder
Writing Part 3

5

a *adjectives added:*	tall, long, white, large, brown
b *adverbs added:*	yesterday, rather, nervously, suddenly
c *direct speech:*	What's your name? You've won a prize!
d *other changes:*	see italics below for all other changes

Yesterday, I went into town to buy a CD. A *tall* man with a *long white beard was standing* outside the shop. He *seemed rather* worried *and he was looking nervously at* a piece of paper. *When he saw me,* he asked, *'What's your name?'* *Although I didn't know him,* I told him. *Suddenly* he smiled. *'You've won a prize!'* he announced, and gave me *a large brown envelope with my name on it.*

Unit 21
page 136

Introduction

3

a top up your mobile **b** switch on **c** a missed call
d hang up **e** call someone back

page 137

Listening

1

Strangers: **a, d**   Friends: **b, c**

2

1 b **2** a **3** d **4** c

Recording script 3 [02]

a
Secretary: Amy Lee's office.
Ivan: Oh, er, hello. May I speak to Mrs Lee?
Secretary: I'm afraid Mrs Lee isn't available this afternoon. Can you call back tomorrow?
Ivan: Er, yes. Thank you.
Secretary: Goodbye.
Ivan: Goodbye.

b
Helen: Hello?
Ivan: Hi. This is Ivan.
Helen: Hi, Ivan.
Ivan: Helen. I'm ringing to ask for your help.
Helen: Oh, yeah?
Ivan: You told me to ring you. The teacher's asked me to write about a journalist.
Helen: Oh, yes.

Ivan: Well, you said a friend of yours is a freelance journalist. She can give me some advice.
Helen: She's a friend of my dad's, really. But she's very nice.
Ivan: Can you give me her phone number?
Helen: Oh, right, er, I've got it here somewhere. Hang on a minute. Mm. Yes. It's 307669. Ask for Mrs Lee. And say you're a friend of Helen Solomon's.
Ivan: OK. Thanks very much.
Helen: That's OK. Let me know how you get on.

c
Helen: Hi. Sorry I can't speak to you just now. Leave your name and number and I'll call you back when I'm free. Wait for the beep!
Ivan: Oh. Helen. This is Ivan. I'm seeing Mrs Lee on Monday afternoon. Thanks for giving me her number. Would you like to meet me afterwards? About four o'clock? I'd like to buy you a coffee or something to say thank you. Ring me if that's OK and say where.

d
Secretary: Amy Lee's office.
Ivan: May I speak to Mrs Lee, please?
Secretary: Could I have your name?
Ivan: Oh, yes. It's Ivan Finn. I'm a friend of Helen Solomon's.
Secretary: One moment, please.
Mrs Lee: Hello, Mr Finn? How can I help you?
Ivan: Er, I'm doing a project about journalism for my media studies course. Helen told me to contact you. Would it be possible for me to interview you one day this week?
Mrs Lee: I see. Well, this week's not good; I'm working to a deadline and I'm having my office painted. But what about Monday at, um, quarter past two?
Ivan: Oh, thanks very much. It's very kind of you to help me.
Mrs Lee: Not at all. I look forward to meeting you.

3

Answers and recording scripts as for previous exercise, in the order b, a, d. 3 [03]

Conversation 1
b I'm ringing to ask for your help.
c Can you give me her phone number?
d Hang on a minute.

Conversation 2
a May I speak to Mrs Lee?
b I'm afraid Mrs Lee isn't available this afternoon.
c Can you call back tomorrow?

Conversation 3
a Could I have your name?
b One moment, please.
c How can I help you?

«Pronunciation»

1

> 307669   three oh seven double six nine

2, 3

> **Answers and recording script 3|05**
>
> **a** three five double seven nine eight
> **b** oh one double two three, two double seven, two oh three
> **c** oh two oh, seven five eight four, double three oh four
> **d** double four, one two seven three, five oh nine, six seven two

Language focus

Making phone calls

1, 2

> **Conversation 1**
> **b** I'm ringing   **c** to ring you   **d** give me the number
> **e** Hang on   **f** Ask for   **g** a friend   **h** Let me know
>
> **Conversation 2**
> **i** May I speak   **j** a friend of   **k** One moment   **l** How can I
> **m** told me   **n** Would you like to   **o** How about
> **p** very kind of   **q** meeting you

page 138

Have something done

1

> **b** has his car washed   **c** has his hair styled
> **d** has his contract checked
> **e** is having his autobiography written

2

> **b** had an indoor swimming pool built.
> **c** had the garden redesigned.
> **d** had all the carpets changed.
>
> **Possible answers**
> **e** She had new furniture made for the living room.
> **f** She had gold taps put on all the basins.

page 139

Reported commands and requests

1

> **Suggested answers**
> **b** Tell the coach to leave the club and not to come back.
> **c** Tell the rest of the team not to go clubbing every night.
> **d** Tell the goalkeeper to have his eyes tested.
> **e** Tell the ref to learn the rules of the game.

> **Corpus spot**
> **a** Please read some of your poems.
> **b** Go to the hospital immediately.
> **c** Please help me.
> **d** Don't lose the stone.
> **e** Call me at nine o'clock.

2

> **b** Michael not to forget his wallet.
> **c** asked her/Angela to phone her dad from the airport.
> **d** asked Mandy not to use her shampoo.
> **e** told Ronnie to phone the doctor immediately.

Possessive pronouns and adjectives

> **c** A classmate of yours said you were ill.
> **d** She saw a friend of hers on TV last week.
> **e** Kamran's lucky because a cousin of his owns a hotel in London.
> **f** A colleague of Pedro's lives in our road.
> **g** I didn't realise that a friend of theirs played football for England.
> **h** I heard that a student of mine met the Prime Minister last week.
> **i** I believe a neighbour of ours has won the lottery.

«Activity» Mobile messages

Recording script 3|06

Helen: Hi. Sorry I can't speak to you just now. Leave your name and number and I'll call you back when I'm free. Wait for the beep!

page 140

Exam folder 21

Reading Part 3

1

> **a** most   **b** less   **c** maximum   **d** allowed   **e** outside

2

> You will read about useful information for people going to the shopping mall.

3

> THE SOUTH LAKES MALL
> The South Lakes Mall offers 200 shops, a swimming pool, restaurants, a bowling alley and two nightclubs as well as 30 acres of parkland with three lakes.
>
> **Opening hours**
> **(1)** Shops   Mon–Fri   10 am–<u>9 pm</u>
>   Sat   9 am–<u>8 pm</u>
>   Sun   10 am–<u>5 pm</u>
> Park   9 am–5 pm in winter
>   <u>9 am–8 pm in summer</u>
> We have thousands of visitors every day, **(2)** <u>our busiest day of the week being Friday</u>. To avoid the crowds, come on a Monday or Tuesday.
>
> **Inside the mall**
> When you arrive, go to **(3)** <u>one of our information offices to get a map. There is one by the main bus stop and another at the bottom of the escalator which goes up to the cinema.</u> The shops are all on the ground floor and you will find everything from specialised furniture stores to clothes shops and department stores as well as restaurants, a bowling alley and a swimming pool. **(4)** <u>On the first floor above the pool</u>

you will find a 12-screen cinema and two nightclubs. If you wish, you can buy entrance tickets for any of these facilities except the nightclubs from the information centres. **(5)** Before 5 pm, entrance tickets to all facilities are reduced for students and the over-sixties.

If you wish to stay overnight, **(6)** the information centres can give you a list of accommodation in the area, ranging from grand hotels to Bed and Breakfast accommodation.

Outside the mall

Make time to visit the 30 acres of parkland which surround the mall. **(7)** Boats for up to six people can be hired and taken out onto one of the lakes for £12 an hour.

Bicycles can be hired every day for £6 an hour. There are 4 km of paths but **(8)** you are not allowed to take hired bicycles beyond the park.

Travel

The mall is located one mile from the M49. Just follow the signs from Junction 13. There is free parking for 10,000 cars and there are six car parks. Car parking spaces are never more than five minutes' walk away from an entrance. **(9)** Remember where your car is parked by looking at the coloured signs – no car park uses the same colour and each level in the car parks is numbered.

It is just as easy to visit the mall by train. There is a rail service every 15 minutes from Central London. **(10)** When you reach Barnwell station, jump on a number 19 bus to the mall. It's a five-minute journey and there's a bus every 15 minutes.

4

| 1 | B | 2 | A | 3 | B | 4 | B | 5 | A | 6 | B | 7 | A | 8 | A | 9 | B | 10 | B |

page 141

Corpus spot

a campsites   **b** shops / shopping centres / (shopping) malls
c police station   **d** car park

Unit 22

page 142

Introduction

1

The photographs show the following: **a** a glowing UFO in the sky in South Carolina, USA; **b** a flying button over Venezuela (a trick photograph); **c** lenticular clouds over Santos, Brazil; **d** the Northern Lights.

page 143

Reading

2

The top photograph matches the report on the left; the bottom photograph matches the report on the bottom right.

Language focus

Reported speech

1

b the soldiers   **c** the soldiers   **d** Brazel
e (Mac) Brazel   **f** (many of) the crew   **g** (many of) the crew
h Stephan Michalak   **i** Stephan Michalak
j Stephan Michalak   **k** Stephan Michalak

2

c was
d had seen
e would never believe the soldiers.
f they had seen a strange UFO above the island.
g had had a ring around it.
h he had gone to search for gold in a lake.
i one of them had landed near him.
j he had approached it.
k he was still feeling ill.

3

b Later they announced that a weather balloon had crashed there.
c They said it was part of a weather balloon.
d Brazel said that he had seen a different kind of material.
e He told the journalists that he would never believe the soldiers.
f Many of the crew said that on 16th January they had seen a strange UFO.
g They said that it had had a ring around it.
h He said he had gone to search for gold in a lake.
i He told people one of them had landed near him.
j He explained that he had approached it.
k He said he was still feeling ill.

page 144

Grammar spot

What people say →	Reporting what people said
(a) Present simple → I see aliens quite often.	**Past simple** She said she saw aliens quite often.
Present continuous → I'm feeling ill.	**(b) Past continuous** She said she was feeling ill.
(c) *will* + verb → We'll meet you later.	***would* + verb** They said they'd (would) meet us later.
(d) Present perfect → I've seen lots of aliens here.	**Past perfect** She said she'd (had) seen lots of aliens there.
Past simple → I saw some aliens last week.	**(e) Past perfect** She said she'd (had) seen some aliens last week.

4

Suggested answers

Direct speech	Reported speech
'Aliens kidnapped me.'	Franck Fontaine told a lot of people that aliens had kidnapped him.
'On 6th November 1979, at Cergy-Pontoise in France, we saw a light all round Franck's car and then Franck disappeared.'	Two of his friends said that on 6th November 1979, at Cergy-Pontoise in France, they had seen a light all round Franck's car and then Franck had disappeared.
'Aliens took me to their spacecraft and I woke up a week later in the middle of a field.'	Franck said aliens had taken him to their spacecraft and he had woken up a week later in the middle of a field.
'The aliens will return in August 1980 and I am meeting them in the field.'	He said the aliens would return in August 1980 and he was meeting them in the field.
'We/I believe him/you.'	Two hundred people said they believed him.

6

b I work in London. **c** We live in New York.
d We don't have any money. / We haven't got any money.
e I visited Paris last year.

7

b We've lost the keys and don't know what to do.
c I haven't seen a UFO yet but I hope to see one soon.
d I've already met some aliens and they speak good English.
e I've never eaten Martian food before.

page 145

8

b She said she didn't enjoy cartoons.
c They said they were both fans of Manchester United.
d She said she hadn't seen her brother for three weeks.
e He said his mum was making him a great birthday cake.
f She said her friend hadn't invited her to her party.

≪Pronunciation≫

1

comb   when   honest

2

b The knives might be in the high cupboard. 4
c I've broken my wrist, my thumb, my knee and my foot. 3
d That foreigner could be a scientist. 3
e You need a bright light to write the receipt. 4
f Let's meet in half an hour. 2

3

Beginning	Middle	End
know knives wrist knee write hour	what answer might cupboard foreigner could scientist bright light receipt half	high thumb

At the beginning of a word, *k* is always silent before *n*, and *w* is always silent before *r*.
In the middle of a word, *gh* is always silent after *i*.
At the end of a word, *b* is always silent after *m*.

Corpus spot

a told **b** said **c** told **d** said **e** told

page 146

Exam folder 22
Listening Part 4

1

b anxious **c** astonished **d** unsure **e** cheerful
f embarrassed **g** grateful **h** cross

2

b 2 **c** 6 **d** 1 **e** 7 **f** 4 **g** 8 **h** 3

3

Dina is a girl and Jason is a boy. They talk about Dina's sister. Her name is Jessica.

4

1 A **2** B **3** B **4** A **5** A **6** B

Recording script **3 08**

Look at the six sentences for this part.
You will hear a conversation between a girl, Dina, and a boy, Jason, about Dina's sister, Jessica.
Decide if each sentence is correct or incorrect.
If it is correct, put a tick (✓) in the box under **A** for **YES**. If it is not correct, put a tick (✓) in the box under **B** for **NO**.
Dina: Hi, Jason. How are you?
Jason: Hey, Dina. It's good to see you. I've got a job just near here. But what are you doing in this part of town? I thought you worked in the city centre.
Dina: Yes, I do. And it's really hard work.
Jason: Yeah?
Dina: Yeah. It's a hotel and we're in the middle of the holiday season, so I'm always busy. But I work on Sundays so it's my day off today. I'm going to see Jessica. You know she has a flat just up the road from here?
Jason: Your sister? What's she doing these days? Is she still sitting at home waiting for the perfect job?
Dina: Well – that's not quite fair.

Jason: Why's that, then?

Dina: She studied really hard at school.

Jason: We all did, in my opinion.

Dina: <u>She's been very unlucky.</u> She has to ask my parents for money, but she hates doing it.

Jason: Perhaps.

Dina: Yeah, it's true. Anyway, she told me something strange on the phone.

Jason: What?

Dina: Well, she said she'd seen a ghost in the road near her flat.

Jason: And you think she did?

Dina: She saw it three times. It was a woman in a long skirt. She walked along the road about seven o'clock and then disappeared near the park gates. <u>I hope I'm going to see her too.</u> I think it's exciting.

Jason: Well, I think you're both mad. Seven o'clock? That's exactly when it begins to get dark at this time of year.

Dina: So?

Jason: You can't see clearly. It's probably someone going home from work in a long coat.

Dina: No, she said she was quite sure it wasn't a real person. What about coming to Jessica's place with me? Then we can all watch.

Jason: Thanks for asking me, but actually, I prefer watching TV to waiting for ghosts.

Dina: OK.

Jason: Let's meet next week. We can go to a film or something. We can have a laugh about your ghost.

Dina: OK, let's meet. But you'll be embarrassed when I tell you I've seen the ghost.

Jason: I doubt it. <u>See you next week. Say hello to Jessica from me.</u>

Dina: Yeah. See you.

Jason: Bye.

page 147

Writing folder
Writing Part 1

> 2 are 3 on 4 cost 5 want 6 old enough
> 7 a long film 8 bored 9 called 10 It's/It is
> 11 were all going 12 wouldn't go

Unit 23
page 148

Introduction

> **Corpus spot**
> a In the first lesson I <u>met</u> a girl from Valencia and now she's my best friend.
> b I <u>made</u> many new friends but I missed my old ones.
> c The film begins at seven, so <u>meet</u> me at ten to seven outside the cinema.

page 149

Listening

1

> **Suggested answers**
> There are no right or wrong answers. Pair 1 might become friends; Pair 2 will probably become friends; Pair 3 probably won't get on with each other.

Recording script 3 09

Conversation 1

Samantha: Alex, I'd like you to meet Monica. Alex, meet Monica. Monica loves rock climbing like you. I'm sure you're going to get on really well.

Monica: Hi, Alex. You don't go to this college, do you?

Alex: No, I don't – Samantha's my cousin. She often invites me to parties here. But actually I'm not very keen on the music. In fact, they usually play the kind of music that I hate.

Monica: Oh, I love this music. I'll never get tired of listening to it. Anyway, even if you don't like the music you can talk to people.

Alex: I've never met anyone here who I'm really interested in talking to.

Monica: What about that girl I saw you with just now?

Alex: She's not my type.

Monica: But this room is full of interesting people. Come on, I'll introduce you to some people that you'll like.

Alex: I'd rather not.

Monica: OK. Have a good evening then. I'm going to enjoy myself.

Alex: Wait a minute. I'm sorry I was rude about everyone here. You see – the truth is, I'm just a bit nervous of people I don't know.

Monica: I see. Why didn't you say that? Well, let's go over there where it's less crowded. We can have a chat about climbing. Where do you usually go?

Conversation 2

Neil: Hi, I'm Neil. This is my first day here.

Francis: Hi, I'm Francis. I've been here for a week. It's not a bad place to work, this restaurant.

Neil: Yeah?

Francis: It's very different from the job I had last summer on a building site. That was really heavy work. At least here we only have to carry a few plates.

Neil: Is everybody friendly here?

Francis: Well, the older waiters aren't really interested in the same kind of things as students doing a holiday job like us.

Neil: Oh.

Francis: But they'll chat to you when they have time. That waiter over there used to play football for Arsenal when he was young.

Neil: Did he?

Francis: Well, he played for them a few times. He's got a friend who sometimes gets free tickets. I'm an Arsenal supporter.

Neil: Really? Me too. There's a match on Wednesday evening which will be really good. I'm quite excited about it because I haven't been to a match this season yet.

Francis: They're playing Chelsea, aren't they?

Neil: That's right.

Francis: I'm not sure if I can go. What time does it start? Oh, there are some customers over there who are waiting for a table. Come on, we'd better start work.

Conversation 3

Peter: Ah, there you are, Kate. Carla wants to meet you. Carla, this is Kate. Kate, this is Carla.

Carla: Hi, Kate.

Kate: Hi, Carla.

Carla: Peter says you're looking for someone to share your flat with.

Kate: That's right. I am actually.

Carla: Well, I'm going to come to university here and it's too far for me to travel to my parents' house every day. Anyway I'm fed up with living there. So could I share your flat?

Kate: Why not?

Carla: Oh, that's great. Does anyone else live there or will it be just the two of us?

Kate: There's one other person who is studying biology.

Carla: Great. It'll be really good to live with people my own age. I want to find a place where I can have parties and my friends can come and stay. My parents don't like me making any noise, but you won't mind, will you?

Kate: What kind of noise? Music is fine. I always have a CD on when I'm in the flat.

Carla: Good, because I play in a band. I play the guitar and I also play the violin, but not in the band.

Kate: Oh, well I do need to study.

Carla: Oh, don't worry. I play an electric guitar which has a volume control and I'm quite good at it.

Kate: That's good news!

Carla: I saw a flat which is very near the university. But it was so tidy I decided I couldn't live there. My parents are always getting angry with me because I'm untidy but I don't expect you're tidy either, are you?

Kate: Well, I do prefer to keep the flat tidy …

Carla: Oh, we're going to be such good friends. Thank you for inviting me to live with you.

2

> **b** false **c** true **d** false **e** true **f** false **g** true
> **h** false **i** true **j** true **k** true **l** false

3

> **Peter:** Carla, this is Kate. Kate, this is Carla.
> **Carla:** Hi, Kate.
> The second way of introducing someone is more formal.

Language focus

Relative clauses

1

> **c** There are some customers over there who are waiting for a table.
> **d** There's one other person who is studying biology.
> **e** I play an electric guitar which has a volume control.
> **f** I saw a flat which is very near the university.

2

> **b** What about that girl who I saw you with just now?
> **c** I'll introduce you to some people who you'll like.
> **d** I'm just a bit nervous of people who I don't know.
> **e** It's very different from the job which I had last summer.

3

> **a** You could use *that* in either set of sentences here instead of *who* or *which*.
> **b** You can leave *who* and *which* out in the second set of sentences. If there is a different subject for the second verb, *that/who/which* are often omitted.

4

> **b** where **c** whose **d** where **e** whose

page 150

> **Grammar spot**
> **Subject relative clauses**
> **a** which
> **b** who
> **Object relative clauses**
> **c** which
> **d** who
> **Relative clauses with *where* and *whose***
> **e** where
> **f** whose

6

> **b** which **c** whose **d** which **e** whose **f** who
> **g** which **h** who

7

> You can put *that* in sentences **a**, **b**, **d**, **f**, **g** and **h**.
> In sentences **b** and **f** the relative pronoun can be omitted.

page 151

Adjectives + prepositions

1

> **b** I'll never get tired of listening to it.
> **c** I'm not very keen on the music.
> **d** This room is full of interesting people.
> **e** I'm nervous of people I don't know.
> **f** It's very different from the job I had last summer.
> **g** They aren't really interested in the same kind of things as students.

h I'm quite excited about the match.
i I'm quite good at it.
j My parents are always getting angry with me.

«Pronunciation»

1

When a word which ends in a consonant is followed by a word which begins with a vowel.

3

b This room is full of interesting people.
c I'm quite good at it.
d She's bad at playing the guitar.
e I'm not very keen on this kind of music.
f I'll never get tired of this song.
g I'm not interested in talking.

Corpus spot

a I began to run because I was afraid <u>of missing</u> the bus.
b I was very worried <u>about</u> the weather before I came to England.
c He was disappointed <u>with</u> his car.
d I am very happy <u>with/about</u> your idea.
e He is very bad <u>at</u> explaining things.
f I am very pleased <u>with</u> the present you sent.

page 152

Exam folder 23
Reading Part 1

Check!
a signs, notices, labels, phone messages, emails, postcards, Post-it notes, text messages
b *a/the/some*, verbs
c guess

1 C **2** C **3** A **4** B **5** A

Corpus spot

a ✓ **b** staying **c** ✓ **d** stayed **e** stayed

page 153

Speaking Part 2

3

a making suggestions:
We'd better do X because ...
Why don't we do X?

b agreeing and disagreeing:
I (don't) agree (that) ...
That's (not) a good idea.

c giving your opinion:
I think ...
In my opinion ...

Unit 24
page 154

Introduction

1

a the first dishwasher **b** a bicycle you can inflate
c the first digital computer **d** the first camera
e an electric serving train at a dinner table
f a Sinclair C5 car (a single seat electric car with pedals)
g a wheelchair which people can sit or lie in and which helps them to stand up **h** a velocipede (a form of transport for land and water – it rolled over the land and floated on the water)

2

1 h the velocipede   **2 e** the electric serving train

Recording script **3** 🔢12

1 It's round and it's made of plastic, or it might be made of glass. It's like a ball but there's a man inside. He's holding something and turning it. It's used for moving across water but it also works on land.
2 It's a kind of railway line which is on a dinner table. It's made of metal. It's used for carrying food around the table.

4

The following have been successful: the first camera, the first dishwasher and the first computer. The electric serving train and the velocipede were not successful. The C5 electric car was not successful because it might be dangerous on busy roads and was very slow. The wheelchair is a new invention and the inflatable bicycle is unlikely to be successful!

page 155

Reading

1

Ben and Jerry's ice cream company

2

escalators (moving stairs); vacuum cleaner

3

Ben and Jerry: **g, b, e**
Charles D. Seeberger: **i, c, a**
Hubert Cecil Booth: **d, h, f**

6

ice cream	escalator	vacuum cleaner
a flavour	a public building	dust
a cone	to transport	to clean
a factory	moving stairs	a machine
a customer	an underground station	dirt
a product	to step on/off	a spot
		a handkerchief

page 156

Language focus

Past passive

1

> Ben and Jerry text: *are sold* is the present passive; *was opened* is in the past passive.

2

> were used   were invented   was placed   was put
> was pushed (up)
>
> **a** were put
> **b** was held, weren't charged
> **c** was opened, were displayed
> **d** was sucked
> **e** is tested, is sold
> **f** –
> **g** was given
> **h** was built, was named, was needed
> **i** were built

> ### Grammar spot
> + was invented
> – weren't charged
> ? was invented

3

> **b** showed the passengers
> **c** served lunch
> **d** didn't tell the passengers
> **e** didn't stamp
> **f** ordered one man to open

4

> **c** was hired by the station manager.
> **d** are held by the company.
> **e** were frightened by 'The Puffing Billy'.
> **f** weren't built by the British.
> **g** was invited to Buckingham Palace by the King and Queen.
> **h** were replaced by clean electric trains.
> **i** are produced by the company all the time.

> ### Corpus spot
> **a** do **b** make **c** made **d** did **e** do **f** do

page 157

Future passive

1

> I think a special car <u>will be invented</u> which <u>will be driven</u> by a computer so a human driver <u>won't be needed</u>. It <u>will be made</u> of plastic and it <u>will be programmed</u> to go on the road or fly through the air. A fee <u>will be paid</u> by car owners at the end of the year to the government. They <u>will be charged</u> according to how many kilometres they have travelled by air and on the road.

> ### Grammar spot
> + will be driven
> – won't be needed
> ? will be paid

«Pronunciation»

1, 2

> **Answers and recording script** 3 13
> **a** Sugar‿and salt are‿added.
> **b** Shops asked them to deliver‿ice cream.
> **c** The mixture‿is frozen.
> **d** There‿are four‿escalators in the station near my house.
> **e** He had a better‿idea.
> **f** Where‿is Ben and Jerry's ice cream sold?

3, 4

> **Answers and recording script** 3 14
> **a** Television was‿invented‿in the 1920s.
> **b** Where‿are‿escalators‿used?
> **c** Ben‿and Jerry's‿ice cream‿is‿sold‿in many places.
> **d** Many shops have‿escalators.
> **e** Some‿inventions‿aren't successful.
> **f** I met him‿at four‿o'clock.
> **g** Some people went‿up‿and down‿all day.
> **h** I've lost your‿address.

page 158

Exam folder 24
Listening Part 3

> ### Check!
> **a** what kind of recording it is, e.g. a recorded message, radio broadcast; what it is about; what you have to do
> **b** read the questions and think about what kind of words can go in each space (there are 20 seconds for reading)
> **c** yes, but the words around the space may be different
> **d** twice

2

> **a** The Weston Museum of Science
> **b** 1 a year   2 a day of the week
>   3 a noun (an exhibition)
>   4 a noun (an activity children would enjoy)
>   5 an ordinal number   6 a place

3

> **1** 1859 **2** Friday(s) **3** planets
> **4** photography/photograph(s) **5** third **6** car park

Recording script ③ 15

You will hear a man talking on the radio about a museum. For each question, fill in the missing information in the numbered space.

Radio presenter: And today we are looking at things to do in the Weston area. One of the big attractions is, of course, the Museum of Science.

It's in South Avenue – it's been there since 1951 but before that it was in a smaller building in **Market Square** for nearly 100 years. // Weston's had a Museum of Science since 1859. So that's something to be proud of.

The museum is open from Saturday to Thursday from **9 am until 5 pm**. // It has longer opening hours on a Friday, when it stays open until 9 pm. The museum shop is open from 10 until 5 every day except Monday, when it closes early.

There's plenty to see in the museum. You can cross a desert or travel through the human body. And there's a **new gallery opening this week with a new exhibition**. // Go there to find out more about the planets – imagine landing somewhere a million miles away from Earth. What would it feel like?

Every week there's a different **children's activity – this week** // the subject is photography. Children can take their own photographs. That's for children between the ages of eight and fourteen.

The museum is on four floors. On the ground floor are the shop and the cloakrooms. The permanent exhibitions are on the first and second floors. By the time you've visited those you'll be thirsty, so carry on to **the café** // on the third floor, which is open all day for drinks and snacks.

One important piece of information. If you visit the museum before **24 July** // you won't be able to use the car park. It's closed for repairs. But you are allowed to park in the hotel car park opposite.

Now the phone …

page 159

Writing folder
Writing Part 3
1

| a 8 | b 3 | c 7 | d 1 | e 6 | f 5 | g 2 | h 4 |

a I really like that band
b I was listening to music
c While I was watching the band
d Although I like music
e The music was so loud
f I used to like folk music
g I enjoy listening to music
h You can have this CD

1 I don't own many CDs.
2 but I don't play an instrument.
3 when I fell asleep.
4 because I don't like it.
5 but now I prefer rock music.
6 that we couldn't talk.
7 my phone was stolen.
8 so get me a ticket too.

2

Suggested answer
Dear Sophie,
I went to a concert last week. My friend bought the tickets *but* she couldn't go *because* she was ill *so* my brother came instead. The band was *so* good *that* I didn't want the music to stop. *Although* my brother doesn't like listening to their CDs, he enjoyed the concert (*or* My brother doesn't like listening to their CDs *but* he enjoyed the concert). *When* the concert finished at 11 o'clock, we went backstage to meet the band.

3

good:	enjoyable, excellent, exciting, fantastic, great, wonderful
bad:	awful, hopeless, terrible, useless
big:	enormous, large
small:	tiny
unusual:	extraordinary, strange, unexpected
famous:	well-known

Units 19–24 Revision
page 160
Telephoning
2

b May I have your name?
c Can you hang on a minute?
d I'm afraid he's not available at the moment.
e Can you call back in about an hour?
f This is Regina.
g I can't speak to you just now.
h I'll call you back in twenty minutes.
i Can you give me their number?

Vocabulary
3

| 1 g | 2 i | 3 d | 4 b | 5 h | 6 f | 7 a | 8 e | 9 c |

page 161
Grammar
4

| 2 B | 3 C | 4 A | 5 A |

5

| 2 A | 3 B | 4 B | 5 C |

6

b invented these machines c phone me d will open
e Don't play football f give my brothers g rang you but you didn't answer h was examined i is fed by our neighbours j she had won k 'll/will be given a lift

7

b who c which d whose e who
f who g where h which/– i which

Unit 25

page 162

Introduction

1

> They show different ways of shopping:
> **a** in a market   **b** in a supermarket   **c** in a shopping mall
> **d** on-line shopping   **e** from a shopping catalogue

Listening

> **b** false   **c** false   **d** true   **e** true   **f** false
> **g** true   **h** false

Recording script 3.16

Darren: Hello?

Andy: Hi, Darren?

Darren: Yeah.

Andy: Look, it's Andy. I'm in town. Can you come and drive me home?

Darren: Where are you?

Andy: In the city centre. You know, Dad gave me some money last week and I wanted to buy a pullover …

Darren: Well, it's a bit late. I want to eat.

Andy: Oh, come on. I've just had a really bad experience.

Darren: What? What's going on?

Andy: It's, like, I was just nearly arrested.

Darren: What for? You only went to buy some clothes! What have you done now?

Andy: Well, first I went into Tempo, you know, the big clothes store?

Darren: Yeah.

Andy: And I looked at the pullovers, and I got one. And then I decided to get a shirt too, but after I'd looked at them I wasn't sure, so I went to a couple of other places to see what they had. A friend told me they were selling some quite cool ones in the market. But when I asked about them, the man who runs the stall said he'd sold them all already. And I bought some shoes and went to the burger bar because it was time for lunch.

Darren: OK.

Andy: Then I went back to Tempo and found some shirts I liked and I said to the assistant I wanted to try them on and he said that was OK. But they weren't any good, so I told the assistant they didn't fit and he put them back on the shelf. They didn't have any other sizes in stock. Then, when I was going out of the shop, this woman came up to me. She asked me if I was leaving the shop. I said I was. She asked me if I'd paid for everything in my bag. I said I had because I knew I'd only got the pullover I bought earlier, and the shoes.

Darren: Right.

Andy: She said she was the store detective and then asked me if I would come to the manager's office with her and I agreed, although I added that I wasn't very happy about it. Everyone was looking at me. It was really bad.

Darren: I believe you!

Andy: In the manager's office, the store detective showed the manager the pullover and the manager asked me how long I'd been in the shop and how many things I had bought. So I told him I'd bought a pullover at about 9.30 but I hadn't bought anything else. I was getting a bit angry and I asked what was going on. Then he asked me whether I had a receipt for the pullover. And of course I couldn't find it. And I tried to explain I'd thrown away the Tempo bag and had put the pullover in the shoe shop bag.

Darren: Oh, Andy.

Andy: Well, I didn't know. But anyway they didn't believe me. They asked me a lot more questions.

Darren: Like what?

Andy: They asked which assistant had served me. I said I didn't remember who had served me. It had been early in the morning. Then the store detective asked the manager if he wanted her to call the police and he said yes.

Darren: Oh, no.

Andy: But then my luck changed. One of the assistants came into the room and I recognised her. She was the one that served me in the morning. I asked her if she remembered me and she did. I've never felt so happy in my life.

Darren: Yeah, I'm sure. OK. So where are you now?

Andy: I'm in the manager's office. He said he was sorry for troubling me and he told me I was welcome to use his phone. Can you come and give me a lift home? There are too many people at the bus stop at this time. I'm really tired and I haven't got enough money for a taxi.

Darren: Sure. I'll be ten minutes. See you outside Tempo.

Andy: Thanks, Darren.

page 163

Language focus

Reported speech

1

> **b** he'd sold them all already.
> **c** I wanted to try them on.
> **d** that was OK.
> **e** they didn't fit.
> **f** I was.

2

> **b** OK/All right, *etc.* but I'm not very happy about it.
> **c** I bought a pullover at about 9.30.
> **d** I threw away the Tempo bag and put the pullover in the shoe shop bag.
> **e** I don't remember who served me.
> **f** I'm sorry for troubling you. You're welcome to use my phone.

3

b Have you paid for everything in your bag?
c Will (or Would) you come to the manager's office with me?
d How long have you been in the shop and how many things have you bought?
e What's going on?
f Do you have (or Have you got) a receipt for the pullover?
g Which assistant served you?
h Do you want me to call the police?
i Do you remember me?

Grammar spot

I asked her if she *liked* it.
He asked me whether I *had* a laptop.
She asked me if I *would come* shopping with her.
I asked what *was happening*.
They asked which assistant *had spoken* to me.

page 164

4

b I spoke c I'd ever worked d why I wanted to work in that shop e how I would travel f I could start

6

b what time I had found it c if/whether I had been alone
d where I lived e how long I had lived there
f if/whether I would be at that address for the next month
g if/whether I had an email address

Too much, too many, not enough

Grammar spot

a too many b too much c enough

a too much b enough c too much d too many; enough
e enough f too much g too many

page 165

«Pronunciation»

1

Answers and recording script 3 17
1 A Did you say ten o'clock?
  B No, I said two o'clock.
2 A Did you say there were five guests?
  B No, I said there were nine guests.
3 A Did you say we had a spelling test?
  B No, I said we had a reading test.
4 A Did you say you came by air?
  B No, I said I came by car.
5 A Did you say she was a doctor?
  B No, I said she was a teacher.
6 A Did you say you came from France?
  B No, I said I came from Greece.

3

b Did you say there were fifteen students?
  No, I said there were sixteen students.
c Did you say we wanted ham sandwiches?
  No, I said we wanted jam sandwiches.
d Did you say she was a model?
  No, I said she was an actress.
e Did you say it was quarter to eleven?
  No, I said it was quarter to seven.

Verbs with two objects

1

b I sent my parents a postcard from London.
c Will you send my boss the bill?
d He wrote me a long letter when he arrived in India.
e On my birthday, the children brought me my breakfast in bed.
f Can you bring us some more bread, please?

2

a Take this note to the headteacher, please.
b Show your passport to the immigration officer.
c We took some fruit to our classmate when he was ill.

page 166

Exam folder 25
Reading Part 3

Check!
a A b A c B

Exam task
1 B 2 B 3 A 4 B 5 A 6 A 7 A 8 B 9 A 10 B

page 167

Corpus spot
a do b malls c high d go e shop

Unit 26
page 168

Introduction

1

a McDonalds b Google c Virgin
d Mercedes-Benz e Coca-Cola

3

They are advertising tissues, washing powder and an airline.

Reading

1

a play computer games
b on Friday at home and on Saturday with his parents
c a surprise party for Robert
d no
e she heard the boys talking about it
f no
g they will make a mess in the house
h nothing

page 169

2

1 D 2 A 3 D 4 C

page 170

3

Suggested answers
b encourages/encouraged c influence d recommends/
recommended e warned / is warning f prevented / are
preventing g apologise

Corpus spot
a I want to warn you <u>about</u> the cold weather here.
b This will encourage me <u>to</u> study harder.
c I explained <u>to</u> her how it was made.
d My illness prevented me <u>from going</u> out.

Language focus

First conditional

Grammar spot

condition	result
IF + ...**present tense**...... ,	............**will**........... .

If only a few people **go** *to the party, it* **won't be** *a problem.*

result	condition
............**will**.............	IF + ...**present tense**..........

He'll have *a really good time* ***if*** *the boys* **organise** *a party for him.*

b will be c will get d won't happen e will stay
f feels g won't have h will be

Unless

Grammar spot

Unless Robert **goes** *to his granny's house, he will be at home.*

1

Suggested answers
b Unless Carolina tells Robert about the party, it will be a surprise.
c Robert will enjoy the party unless the boys ask too many people.
d Unless the boys organise a party for Robert, he won't have one.
e Robert's parents won't know about the party unless Carolina tells them.

2

Suggested answers
b I can come shopping with you if you lend me some money.
c I won't tell anyone if you tell me the secret.
d I won't pass my exam unless you help me with my revision.
e The letter will get there tomorrow if you post it by five o'clock.

page 171

If and *when*

Grammar spot

1
In sentence A the speaker knows that Robert's parents will come home.
In sentence B the speaker is not sure where Robert's parents are.

2
In sentence B Robert will definitely answer the door (the speaker is sure).
In sentence A Robert will possibly answer the door (the speaker isn't sure).

b if c if/when d If e When f if g when
h If/When i if

«Pronunciation»

1

Answers and recording script 3 18

Joanna:	<u>What's</u> the <u>time</u>?
Michael:	<u>Five</u> to <u>nine</u>.
Joanna:	Oh <u>dear</u>.
Michael:	<u>What's</u> the <u>problem</u>?
Joanna:	It doesn't <u>matter</u>.
Michael:	<u>Tell</u> me.
Joanna:	I'm <u>late</u> for <u>college</u>. Can you <u>give</u> me a <u>lift</u>?
Michael:	Of <u>course</u> I <u>can</u>.
Joanna:	<u>Thank</u> you.
Michael:	You're <u>welcome</u>.

Activity Adverts

Suggested answers
If you buy this fridge, your food will stay fresher. / When you use this fridge, your food will taste good.
If you travel with this airline, you'll be very comfortable. / Unless you fly with this airline, you'll feel tired.

Activity Superstitions

Answers for British culture
If a black cat crosses your path, you will have good luck.
If you break a mirror, you will have seven years' bad luck.
If you see a ladybird, you will have good luck.
If you pick up a horseshoe, you will have good luck.
If you see a rainbow, you will have good luck.
If you walk under a ladder, you will have bad luck.
If you open an umbrella indoors, you will have bad luck.

page 172

Exam folder 26
Speaking Part 1

> **Check!**
>
> **a** four – two examiners (one doesn't speak) and two candidates
> **b** the examiner
> **c** some of these: where you live / come from, what job you do / what you are studying, why you're learning English, your interests, your daily life
> **d** Could you speak more slowly, please?
> Could you repeat that, please?
> **e** two or three minutes, therefore only a minute or so for each candidate

Speaking Part 2

> **Check!**
>
> **a** some pictures to look at
> **b** the other candidate
> **c** Could you speak more slowly, please?
> Could you repeat that, please?
> **d** about two or three minutes
> **e** the examiner will ask a question

page 173

Writing folder
Writing Part 3

1

> **a** after **b** Next **c** While **d** when

2

> **1** g **2** e **3** d **4** a **5** c **6** j **7** f **8** h **9** b **10** i

Unit 27

page 174

Introduction

3

> **a** shining **b** sky **c** silver **d** shining **e** road
> **f** hard **g** high **h** out **i** never **j** gold **k** land

page 175

Listening

2, 3

> **a** a musical instrument
> **b** someone who looks after children in their home
> **c** someone who works for no money
> **d** a wooden path
> **e** someone who studies very old buildings and objects
> **f** a fire that people build when they are camping
> **g** part of a house which is underground

Recording script 3 20

Host: Hi, everyone, and welcome to International Chat, our phone-in programme for students everywhere. Today's subject is working abroad and we'd like to hear from anyone who's done this. Many employers and universities say that before you start a course or a job at home, it's a good idea to spend some time travelling in other countries. Some students are helped by their parents, others have to find a job. We'd like to hear about your experiences.
And our first caller is Joe. Joe, tell us about your experience.

Joe: Well, I had a great time in Ireland. I stayed on a traditional farm where I picked potatoes and looked after the cows. I did repairs to the farmhouse too. I was given a room and my food and every evening the old farmer played his accordion and sang Irish songs and told stories. His wife was a wonderful cook. <u>Her home-made bread</u> was out of this world.

Host: Well done, Joe, you obviously enjoyed yourself there. And now we go to Natasha. Where did you work, Natasha?

Natasha: I'd reached Finland, and I was in Helsinki. <u>I earned about £110 each week</u> for five days' work. I was employed as a nanny. I helped the older children get ready for school in the morning and then looked after the little one **all** day.

Host: And did you find the job by yourself?

Natasha: Well, <u>luckily, a Finnish friend helped me to write a little notice</u> about myself in Finnish and we put it in some playgroups. Lots of families like to have some help with the children and they prefer someone who can speak English, but you need to advertise in Finnish.

Host: Thanks for that tip, Natasha. And now we go to Owen from Lancashire. Did you earn money abroad too?

Owen: No. I wasn't paid, I was a volunteer. I wanted to do something to help the environment. I was <u>in Canada</u> and I helped to build boardwalks on Vancouver Island. These allow more people to walk in the forest.

Host: Is that good for the environment?

Owen: Yes, it'll help prevent the forest from being destroyed by people who want to cut down the trees.

Host: And did you have a good time?

Owen: <u>Obviously</u>, I liked helping to save the forest. <u>It was fairly wet there, it rained</u> nearly **every** day, and it was hard work, but it was fun. I liked **all** the people there and the forest was wonderful – the big trees, the wild fruit and the mushrooms and the mist.

Host: Well, that sounds magic, doesn't it? And let's hear from Jennifer, who worked in very different weather, I think.

Jennifer: That's right. I was in the desert, in the Middle East, helping archaeologists. <u>Of course</u>, the sun was really hot during the day, but it was very cold at night.

Some people might think it's very romantic to dig up old buildings which were buried for hundreds or thousands of years, but <u>unfortunately</u> digging is very hard work. <u>Actually</u>, we needed to be quite fit and know how to look after ourselves. You quickly get sore hands and <u>backache.</u>

Host: And what about the accommodation?

Jennifer: Oh, the camp was great. **Each of** the workers had a small tent. There were people from every part of the world and after we finished working, there was normally a campfire and a couple of musicians. But most of all, it was wonderful to spend time in the desert which was so beautiful and <u>empty.</u> Very different from Manchester, where I'm studying now.

Host: Yeah, I can believe that. Thank you, Jennifer. And we have time for one more caller. And it's Martin, who found ways of earning money in Los Angeles, in the USA.

Martin: Hello. Yes, I was staying with my <u>uncle.</u> He knew an old man who wanted some help in his house and arranged for us to meet. He gave me free food and I was paid $12 an hour. I painted some rooms for him, which I hadn't done before. <u>Surprisingly</u>, his <u>landlady</u> was so satisfied with the job I did that she asked me to paint her basement and then a friend asked me as well. I was employed by lots of people. **Each** person told their friends about me. I had a wonderful time and earned quite a lot of money. <u>In fact</u>, I had an email from someone last week offering me work there next summer.

Host: Well, that's great. And that's all we have time for. But I hope our listeners will be encouraged by those stories and start making their own plans for travelling and working abroad.

5

b (home-made) bread **c** 110 **d** a (little) notice **e** Canada **f** (fairly) wet/rainy **g** back **h** empty **i** his uncle **j** landlady

Language focus
Adverbs at the beginning of sentences

1

b Obviously **c** Of course **d** Unfortunately **e** Actually **f** Surprisingly **g** In fact

2

luckily = fortunately; in fact = actually
obviously = of course; unluckily = unfortunately

page 176
Reflexive pronouns

1

b talking to yourself **c** hurt herself **d** help yourselves **e** didn't enjoy ourselves **f** ask myself **g** look after themselves

Grammar spot
a Picture 1 **b** Picture 2

Every, each, all

Grammar spot
a
We use *each* and *every* + a *singular* countable noun.
We use *each of* + a *plural* countable noun.
We use *all* + a *plural* noun or an uncountable noun.
b
All day means *a complete day.*
Every day means *more than one day.*

b each **c** every **d** All **e** all **f** each **g** all **h** each

«Pronunciation»

1

/ɪə/ Here /eə/ chair

2

/eə/		/ɪə/	
rarely	pears	*fear*	volunteers
fair	Where	beard	engineer
hair	pairs	dear	steered
care	carefully	near	
stairs		appear	
There's			

page 177
Using the passive

1

b paid me. **c** buried the buildings for hundreds of years. **d** employed me. **e** will encourage our listeners.

2

He feels he was doing something useful.

3

b are started (by tourists) **c** was cleaned (by volunteers) **d** were collected **e** will be employed (by the government) **f** are damaged (by pollution) **g** will not/won't be spoiled

page 178
Exam folder 27
Reading Part 2

Check!
a five **b** eight
c three (students do not need to understand every word of every text but they need to read each text carefully)
d no **e** underline the important information
f that the answer contains everything that the person wants

page 179

Corpus spot

a trip   b journey   c travel

Unit 28

page 180

Introduction

2

a 3 David Beckham   b 1 Kate Winslet   c 5 Madonna
d 2 Barack Obama   e 4 Prince Harry

page 181

Reading

1

A celebrity chef   B stylist   C fashion designer
D personal assistant   E personal trainer   F bodyguard

2

Job A
1 to do the cooking themselves (not really to get their hands dirty)
2 I take care of
Job B
3 choose clothes for the celebrity
4 because a celebrity has to look wonderful at all times
Job C
5 everyone wants to see him/her
6 new and modern
7 celebrities might not want his/her clothes any more
Job D
8 all the jobs the celebrity doesn't want to do
9 when the celebrity is angry about something
Job E
10 because the celebrity wants to look good
11 the celebrity might fall in love with the trainer
Job F
12 because he/she has to make sure the celebrity is safe and always be ready for a problem
13 he/she sometimes has to work long hours

3

Possible advantages
Having lots of money
Not having to do boring jobs, e.g. cleaning
Travel
Being on TV
Having expensive clothes

Possible disadvantages
Photographers following you
People writing things about you that aren't true
Not having a normal life
Not being able to trust people
Having to stay famous

page 182

Language focus

Second conditional

Grammar spot

If I *had* a stylist, I *would look* good all the time.
I *would look* good all the time if I *had* a stylist.

2

b If I *didn't have* so much homework to do, I'*d go* out with my friends.
c I'*d buy* a new computer if I *had* plenty of money.
d If I *owned* a plane, I'*d fly* in it every day.
e If Andrea *got up* earlier, she *wouldn't be* late every day.
f If my neighbours *were* friendly, I'*d invite* them to my party.
g If Suzi *was/were* old enough, she'*d learn* to drive.
h My brother *would teach* you the guitar if he *had* time.

3

Possible answers
c I would fly it to school every day.   d you wouldn't come to this class.   e I'll be very tired tomorrow.   f I'll never finish it.   g everyone would fall in love with you.   h I'd have more free time.

Expressions with prepositions

1

b by   c in   d at   on   e in   f in   g at
h in   i at   j on   k in   l At   m in

2

AT	breakfast, first, last, school
BY	bus, car, mistake, post
IN	stock, town
ON	business, foot

page 183

« **Pronunciation** »

1

b 've have   c 'll will   d 'd had   e 'd would
f 're are   g 's has   h 'll will   i 's is

3

Recording script 3 23

a I'd lend it to you
b I've almost finished
c They'll be late
d They'd already arrived
e She'd be happier
f You're not listening
g He's played the trumpet in public
h We'll ring you
i She's coming home

4

Answers and recording script **3** **24**
a They(d)already left.
b He(ll)help you.
c The pop star's leaving. ✓
d It'd be too dark to see anything. ✓
e I(d)seen the programme before.
f She(s)got plenty of money.

page 184

Exam folder 28
Listening Part 2

Check!

a what you will hear / who will speak
b choose A, B or C
c read the questions (candidates are given 45 seconds to do this)
d they give you some idea about what you will hear
e twice
f wait till the second time you hear it, and if you still don't know, guess

1

1 B   2 C   3 A   4 C   5 B   6 A

2, 3

Recording script **3** **25**

You will hear an interview with a young actor called Paul. For each question, put a tick in the correct box.

Interviewer: This week we're interviewing Paul Mason, who became famous for playing the good-looking teenage son called Frank in the soap opera, *Along our street*. Paul, when did you first join the soap opera?

Paul: I started playing Frank (in the soap opera in 2007.) (I was just 15 years old.) I'd been on TV a couple of times before. I was in a children's drama series when I was about ten years old but I didn't actually say anything and (I appeared on a quiz show, again for children's TV, when) (I was about 13.)

Interviewer: So, did you enjoy acting in the soap opera?

Paul: I did – the boy I played, Frank, was very much like me – he had a (nicer personality than me,) though. But I played Frank for four years and I really needed to get experience and have the chance to play (lots of different parts.) After two or three years it was time to move on. But Frank was such a big part in the soap opera, it was difficult for me to leave.

Interviewer: You became very popular, especially with teenage girls.

Paul: I had lots of girlfriends, yes. And (I loved people) (coming up to me in the street,) wanting my autograph. I was always busy, (never tired) – I didn't need much sleep. Everyone wanted to be my friend but it was only because I was rich and famous. They weren't real friends. I didn't know who I could trust and I wasn't ready for that. I was too young.

Interviewer: So what did you do next?

Paul: I was in a play in a London theatre and because I'd spent so long in front of a TV camera I did everything wrong on the stage – I'd never acted in front of an audience before and (it frightened me.) I got better but it was (much more difficult for me than TV.)

Interviewer: And what about the future?

Paul: (I'm giving TV a break. I've made a film) called *The Last Journey*, which will be in the cinemas in two months. But I'm hoping to do more plays in theatres. I intend to be one of the actors people will remember – not just on TV but for playing serious parts on the stage too.

Interviewer: How do your parents feel about your success?

Paul: Neither of them are actors but they knew that was what I wanted to do and (they've always supported me.) (They're very proud of me.) They're anxious, though, that suddenly one day I won't have any work or it will change me – it's not like working in an office, which is what they both do.

page 185

Writing folder
Writing Part 1

2 remember to
3 do you have / have you got
4 lent
5 are
6 whose
7 too expensive
8 buy anything
9 owns
10 but
11 we hurry
12 tired (that)

Corpus spot

a Could you <u>lend</u> me that book for two weeks?
b ✓
c I <u>lent</u> Tom my bicycle.
d ✓
e When I got home, I didn't have the beautiful scarf my mother had <u>lent</u> me.

Corpus spot

a There <u>are</u> a lot of interesting historic buildings.
b There <u>are</u> three films to choose from.
c In the centre there <u>is</u> a new club.
d There <u>are</u> a lot of things to do in my town.
e You could go to the National Museum where <u>there</u> is a painting by Michelangelo.
f Sometimes there <u>is</u> a special guest on the show.
g There <u>are</u> two cupboards in my room.
h We will go to a big park where <u>there</u> is a roller coaster.

Unit 29

page 186

Introduction

1

> **Suggested answers** (other answers also possible)
> **B** bananas, bread, bowl, basket
> **C** cucumber, cheese, chicken, cups, crisps, cola, cake, chocolate
> **E/F/G** egg, fizzy drink, fruit, fruit juice, fork, glass, grape
> **K/L** knife, lemon, lemonade, lettuce
> **O/T** oil, onion, orange, tart, tomato
> **P** pear, pepper, pie, plate, pizza
> **S** sausage, strawberry, spoon, salad, salt

4

> **b** oil **c** chips **d** coffee **e** cream **f** fish
> **g** hotdog **h** jam **i** milk **j** sugar **k** cabbage **l** peanut
> **m** salt **n** spinach **o** mushroom

5

> **Suggested answers**
> *Healthy foods:*   cabbage, fish, jam, milk, mushroom,
>   peanut, spinach
> *Unhealthy foods:*   burger, chips, coffee, cream, hotdog, oil,
>   salt, sugar

> **Corpus spot**
> **a** We decided to <u>have</u> our dinner in a pizzeria.
> **b** What about <u>having</u> a cup of coffee together?
> **c** That restaurant is the best place to <u>have</u> a romantic meal.
> **d** After the film we'll <u>have</u> a drink in the bar.
> **e** We went to the beach and <u>had</u> an ice cream there.

page 187

Listening

2

> **a** Conversation 4   **b** Conversation 5
> **c** Conversation 3   **d** Conversation 2   **e** Conversation 1

Recording script 3 26

Conversation 1
Alison: So, let's go and eat. I'm hungry.
Daniel: So <u>am I</u>. Where shall we go?
Alison: There are plenty of restaurants round here. Do you like Mexican food? Or what about Thai?
Beata: Can you tell me what Thai food tastes like? I've never tried it.
Daniel: No, nor <u>have I</u>.
Alison: Well, I love it. It's quite spicy.
Beata: Oh, is it? I'm not very keen on hot spices.
Daniel: No, neither <u>am I</u>.
Alison: OK. Er, so not Thai or Mexican. There's a good Italian restaurant further up the road.
Daniel: Oh, I love Italian food.
Beata: Really? So <u>do I</u>.
Alison: Right, let's go there then.

Conversation 2
Graham: Good evening. Table for two?
Greta: For three, please. We're meeting a friend.
Graham: Certainly. Inside or outside?
Greta: I don't like sitting outside.
Brigitte: Neither <u>do I</u>, so inside, please.
Graham: Thank you. There's a table just there, near the window.
Brigitte: That'll be all right.
Greta: Yes, it's fine.
Graham: Would you like to order any drinks before your friend arrives?
Brigitte: Er, yes. I'm really thirsty. I can't wait.
Greta: Neither <u>can I</u>.
Brigitte: I'd like an orange juice, please.
Tina: Hi! Sorry I'm late. I got lost.
Brigitte: So <u>did I</u>. It's hard to find, isn't it? Never mind. Come and sit down. We're just getting some drinks.
Tina: I'll have a mineral water, I think.
Greta: So <u>will I</u>.
Graham: Still or sparkling?
Tina: Still, please.
Graham: Thank you. I'll bring the menu in a moment.
Greta: Thank you.

Conversation 3
Bob: Now, what are we going to have?
Carl: What do you recommend?
Bob: They do home-made soup, that's usually very nice. And there's always a hot dish.
Carl: Oh, yeah. I see. 'Today's special', it says on the board. <u>Can you explain what that is?</u>
Bob: It says underneath, look. Lancashire Hotpot.
Carl: It sounds a bit funny. <u>I'd like to know if it's got meat in it.</u>
Bob: It's made of lamb with potatoes and onions, cooked for a long time. A traditional dish from the north of England. Very good on a cold day like today.
Carl: Oh, right. I'm a vegetarian so I won't have that.
Bob: OK. We'll ask for a menu. Would you like a starter?
Carl: No, thanks. I'll just have a main course. I don't want to fall asleep this afternoon.
Bob: No, neither do I. OK, now, where's the waiter?

Conversation 4
Gary: Yes?
Tammy: One burger, one milkshake, one vegeburger and one cappuccino, please.
Gary: What flavour milkshake?
Tammy: Oh, sorry. Rosie, <u>do you know what flavour milkshake your friend wants</u>?
Rosie: Oh, she didn't say.
Tammy: Oh, typical.
Rosie: <u>Can you tell us what flavours you've got?</u>
Gary: Chocolate, strawberry, banana and vanilla.
Rosie: She'd like strawberry, I think.
Gary: OK. Now do you want to eat in or take away?

Tammy: Take away. Oh, and one portion of chips.

Gary: OK. That's thirteen pounds twenty.

Tammy: Here you are.

Gary: Enjoy your meal.

Rosie: Thank you.

Conversation 5

Nigel: Excuse me!

Marco: Yes? Can I help you?

Nigel: I hope so. You see, we ordered a tuna salad and a baked potato with cheese fifteen minutes ago! <u>Can you find out if there's a problem?</u>

Marco: I'm sorry, we are very busy, as you see.

Nigel: But we said we were in a hurry and the waitress promised to be quick.

Laura: <u>Can you find out if we're going to get our food soon?</u> We have to catch a train at one fifty-five.

Marco: OK. <u>Can you remember what your waitress looked like?</u>

Nigel: Oh, here she comes now.

Anna: I'm ever so sorry. Someone else took your order by mistake.

Nigel: All right. Thank you. Now we can eat.

Laura: This potato isn't properly cooked. Part of it is almost raw!

Nigel: Oh, no. Well, that's it. I'm going to see the manager.

Language focus

So do I and *neither/nor do I*

1

| Conversation 1 | **b** have I | **c** am I | **d** do I |
| Conversation 2 | **e** do I | **f** can I | **g** did I | **h** will I |

page 188

Corpus spot

We <u>were</u> hungry so we stopped for a meal.
We use *to be* before adjectives such as *thirsty, hot, cold, lucky, sad, afraid*.

a At first, I <u>was</u> afraid, but then I saw my family.
b We <u>were</u> lucky because the weather was very nice.
c I <u>was</u> very surprised when she told me.
d I'll <u>be</u> cold if I don't wear my scarf.
e When I read it I <u>was</u> shocked.
f I <u>am</u> hot and I want to go for a swim.

Grammar spot

I've really enjoyed this evening.	So have I.
I've never tried this before.	Neither/Nor have I.
They enjoyed the main course.	So did I/we.
We didn't want a big meal.	Neither/Nor did I.
I'll come here again.	So will I.
I won't finish all this.	Neither/Nor will I.
He's going to give the waiter a tip.	So am I.
I can't eat any more.	Neither/Nor can I.
We'd like to come here again.	So would I.

Polite question forms

1 and Grammar spot (page 189)

Conversation 3

Carl: <u>What is that?</u> (Can you explain what that is?)
Carl: <u>Has it got meat in it?</u> (I'd like to know if it's got meat in it.)

Conversation 4

Tammy: … <u>what flavour milkshake does your friend want?</u> (do you know what flavour milkshake your friend wants?)

Rosie: <u>What flavours have you got?</u> (Can you tell us what flavours you've got?)

Conversation 5

Nigel: … <u>Is there a problem?</u> (Can you find out if there's a problem?)

Laura: <u>Are we going to get our food soon?</u> (Can you find out if we're going to get our food soon?)

Marco: <u>What did your waitress look like?</u> (Can you remember what your waitress looked like?)

<u>Yes/No</u> questions use *if* when reported.

page 189

2

Possible answers

c (Can you find out) where the toilet is?
d (Can you remember) if they serve vegetarian dishes?
e (I'd like to know) what flavour ice cream they've got.
f (I'd like to know) if we can sit outside.
g (Can you tell me) when this café closes?
h (Do you know) what the name of this dish is? / the name of this dish?

⟪Pronunciation⟫

1

Answers and recording script 3 **27**

<u>a</u> cup <u>of</u> coffee /ə/ cup /əv/ coffee

2

Answers and recording script 3 **28**

<u>a</u> /ə/ glass <u>of</u> /əv/ milk <u>and</u> /ən/ <u>some</u> /səm/ pieces <u>of</u> /əv/ cake
<u>some</u> /səm/ ice cream <u>but</u> /bət/ no burgers /bɜːgəz/

3

Answers and recording script 3 29
It's made <u>of</u> /əv/ eggs <u>and</u> /ən/ sugar. /ˈʃʊgə/
He wants <u>a</u> /ə/ cup <u>of</u> /əv/ tea <u>and</u> /ən/ <u>a</u> /ə/ sandwich.
I'd like <u>a</u> /ə/ slice <u>of</u> /əv/ meat <u>and</u> /ən/ <u>some</u> /səm/ potatoes
/pəˈteɪtəʊz/.
You <u>can</u> /kən/ have <u>a</u> /ə/ bag <u>of</u> /əv/ crisps <u>but</u> /bət/ not <u>a</u>
/ə/ packet <u>of</u> /əv/ biscuits.
They've got fish <u>and</u> /ən/ chips <u>and</u> /ən/ meat <u>and</u> /ən/ rice
<u>but</u> /bət/ no bread <u>and</u> /ən/ cheese.

page 190

Exam folder 29
Reading Part 4

Check!

a no (Questions 1 and 5 test information from the whole text.
The others are in the order of information in the text.)
b yes (One or two words may give the answer to one of the
detail questions.)

Exam task
1 B   **2** B   **3** C   **4** D   **5** A

Unit 30
page 192

Introduction

Corpus spot

a I <u>would</u> like to hear from you soon.
b ✓
c I <u>would</u> like you to join me and my friends on Saturday.
d ✓
e Would you like <u>to</u> go to the cinema with me?
f ✓

page 193

Reading and Language focus
Revision of tenses

1

Jake:	sit speaks notices am going to ask will say
	was chosen playing
Lucy:	whistle think smile see doesn't like
	was picked 'll go

2

Jake (the correct order is given under Exercise 5)
B: was looking   saw   had   ran
C: came   scored   chatted   to ask   saying   'll write
D: saw   laughed   were changing   like
E: wants   thinks   'll ask

Lucy (the correct order is given under Exercise 5)
G: didn't seem   to help   're meeting / 're going to meet
H: ask   'll have   bumped   had just had   put
I: watched   scored   chatted   had never played
   will I do   isn't   going   'll be
J: was talking   walked   to laugh / laughing

page 194
4

a because she wanted to see Jake
b to see Gary Smart
c because he was afraid of saying the wrong thing
d because he might not be interested in her
e they were embarrassed
f that they thought he was a joke
g that they were going out together
h he's not her type
i as a way of seeing him
j because he thought she liked Gary

5

Jake	Tuesday C	Wednesday D	Thursday B	Friday E
Lucy	Tuesday I	Wednesday J	Thursday H	Friday G

6

a because he talked about Gary Smart a lot
b because he was afraid she didn't like him
c in her maths book
d excited
e yes
f This is a story from a teenage magazine rather than true life.

Recording script 3 31

Lucy: Monday. Met Jake in the library and he was so sweet
and funny and shy and clever and gorgeous! He talked a
lot about Gary Smart. I thought maybe he was missing
a football practice with him or something but then I
realised that he thought Gary was my boyfriend! I told
him that wasn't true and we had a great time after that
talking and laughing. We did hardly any maths and then
we walked home together.

Jake: Monday. I didn't ask Lucy to go out with me after
we finished working in the library because I didn't want
to spoil things. She said she likes smart, funny guys, so
that means I'm not the one for her. But I can't forget her.
Maybe a short note would be best …

Lucy: Tuesday. Wow! I got a letter from Jake!! After
handing back my maths book at school, he walked away.
When I opened it, there was a letter from him, saying he
liked me and inviting me to go bowling. We're meeting
after school tonight. I don't know what to wear or say, but
I can't wait!

Jake: Wednesday. We went bowling and we had a drink in
the café afterwards. I really think she likes me and wants
to go out with me. I can't believe it. Life is great.

Lucy: Wednesday. We went bowling and then sat in the café talking. When we sat down I told him that I had been so pleased to get his note and that I felt the same as him. We both laughed. I'm meeting him tomorrow too.

Vocabulary spot

mad = angry   guy = boy/man*
smart = clever   mate = friend   cool = good
my type = the kind of boy/girl I like
*NB When *guys* refers to a group of people, it can sometimes include women too.

Hardly

Grammar spot

Hardly + verb
Hardly goes *before* the verb.

Hardly + noun
Any and *anybody* (also *anything, anyone, anywhere*) go after *hardly*. *Any* goes after *hardly* and before a noun.

1

b I hardly (ever) see her
c I hardly slept
d she hardly danced
e I hardly remember it

2

b Hardly anybody/anyone c hardly any d Hardly anybody/anyone e hardly anything f hardly any

page 195

Before and *after -ing*

Grammar spot

The *-ing* form of the verb follows *before* and *after*.

1

Suggested answers

b After playing in the match, Jake talked to Lucy.
c Before meeting Jake in the library, Lucy asked him for help with her maths.
d After seeing Lucy with Gary, Jake felt sad.
e Before going out with Jake, Lucy asked Sophie to do her hair.
f After meeting Lucy in the library, Jake decided to write her a letter.
g After getting a letter from Jake, Lucy told him she liked him.

Saying goodbye

1 g   2 b   3 a   4 e   5 f   6 c   7 d

page 196

Exam folder 30
Listening Part 4

Check!

a two
b read the questions

Exam task

1 B   2 A   3 A   4 B   5 B   6 B

Recording script 3 32

Look at the six sentences for this part. You will hear a conversation between a boy, Andy, and a girl, Sarah, about dancing. Decide if each sentence is correct or incorrect. If it is correct, put a tick in the box under **A** for **YES**. If it is not correct, put a tick in the box under **B** for **NO**.

Sarah: Hi, Andy. Are you coming to the drama class?
Andy: Sorry, I'm busy.
Sarah: Not another computer class. You ought to do something different occasionally.
Andy: I only do that class on Thursdays now. I'm going to a dance class today.
Sarah: Really? I didn't know you were interested in dancing. Why haven't you ever said anything?
Andy: Well, nobody knows really, except my parents. My friends would think it was a huge joke. They prefer playing football.
Sarah: But there's nothing wrong with boys dancing, you know. I read somewhere that dancers are often fitter and stronger than footballers. It would be good for your friends to know – why not invite them to watch you dance one day, then they might understand.
Andy: I'm not sure.
Sarah: When did you start dancing?
Andy: When I was seven. My auntie, who's a ballet teacher, used to look after me, so she had to take me to her classes. I had to sit and watch. Then one day I persuaded her to let me join in. She wasn't very keen on the idea but I loved it.
Sarah: So, you've done classes ever since?
Andy: I stopped when I was about eleven. But three years ago I decided to join another class. Usually I'm the only boy but there are two other boys who sometimes go.
Sarah: That's nice for you.
Andy: I actually prefer it when they're not there because they're not really serious about it and I can't concentrate.
Sarah: So, you're really serious about it.
Andy: I want to go to the Dance Academy in London next year.
Sarah: Wow! And what do your parents think?
Andy: They're not keen. They don't think it's a good career. It only lasts a few years and it's difficult to get jobs. But I want to do it.

Sarah: <u>Well, you must persuade them.</u> If that's what you really want to do, you'll never forgive yourself if you don't try.

Andy: Thanks. I'll let you know what happens.

Speaking Part 3

> **Check!**
> a what you can see in the photograph
> b I don't know the word for this, but it's a kind of …
> c one minute

Speaking Part 4

> **Check!**
> a the other student   b invent some
> c the conversation will last about three minutes

page 197

Writing folder
Writing Part 1

> 1 such a   2 as/so crowded   3 we chose
> 4 were/was   5 didn't include

Writing Part 2

> **Sample answer**
> Dear Jerry,
> My friends and I are going to the cinema next Friday to see an adventure film called *Danger Country*. Would you like to come with us? We're meeting at 6.15 in the café next to the cinema. Hope you can come.
> Daniel

Writing Part 3

> **Sample answers**
> Dear Kim,
> Thank you for your letter. You're very lucky because you can choose your holiday. Both places are good, I think, but in different ways.
>   If I had your choice, I would go to the seaside with your friend's family. You will be with your friend, so that will be fun. Also, you will see a new place. It would be great to be at the seaside in the summer weather.
>   On the other hand, if you don't go away with your family, perhaps you will miss them. Have you talked to your parents? What do they say?
>
> Love,
> Nancy
> _____
> When we set out, the sky was blue and the sun was shining. My friends owned the boat and they went sailing every weekend. At first, I enjoyed it. The water was calm and the sun was hot. But suddenly the sun was covered by clouds and it started to rain. It also became windy. I was very frightened but my friends were pleased because sailing was boring without the wind. After two hours we could see the beach again. I decided that I didn't really like sailing but my friends went again the next day.

Units 25–30 Revision
page 198
Vocabulary

2

> b peanut   c dessert   d egg   e pepper   f glass
> g bread   h orange

Grammar

3

> c I wanted to know when he had decided to be a football manager.
> d I asked him what other jobs he had done.
> e I asked him if/whether he would always work as a football manager.
> f I wanted to know which countries he had visited.
> g I asked him if he worked hard.
> h I wanted to know how much money he earned.
> i I asked him if he had any hobbies.
> j I asked him what would happen to his job if the team lost again.

4

> b all   c too much   d too many   e When
> f hardly   g every   h unless   i enough   j If if

page 199

5

> b had   c was/were   d 'd/would stay   e is   f 'll/will have
> g 'll/will catch   h was/were   i 'd/would go   j visit
> k 'll/will buy   l spoke   m 'd/would be   n get
> o 'll/will show

Vocabulary

6

> b afford   c store   d size   e try   f fitting
> g matches   h fit   i stock   j bring   k change
> l refund   m receipt

Common mistakes

7

> Dear Lizzie,
> Thanks for the <u>beautiful</u> scarf. <u>It's</u> perfect. I had a great birthday with Emily <u>and</u> Paul. <u>At</u> lunchtime <u>we tried</u> the Mexican <u>restaurant</u> in the <u>shopping</u> mall. Have you ever <u>been there</u>? The food <u>was delicious</u> but it was <u>terribly</u> crowded. I look forward to <u>hearing</u> from you.
> Love,
> Cornelia

CARDIFF AND VALE COLLEGE